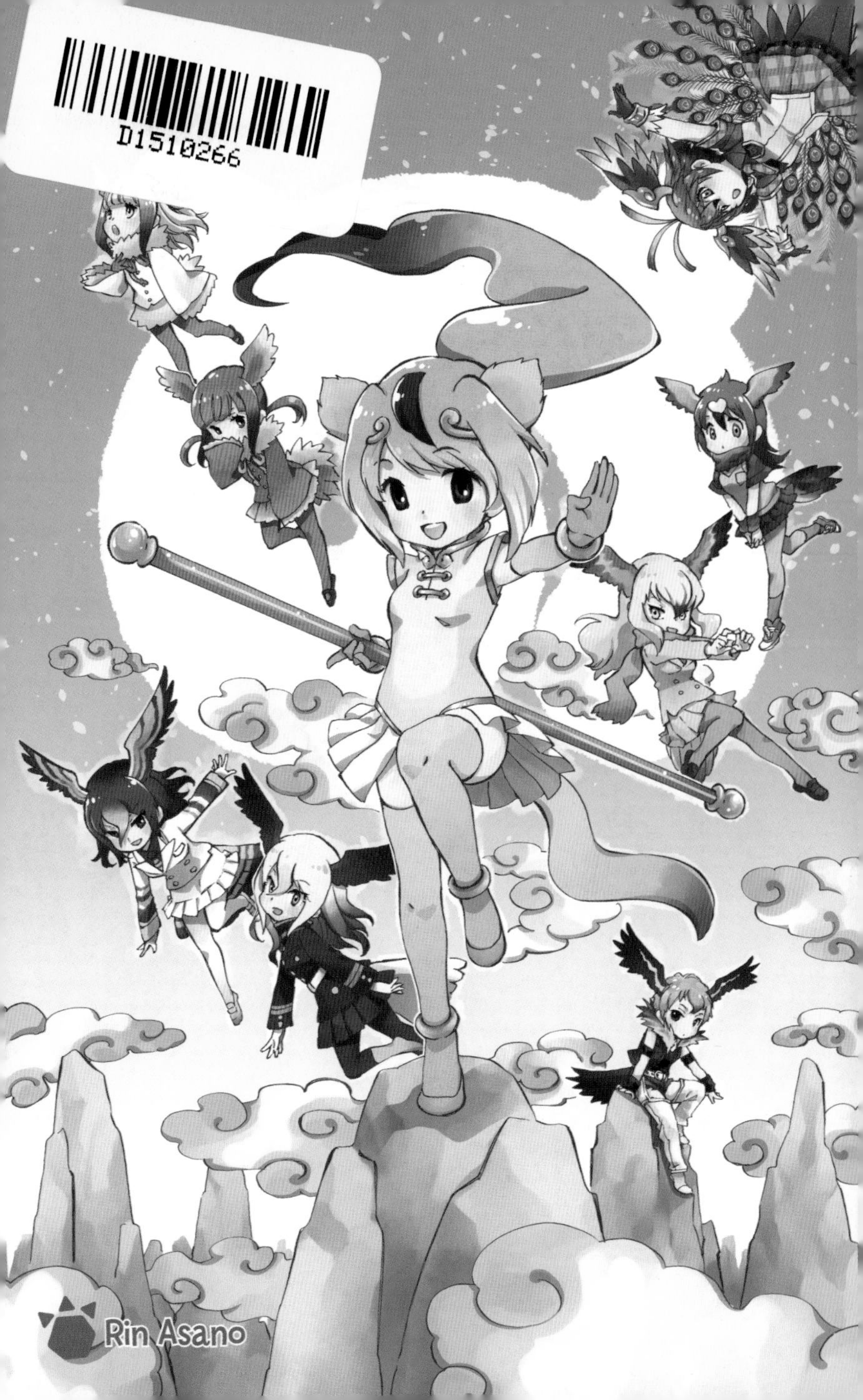
Rin Asano

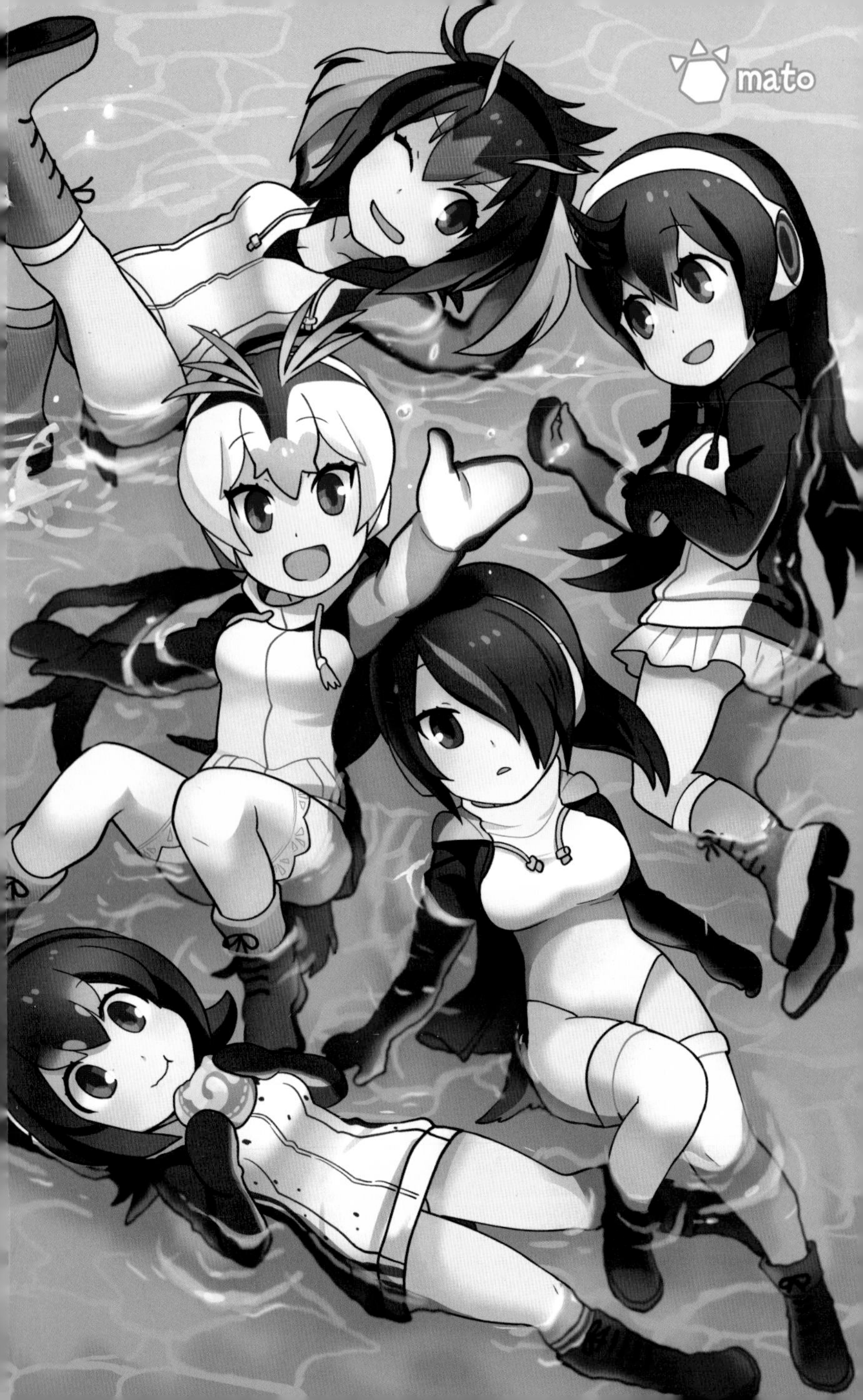
mato

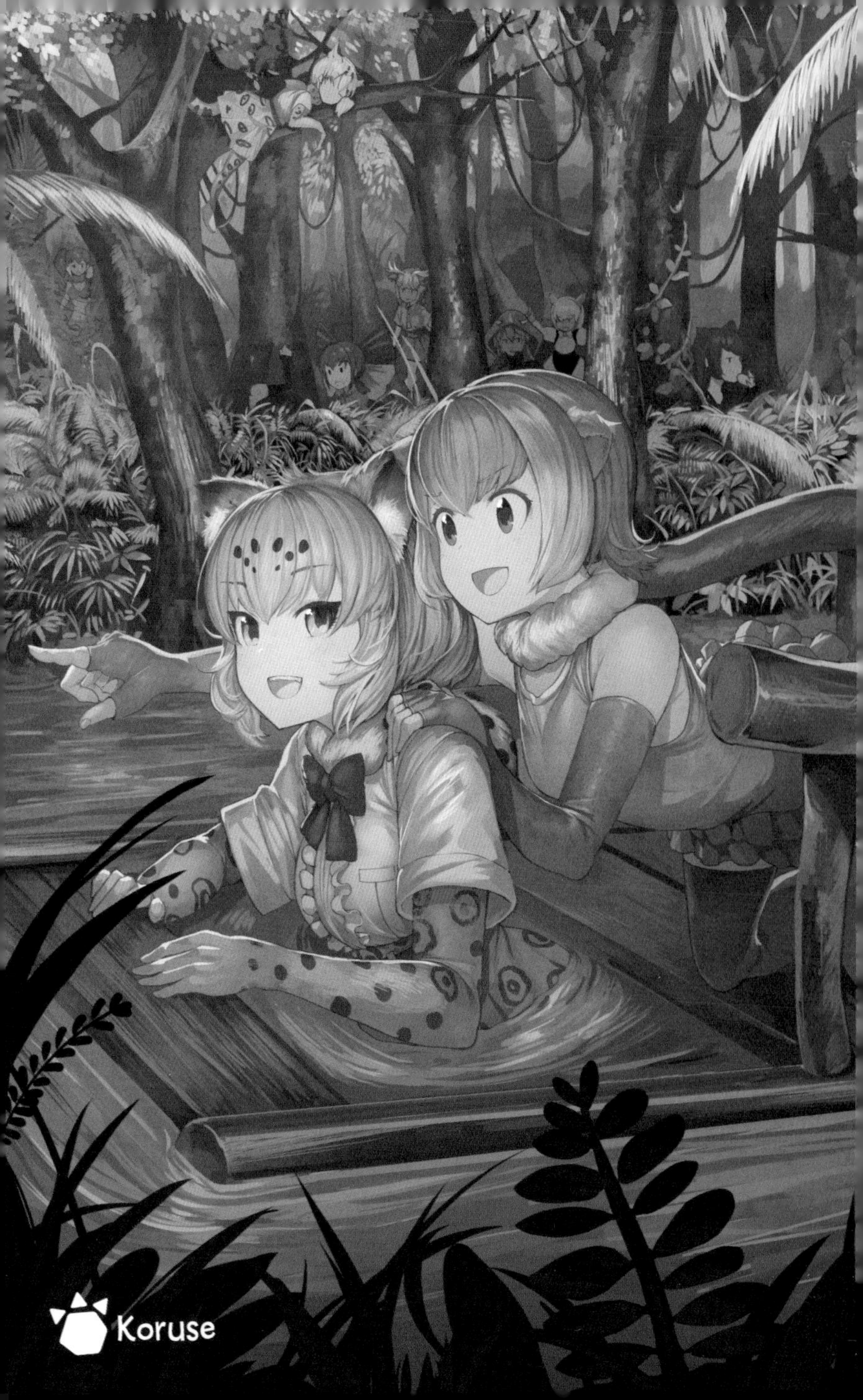
Koruse

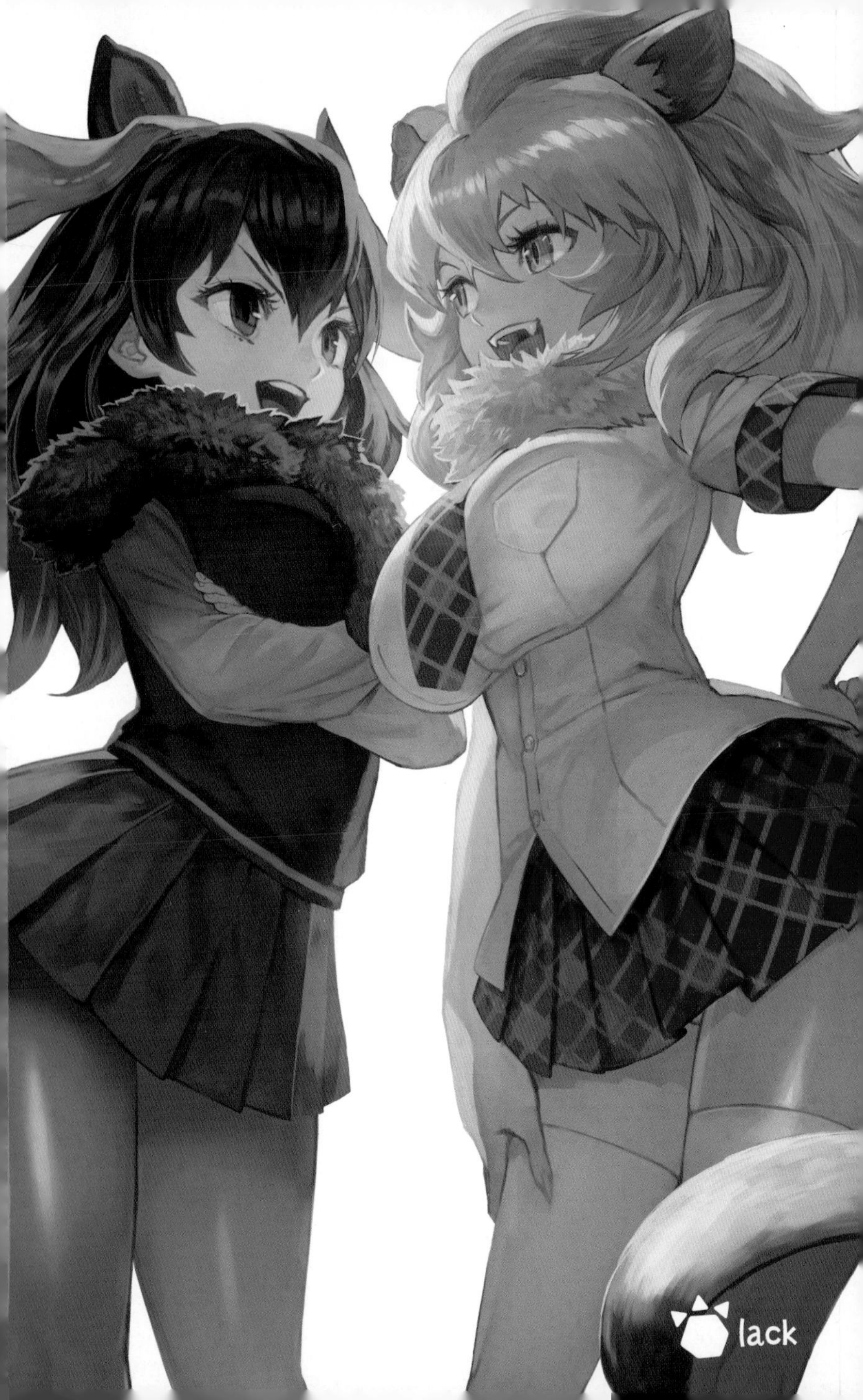
lack

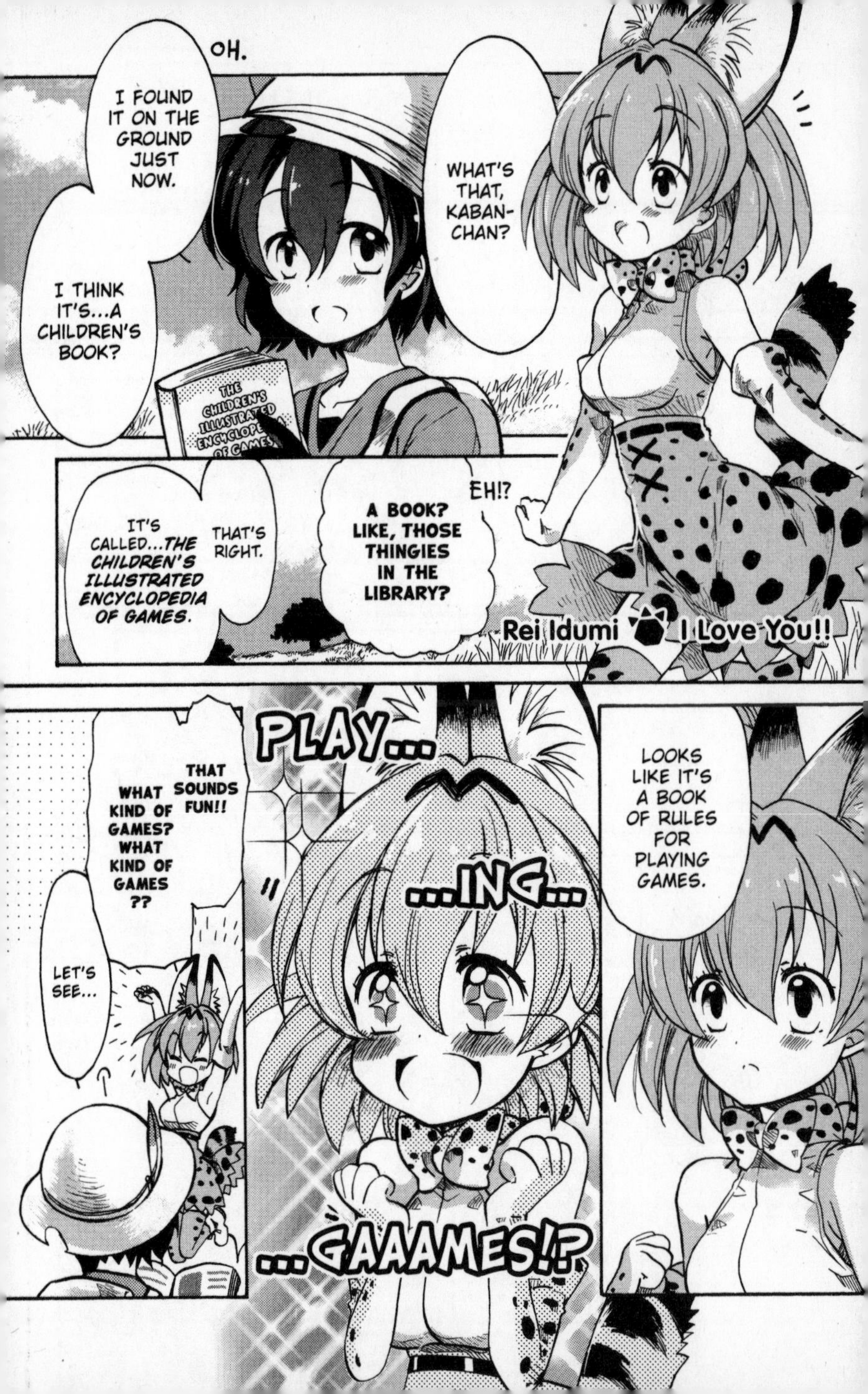
WHAT'S THAT, KABAN-CHAN?
OH.
I FOUND IT ON THE GROUND JUST NOW.
I THINK IT'S...A CHILDREN'S BOOK?
EH!?
A BOOK? LIKE, THOSE THINGIES IN THE LIBRARY?
THAT'S RIGHT.
IT'S CALLED...*THE CHILDREN'S ILLUSTRATED ENCYCLOPEDIA OF GAMES*.
Rei Idumi I Love You!!
LOOKS LIKE IT'S A BOOK OF RULES FOR PLAYING GAMES.
PLAY...
...ING...
...GAAAMES!?
THAT SOUNDS FUN!!
WHAT KIND OF GAMES? WHAT KIND OF GAMES??
LET'S SEE...

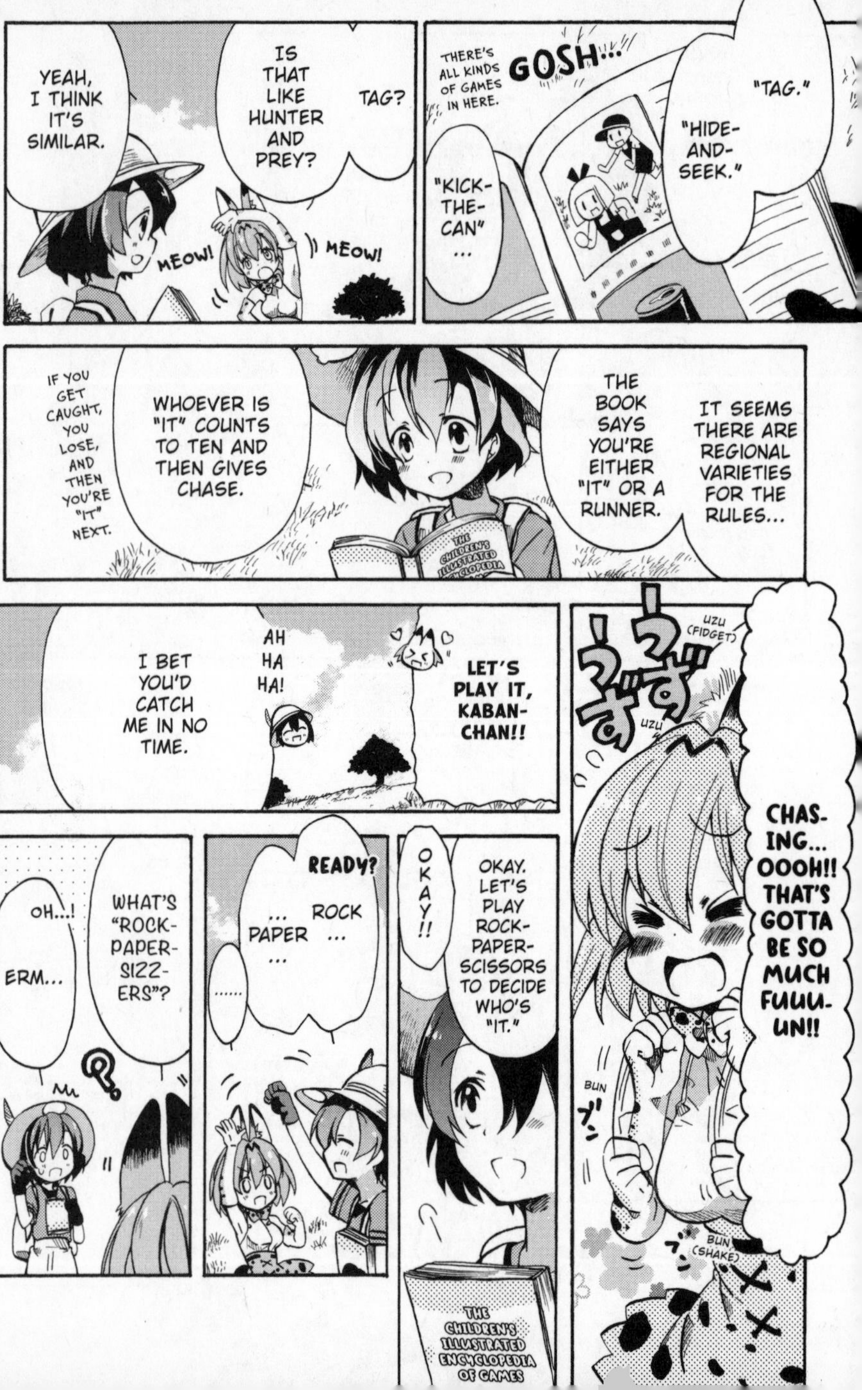
"TAG."
"HIDE-AND-SEEK."
GOSH...
THERE'S ALL KINDS OF GAMES IN HERE.
"KICK-THE-CAN"...
TAG? IS THAT LIKE HUNTER AND PREY?
MEOW!
MEOW!
YEAH, I THINK IT'S SIMILAR.
IT SEEMS THERE ARE REGIONAL VARIETIES FOR THE RULES...
THE BOOK SAYS YOU'RE EITHER "IT" OR A RUNNER.
THE CHILDREN'S ILLUSTRATED ENCYCLOPEDIA
WHOEVER IS "IT" COUNTS TO TEN AND THEN GIVES CHASE.
IF YOU GET CAUGHT, YOU LOSE, AND THEN YOU'RE "IT" NEXT.
UZU (FIDGET)
UZU
CHASING... OOOH!! THAT'S GOTTA BE SO MUCH FUUUUN!!
BUN
BUN (SHAKE)
LET'S PLAY IT, KABAN-CHAN!!
AH HA HA!
I BET YOU'D CATCH ME IN NO TIME.
OKAY. LET'S PLAY ROCK-PAPER-SCISSORS TO DECIDE WHO'S "IT."
OKAY!!
THE CHILDREN'S ILLUSTRATED ENCYCLOPEDIA OF GAMES
READY?
ROCK ... PAPER ...
......
WHAT'S "ROCK-PAPER-SIZZ-ERS"?
OH...! ERM...

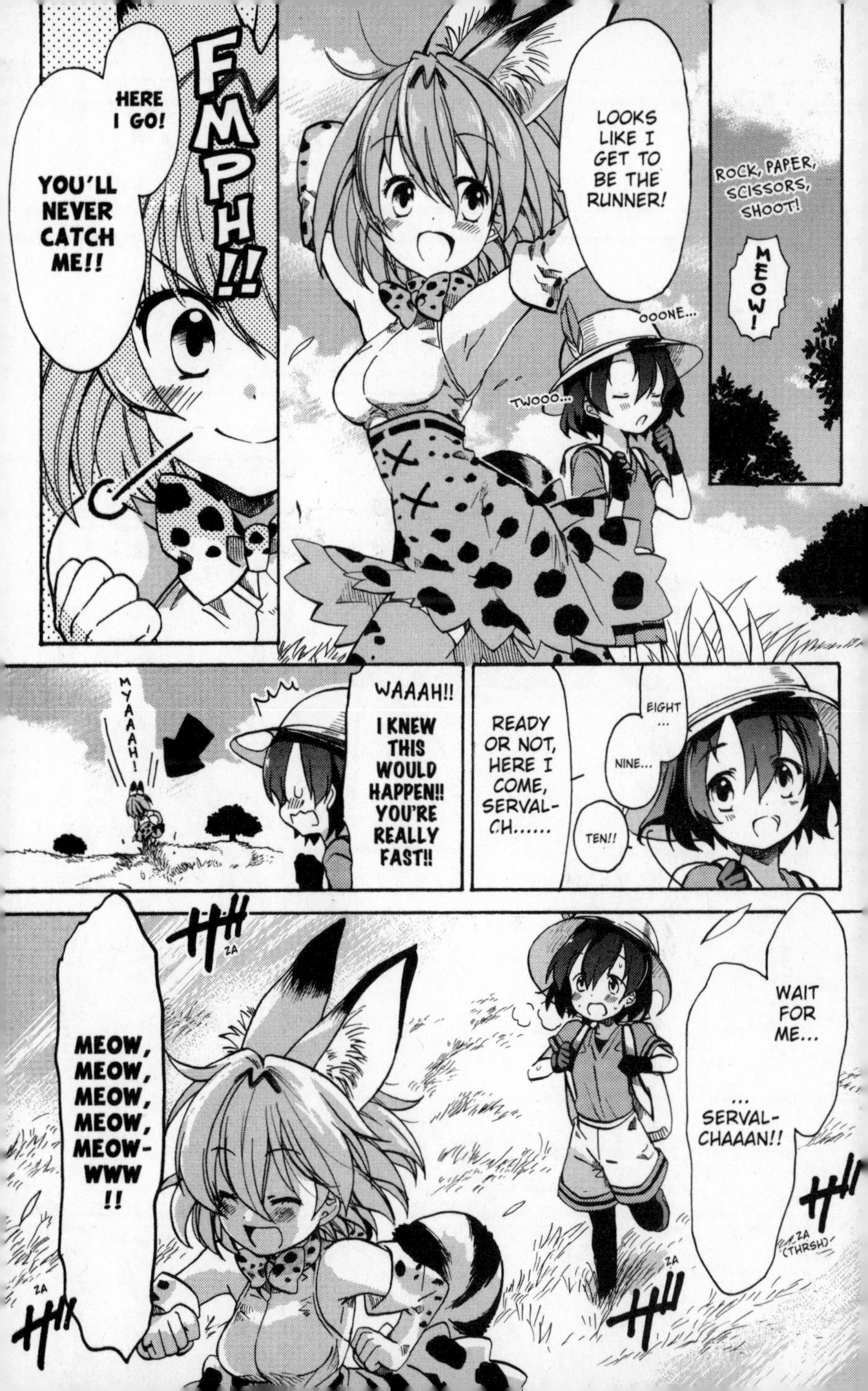
ROCK, PAPER, SCISSORS, SHOOT!
MEOW!
LOOKS LIKE I GET TO BE THE RUNNER!
OOONE...
TWOOO...
FMPH!!
HERE I GO!
YOU'LL NEVER CATCH ME!!
EIGHT...
NINE...
TEN!!
READY OR NOT, HERE I COME, SERVAL-CH......
WAAAH!!
I KNEW THIS WOULD HAPPEN!! YOU'RE REALLY FAST!!
MYAAAH!
WAIT FOR ME...
... SERVAL-CHAAAN!!
ZA (THRSH)
ZA
MEOW, MEOW, MEOW, MEOW, MEOW-WWW!!
ZA
ZA

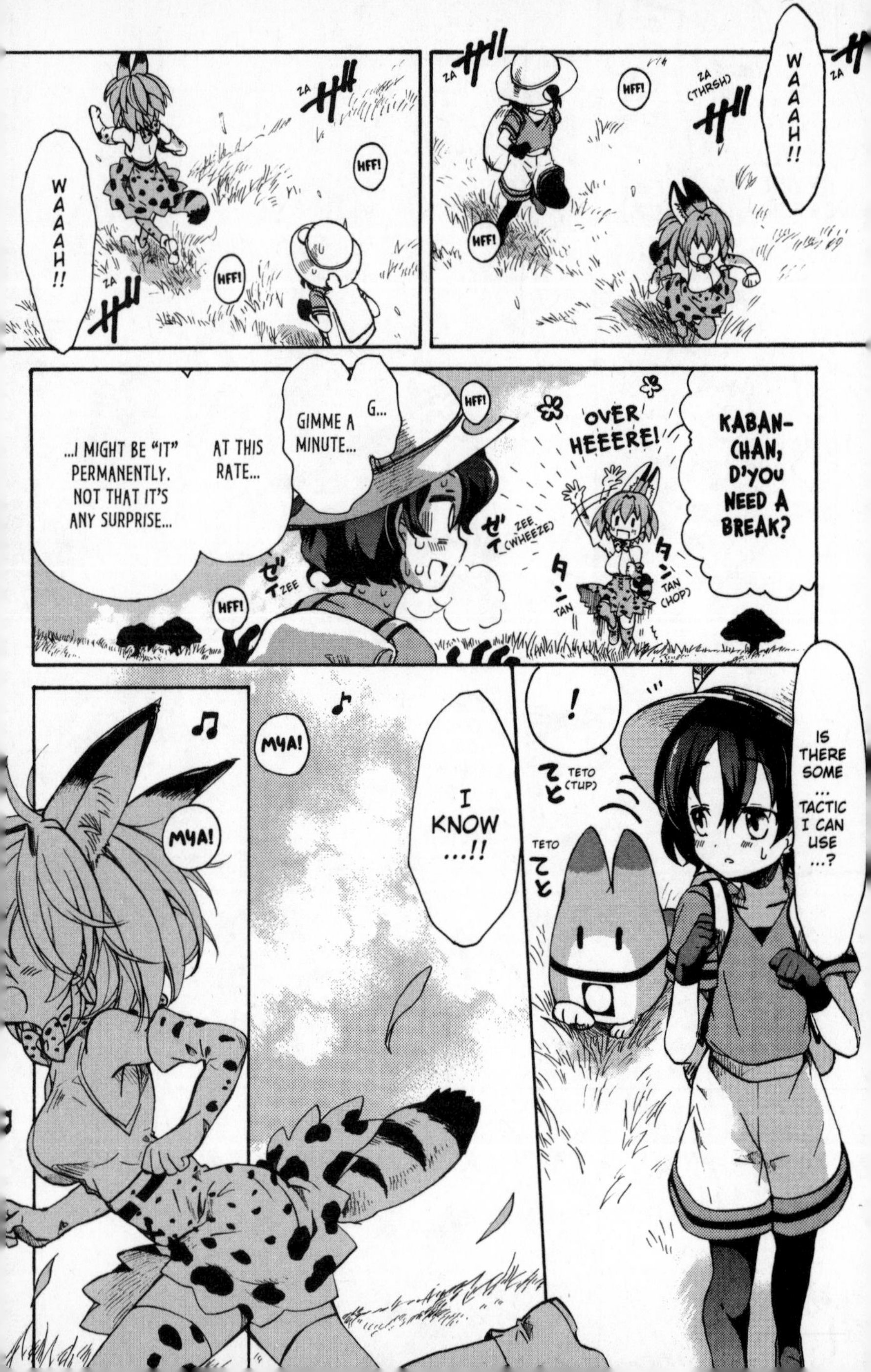
ZA
WAAAH!!
ZA (THRSH)
HFF!
ZA
HFF!
ZA
HFF!
HFF!
WAAAH!!
ZA
KABAN-CHAN, D'YOU NEED A BREAK?
OVER HEEERE!
タン TAN (HOP)
タン TAN
HFF!
G...
GIMME A MINUTE...
ゼイ ZEE (WHEEZE)
ゼイ ZEE
HFF!
AT THIS RATE...
...I MIGHT BE "IT" PERMANENTLY. NOT THAT IT'S ANY SURPRISE...
IS THERE SOME ... TACTIC I CAN USE ...?
!
てと TETO (TUP)
TETO てと
I KNOW ...!!
MYA!
MYA!

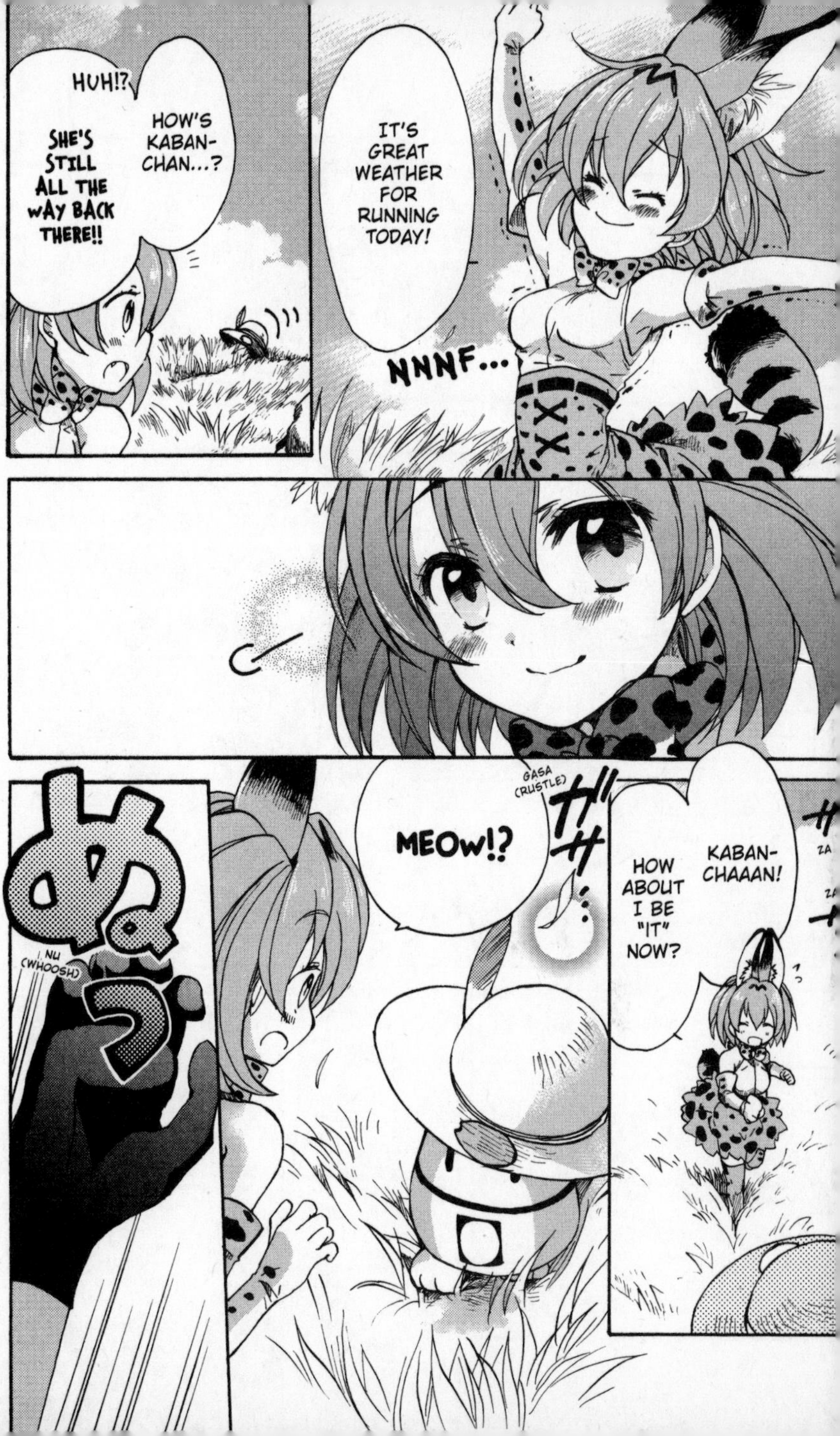
IT'S GREAT WEATHER FOR RUNNING TODAY!
NNNF...
HUH!?
HOW'S KABAN-CHAN...?
SHE'S STILL ALL THE WAY BACK THERE!!
KABAN-CHAAAN!
HOW ABOUT I BE "IT" NOW?
ZA
ZA
GASA (RUSTLE)
MEOW!?
NU (WHOOSH)

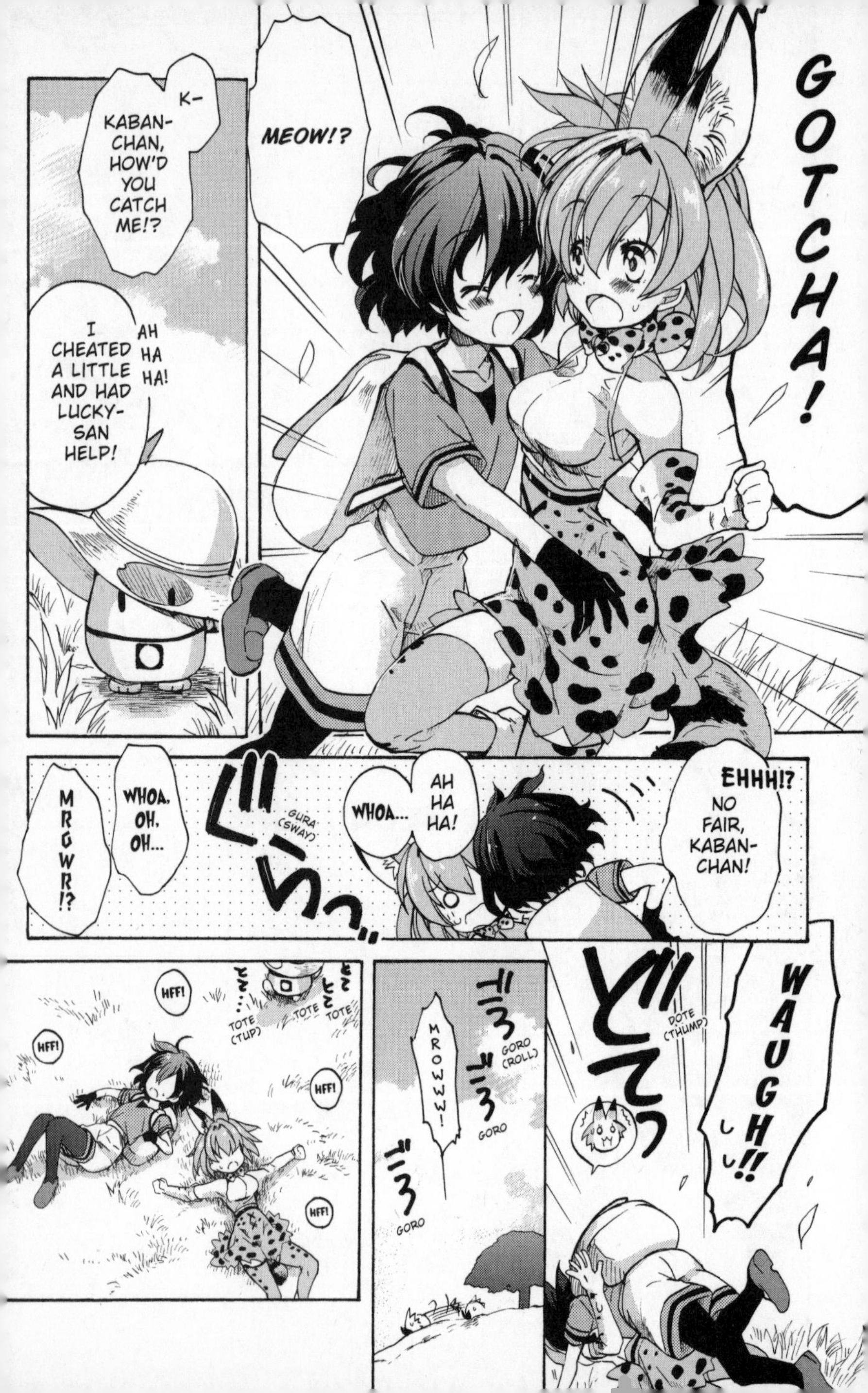
GOTCHA!
MEOW!?
K- KABAN-CHAN, HOW'D YOU CATCH ME!?
AH HA HA!
I CHEATED A LITTLE AND HAD LUCKY-SAN HELP!
EHHH!? NO FAIR, KABAN-CHAN!
AH HA HA!
WHOA...
ぐらっ
GURA (SWAY)
WHOA. OH, OH...
MRGWR!?
WAUGH!!
どてっ
DOTE (THUMP)
ごろ
GORO (ROLL)
MROWWW!
ごろ
GORO
ごろ
GORO
TOTE (TUP)
TOTE
TOTE
HFF!
HFF!
HFF!
HFF!

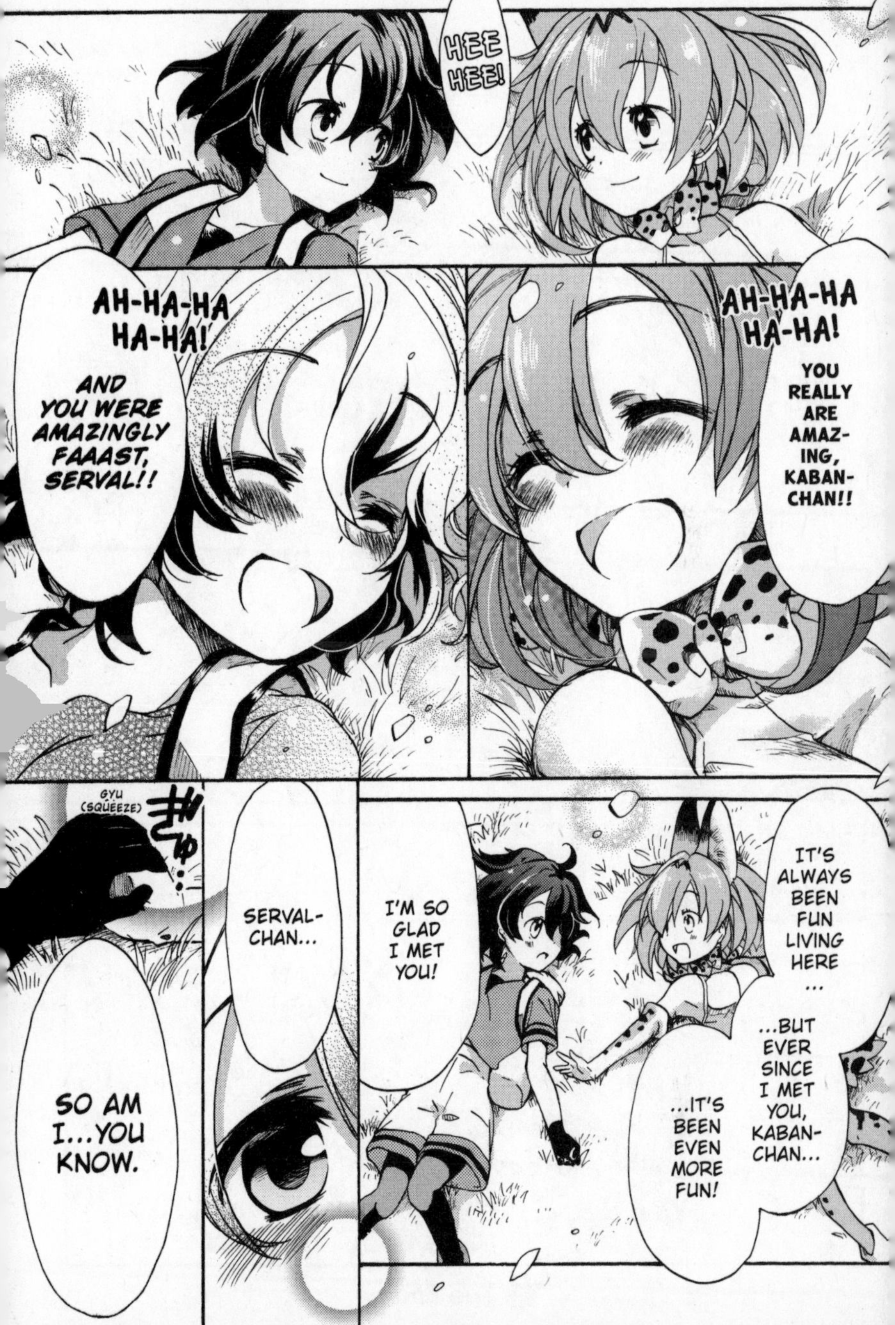
HEE HEE!
AH-HA-HA HA-HA!
YOU REALLY ARE AMAZ-ING, KABAN-CHAN!!
AH-HA-HA HA-HA!
AND YOU WERE AMAZINGLY FAAAST, SERVAL!!
IT'S ALWAYS BEEN FUN LIVING HERE...
...BUT EVER SINCE I MET YOU, KABAN-CHAN...
...IT'S BEEN EVEN MORE FUN!
I'M SO GLAD I MET YOU!
SERVAL-CHAN...
GYU (SQUEEZE)
SO AM I...YOU KNOW.

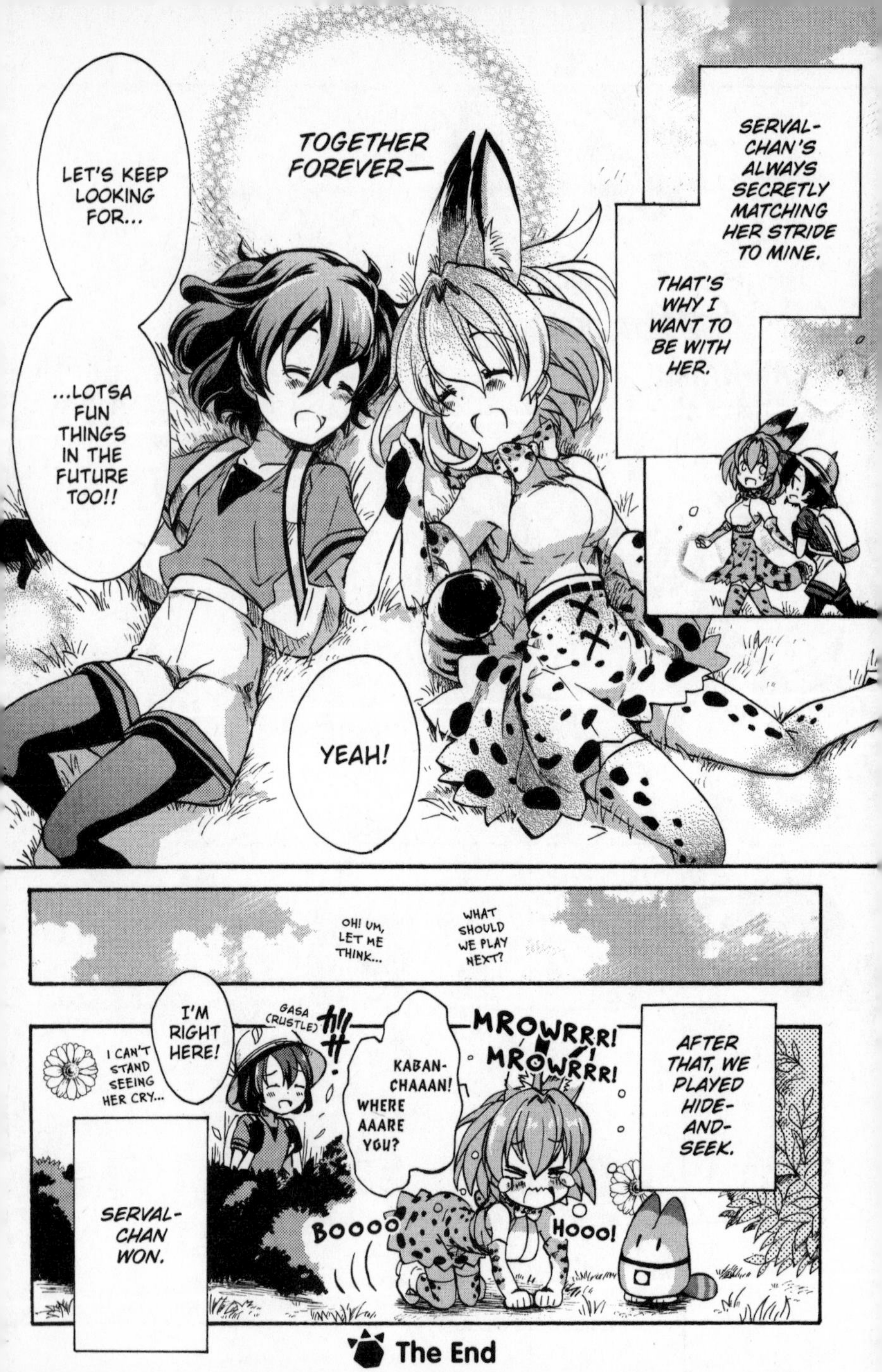
SERVAL-CHAN'S ALWAYS SECRETLY MATCHING HER STRIDE TO MINE.
THAT'S WHY I WANT TO BE WITH HER.
TOGETHER FOREVER—
LET'S KEEP LOOKING FOR...
...LOTSA FUN THINGS IN THE FUTURE TOO!!
YEAH!
WHAT SHOULD WE PLAY NEXT?
OH! UM, LET ME THINK...
AFTER THAT, WE PLAYED HIDE-AND-SEEK.
MROWRRR! MROWRRR!
KABAN-CHAAAN! WHERE AAARE YOU?
GASA (RUSTLE)
I'M RIGHT HERE!
I CAN'T STAND SEEING HER CRY...
BOOOO HOOO!
SERVAL-CHAN WON.

The End

Everyday PPP

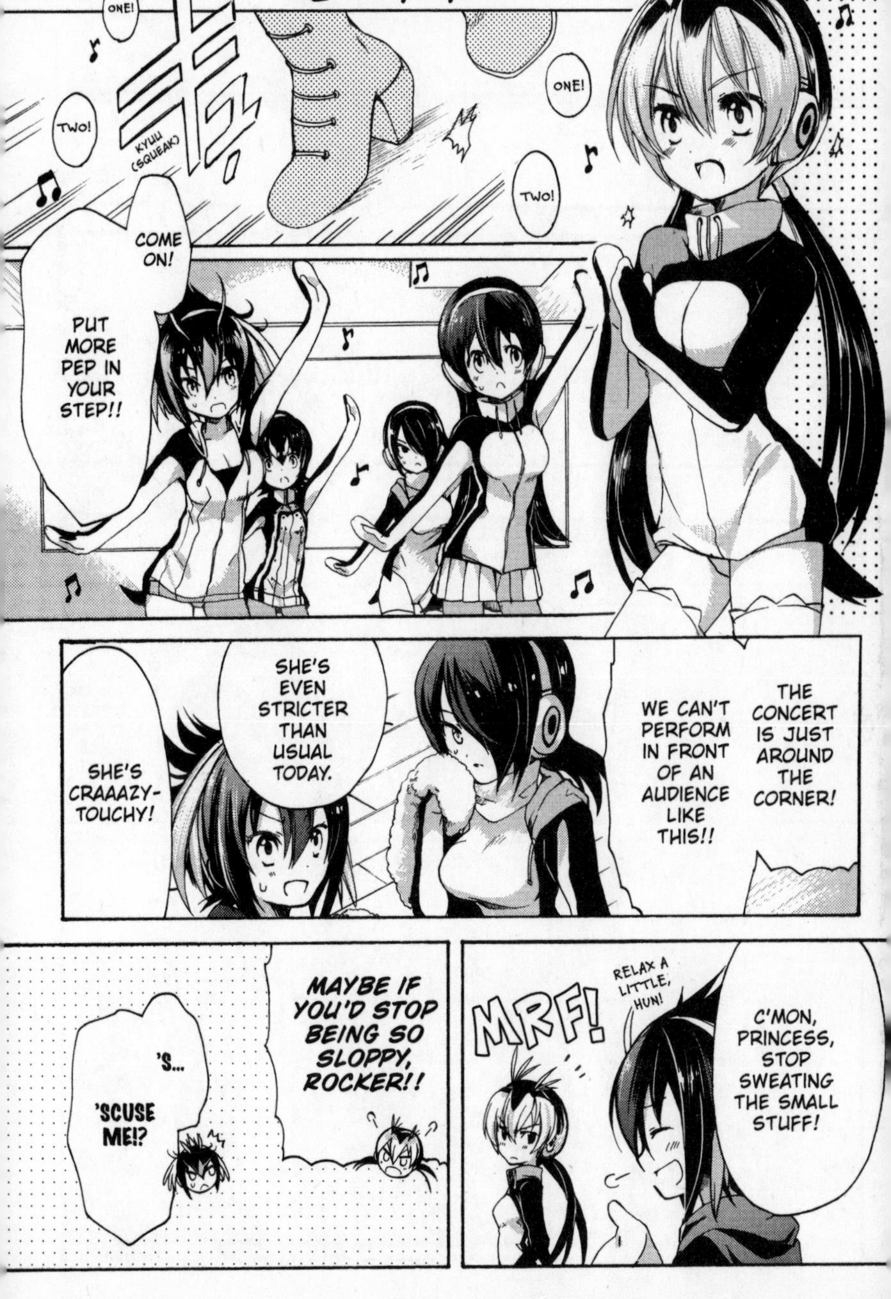
ONE!
TWO!
ONE!
TWO!
KYUU (SQUEAK)
COME ON!
PUT MORE PEP IN YOUR STEP!!
THE CONCERT IS JUST AROUND THE CORNER!
WE CAN'T PERFORM IN FRONT OF AN AUDIENCE LIKE THIS!!
SHE'S EVEN STRICTER THAN USUAL TODAY.
SHE'S CRAAAZY-TOUCHY!
C'MON, PRINCESS, STOP SWEATING THE SMALL STUFF!
RELAX A LITTLE, HUN!
MRF!
MAYBE IF YOU'D STOP BEING SO SLOPPY, ROCKER!!
'S...
'SCUSE ME!?

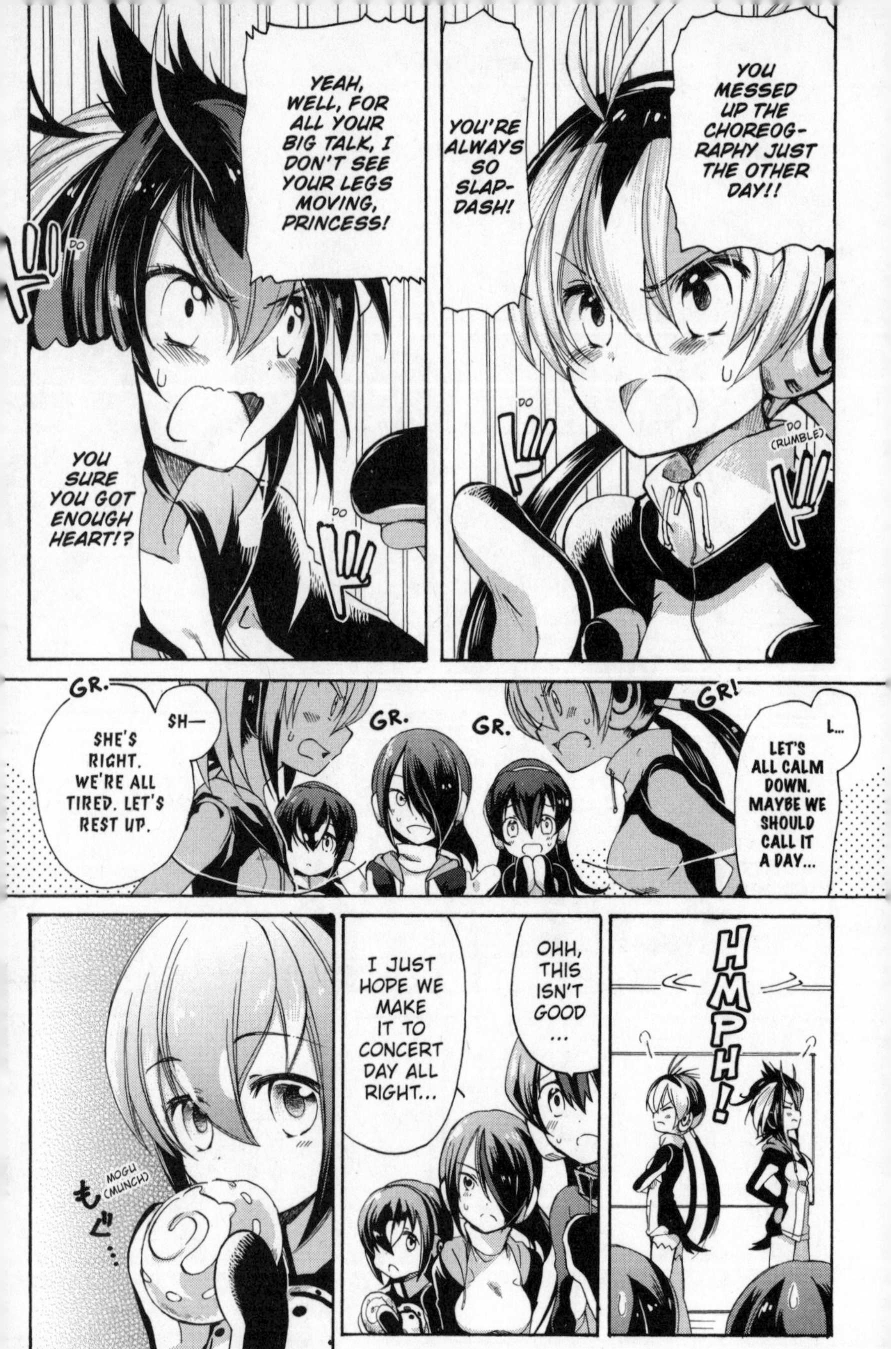
YOU MESSED UP THE CHOREOGRAPHY JUST THE OTHER DAY!!
YOU'RE ALWAYS SO SLAPDASH!
DO
DO (RUMBLE)
YEAH, WELL, FOR ALL YOUR BIG TALK, I DON'T SEE YOUR LEGS MOVING, PRINCESS!
DO
YOU SURE YOU GOT ENOUGH HEART!?
DO
GR!
L...
LET'S ALL CALM DOWN. MAYBE WE SHOULD CALL IT A DAY...
GR.
GR.
GR.
SH—
SHE'S RIGHT. WE'RE ALL TIRED. LET'S REST UP.
HMPH!
OHH, THIS ISN'T GOOD...
I JUST HOPE WE MAKE IT TO CONCERT DAY ALL RIGHT...
MOGU (MUNCH)

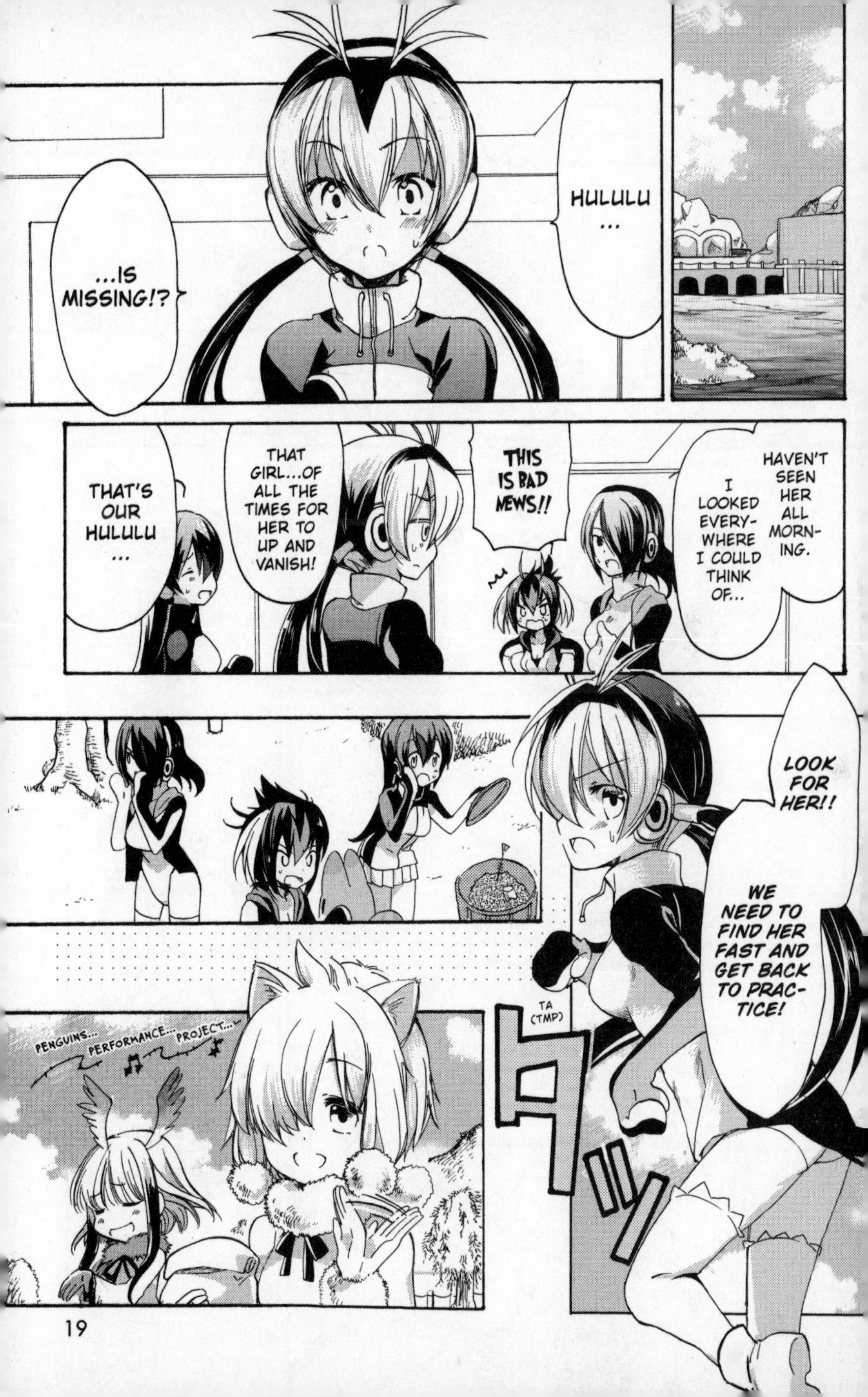
HULULU ...
...IS MISSING!?
I LOOKED EVERY-WHERE I COULD THINK OF... HAVEN'T SEEN HER ALL MORN-ING.
THIS IS BAD NEWS!!
THAT GIRL...OF ALL THE TIMES FOR HER TO UP AND VANISH!
THAT'S OUR HULULU ...
LOOK FOR HER!!
WE NEED TO FIND HER FAST AND GET BACK TO PRAC-TICE!
TA (TMP)
PENGUINS... PERFORMANCE... PROJECT...

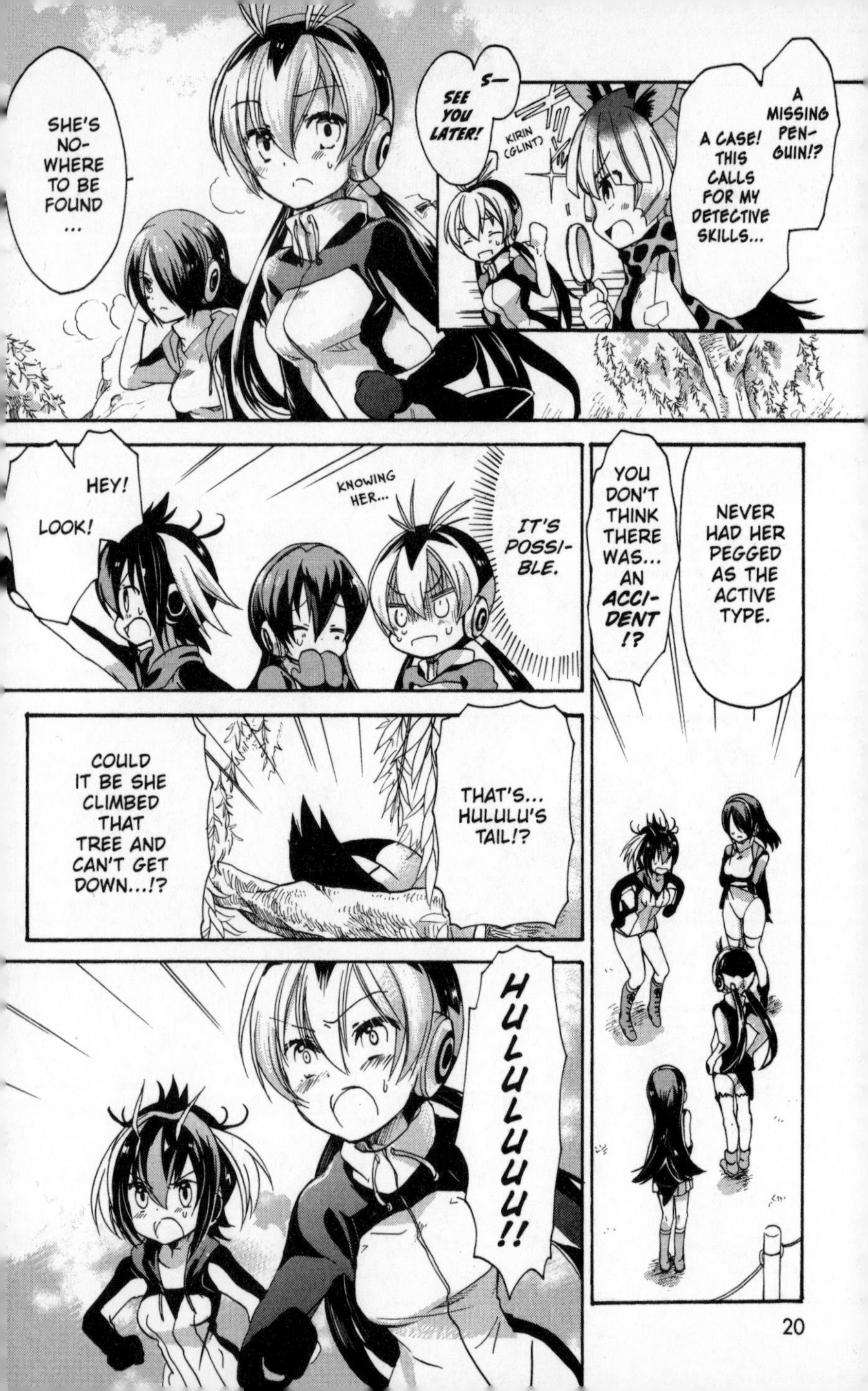
A MISSING PEN-GUIN!?
A CASE! THIS CALLS FOR MY DETECTIVE SKILLS...
KIRIN (GLINT)
S— SEE YOU LATER!
SHE'S NO-WHERE TO BE FOUND...
NEVER HAD HER PEGGED AS THE ACTIVE TYPE.
YOU DON'T THINK THERE WAS... AN ACCI-DENT!?
IT'S POSSI-BLE.
KNOWING HER...
HEY!
LOOK!
THAT'S... HULULU'S TAIL!?
COULD IT BE SHE CLIMBED THAT TREE AND CAN'T GET DOWN...!?
HULULUUUU!!

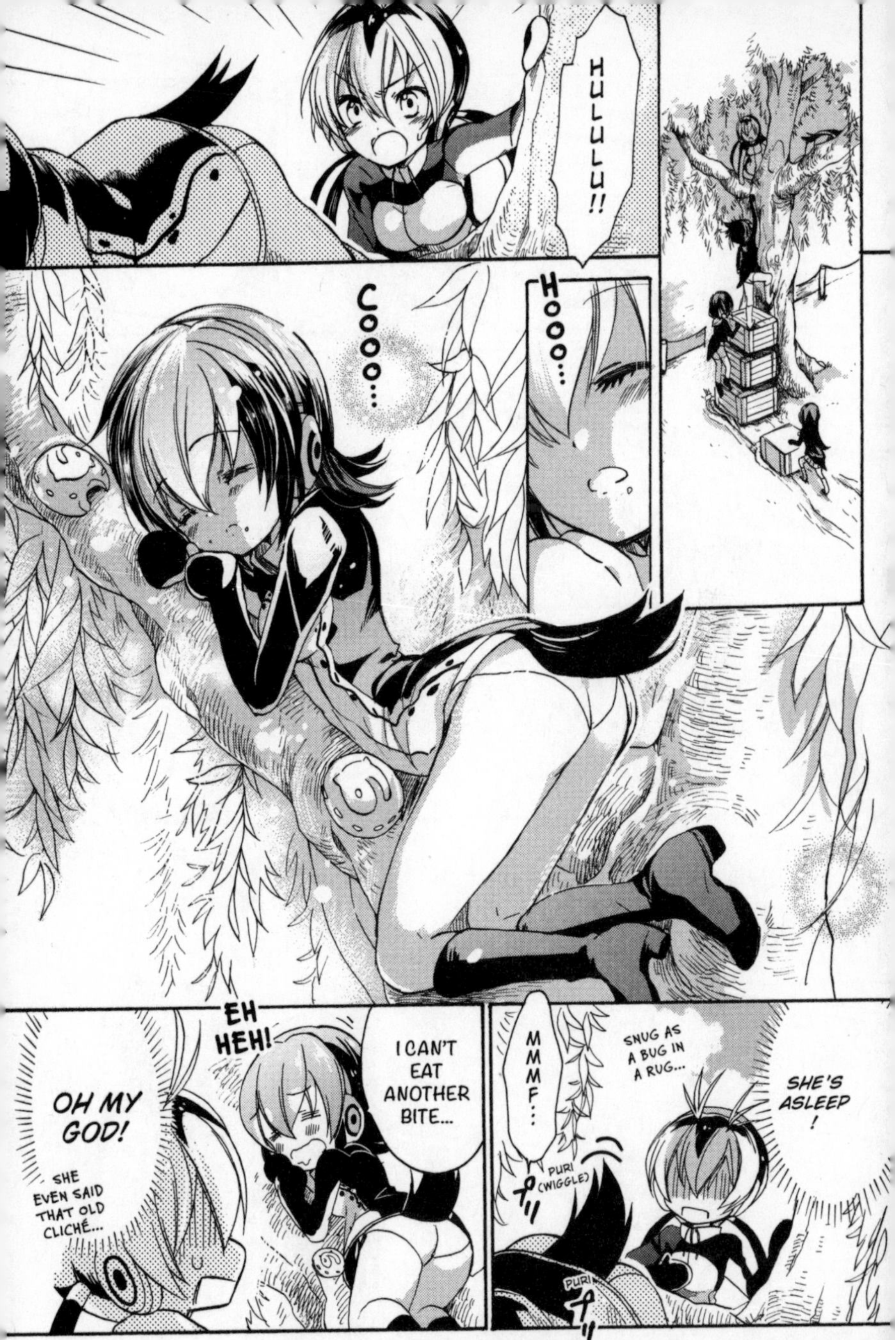
HULULU!!
HOOO...
COOO...
SHE'S ASLEEP!
SNUG AS A BUG IN A RUG...
MMMF...
PURI (WIGGLE)
PURI
I CAN'T EAT ANOTHER BITE...
EH HEH!
OH MY GOD!
SHE EVEN SAID THAT OLD CLICHÉ...

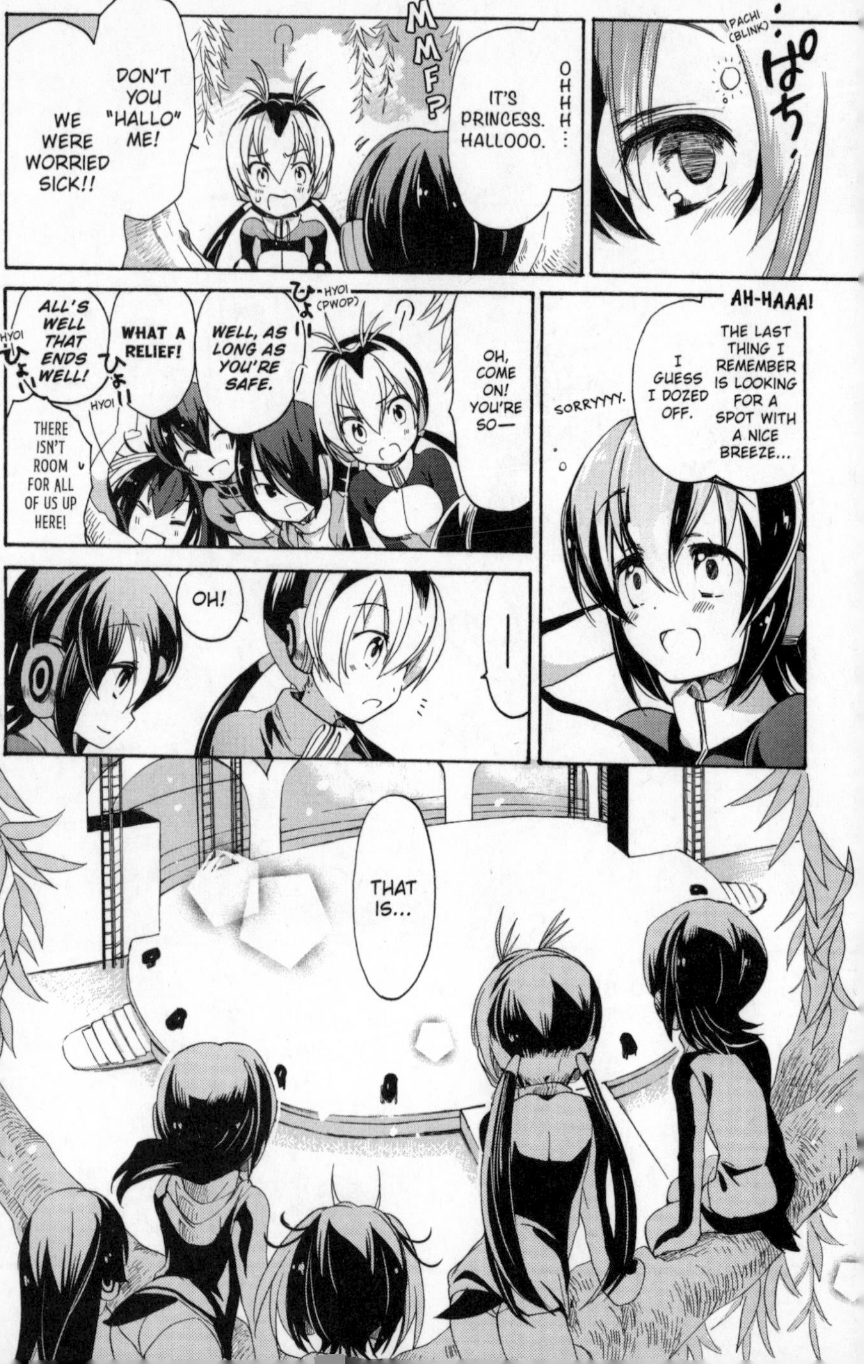

PACHI (BLINK)
ぱち
...
OHHH...
IT'S PRINCESS. HALLOOO.
MMF?
DON'T YOU "HALLO" ME!
WE WERE WORRIED SICK!!
AH-HAAA!
THE LAST THING I REMEMBER IS LOOKING FOR A SPOT WITH A NICE BREEZE...
I GUESS I DOZED OFF.
SORRYYYY.
OH, COME ON! YOU'RE SO—
ひょい
HYOI (PWOP)
WELL, AS LONG AS YOU'RE SAFE.
ひょい
HYOI
WHAT A RELIEF!
ひょい
HYOI
ALL'S WELL THAT ENDS WELL!
THERE ISN'T ROOM FOR ALL OF US UP HERE!
OH!
THAT IS...

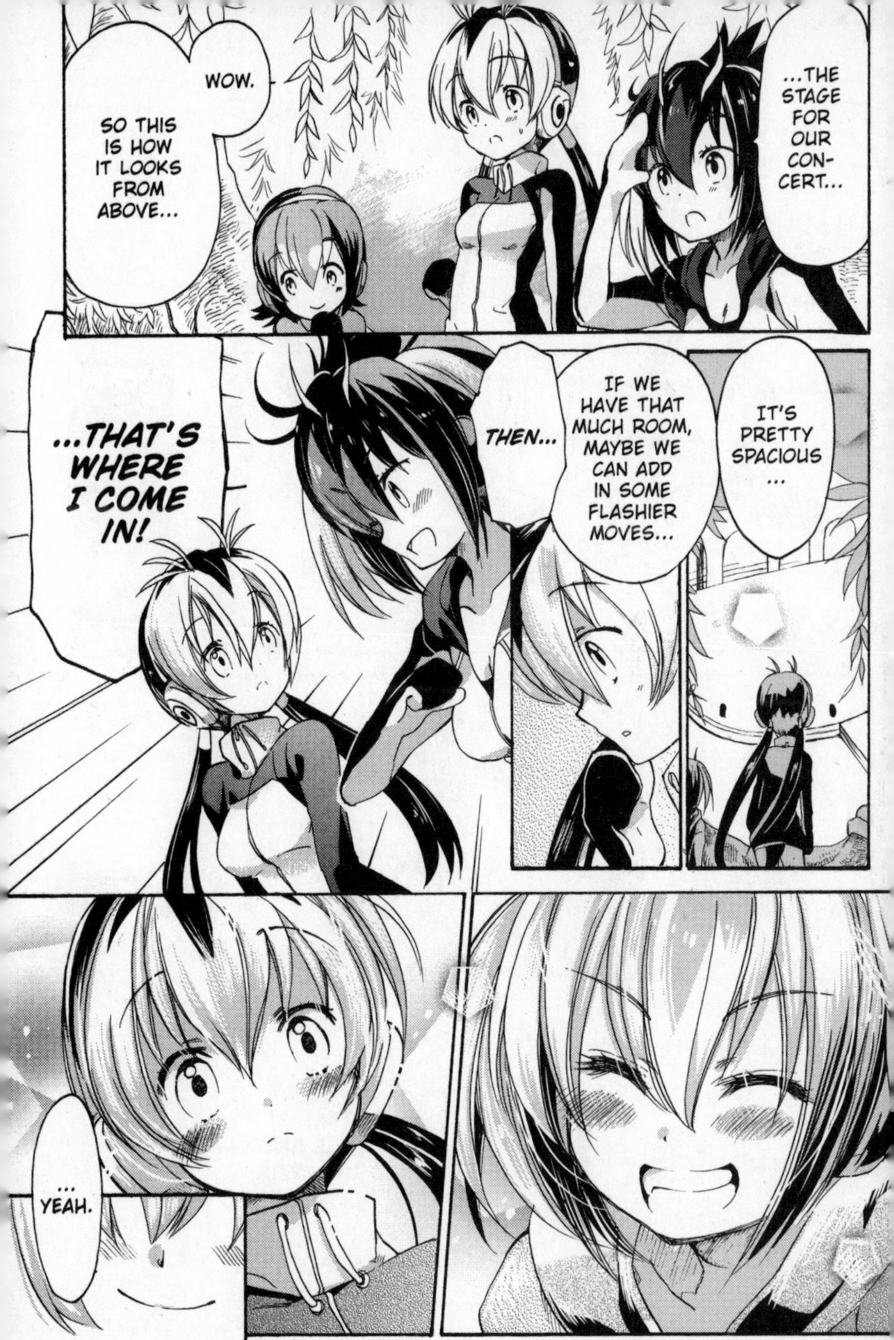
...THE STAGE FOR OUR CONCERT...
WOW.
SO THIS IS HOW IT LOOKS FROM ABOVE...
IT'S PRETTY SPACIOUS ...
IF WE HAVE THAT MUCH ROOM, MAYBE WE CAN ADD IN SOME FLASHIER MOVES...
THEN...
...THAT'S WHERE I COME IN!
... YEAH.

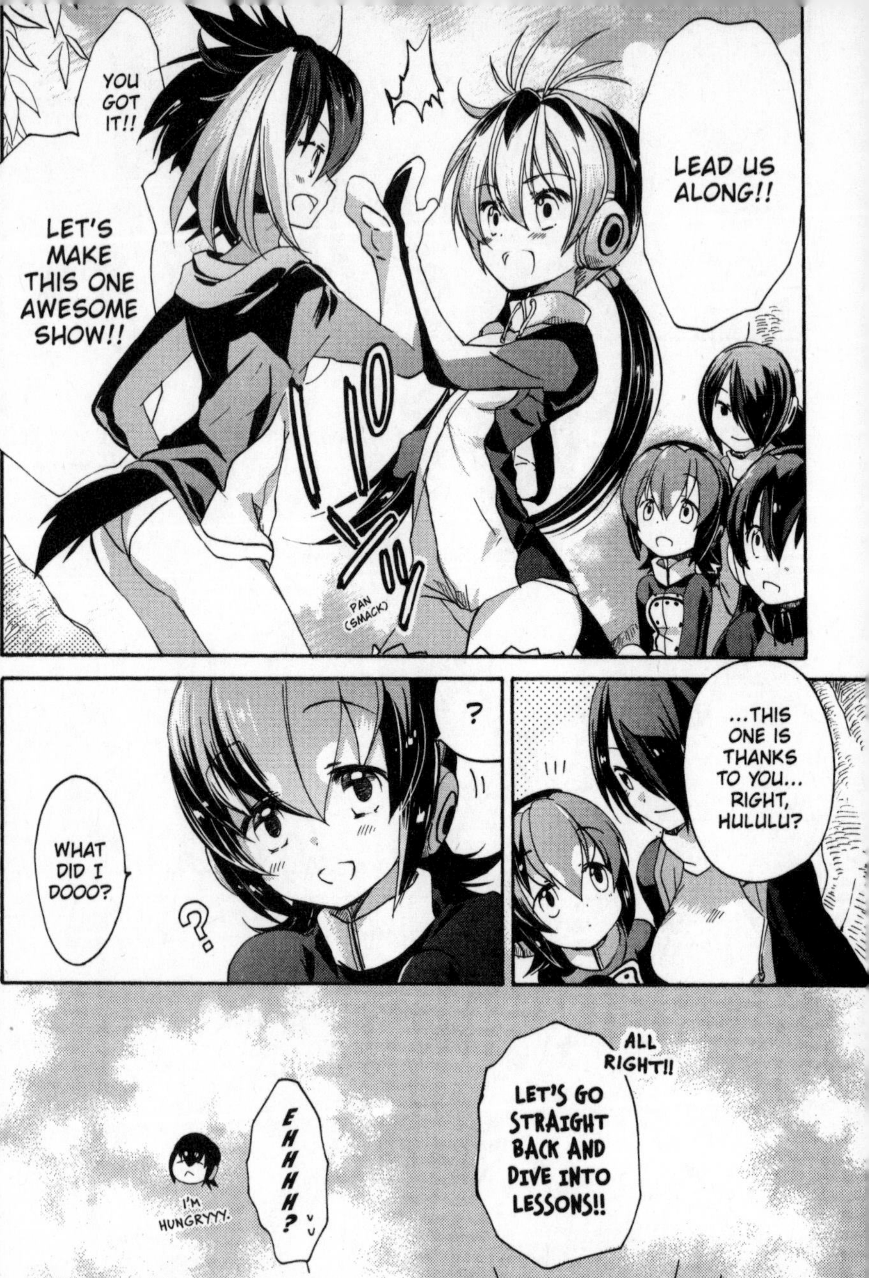
LEAD US ALONG!!
YOU GOT IT!!
LET'S MAKE THIS ONE AWESOME SHOW!!
PAN (SMACK)
...THIS ONE IS THANKS TO YOU... RIGHT, HULULU?
?
WHAT DID I DOOO?
ALL RIGHT!!
LET'S GO STRAIGHT BACK AND DIVE INTO LESSONS!!
EHHHH?
I'M HUNGRYYY.

The End

Yasuyuki Kosaka ◆ Crested Ibis's Errand

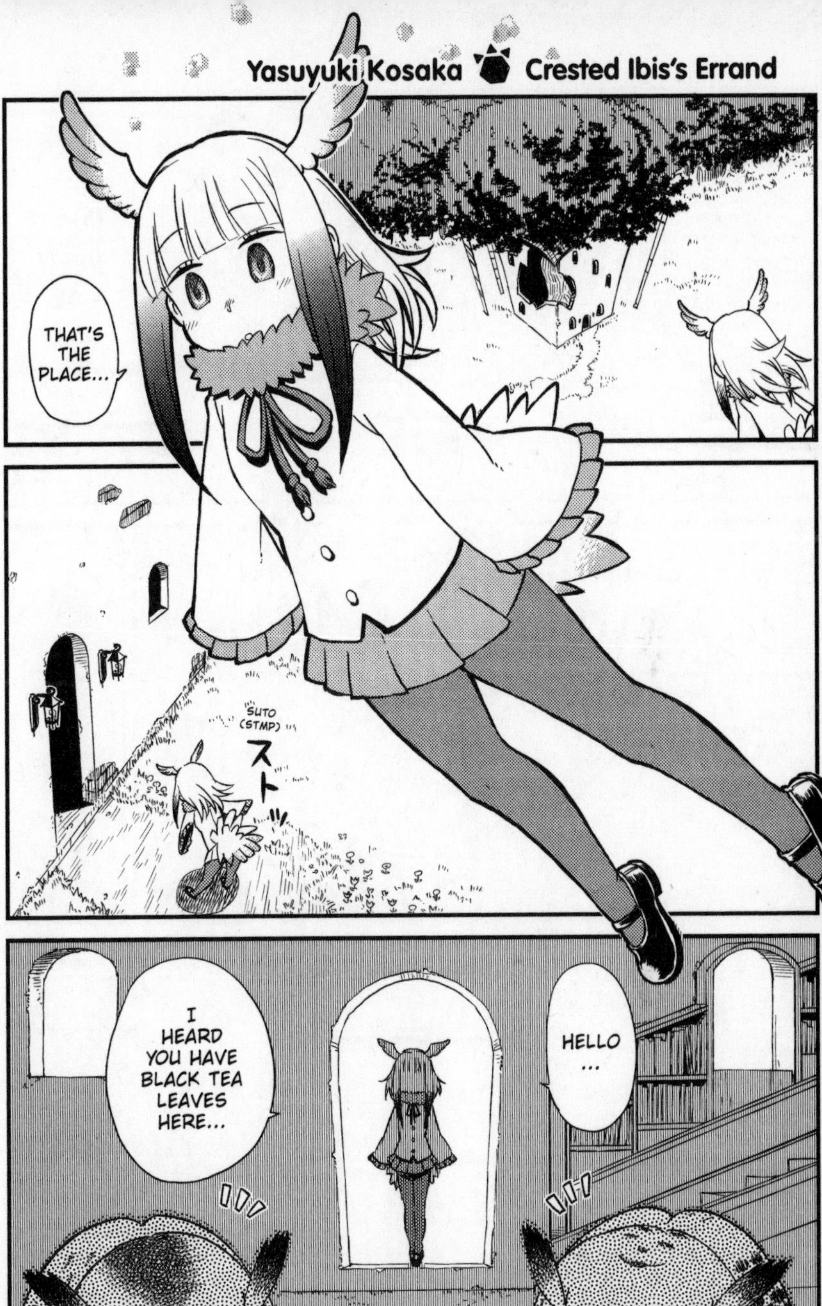

THAT'S THE PLACE...
SUTO (STMP)
スト
HELLO ...
I HEARD YOU HAVE BLACK TEA LEAVES HERE...

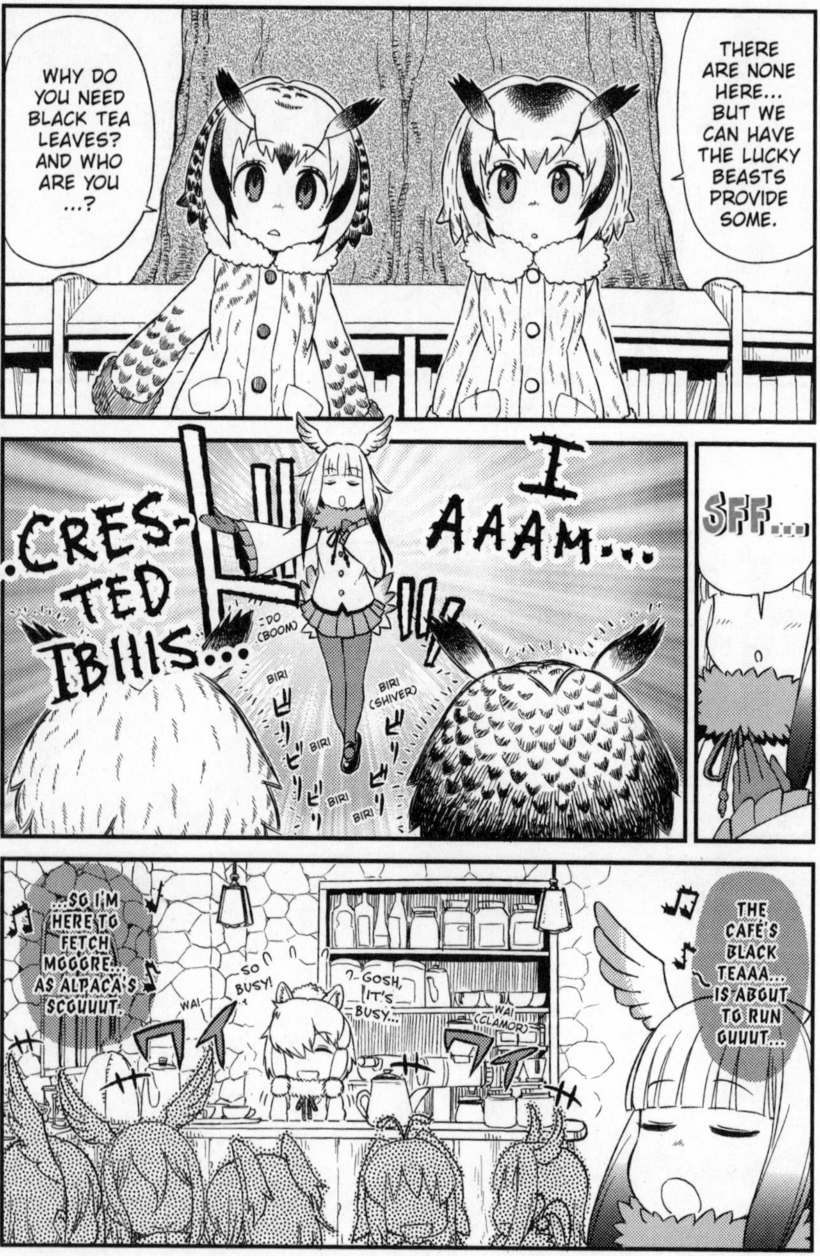
THERE ARE NONE HERE... BUT WE CAN HAVE THE LUCKY BEASTS PROVIDE SOME.
WHY DO YOU NEED BLACK TEA LEAVES? AND WHO ARE YOU ...?
SFF...
I AAAM...
..CRES-TED IBIIIS...
DO (BOOM)
BIRI (SHIVER)
BIRI
BIRI
BIRI
BIRI
THE CAFÉ'S BLACK TEAAA... IS ABOUT TO RUN OUUUT...
WAI (CLAMOR)
GOSH, IT'S BUSY...
SO BUSY!
WAI
...SO I'M HERE TO FETCH MOOORE AS ALPACA'S SCOUUUT.

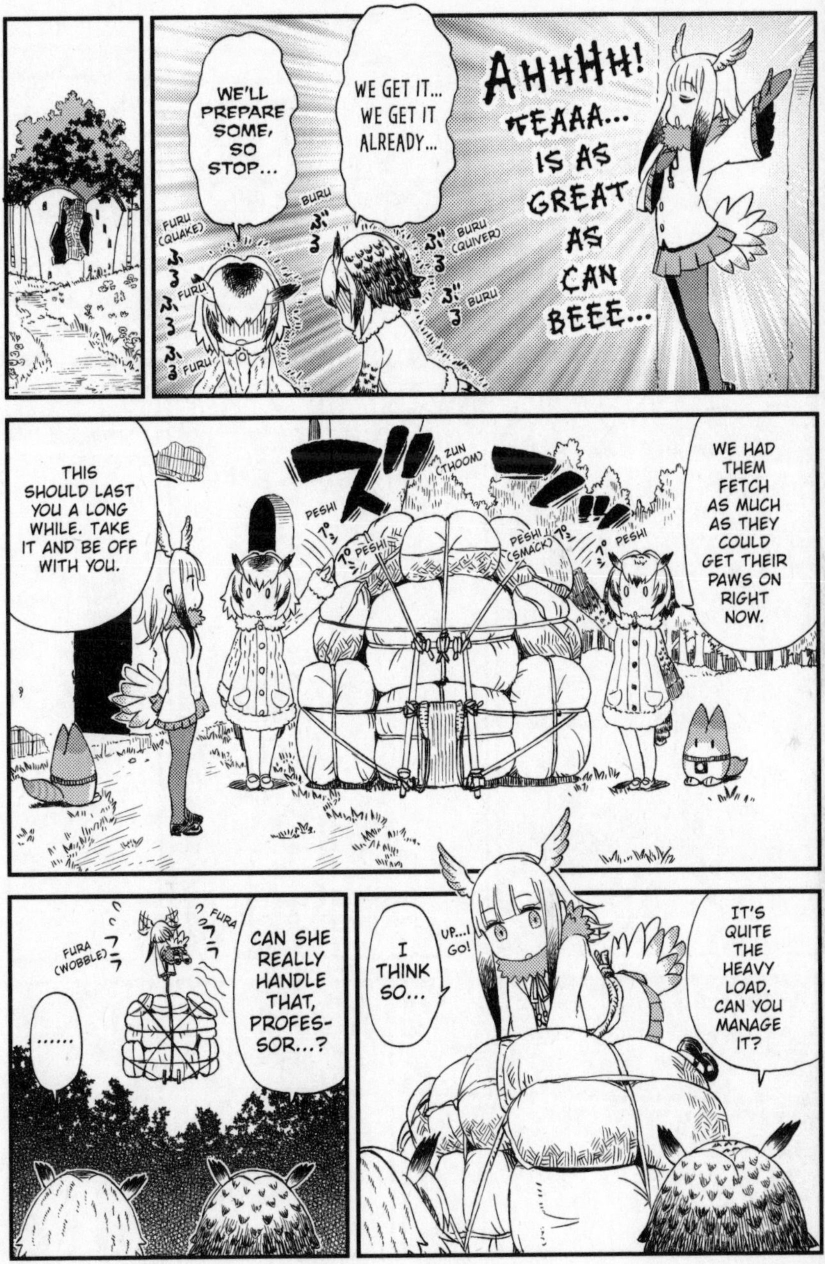
AHHHH! TEAAA... IS AS GREAT AS CAN BEEE...
BURU (QUIVER) ぶる
BURU ぶる
WE GET IT... WE GET IT ALREADY...
BURU ぶる
WE'LL PREPARE SOME, SO STOP...
FURU (QUAKE) ふる
FURU ふる
FURU ふる
WE HAD THEM FETCH AS MUCH AS THEY COULD GET THEIR PAWS ON RIGHT NOW.
ズーン
ZUN (THOOM)
PESHI
PESHI (SMACK)
PESHI
PESHI
THIS SHOULD LAST YOU A LONG WHILE. TAKE IT AND BE OFF WITH YOU.
IT'S QUITE THE HEAVY LOAD. CAN YOU MANAGE IT?
UP...! GO!
I THINK SO...
CAN SHE REALLY HANDLE THAT, PROFES-SOR...?
FURA
FURA (WOBBLE)
......

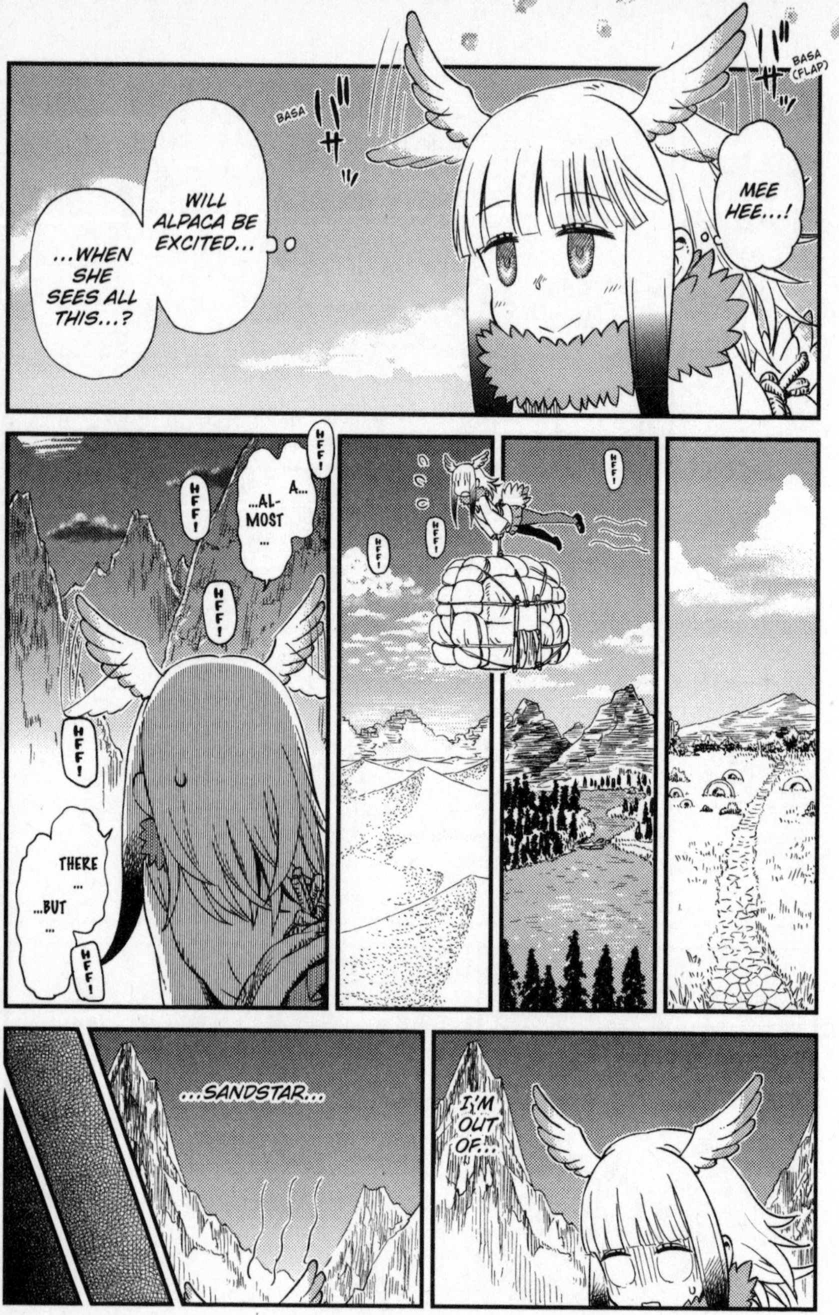
BASA (FLAP)
MEE HEE...!
BASA
WILL ALPACA BE EXCITED...
...WHEN SHE SEES ALL THIS...?
HFF!
HFF!
HFF!
HFF!
A...
...AL-MOST ...
HFF!
HFF!
HFF!
THERE ... ...BUT ...
HFF!
I'M OUT OF...
...SANDSTAR...

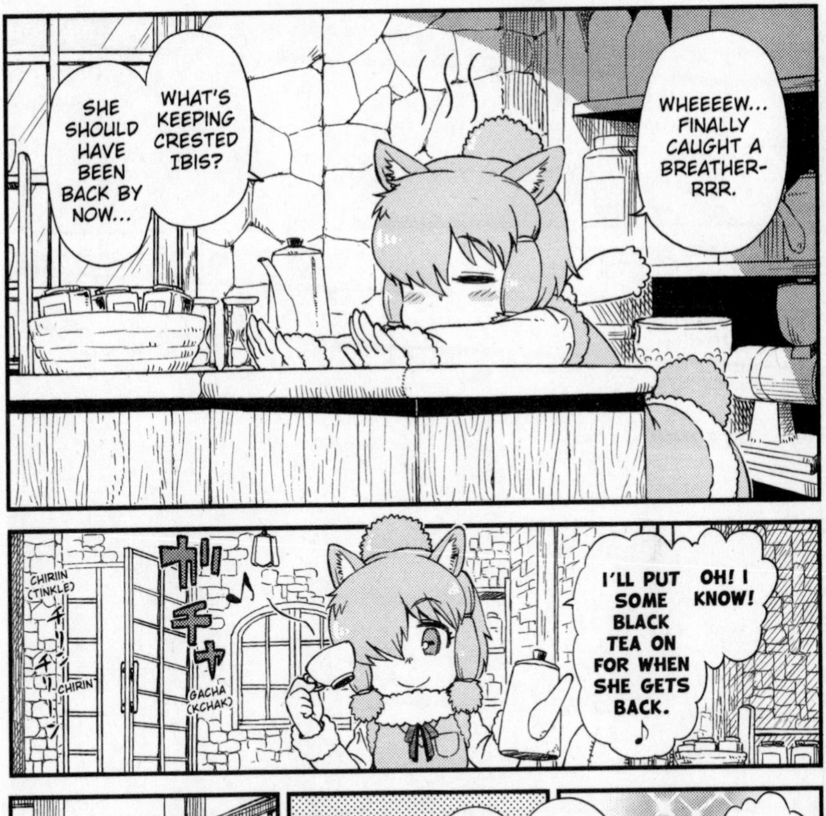
WHEEEEW... FINALLY CAUGHT A BREATHER-RRR.
WHAT'S KEEPING CRESTED IBIS?
SHE SHOULD HAVE BEEN BACK BY NOW...
OH! I KNOW!
I'LL PUT SOME BLACK TEA ON FOR WHEN SHE GETS BACK. ♪
ガチャ
GACHA (KCHAK)
チリーン
CHIRIIN (TINKLE)
チリーン
CHIRIN
AH! WELCOME BAAACK!
THANKS FOR THE HEEELP. IT WAS A LONG TRIP, RIIIGHT?
I'LL FIX YOU UP A CUPPA TEA RIGHT A...
BOSS ...?

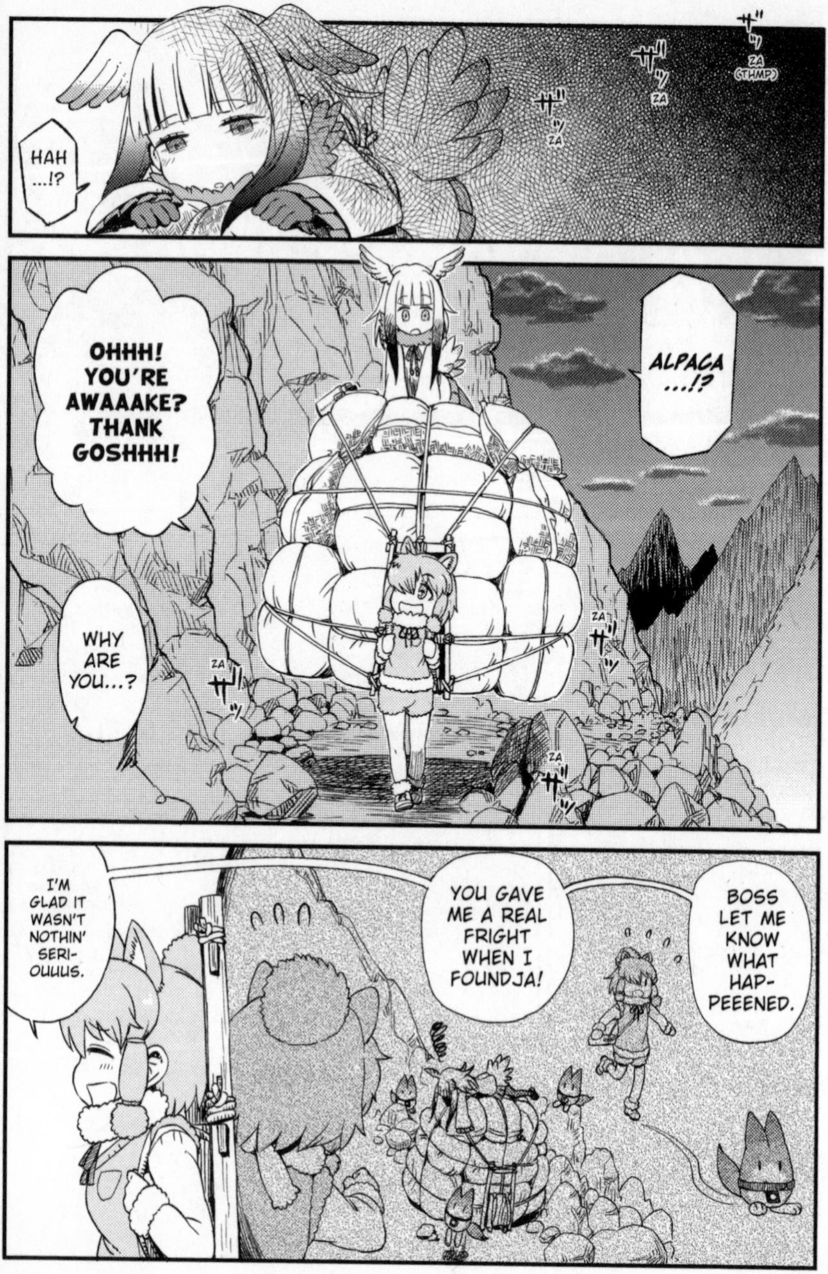
ZA (THMP)
ZA
ZA
HAH ...!?
ALPACA ...!?
OHHH! YOU'RE AWAAAKE? THANK GOSHHH!
ZA
ZA
WHY ARE YOU...?
ZA
BOSS LET ME KNOW WHAT HAP-PEEENED.
YOU GAVE ME A REAL FRIGHT WHEN I FOUNDJA!
I'M GLAD IT WASN'T NOTHIN' SERI-OUUUS.

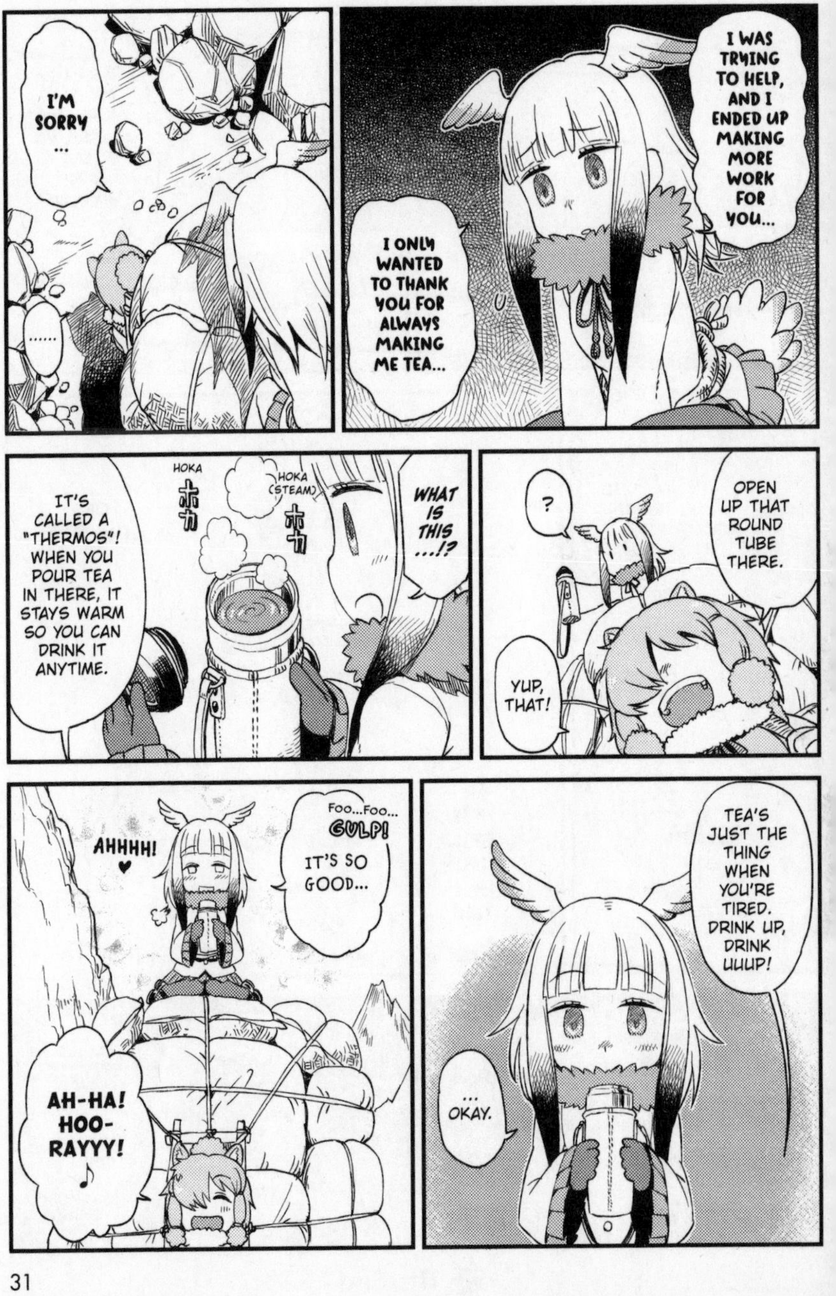
I WAS TRYING TO HELP, AND I ENDED UP MAKING MORE WORK FOR YOU...
I ONLY WANTED TO THANK YOU FOR ALWAYS MAKING ME TEA...
I'M SORRY ...
......
OPEN UP THAT ROUND TUBE THERE.
?
YUP, THAT!
WHAT IS THIS ...!?
HOKA (STEAM)
ホカ
HOKA
ホカ
IT'S CALLED A "THERMOS"! WHEN YOU POUR TEA IN THERE, IT STAYS WARM SO YOU CAN DRINK IT ANYTIME.
TEA'S JUST THE THING WHEN YOU'RE TIRED. DRINK UP, DRINK UUUP!
... OKAY.
Foo...Foo... GULP!
IT'S SO GOOD...
AHHHH! ♥
AH-HA! HOO-RAYYY! ♪

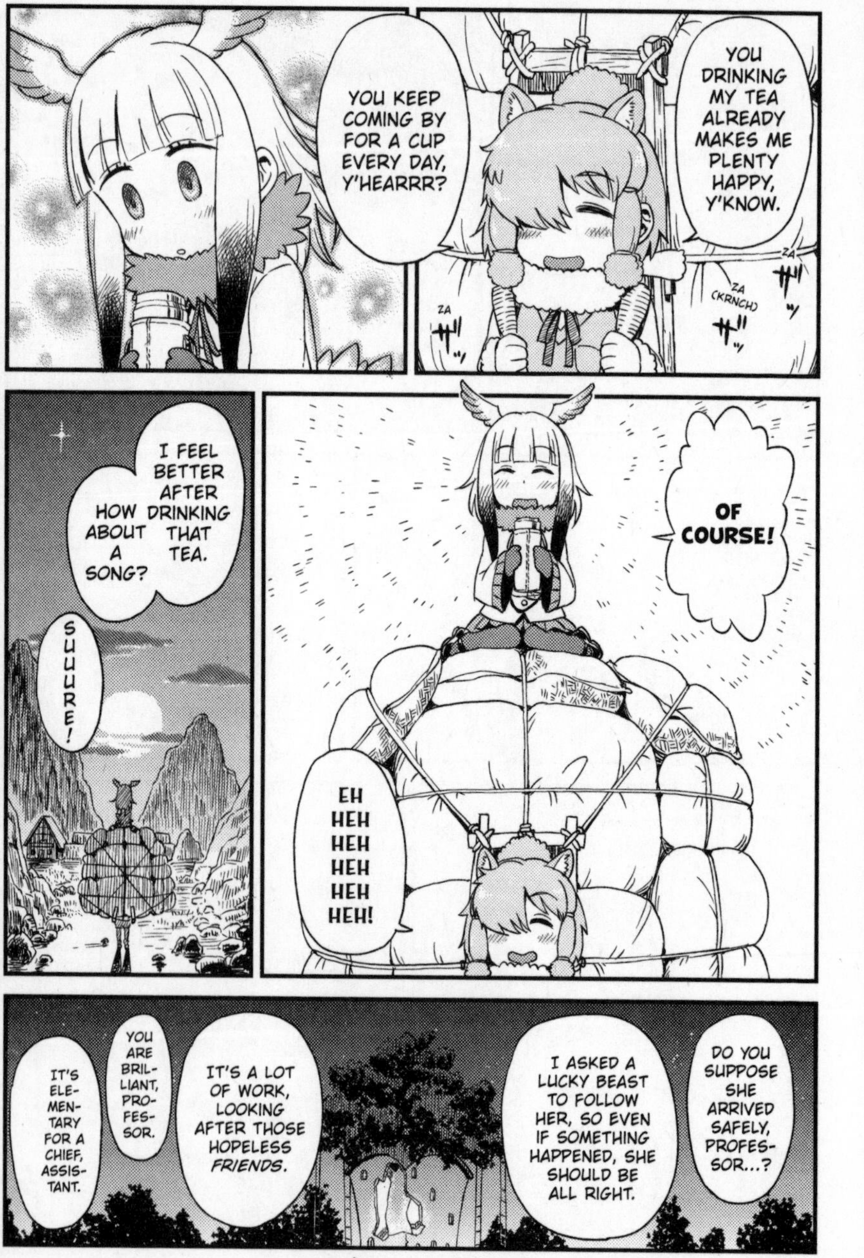
YOU DRINKING MY TEA ALREADY MAKES ME PLENTY HAPPY, Y'KNOW.
ZA
ZA (KRNCH)
ZA
YOU KEEP COMING BY FOR A CUP EVERY DAY, Y'HEARRR?
OF COURSE!
EH HEH HEH HEH HEH HEH!
I FEEL BETTER AFTER DRINKING THAT TEA.
HOW ABOUT A SONG?
SUUURE!
DO YOU SUPPOSE SHE ARRIVED SAFELY, PROFES-SOR...?
I ASKED A LUCKY BEAST TO FOLLOW HER, SO EVEN IF SOMETHING HAPPENED, SHE SHOULD BE ALL RIGHT.
IT'S A LOT OF WORK, LOOKING AFTER THOSE HOPELESS *FRIENDS*.
YOU ARE BRIL-LIANT, PRO-FES-SOR.
IT'S ELE-MEN-TARY FOR A CHIEF, ASSIS-TANT.

The End

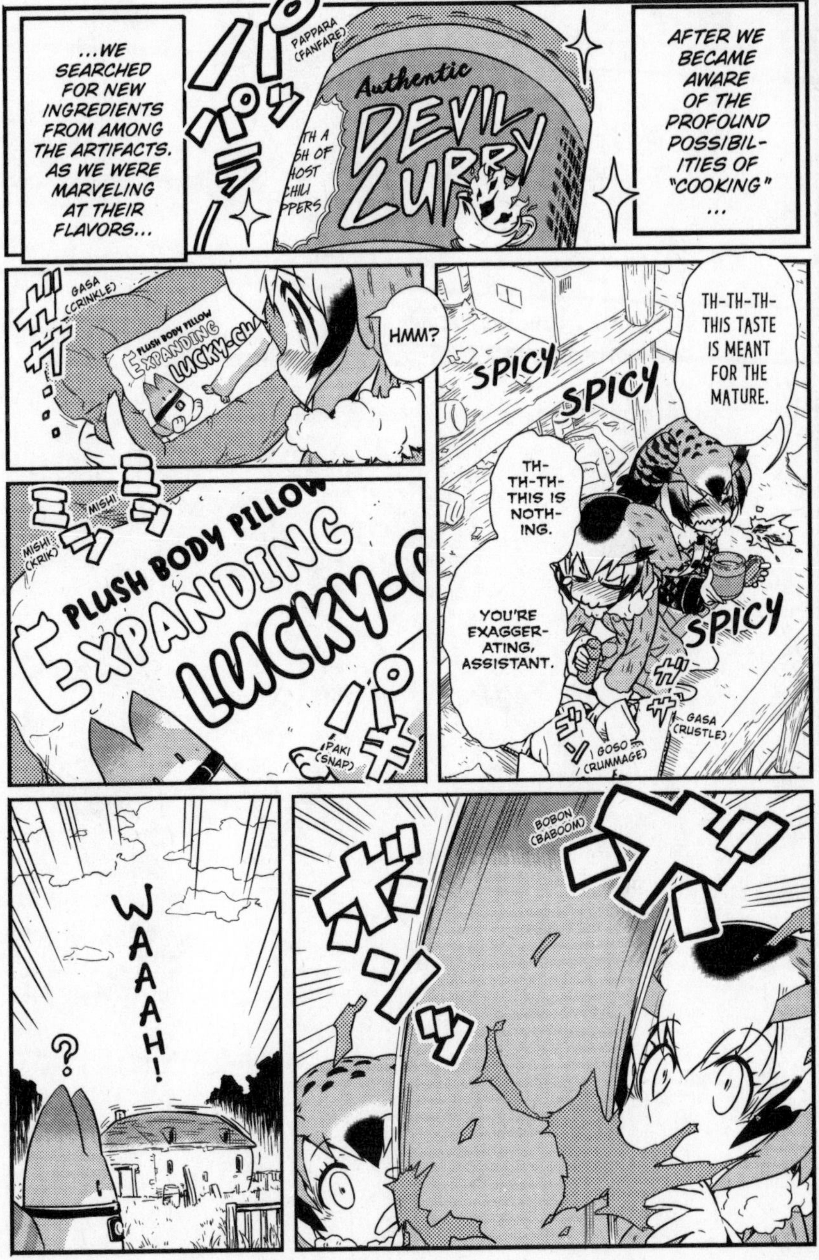
AFTER WE BECAME AWARE OF THE PROFOUND POSSIBILI-TIES OF "COOKING" ...
PAPPARA (FANFARE)
Authentic
DEVIL CURRY
...WE SEARCHED FOR NEW INGREDIENTS FROM AMONG THE ARTIFACTS. AS WE WERE MARVELING AT THEIR FLAVORS...
TH-TH-TH-THIS TASTE IS MEANT FOR THE MATURE.
SPICY
SPICY
TH-TH-TH-THIS IS NOTH-ING.
YOU'RE EXAGGER-ATING, ASSISTANT.
SPICY
GASA (RUSTLE)
GOSO (RUMMAGE)
HMM?
GASA (CRINKLE)
PLUSH BODY PILLOW
EXPANDING LUCKY-CH
MISHI
MISHI (KRIK)
PLUSH BODY PILLOW
EXPANDING LUCKY-C
PAKI (SNAP)
BOBON (BABOOM)
WAAAAH!
?

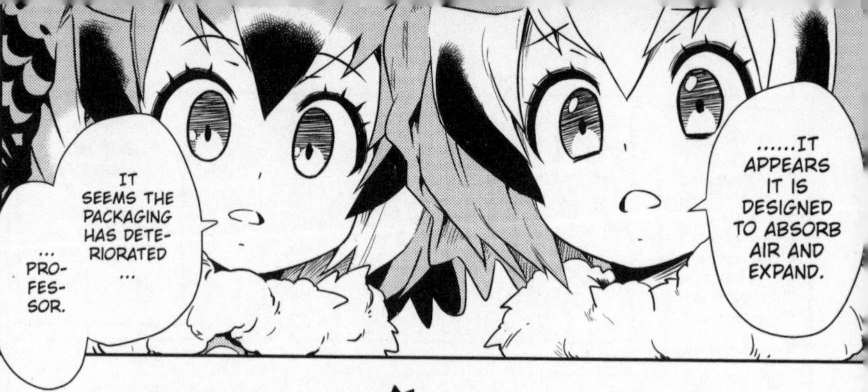
......IT APPEARS IT IS DESIGNED TO ABSORB AIR AND EXPAND.
IT SEEMS THE PACKAGING HAS DETERIORATED ... ... PROFESSOR.

Tomohiro Marukawa
The Professor, the Assistant & the Body Pillow

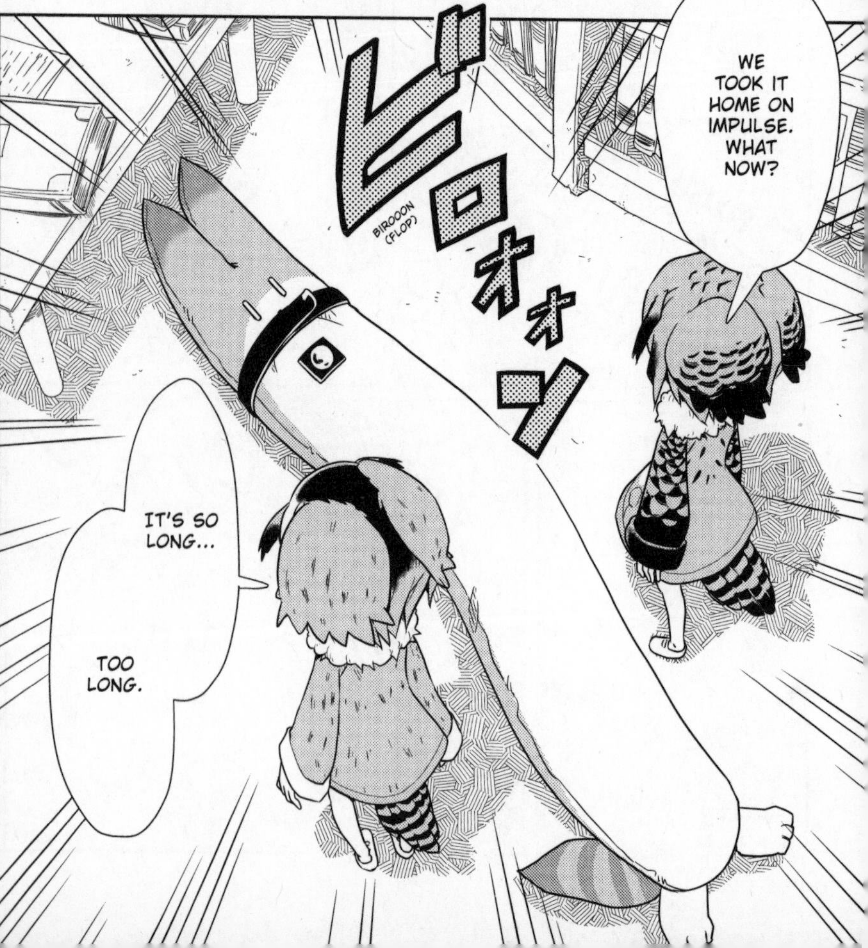
WE TOOK IT HOME ON IMPULSE. WHAT NOW?
BIROOON (FLOP)
IT'S SO LONG...
TOO LONG.

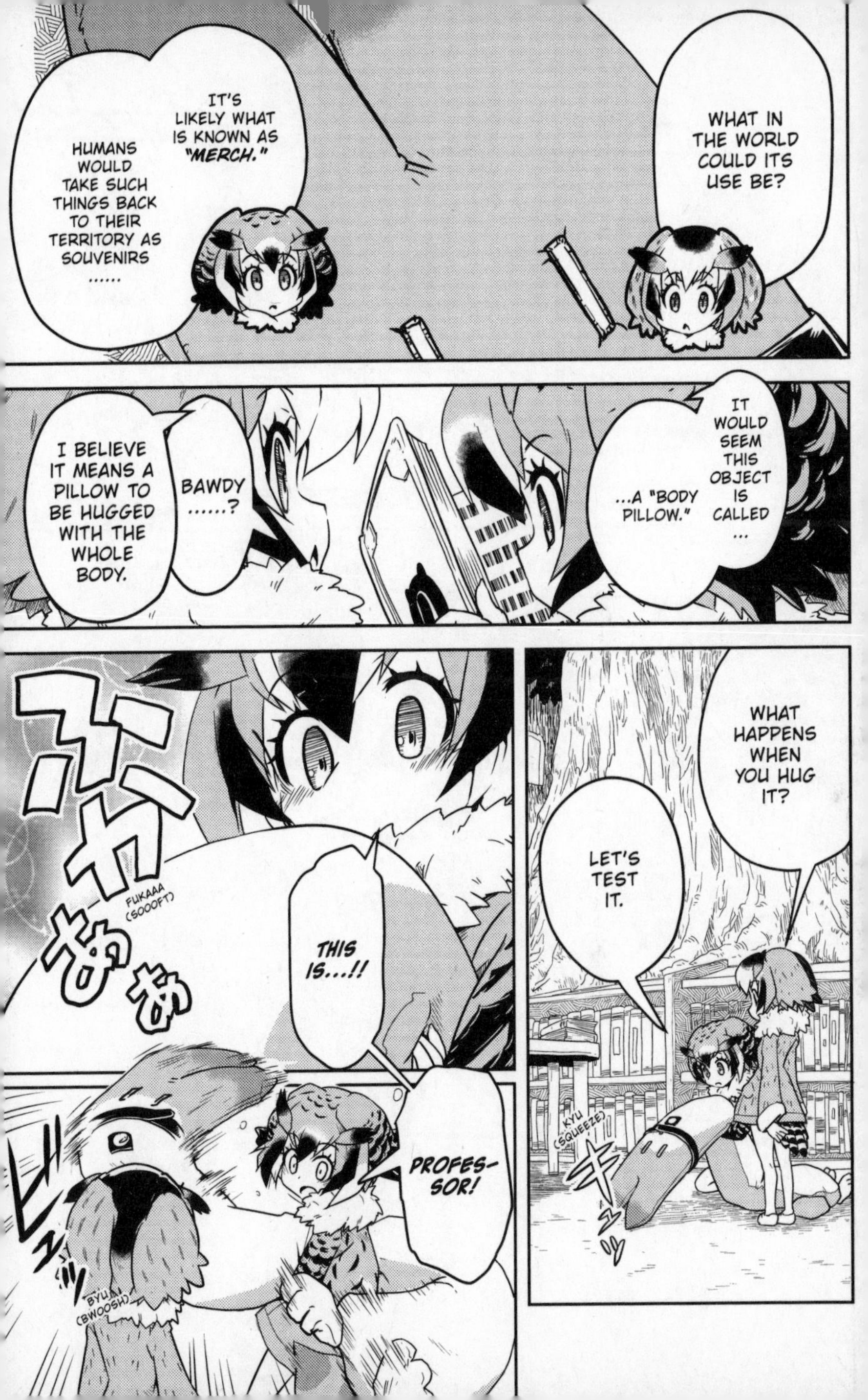
WHAT IN THE WORLD COULD ITS USE BE?
IT'S LIKELY WHAT IS KNOWN AS "MERCH."
HUMANS WOULD TAKE SUCH THINGS BACK TO THEIR TERRITORY AS SOUVENIRS ......
IT WOULD SEEM THIS OBJECT IS CALLED ...
...A "BODY PILLOW."
BAWDY ......?
I BELIEVE IT MEANS A PILLOW TO BE HUGGED WITH THE WHOLE BODY.
WHAT HAPPENS WHEN YOU HUG IT?
LET'S TEST IT.
KYU (SQUEEZE)
FUKAAA (SOOOFT)
THIS IS...!!
PROFES-SOR!
BYU (BWOOSH)

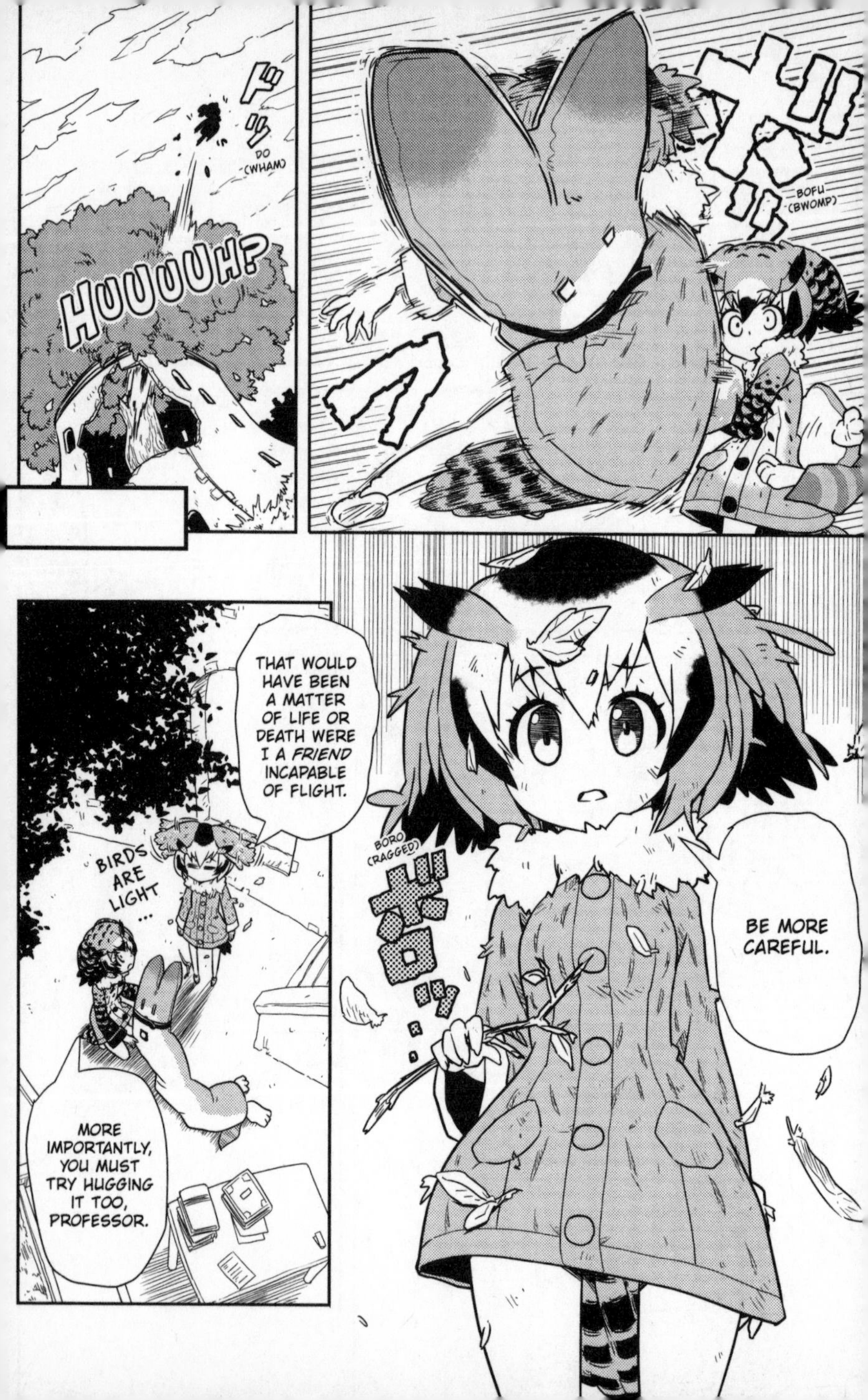
BOFU (BWOMP)
DO (WHAM)
HUUUUH?
BORO (RAGGED)
BE MORE CAREFUL.
THAT WOULD HAVE BEEN A MATTER OF LIFE OR DEATH WERE I A *FRIEND* INCAPABLE OF FLIGHT.
BIRDS ARE LIGHT...
MORE IMPORTANTLY, YOU MUST TRY HUGGING IT TOO, PROFESSOR.

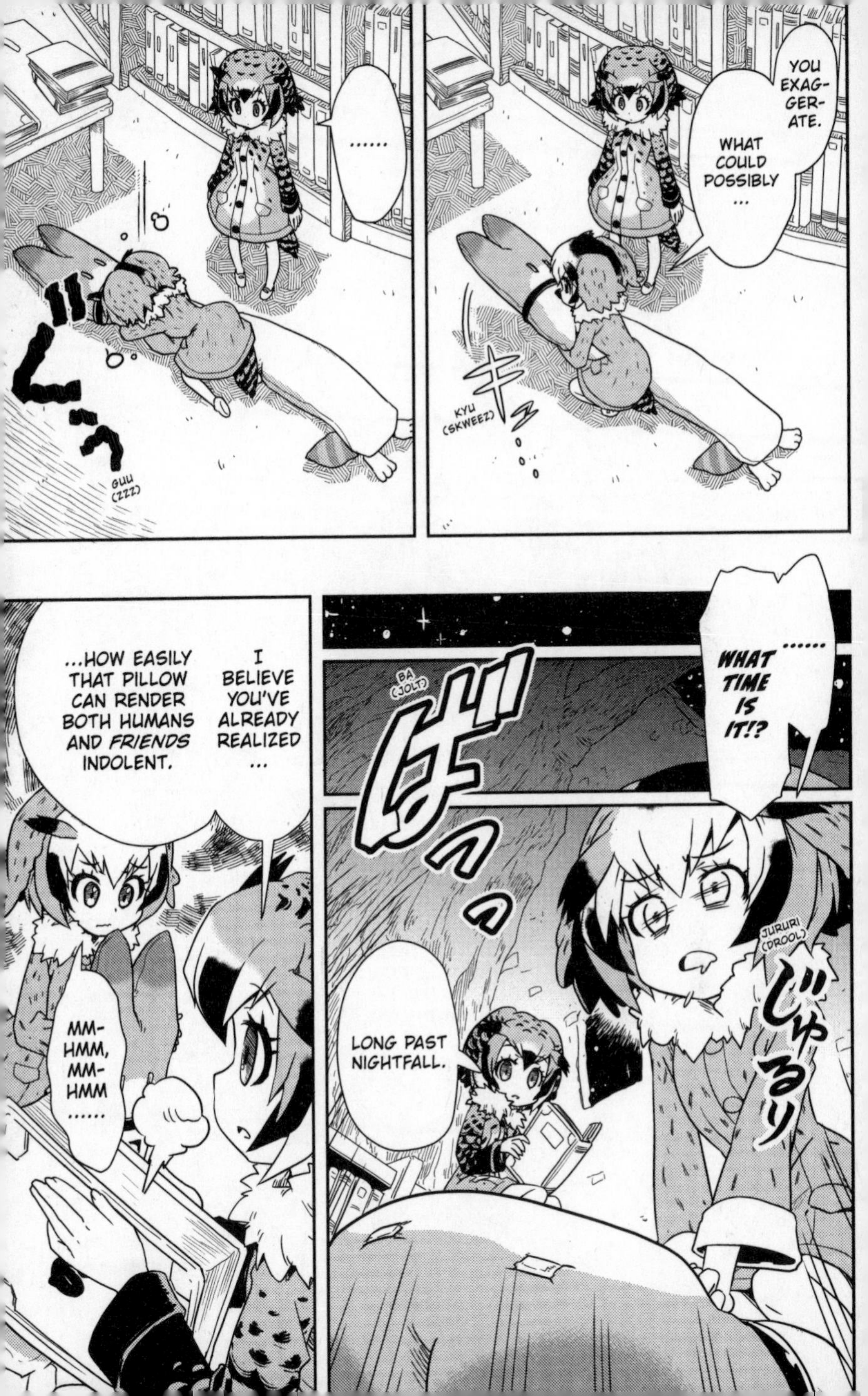
YOU EXAG-GER-ATE.
WHAT COULD POSSIBLY ...
キュ
KYU (SKWEEZ)
......
ぐぅ
GUU (ZZZ)
...... *WHAT TIME IS IT!?*
ばっ
BA (JOLT)
LONG PAST NIGHTFALL.
じゅるり
JURURI (DROOL)
I BELIEVE YOU'VE ALREADY REALIZED ...
...HOW EASILY THAT PILLOW CAN RENDER BOTH HUMANS AND *FRIENDS* INDOLENT.
MM-HMM, MM-HMM ......

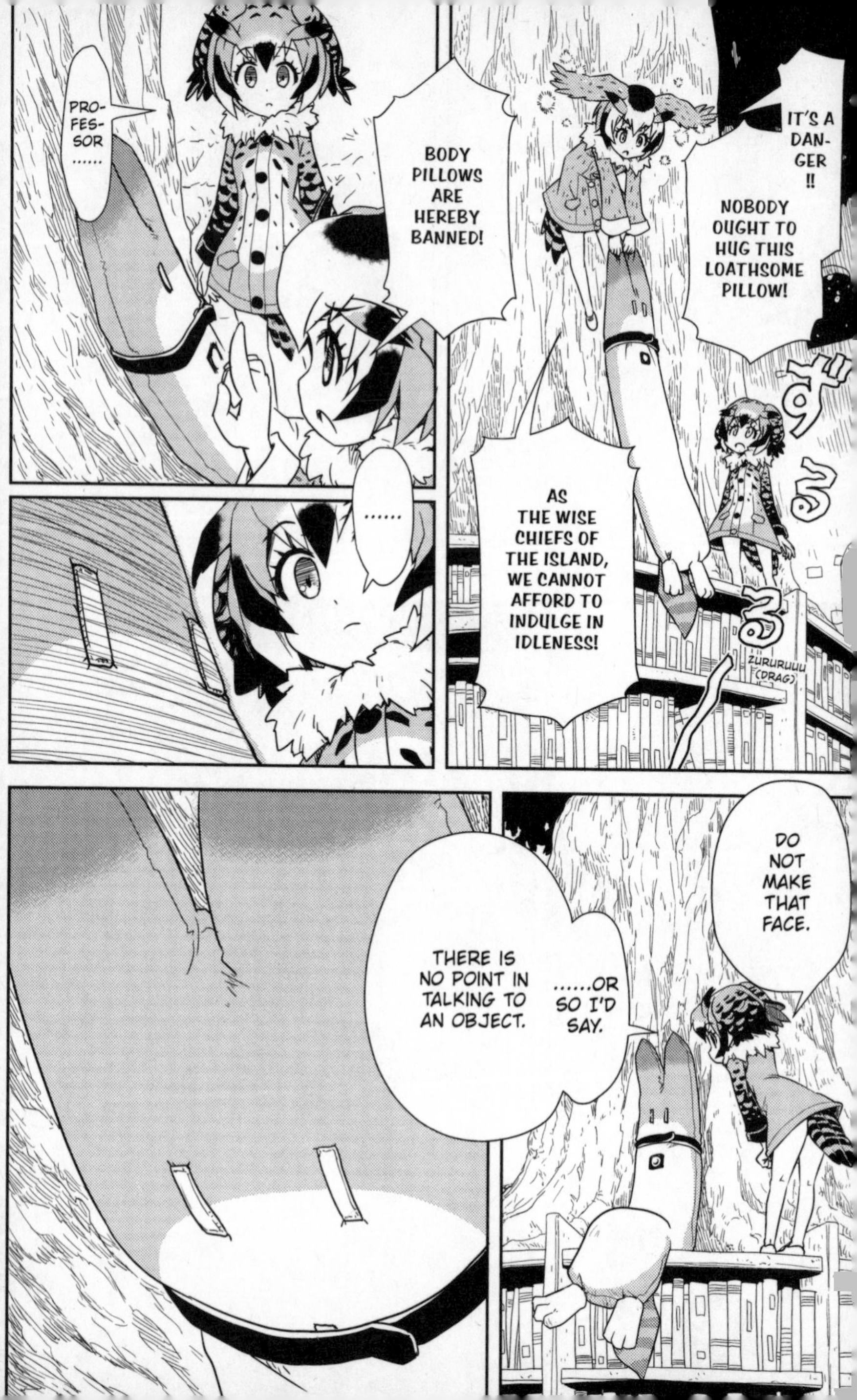
IT'S A DANGER!!
NOBODY OUGHT TO HUG THIS LOATHSOME PILLOW!
ずるるる
ZURURUUU (DRAG)
AS THE WISE CHIEFS OF THE ISLAND, WE CANNOT AFFORD TO INDULGE IN IDLENESS!
BODY PILLOWS ARE HEREBY BANNED!
PRO-FES-SOR ......
......
DO NOT MAKE THAT FACE.
......OR SO I'D SAY.
THERE IS NO POINT IN TALKING TO AN OBJECT.

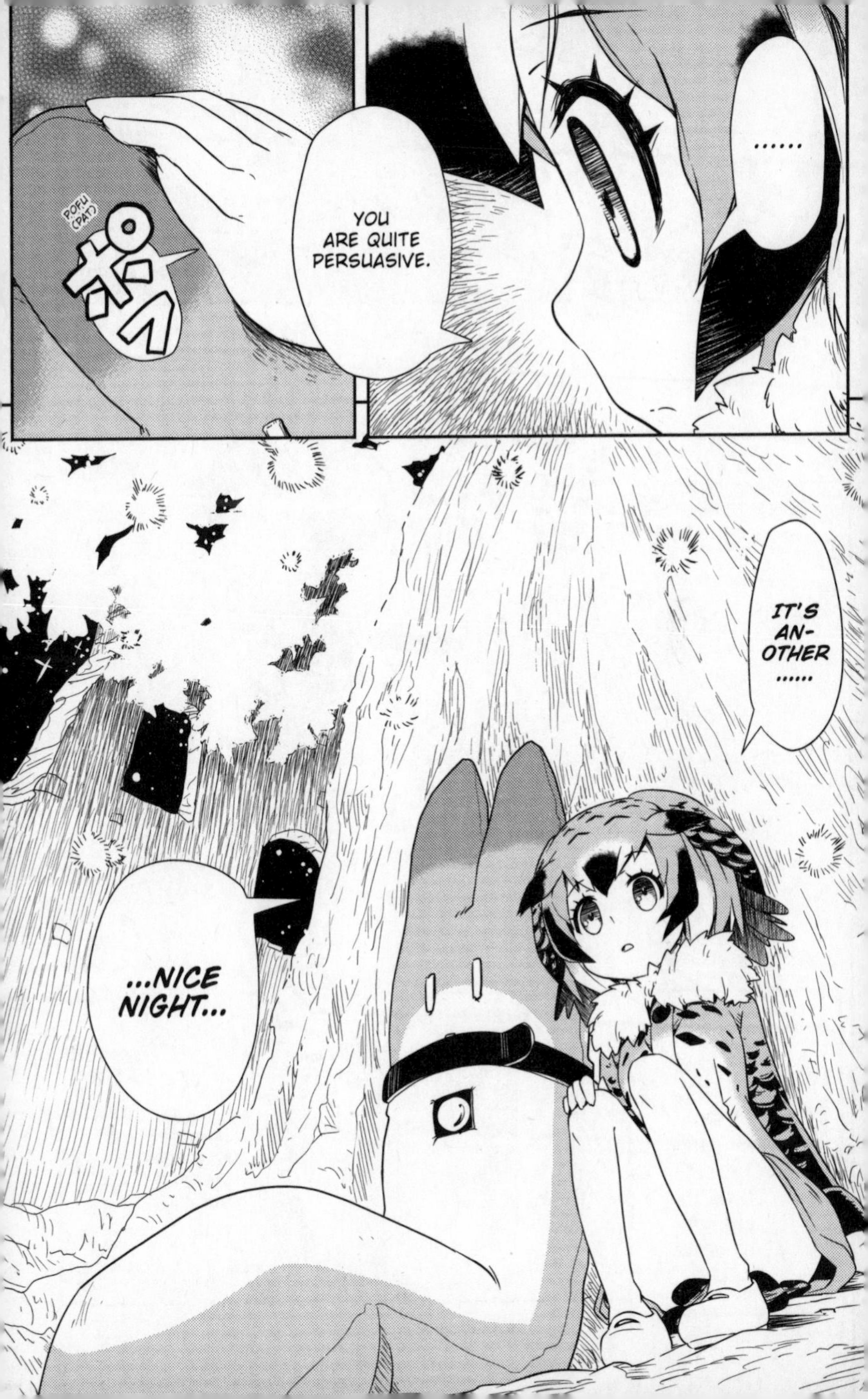
......
YOU ARE QUITE PERSUASIVE.
POFU (PAT)
IT'S AN-OTHER ......
...NICE NIGHT...

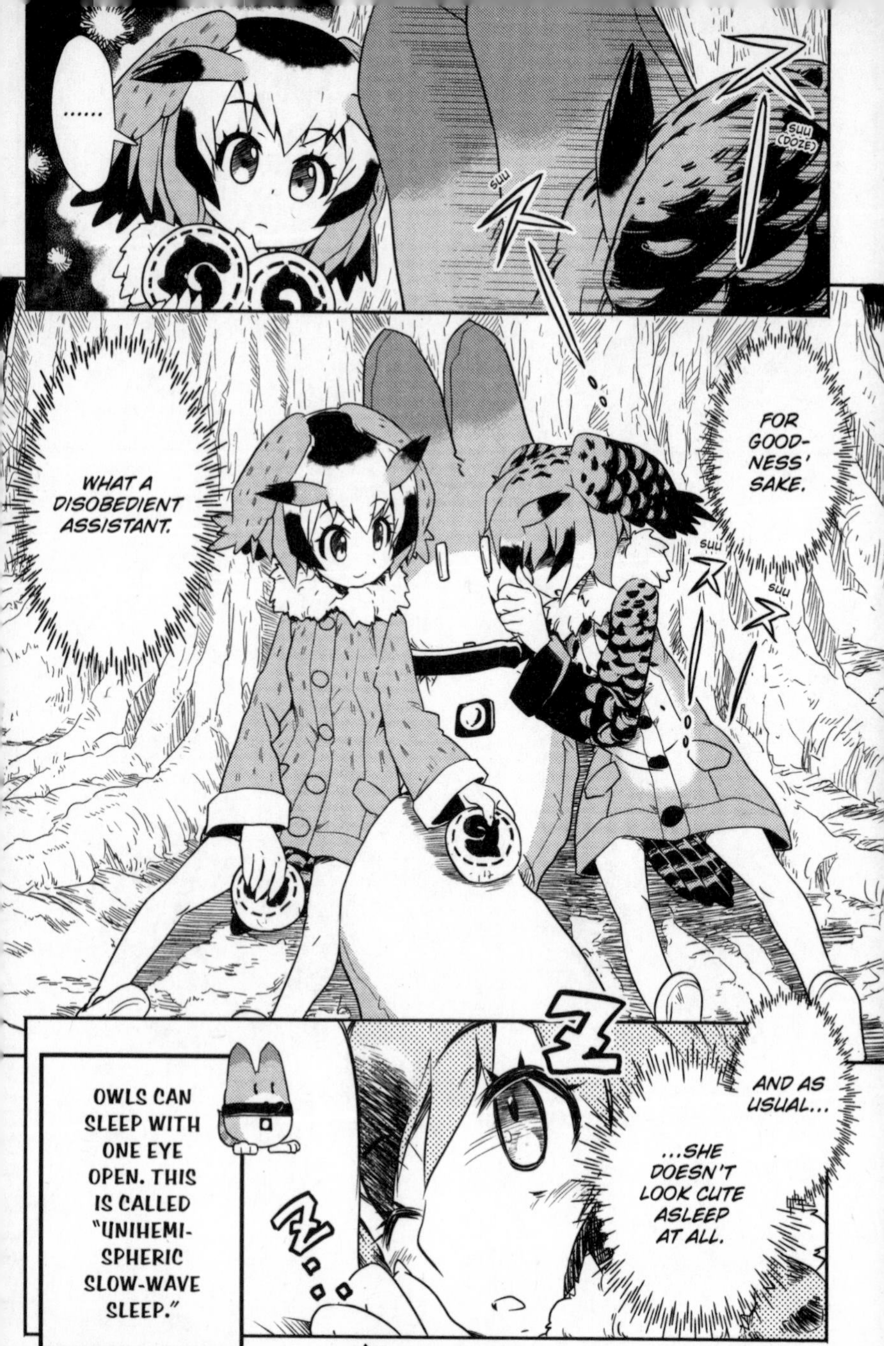
SUU (DOZE)
SUU
......
FOR GOODNESS' SAKE.
SUU
SUU
WHAT A DISOBEDIENT ASSISTANT.
AND AS USUAL...
...SHE DOESN'T LOOK CUTE ASLEEP AT ALL.
Z
Z
OWLS CAN SLEEP WITH ONE EYE OPEN. THIS IS CALLED "UNIHEMI-SPHERIC SLOW-WAVE SLEEP."

The End

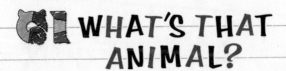

Kemono Friends

Question

01 WHAT'S THAT ANIMAL?

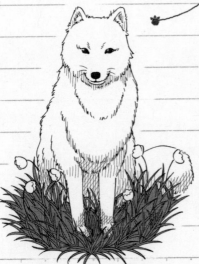

HINT:

Their short ears and snouts are adapted to a climate of extreme cold. In the winter, their coats are white or blue-gray, but come summertime, they turn gray or brown.

Turn the page for the answer!

A1
ARCTIC FOX

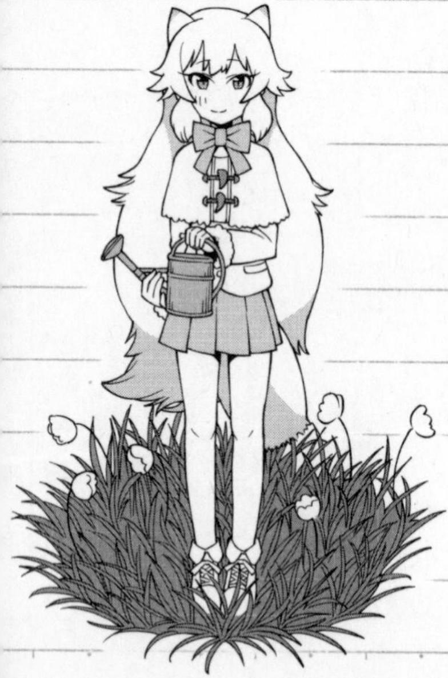

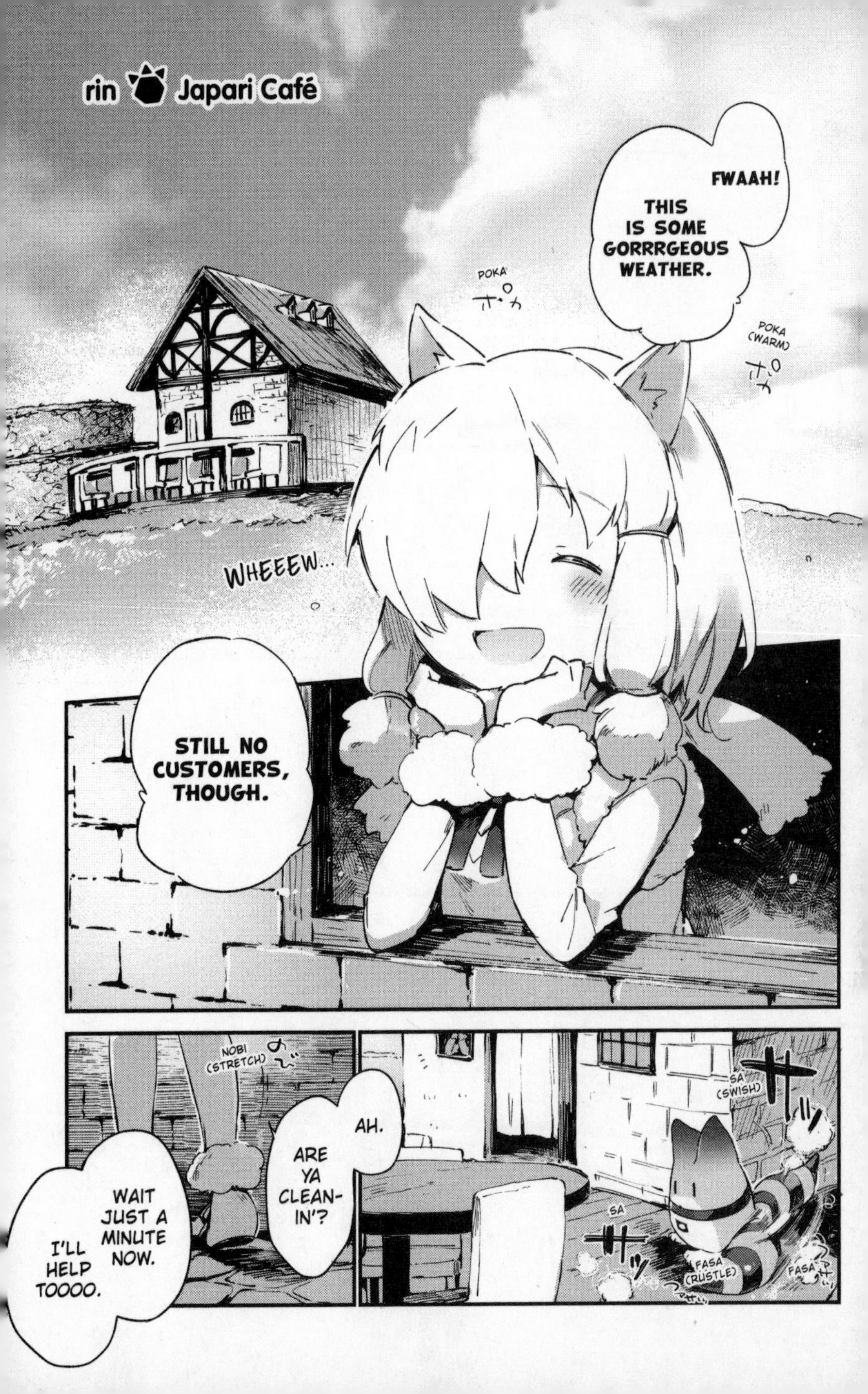
rin Japari Café
FWAAH! THIS IS SOME GORRRGEOUS WEATHER.
POKA (WARM)
POKA
WHEEEW...
STILL NO CUSTOMERS, THOUGH.
SA (SWISH)
SA
FASA (RUSTLE)
FASA
NOBI (STRETCH)
AH.
ARE YA CLEAN-IN'?
WAIT JUST A MINUTE NOW.
I'LL HELP TOOOO.

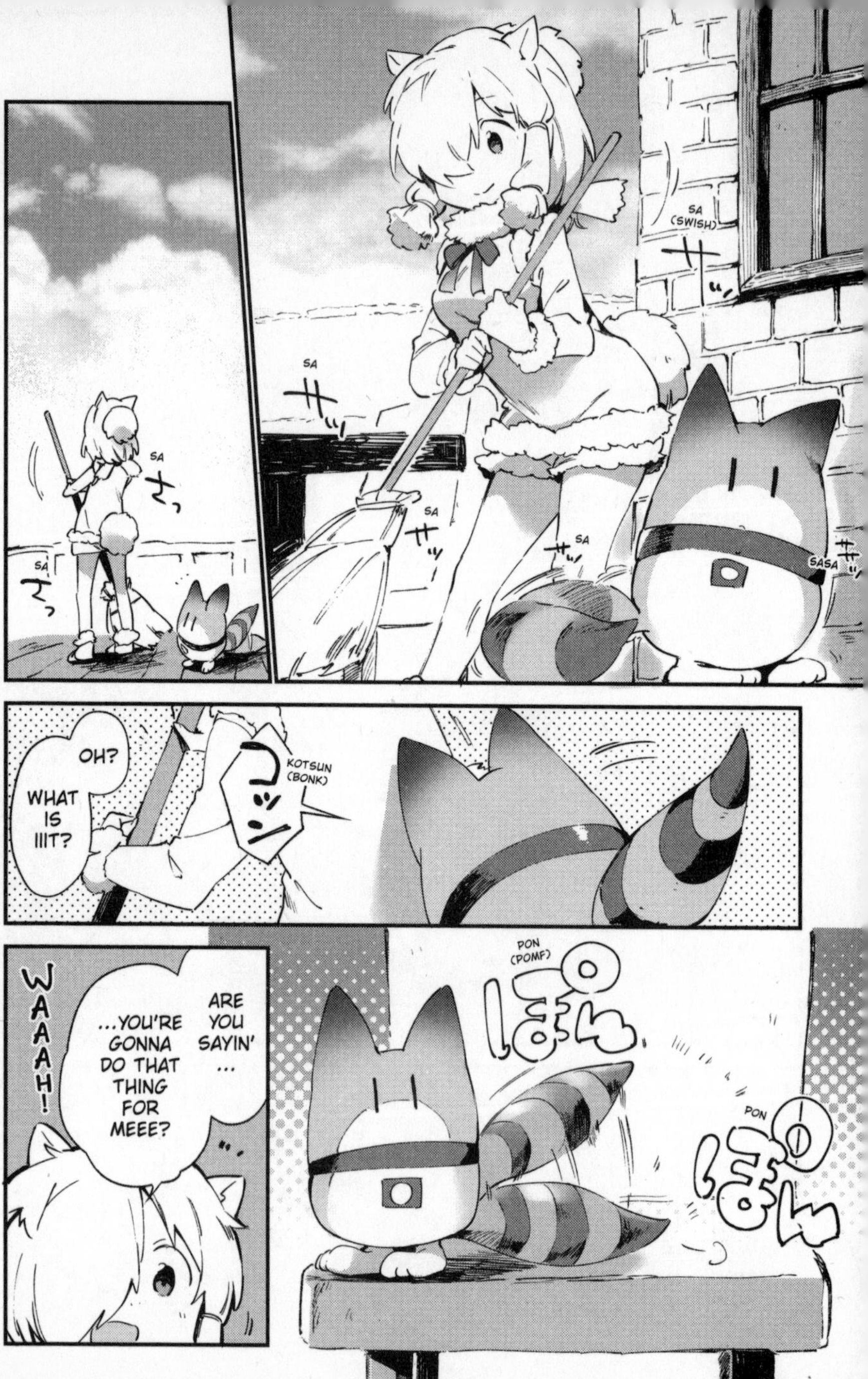
SA (SWISH)
SA
SA
SA
SASA
SA
SA
OH?
WHAT IS IIIT?
KOTSUN (BONK)
PON (POMF)
PON
ARE YOU SAYIN' ...
...YOU'RE GONNA DO THAT THING FOR MEEE?
WAAAAH!

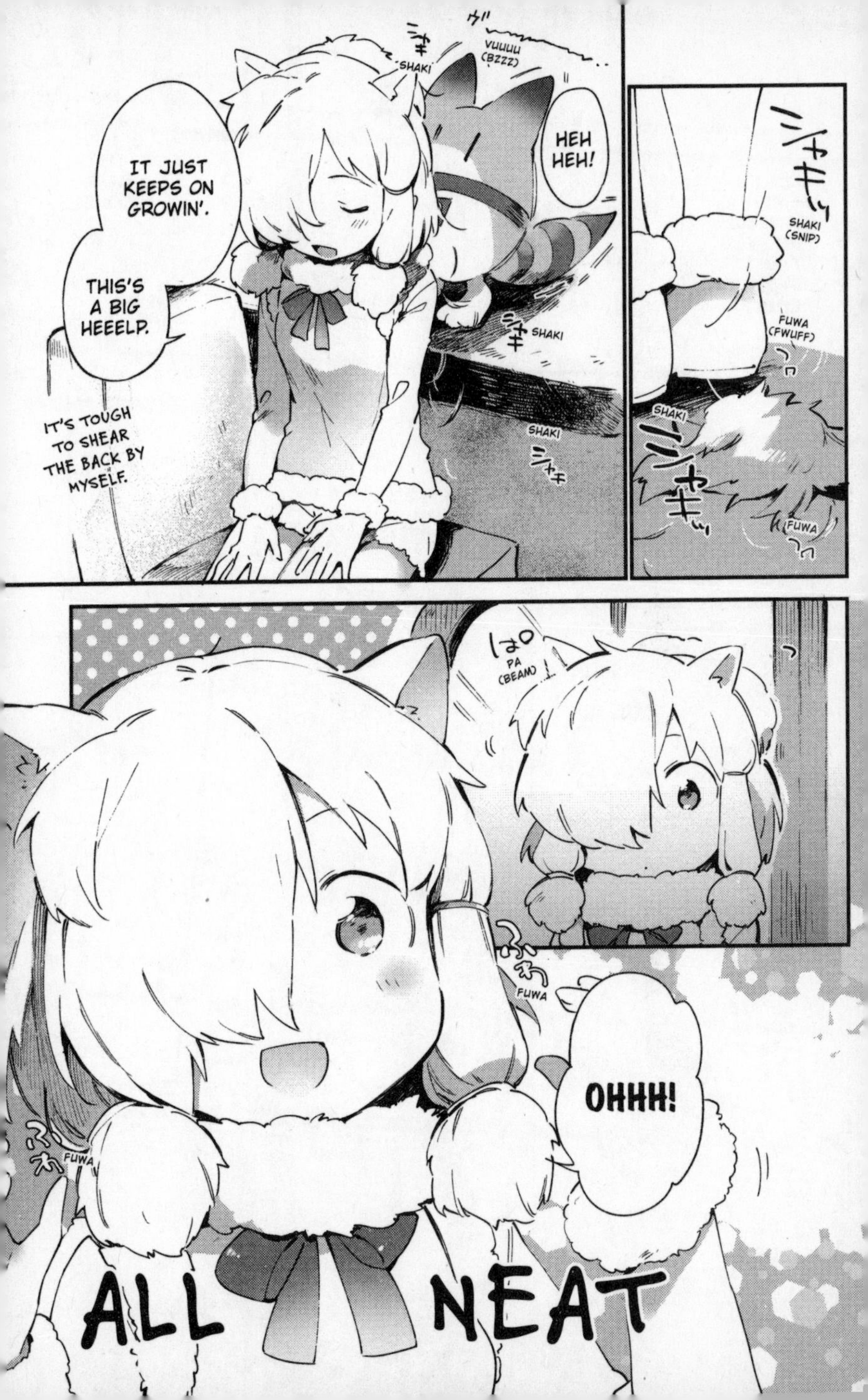

シャキッ
SHAKI (SNIP)
FUWA (FWUFF)
SHAKI
シャキッ
FUWA
VUUUU (BZZZ)
SHAKI
HEH HEH!
IT JUST KEEPS ON GROWIN'.
THIS'S A BIG HEEELP.
SHAKI
SHAKI
IT'S TOUGH TO SHEAR THE BACK BY MYSELF.
ぱっ
PA (BEAM)
ふわ
FUWA
OHHH!
ふわ
FUWA
ALL NEAT

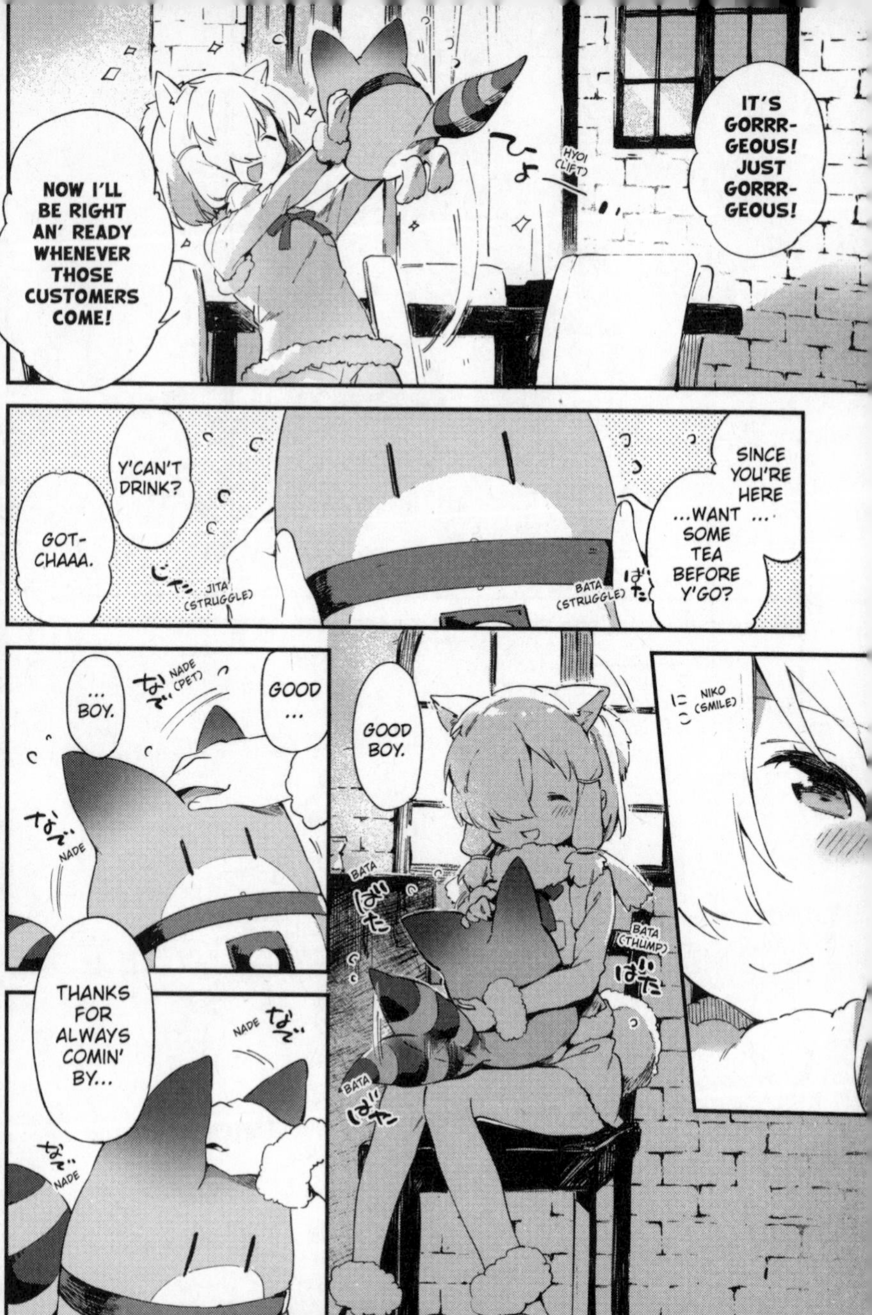
IT'S GORRR-GEOUS! JUST GORRR-GEOUS!
ひょ HYOI (LIFT)
NOW I'LL BE RIGHT AN' READY WHENEVER THOSE CUSTOMERS COME!
SINCE YOU'RE HERE ...WANT ... SOME TEA BEFORE Y'GO?
ばた BATA (STRUGGLE)
Y'CAN'T DRINK?
じた JITA (STRUGGLE)
GOT-CHAAA.
にこ NIKO (SMILE)
GOOD BOY.
ばた BATA
ばた BATA (THUMP)
ばた BATA
GOOD ...
... BOY.
なで NADE (PET)
なで NADE
THANKS FOR ALWAYS COMIN' BY...
なで NADE
なで NADE

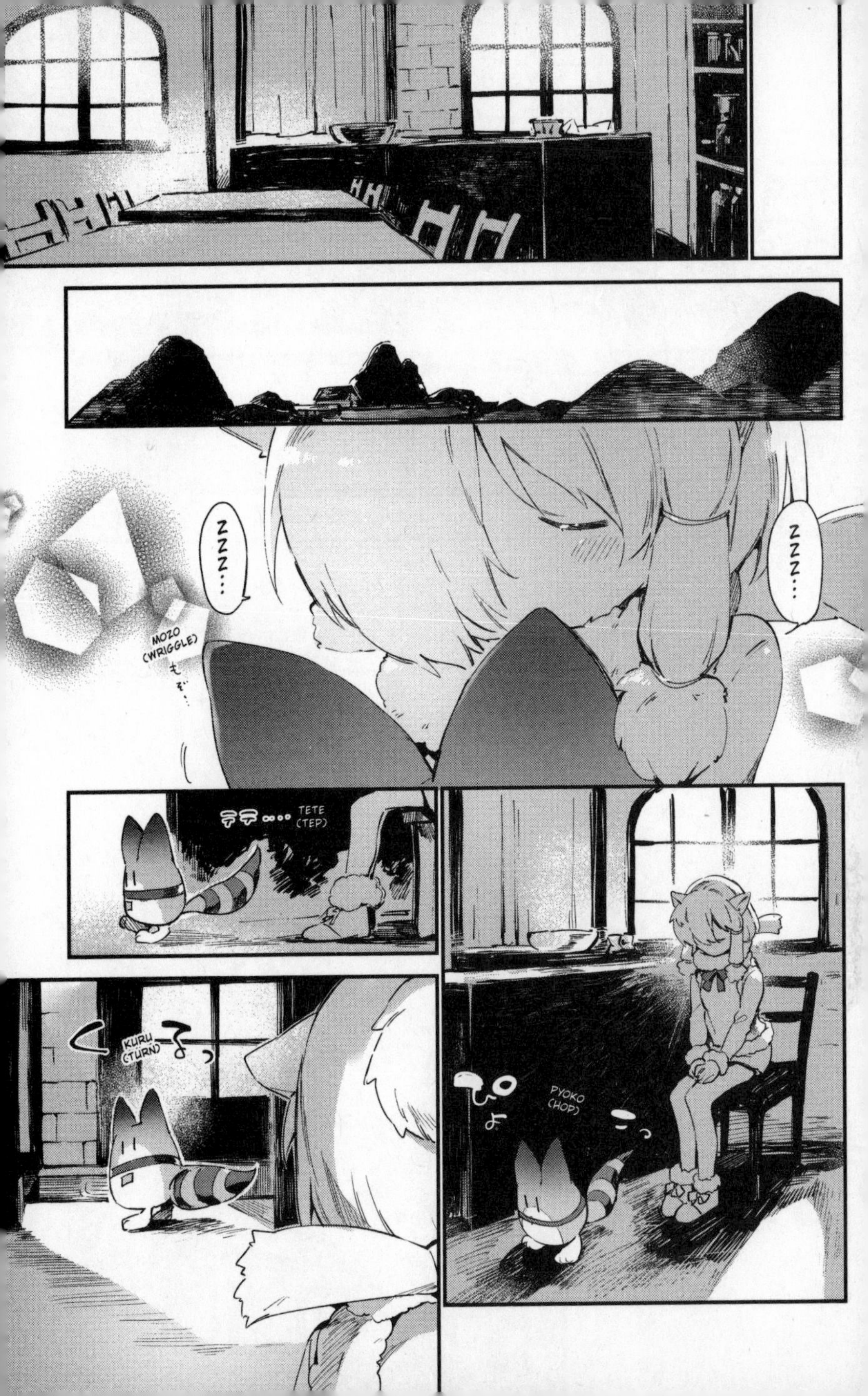
ZZZ...
ZZZ...
MOZO (WRIGGLE)
もぞ…
PYOKO (HOP)
テテ…
TETE (TEP)
KURU (TURN)

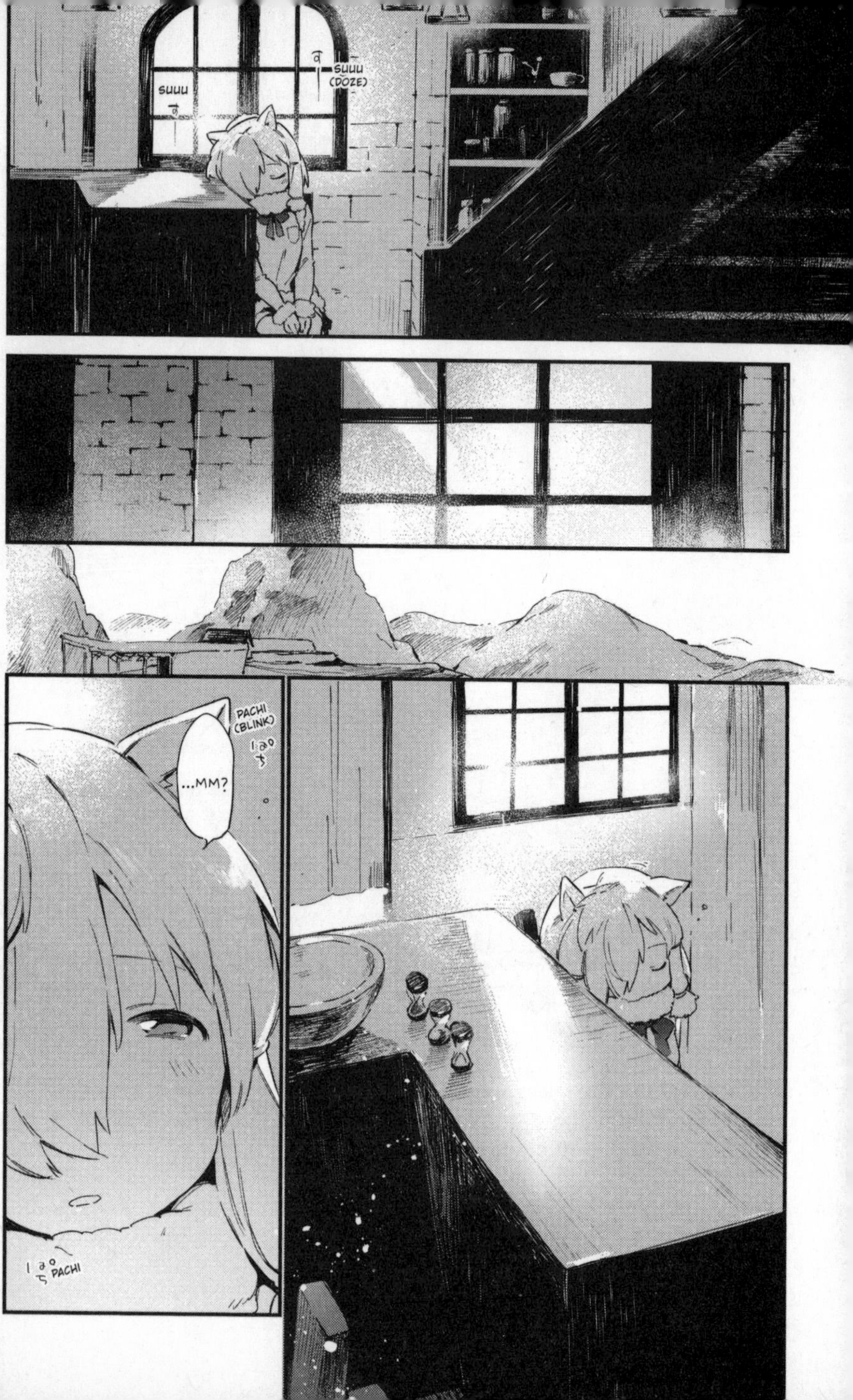
す
SUUU (DOZE)
す
SUUU
ぱち
PACHI (BLINK)
...MM?
ぱち
PACHI

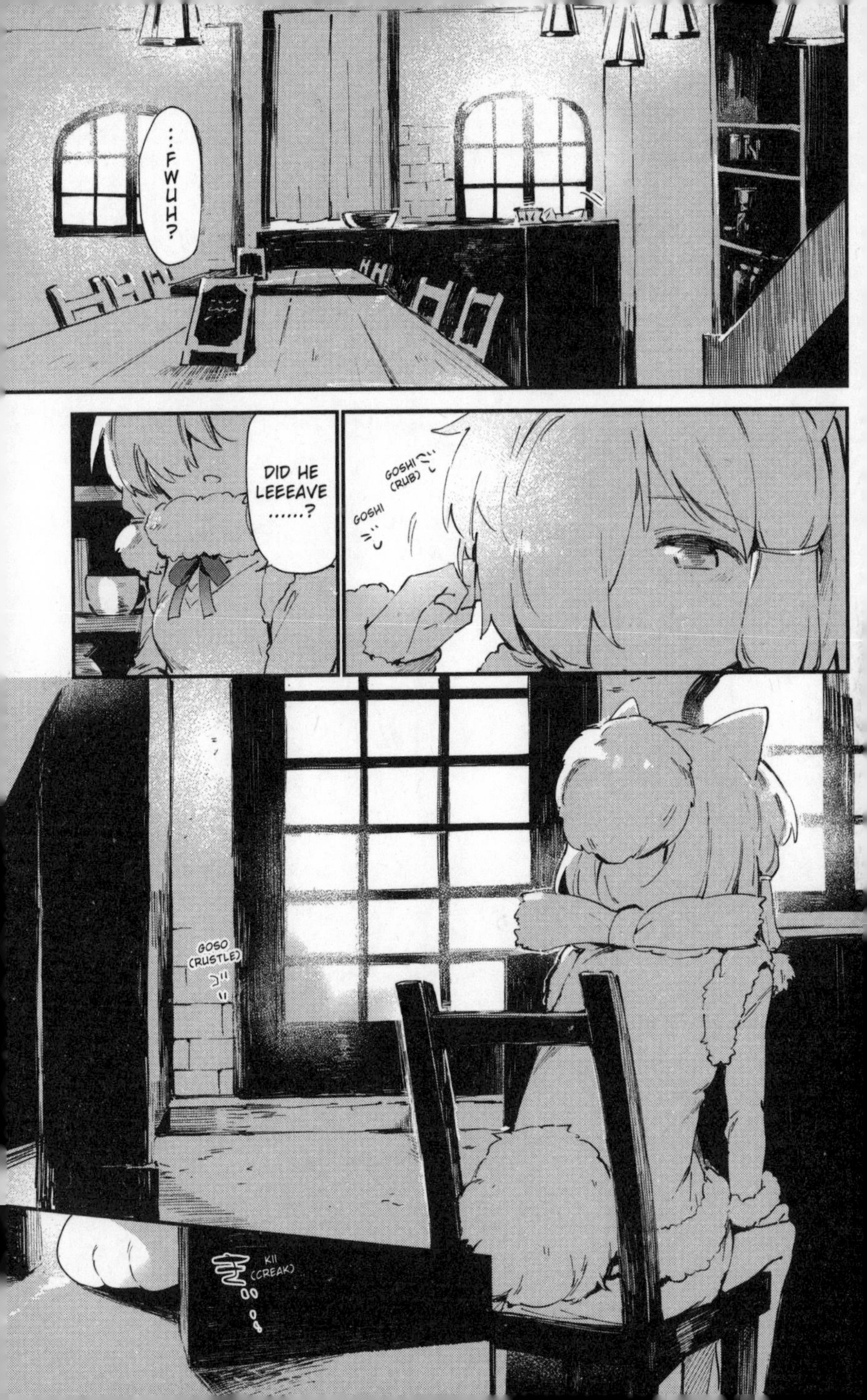
...FWUH?
GOSHI (RUB)
GOSHI
DID HE LEEEAVE ......?
GOSO (RUSTLE)
KII (CREAK)

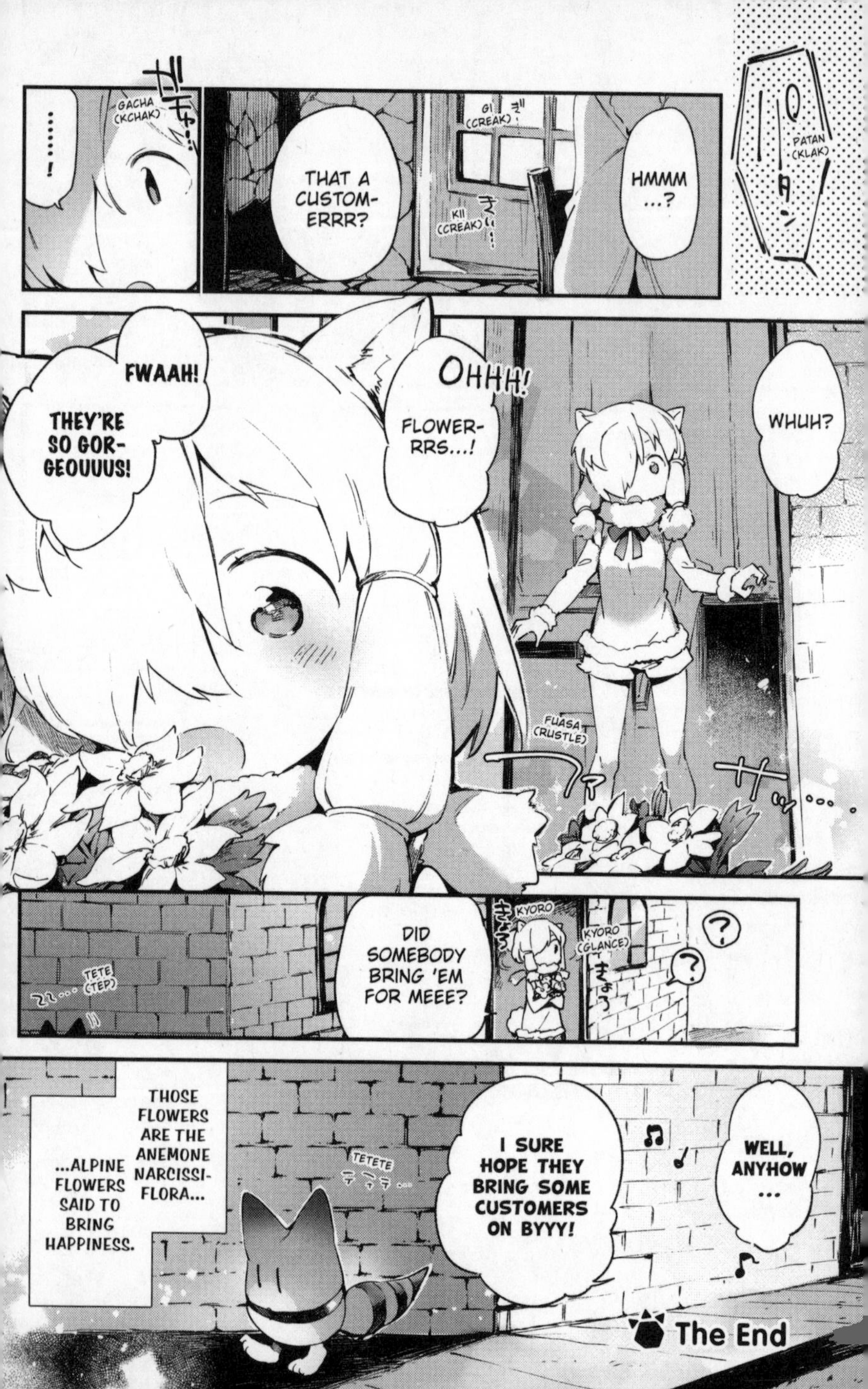
PATAN (KLAK)
HMMM...?
GI (CREAK)
THAT A CUSTOM-ERRR?
KII (CREAK)
GACHA (KCHAK)
......!
WHUH?
OHHH!
FLOWER-RRS...!
FWAAH!
THEY'RE SO GOR-GEOUUUS!
FUASA (RUSTLE)
KYORO
KYORO (GLANCE)
DID SOMEBODY BRING 'EM FOR MEEE?
TETE (TEP)
WELL, ANYHOW...
I SURE HOPE THEY BRING SOME CUSTOMERS ON BYYY!
TETETE
THOSE FLOWERS ARE THE ANEMONE NARCISSIFLORA...
...ALPINE FLOWERS SAID TO BRING HAPPINESS.
The End

Ikumi Hino ⬟ Cerulean Hunters, Go!

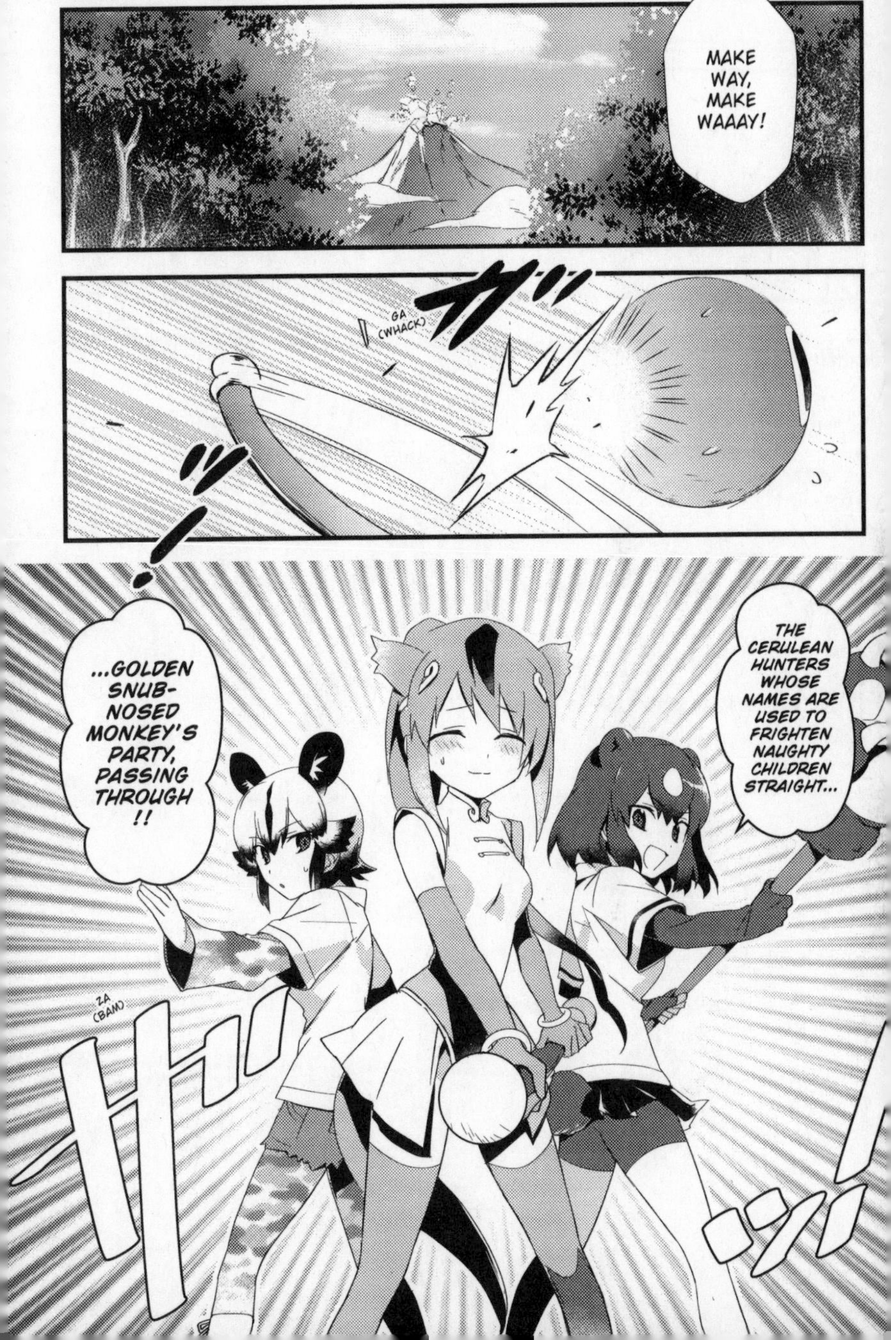
MAKE WAY, MAKE WAAAY!
GA (WHACK)
THE CERULEAN HUNTERS WHOSE NAMES ARE USED TO FRIGHTEN NAUGHTY CHILDREN STRAIGHT...
...GOLDEN SNUB-NOSED MONKEY'S PARTY, PASSING THROUGH!!
ZA (BAM)

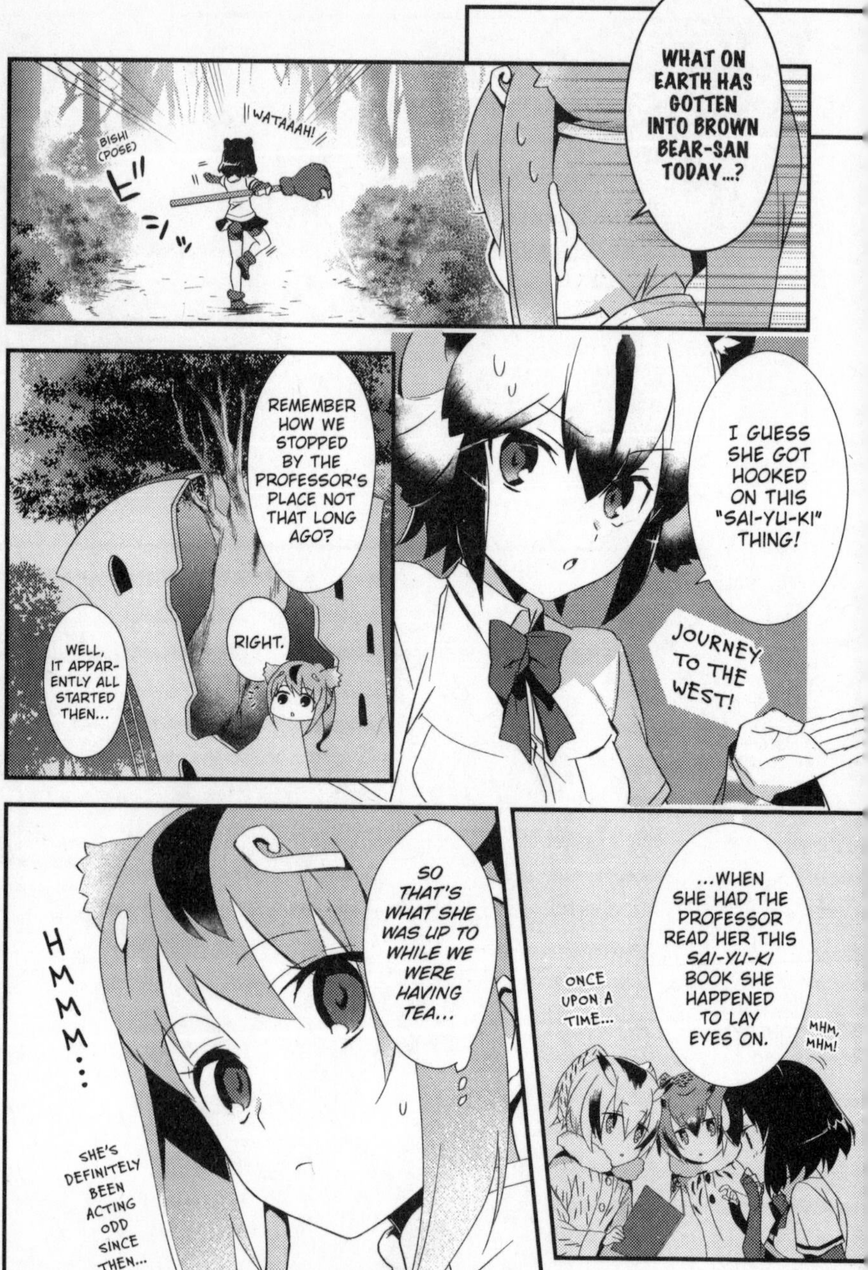
WHAT ON EARTH HAS GOTTEN INTO BROWN BEAR-SAN TODAY...?
WATAAAH!
BISHI (POSE)
I GUESS SHE GOT HOOKED ON THIS "SAI-YU-KI" THING!
JOURNEY TO THE WEST!
REMEMBER HOW WE STOPPED BY THE PROFESSOR'S PLACE NOT THAT LONG AGO?
RIGHT.
WELL, IT APPARENTLY ALL STARTED THEN...
...WHEN SHE HAD THE PROFESSOR READ HER THIS *SAI-YU-KI* BOOK SHE HAPPENED TO LAY EYES ON.
MHM, MHM!
ONCE UPON A TIME...
SO THAT'S WHAT SHE WAS UP TO WHILE WE WERE HAVING TEA...
HMMM...
SHE'S DEFINITELY BEEN ACTING ODD SINCE THEN...

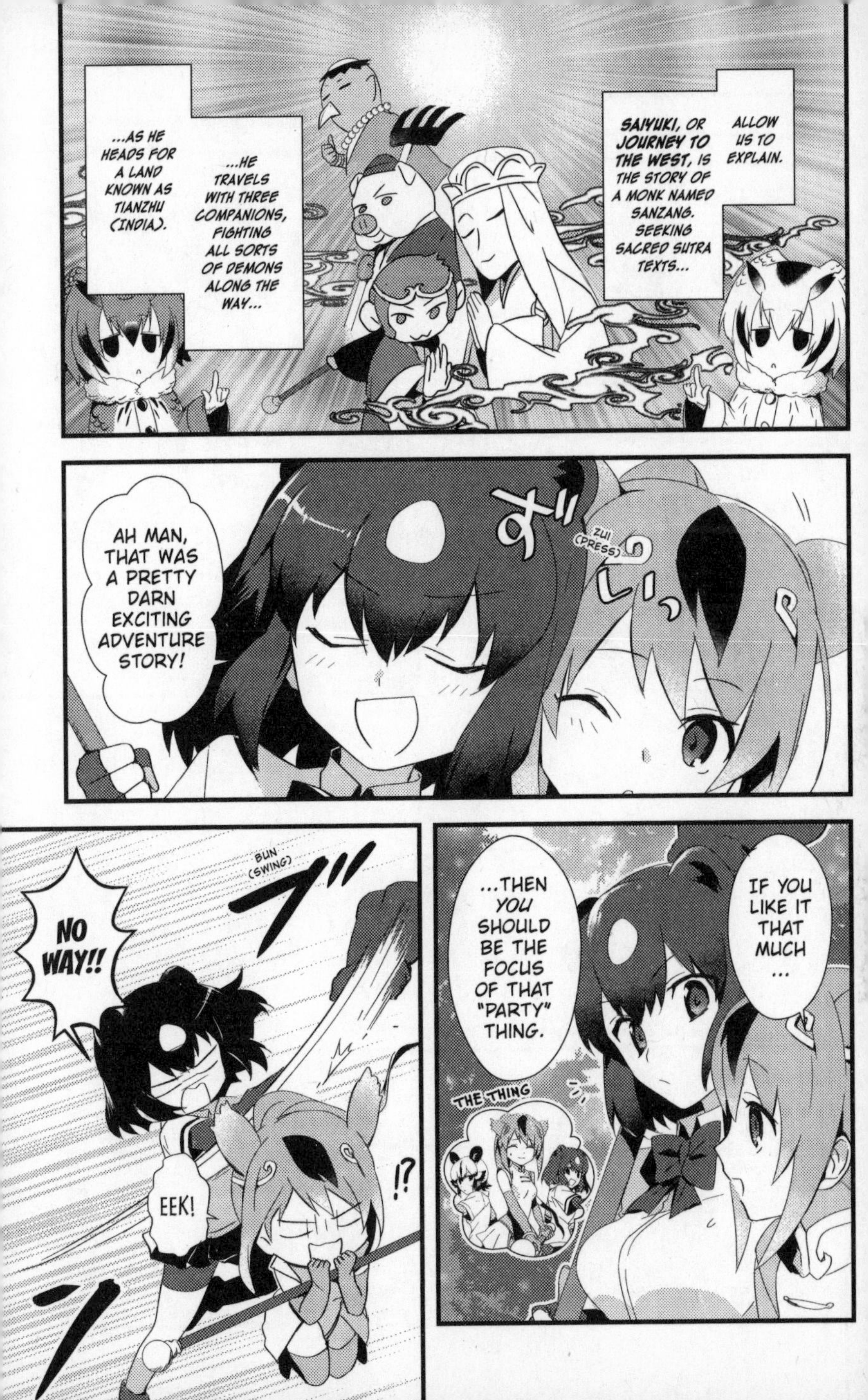
ALLOW US TO EXPLAIN.
SAIYUKI, OR JOURNEY TO THE WEST, IS THE STORY OF A MONK NAMED SANZANG. SEEKING SACRED SUTRA TEXTS...
...HE TRAVELS WITH THREE COMPANIONS, FIGHTING ALL SORTS OF DEMONS ALONG THE WAY...
...AS HE HEADS FOR A LAND KNOWN AS TIANZHU (INDIA).
ZUI (PRESS)
AH MAN, THAT WAS A PRETTY DARN EXCITING ADVENTURE STORY!
IF YOU LIKE IT THAT MUCH ...
...THEN YOU SHOULD BE THE FOCUS OF THAT "PARTY" THING.
THE THING
BUN (SWING)
NO WAY!!
!?
EEK!

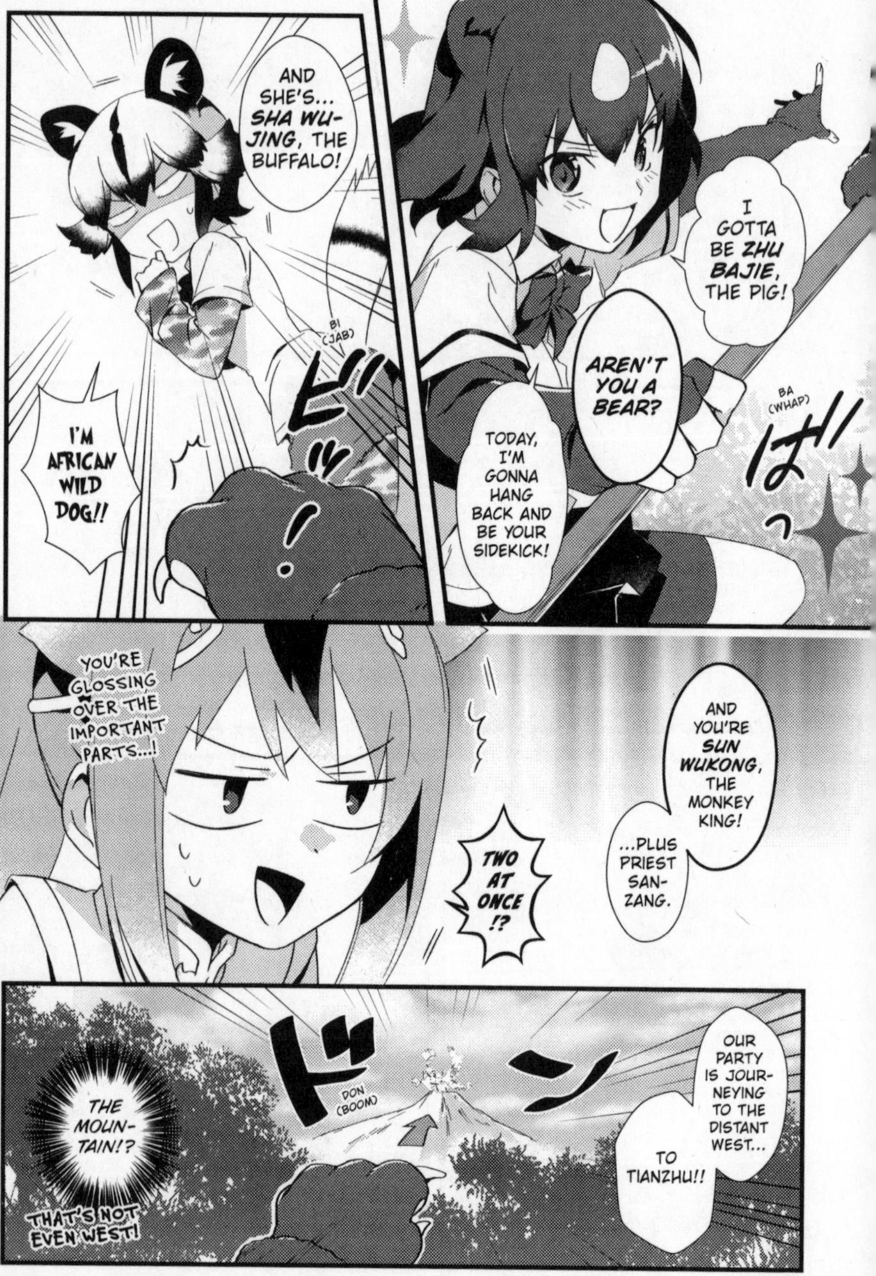
I GOTTA BE ZHU BAJIE, THE PIG!
AREN'T YOU A BEAR?
TODAY, I'M GONNA HANG BACK AND BE YOUR SIDEKICK!
BA (WHAP)
AND SHE'S... SHA WU-JING, THE BUFFALO!
BI (JAB)
I'M AFRICAN WILD DOG!!
AND YOU'RE SUN WUKONG, THE MONKEY KING!
...PLUS PRIEST SAN-ZANG.
TWO AT ONCE!?
YOU'RE GLOSSING OVER THE IMPORTANT PARTS...!
OUR PARTY IS JOUR-NEYING TO THE DISTANT WEST...
TO TIANZHU!!
DON (BOOM)
THE MOUN-TAIN!?
THAT'S NOT EVEN WEST!

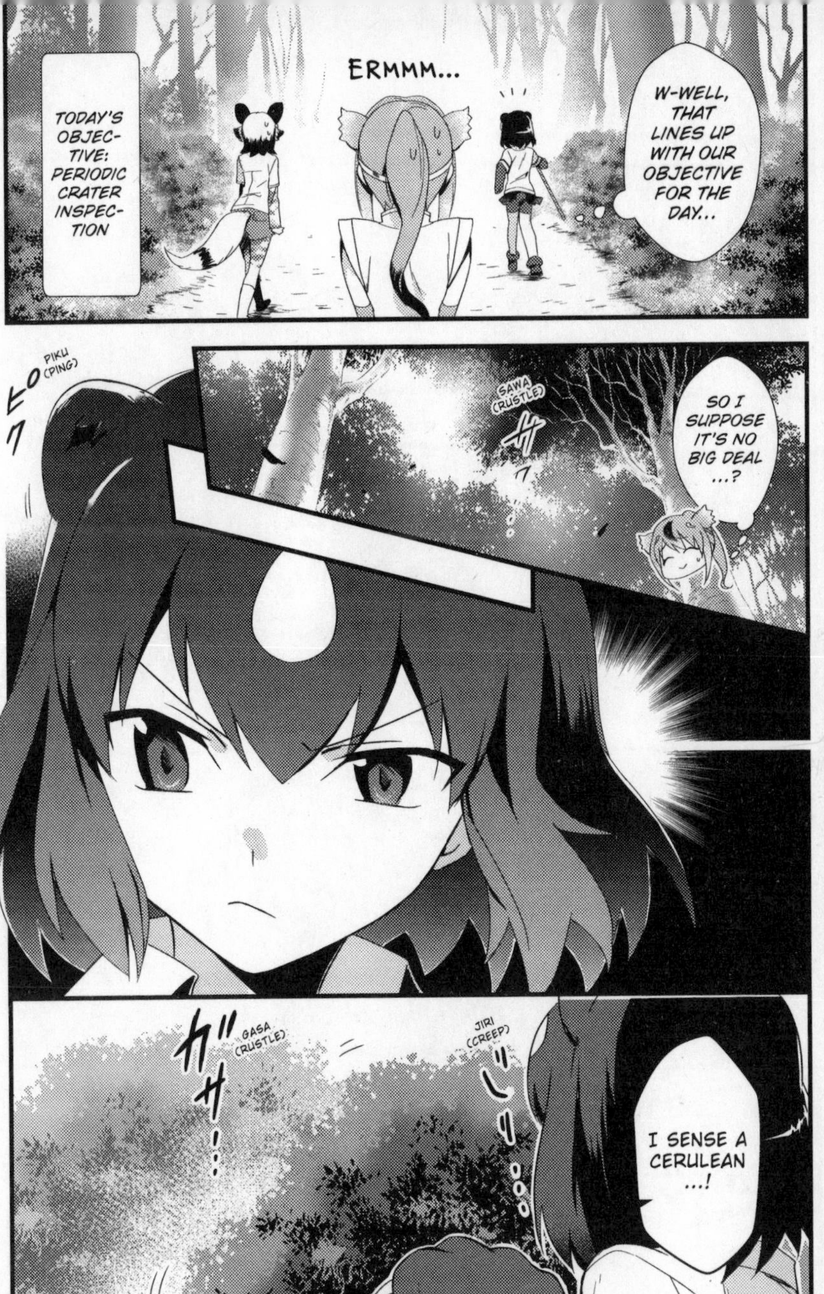
W-WELL, THAT LINES UP WITH OUR OBJECTIVE FOR THE DAY...
ERMMM...
TODAY'S OBJECTIVE: PERIODIC CRATER INSPECTION
SO I SUPPOSE IT'S NO BIG DEAL ...?
SAWA (RUSTLE)
PIKU (PING)
I SENSE A CERULEAN ...!
JIRI (CREEP)
GASA (RUSTLE)

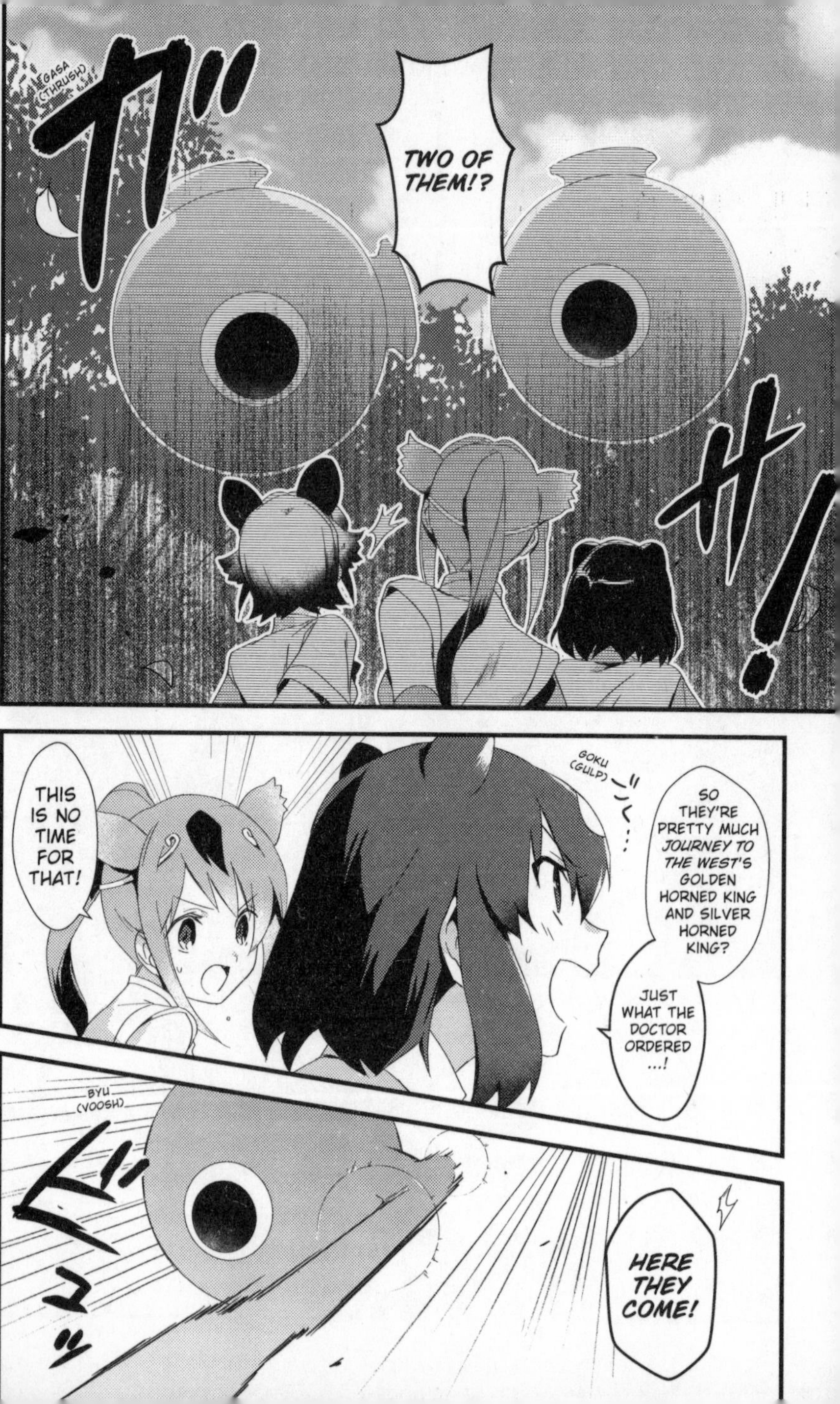
TWO OF THEM!?
GASA (THRUSH)
GOKU (GULP)
SO THEY'RE PRETTY MUCH *JOURNEY TO THE WEST*'S GOLDEN HORNED KING AND SILVER HORNED KING?
JUST WHAT THE DOCTOR ORDERED ...!
THIS IS NO TIME FOR THAT!
HERE THEY COME!
BYU (VOOSH)

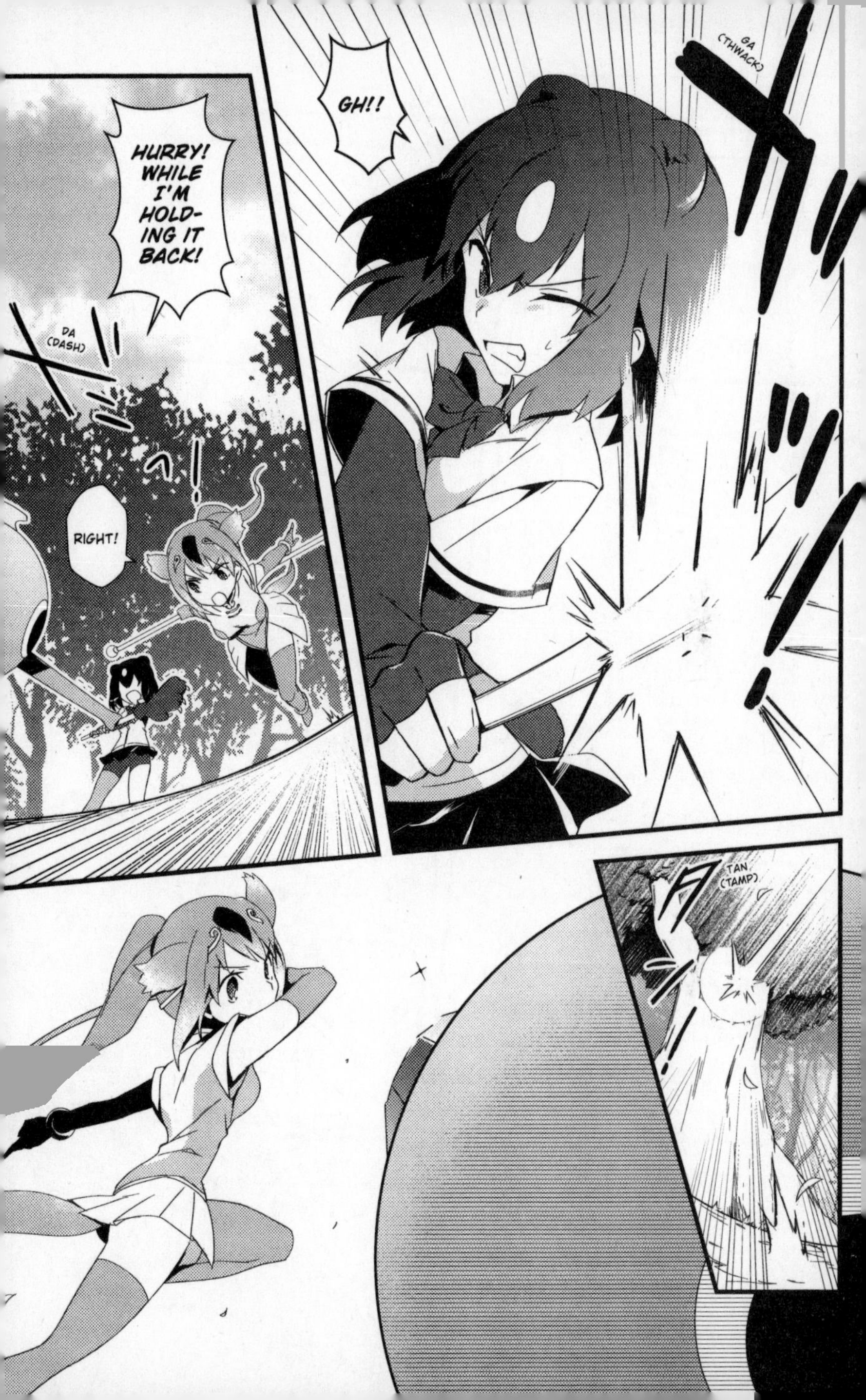
GA (THWACK)
GH!!
HURRY! WHILE I'M HOLDING IT BACK!
DA (DASH)
RIGHT!
TAN (TAMP)

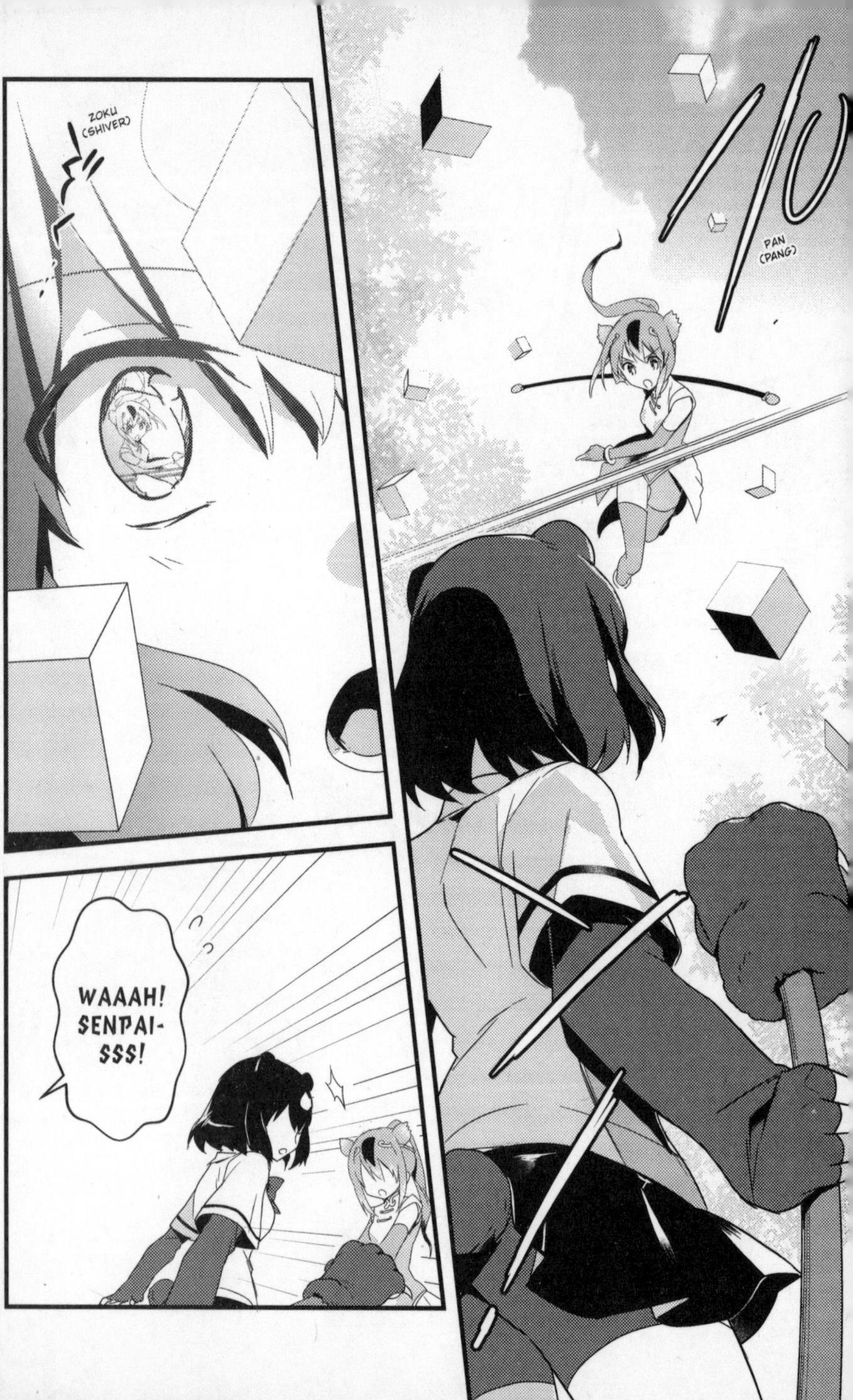
PAN (PANG)
ZOKU (SHIVER)
WAAAH! SENPAI-SSS!

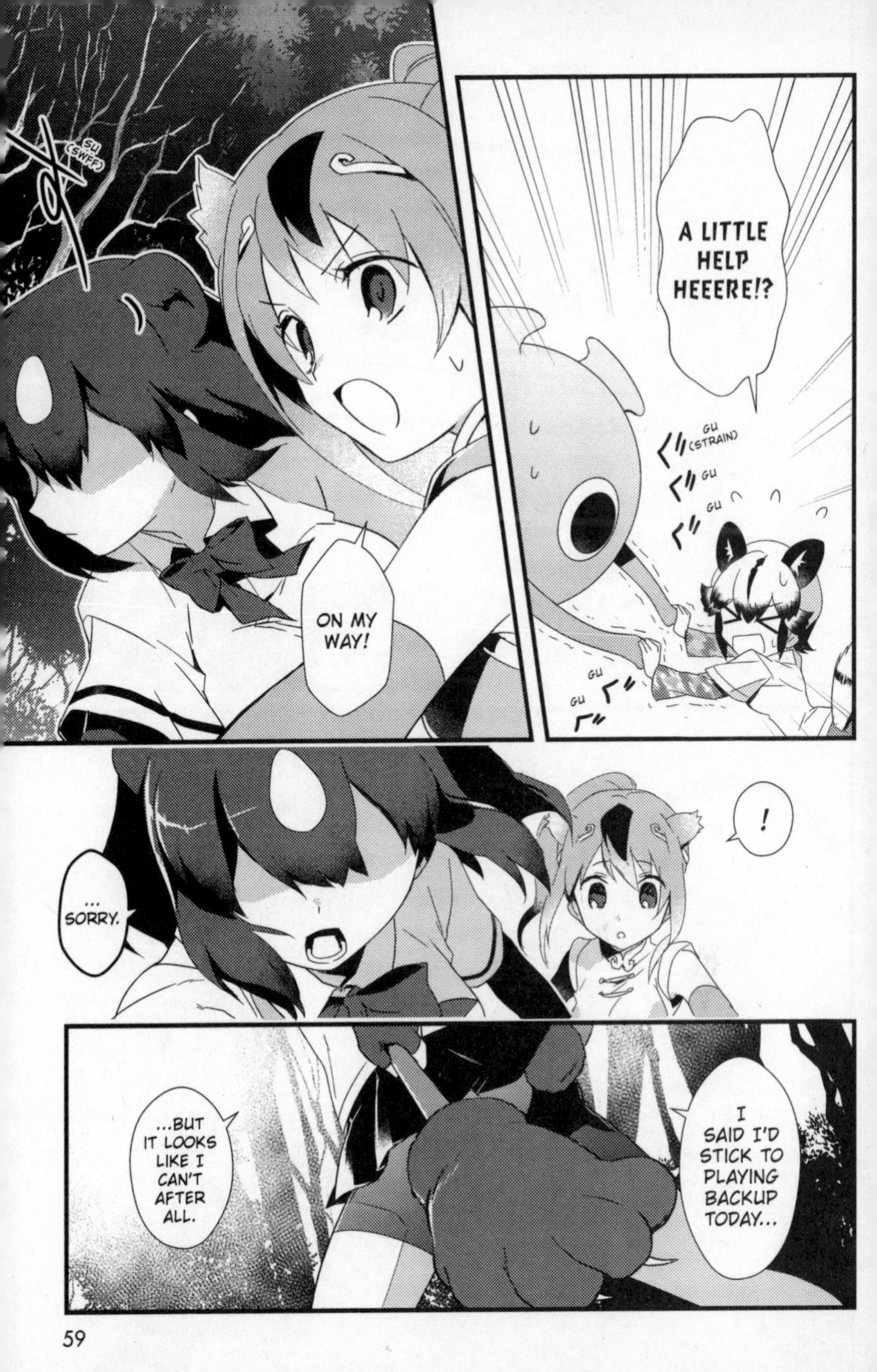
A LITTLE HELP HEEERE!?
GU (STRAIN)
GU
GU
GU
GU
SU (SWFF)
ON MY WAY!
!
... SORRY.
I SAID I'D STICK TO PLAYING BACKUP TODAY...
...BUT IT LOOKS LIKE I CAN'T AFTER ALL.

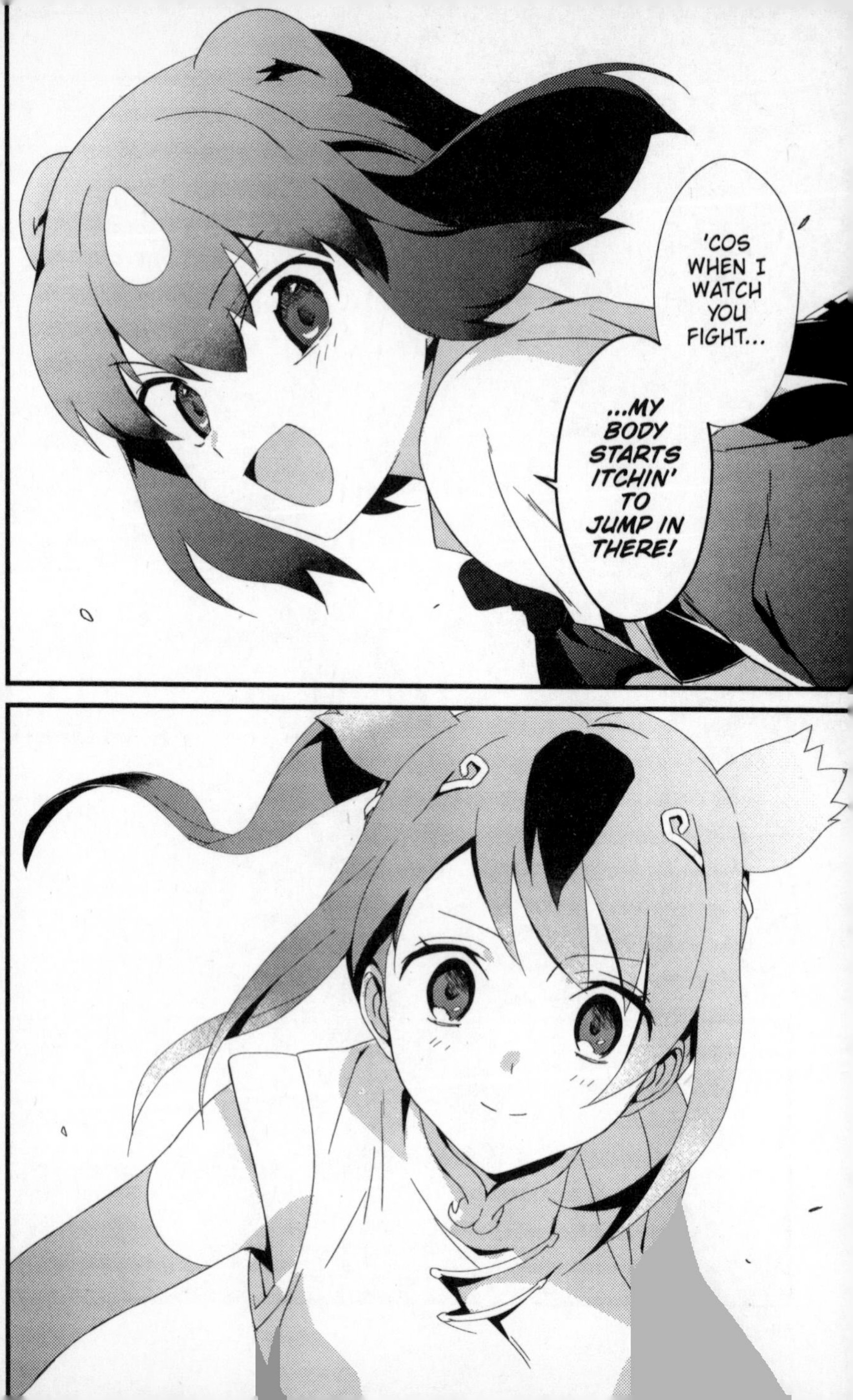
'COS WHEN I WATCH YOU FIGHT...
...MY BODY STARTS ITCHIN' TO JUMP IN THERE!

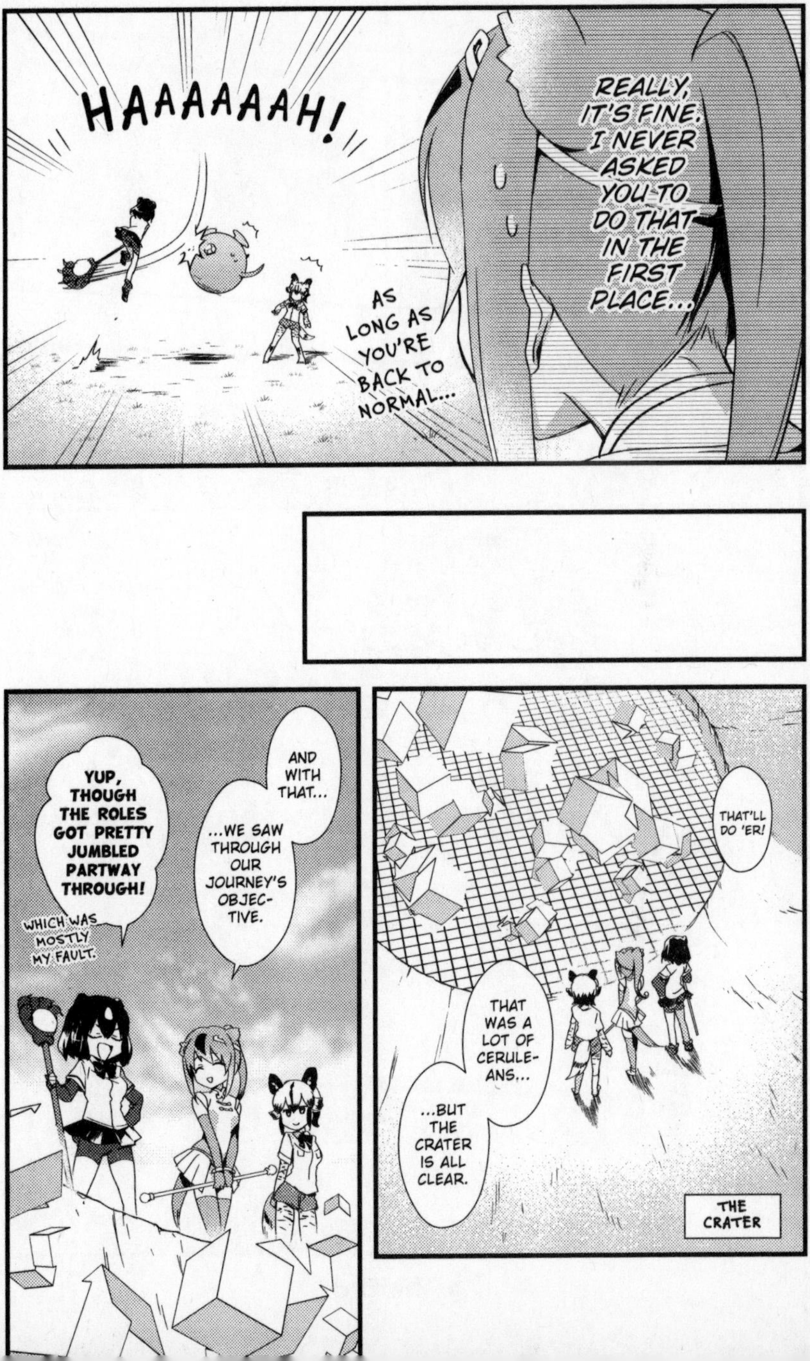
REALLY, IT'S FINE. I NEVER ASKED YOU TO DO THAT IN THE FIRST PLACE...
AS LONG AS YOU'RE BACK TO NORMAL...
HAAAAAAH!
THE CRATER
THAT'LL DO 'ER!
THAT WAS A LOT OF CERULE-ANS...
...BUT THE CRATER IS ALL CLEAR.
AND WITH THAT...
...WE SAW THROUGH OUR JOURNEY'S OBJEC-TIVE.
YUP, THOUGH THE ROLES GOT PRETTY JUMBLED PARTWAY THROUGH!
WHICH WAS MOSTLY MY FAULT.

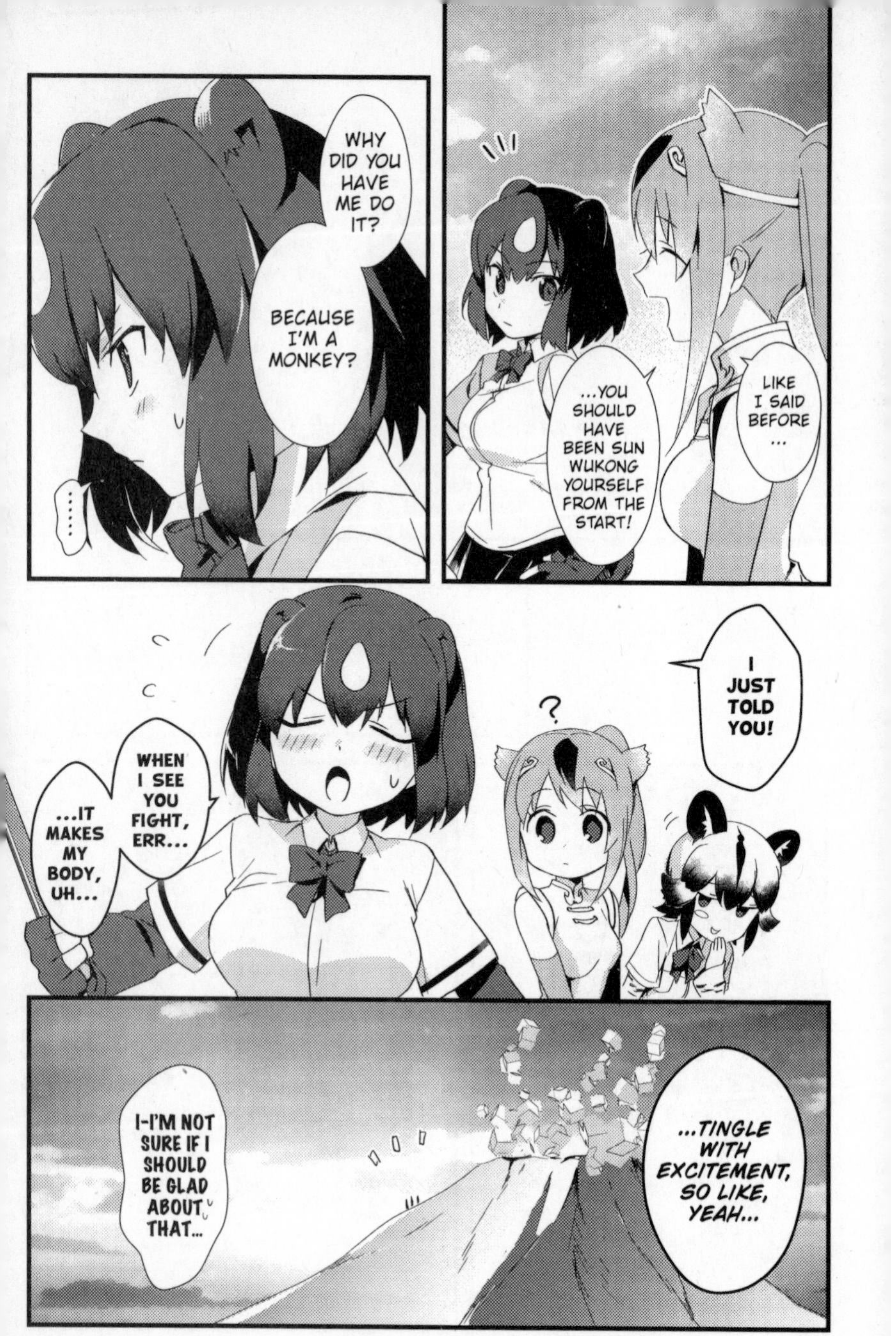
LIKE I SAID BEFORE ...
...YOU SHOULD HAVE BEEN SUN WUKONG YOURSELF FROM THE START!
WHY DID YOU HAVE ME DO IT?
BECAUSE I'M A MONKEY?
......
I JUST TOLD YOU!
?
WHEN I SEE YOU FIGHT, ERR...
...IT MAKES MY BODY, UH...
...TINGLE WITH EXCITEMENT, SO LIKE, YEAH...
I-I'M NOT SURE IF I SHOULD BE GLAD ABOUT THAT...

The End

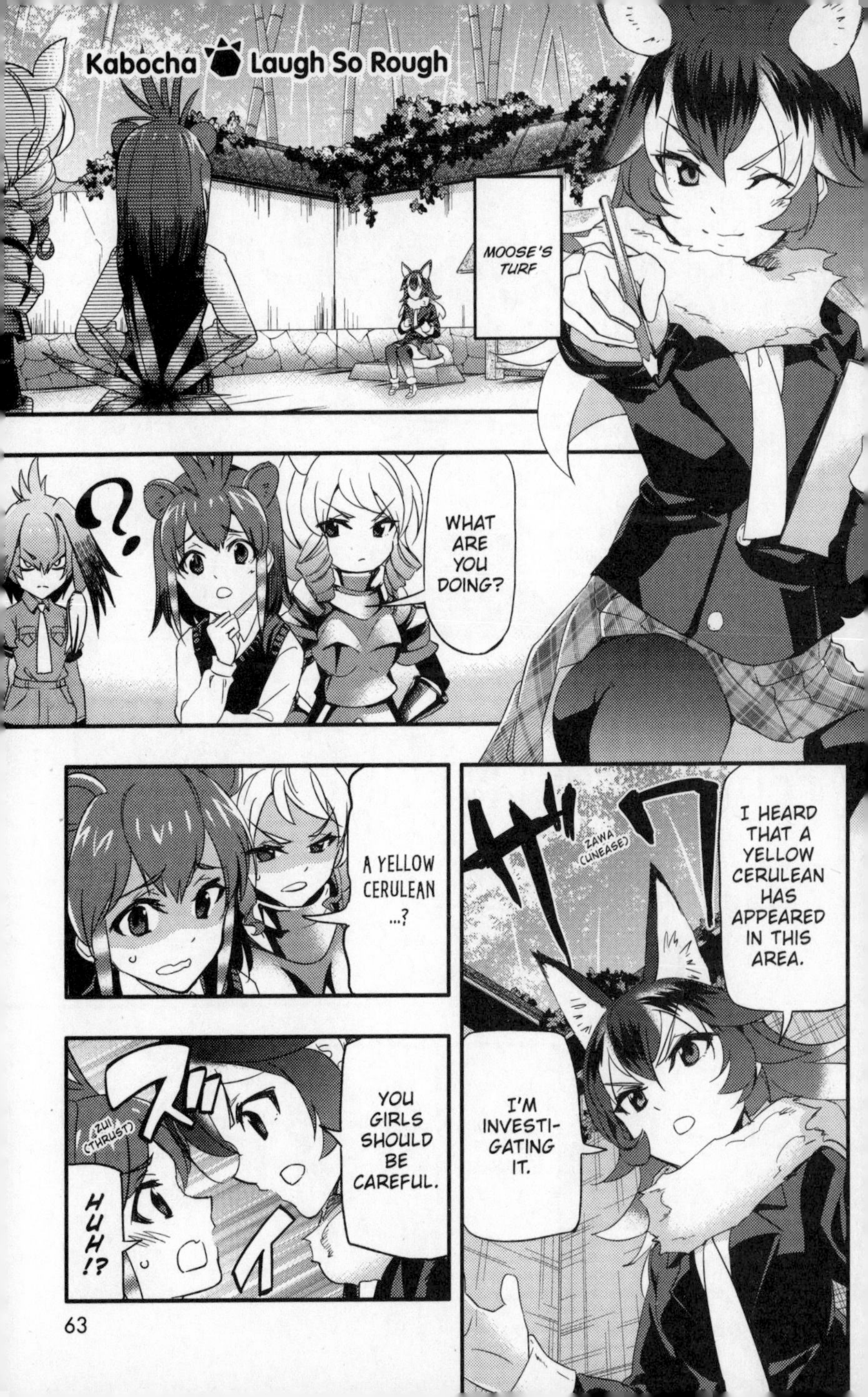
Kabocha Laugh So Rough
MOOSE'S TURF
WHAT ARE YOU DOING?
ZAWA (UNEASE)
I HEARD THAT A YELLOW CERULEAN HAS APPEARED IN THIS AREA.
I'M INVESTIGATING IT.
A YELLOW CERULEAN ...?
YOU GIRLS SHOULD BE CAREFUL.
ZUI (THRUST)
HUH!?

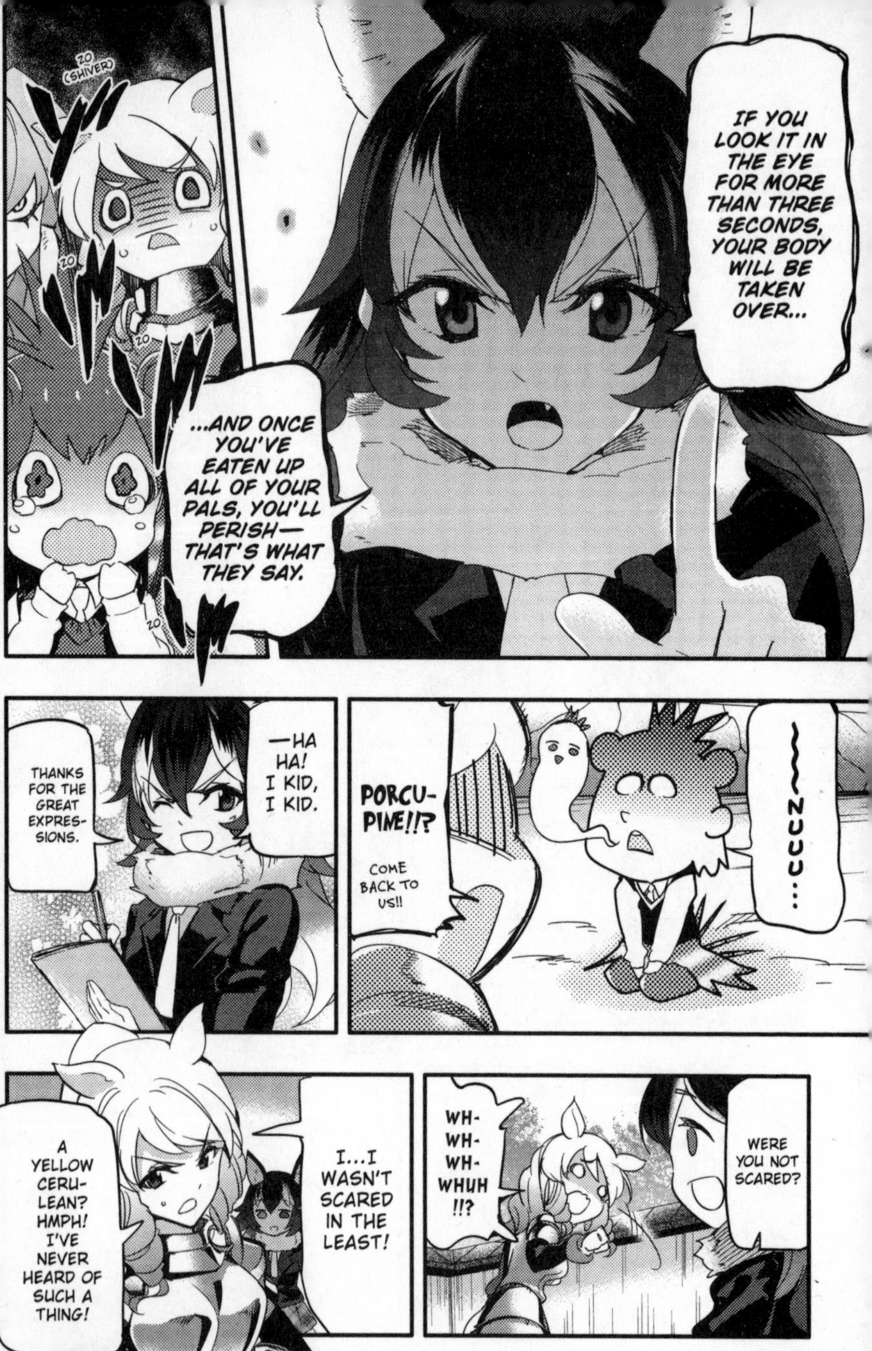
IF YOU LOOK IT IN THE EYE FOR MORE THAN THREE SECONDS, YOUR BODY WILL BE TAKEN OVER...
...AND ONCE YOU'VE EATEN UP ALL OF YOUR PALS, YOU'LL PERISH—THAT'S WHAT THEY SAY.
ZO (SHIVER)
ZO
ZO
ZO
~~NUUU...
PORCU-PINE!!?
COME BACK TO US!!
—HA HA! I KID, I KID.
THANKS FOR THE GREAT EXPRES-SIONS.
WERE YOU NOT SCARED?
WH-WH-WH-WHUH!!?
I...I WASN'T SCARED IN THE LEAST!
A YELLOW CERU-LEAN? HMPH! I'VE NEVER HEARD OF SUCH A THING!

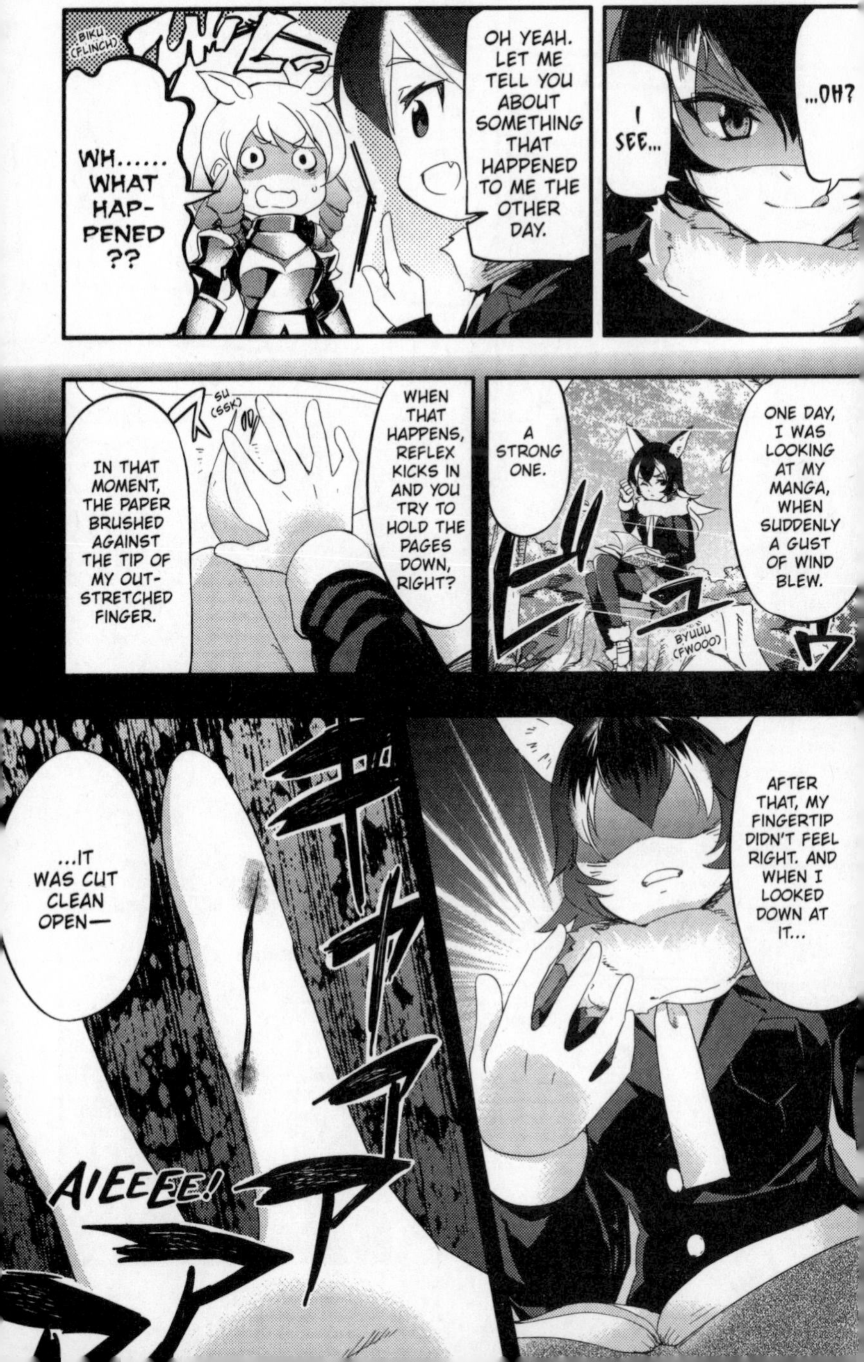
...OH?
I SEE...
OH YEAH. LET ME TELL YOU ABOUT SOMETHING THAT HAPPENED TO ME THE OTHER DAY.
BIKU (FLINCH)
WH...... WHAT HAPPENED??
ONE DAY, I WAS LOOKING AT MY MANGA, WHEN SUDDENLY A GUST OF WIND BLEW.
A STRONG ONE.
BYUUU (FWOOO)
WHEN THAT HAPPENS, REFLEX KICKS IN AND YOU TRY TO HOLD THE PAGES DOWN, RIGHT?
SU (SSK)
IN THAT MOMENT, THE PAPER BRUSHED AGAINST THE TIP OF MY OUT-STRETCHED FINGER.
AFTER THAT, MY FINGERTIP DIDN'T FEEL RIGHT. AND WHEN I LOOKED DOWN AT IT...
...IT WAS CUT CLEAN OPEN—
AIEEEEE!

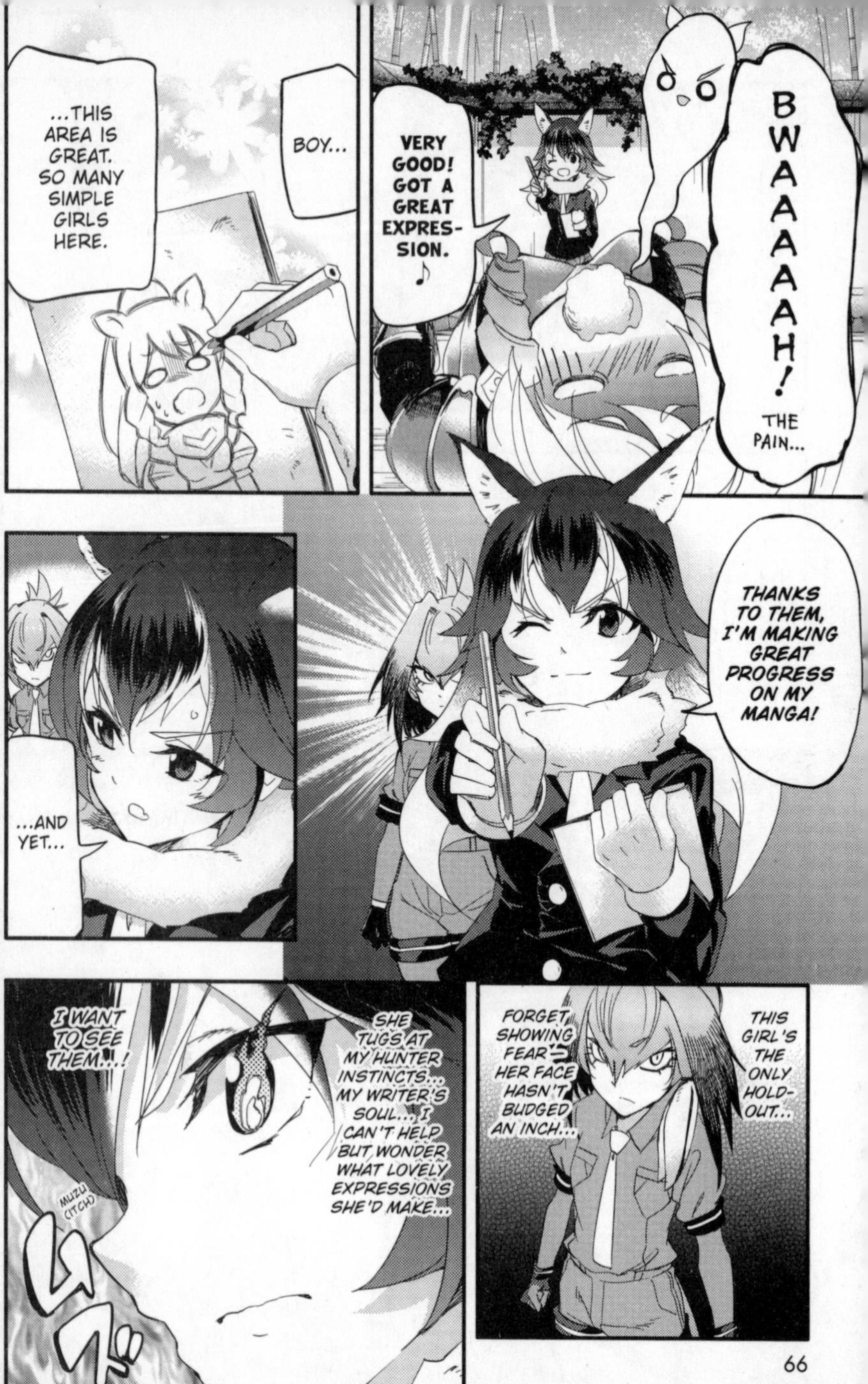
BWAAAAAAH!
THE PAIN...
VERY GOOD! GOT A GREAT EXPRESSION. ♪
BOY...
...THIS AREA IS GREAT. SO MANY SIMPLE GIRLS HERE.
THANKS TO THEM, I'M MAKING GREAT PROGRESS ON MY MANGA!
...AND YET...
THIS GIRL'S THE ONLY HOLD-OUT...
FORGET SHOWING FEAR— HER FACE HASN'T BUDGED AN INCH...
SHE TUGS AT MY HUNTER INSTINCTS... MY WRITER'S SOUL... I CAN'T HELP BUT WONDER WHAT LOVELY EXPRESSIONS SHE'D MAKE...
I WANT TO SEE THEM...!
MUZU (ITCH)

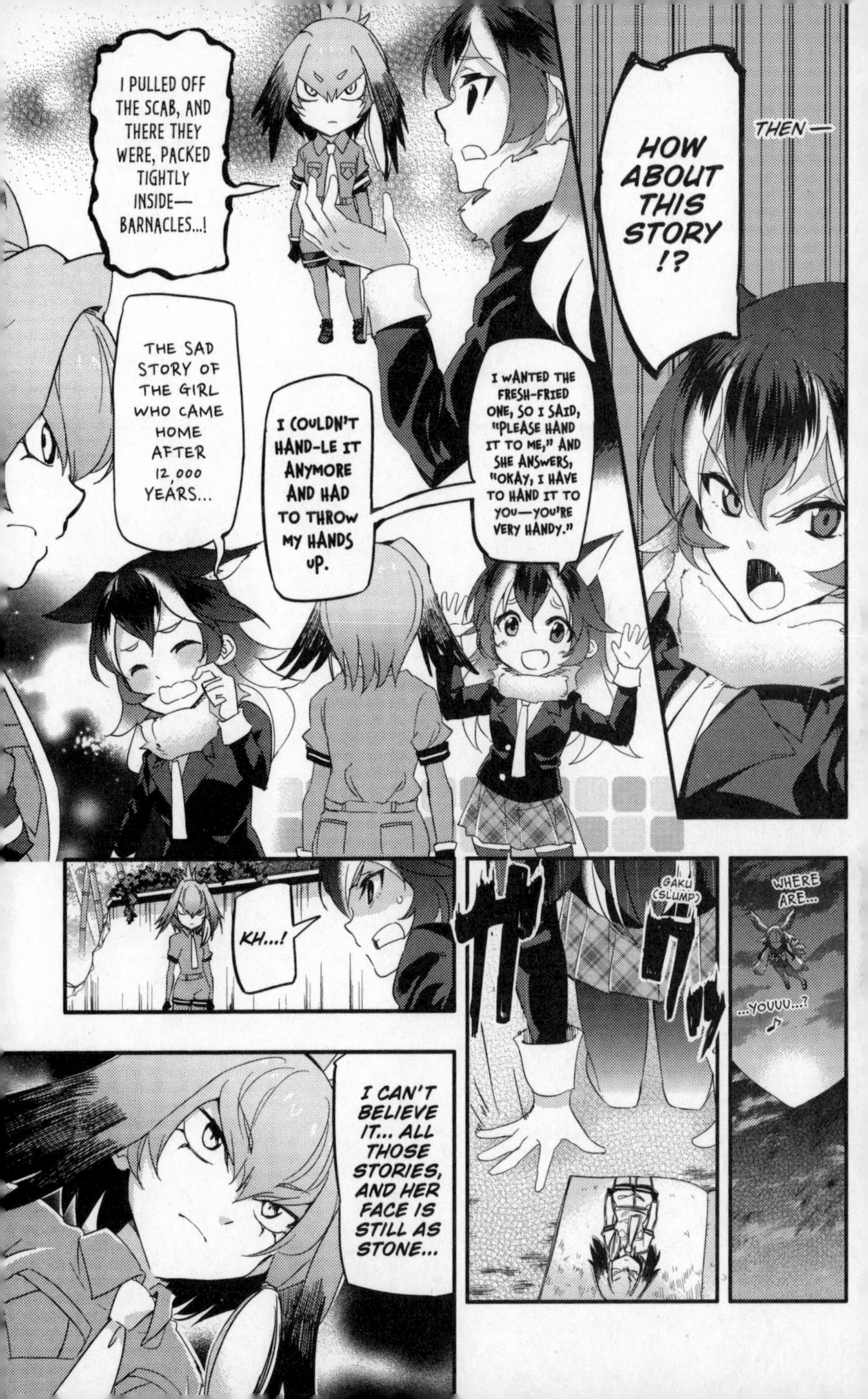
THEN—
HOW ABOUT THIS STORY!?
I PULLED OFF THE SCAB, AND THERE THEY WERE, PACKED TIGHTLY INSIDE—BARNACLES...!
I WANTED THE FRESH-FRIED ONE, SO I SAID, "PLEASE HAND IT TO ME," AND SHE ANSWERS, "OKAY, I HAVE TO HAND IT TO YOU—YOU'RE VERY HANDY."
I COULDN'T HAND-LE IT ANYMORE AND HAD TO THROW MY HANDS UP.
THE SAD STORY OF THE GIRL WHO CAME HOME AFTER 12,000 YEARS...
WHERE ARE...
...YOUUU...? ♪
GAKU (SLUMP)
KH...!
I CAN'T BELIEVE IT... ALL THOSE STORIES, AND HER FACE IS STILL AS STONE...

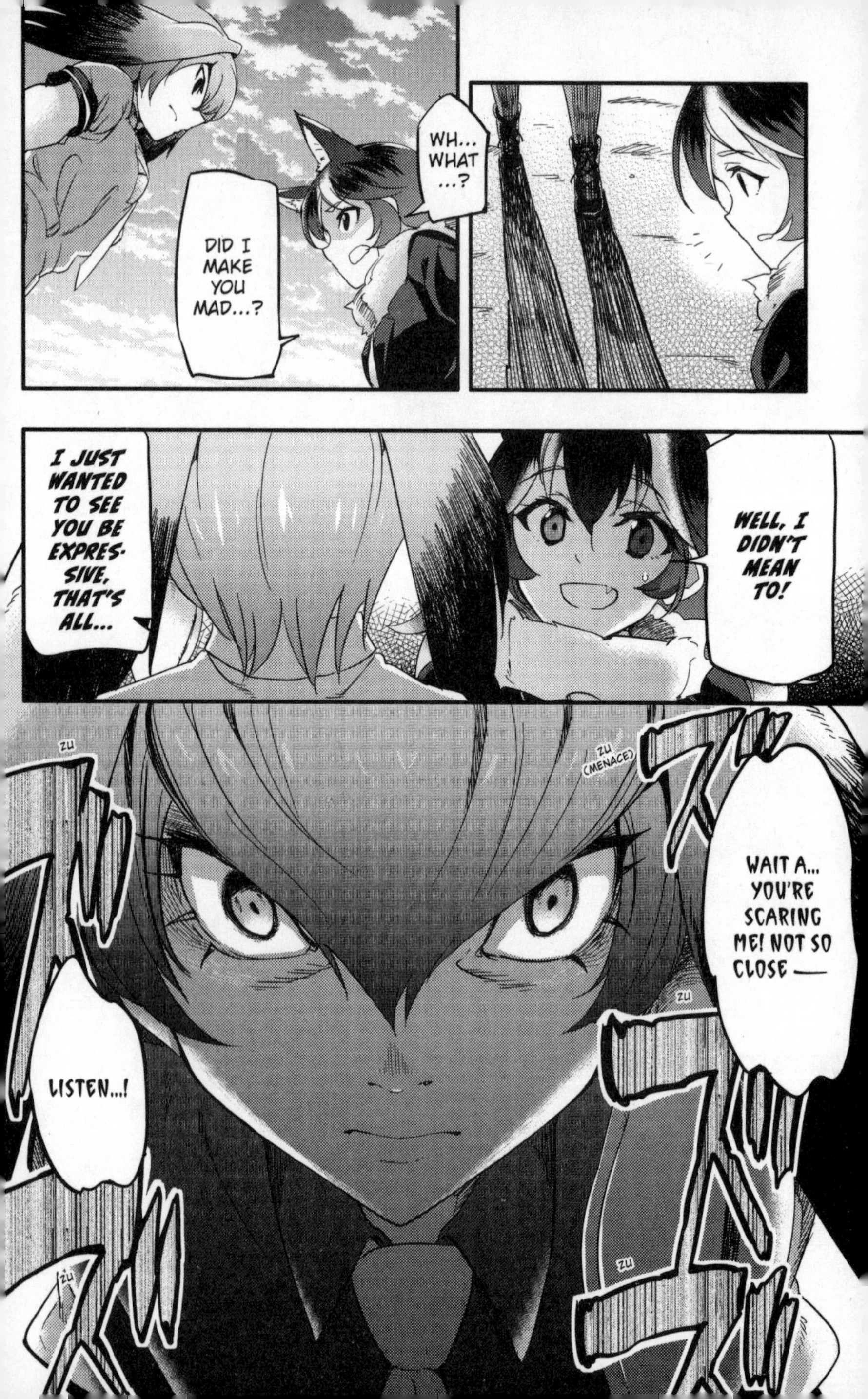
WH... WHAT ...?
DID I MAKE YOU MAD...?
WELL, I DIDN'T MEAN TO!
I JUST WANTED TO SEE YOU BE EXPRES-SIVE, THAT'S ALL...
ZU (MENACE)
WAIT A... YOU'RE SCARING ME! NOT SO CLOSE —
ZU
ZU
ZU
ZU
LISTEN...!

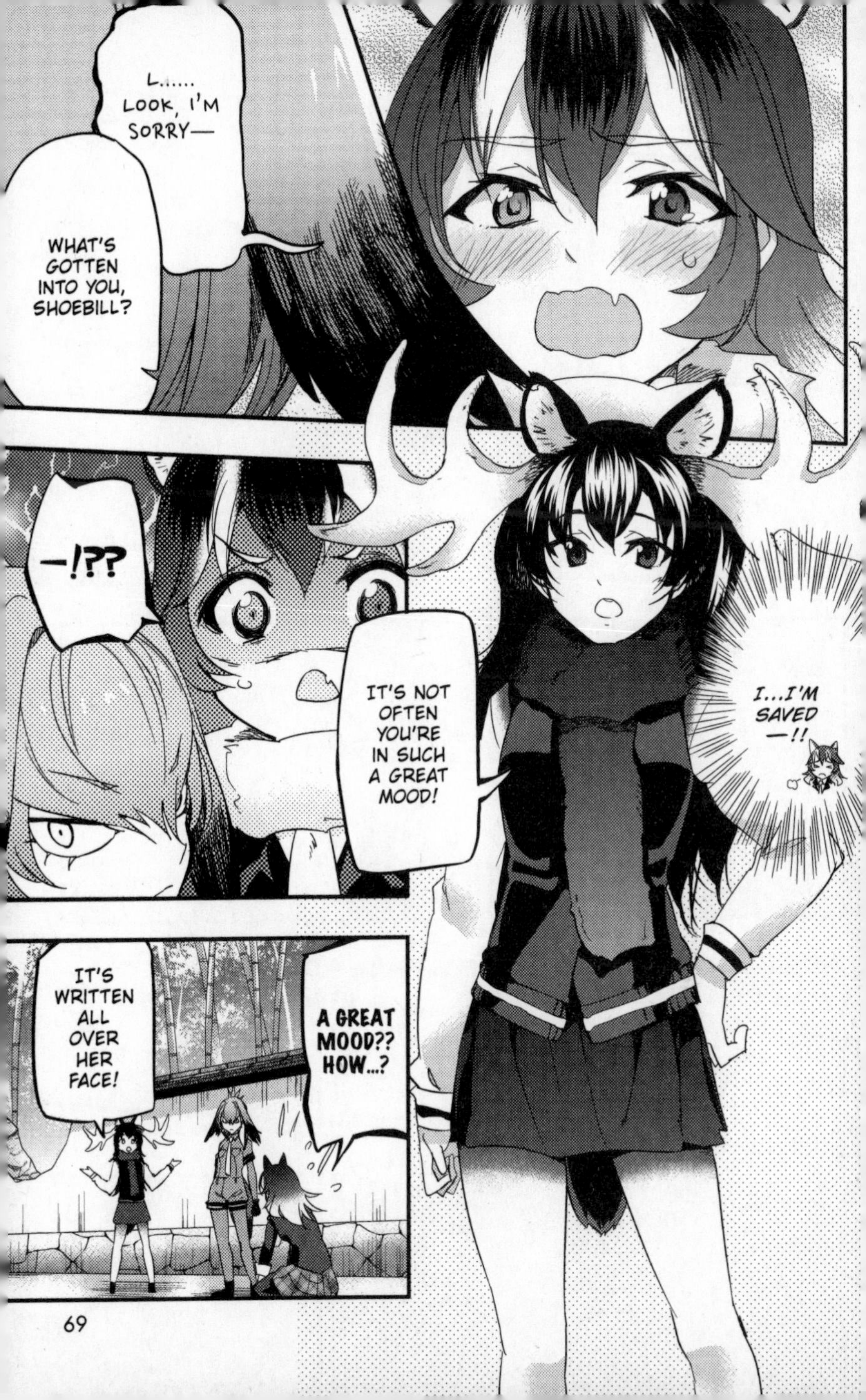
L...... LOOK, I'M SORRY—
WHAT'S GOTTEN INTO YOU, SHOEBILL?
IT'S NOT OFTEN YOU'RE IN SUCH A GREAT MOOD!
I...I'M SAVED—!!
—!??
A GREAT MOOD?? HOW...?
IT'S WRITTEN ALL OVER HER FACE!

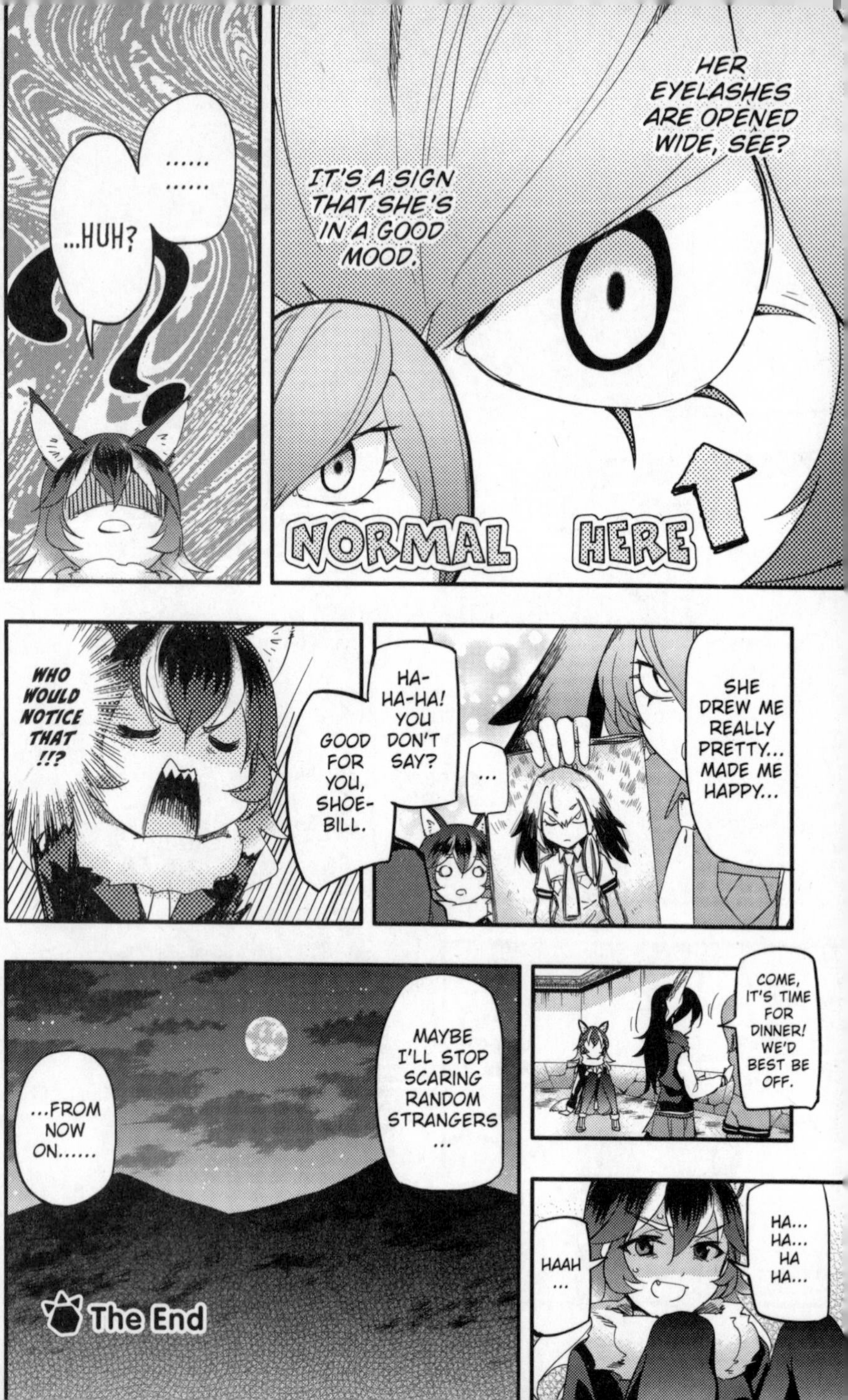
HER EYELASHES ARE OPENED WIDE, SEE?
IT'S A SIGN THAT SHE'S IN A GOOD MOOD.
HERE
NORMAL
....
...HUH?
SHE DREW ME REALLY PRETTY... MADE ME HAPPY...
...
HA-HA-HA! YOU DON'T SAY?
GOOD FOR YOU, SHOE-BILL.
WHO WOULD NOTICE THAT!!?
COME, IT'S TIME FOR DINNER! WE'D BEST BE OFF.
HA... HA... HA HA...
HAAH ...
MAYBE I'LL STOP SCARING RANDOM STRANGERS ...
...FROM NOW ON......
The End

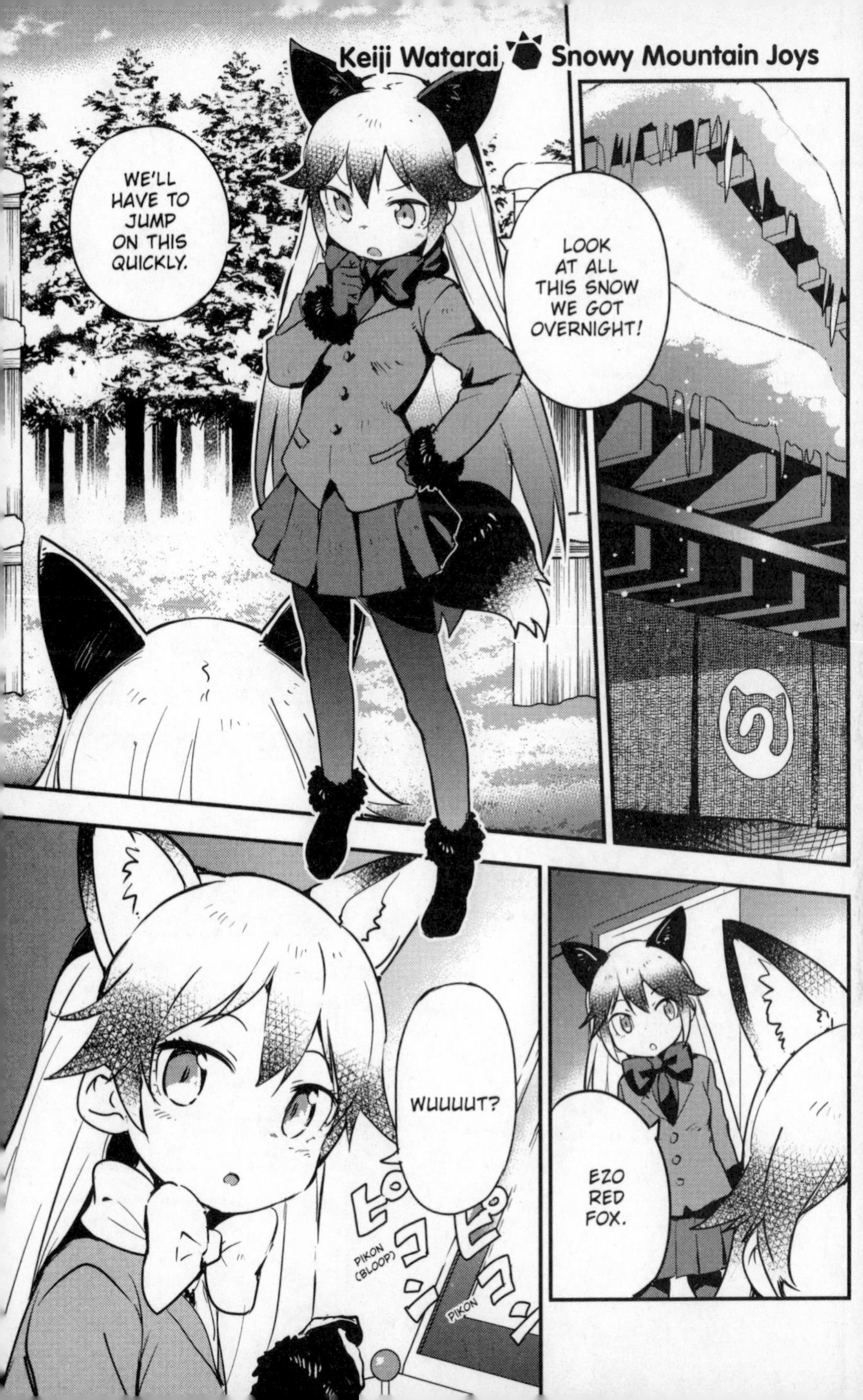
Keiji Watarai Snowy Mountain Joys
LOOK AT ALL THIS SNOW WE GOT OVERNIGHT!
WE'LL HAVE TO JUMP ON THIS QUICKLY.
EZO RED FOX.
WUUUUT?
PIKON (BLOOP)
PIKON

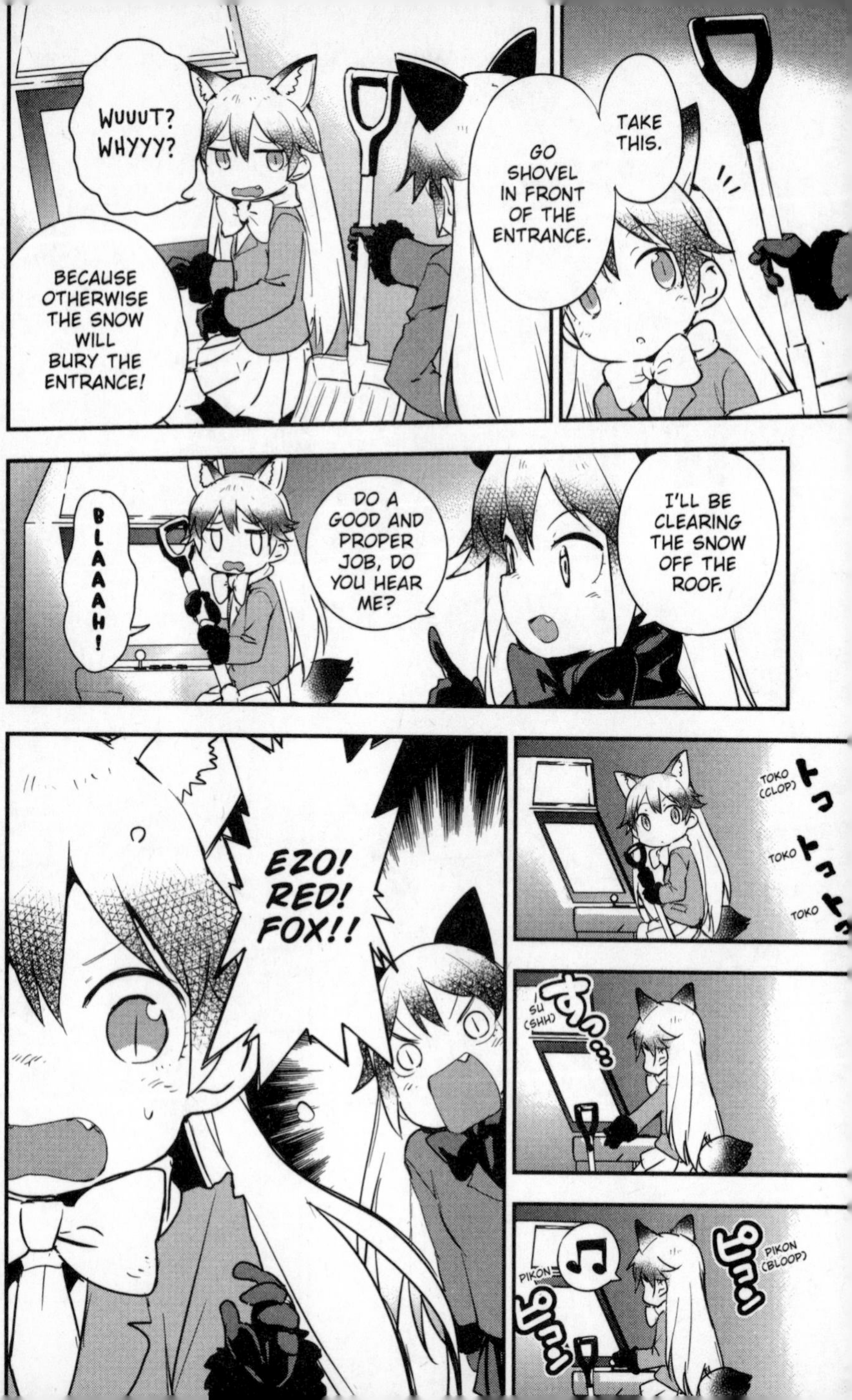
TAKE THIS.
GO SHOVEL IN FRONT OF THE ENTRANCE.
WUUUT? WHYYY?
BECAUSE OTHERWISE THE SNOW WILL BURY THE ENTRANCE!
I'LL BE CLEARING THE SNOW OFF THE ROOF.
DO A GOOD AND PROPER JOB, DO YOU HEAR ME?
BLAAAAH!
トコ TOKO (CLOP)
トコ TOKO
トコ TOKO
すっ… SU (SHH)
ピコン PIKON (BLOOP)
ピコン PIKON
EZO! RED! FOX!!

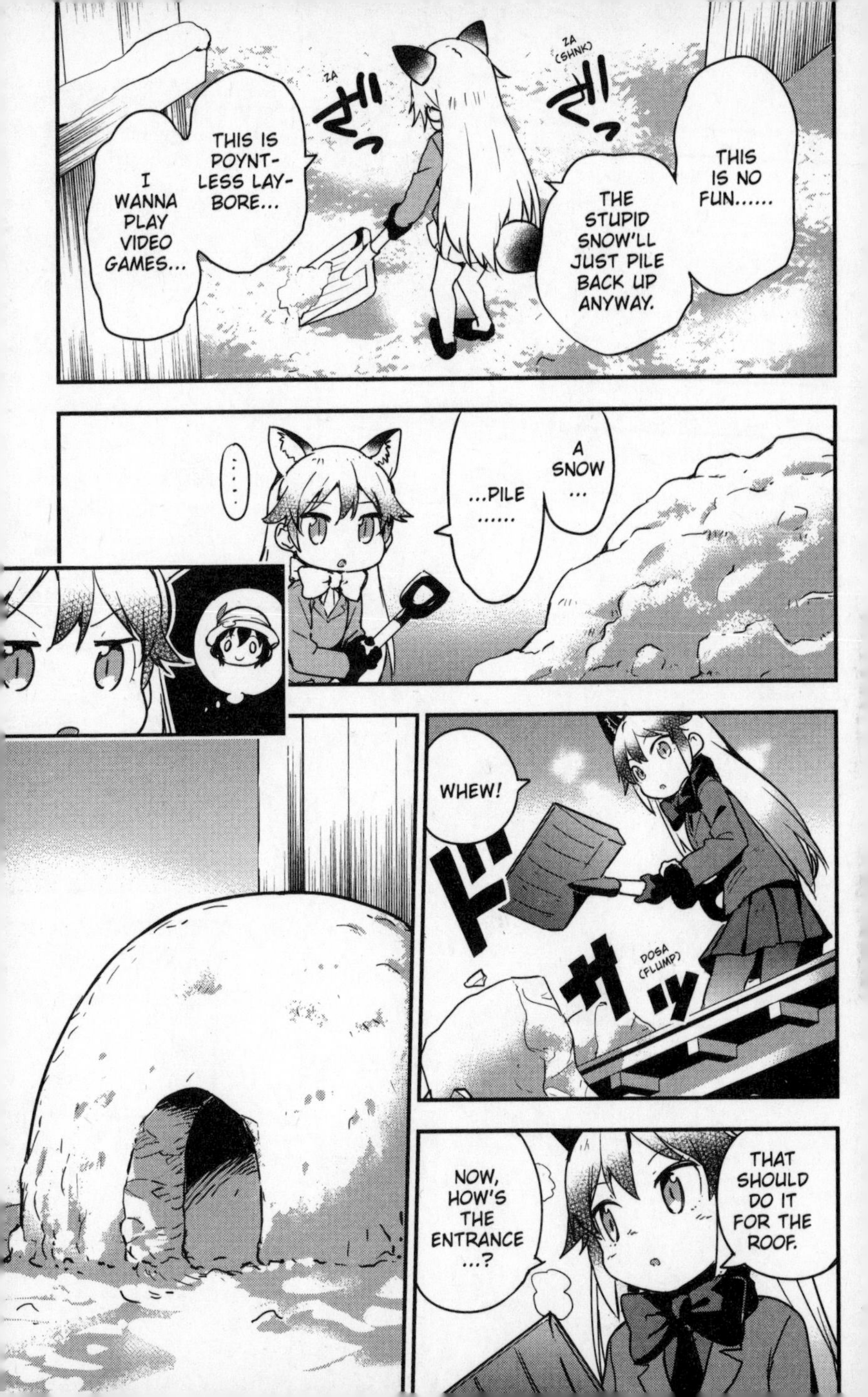
ZA (SHNK)
THIS IS NO FUN......
THE STUPID SNOW'LL JUST PILE BACK UP ANYWAY.
ZA
THIS IS POYNT-LESS LAY-BORE...
I WANNA PLAY VIDEO GAMES...
A SNOW ...
...PILE ......
......
WHEW!
DOSA (FLUMP)
THAT SHOULD DO IT FOR THE ROOF.
NOW, HOW'S THE ENTRANCE ...?

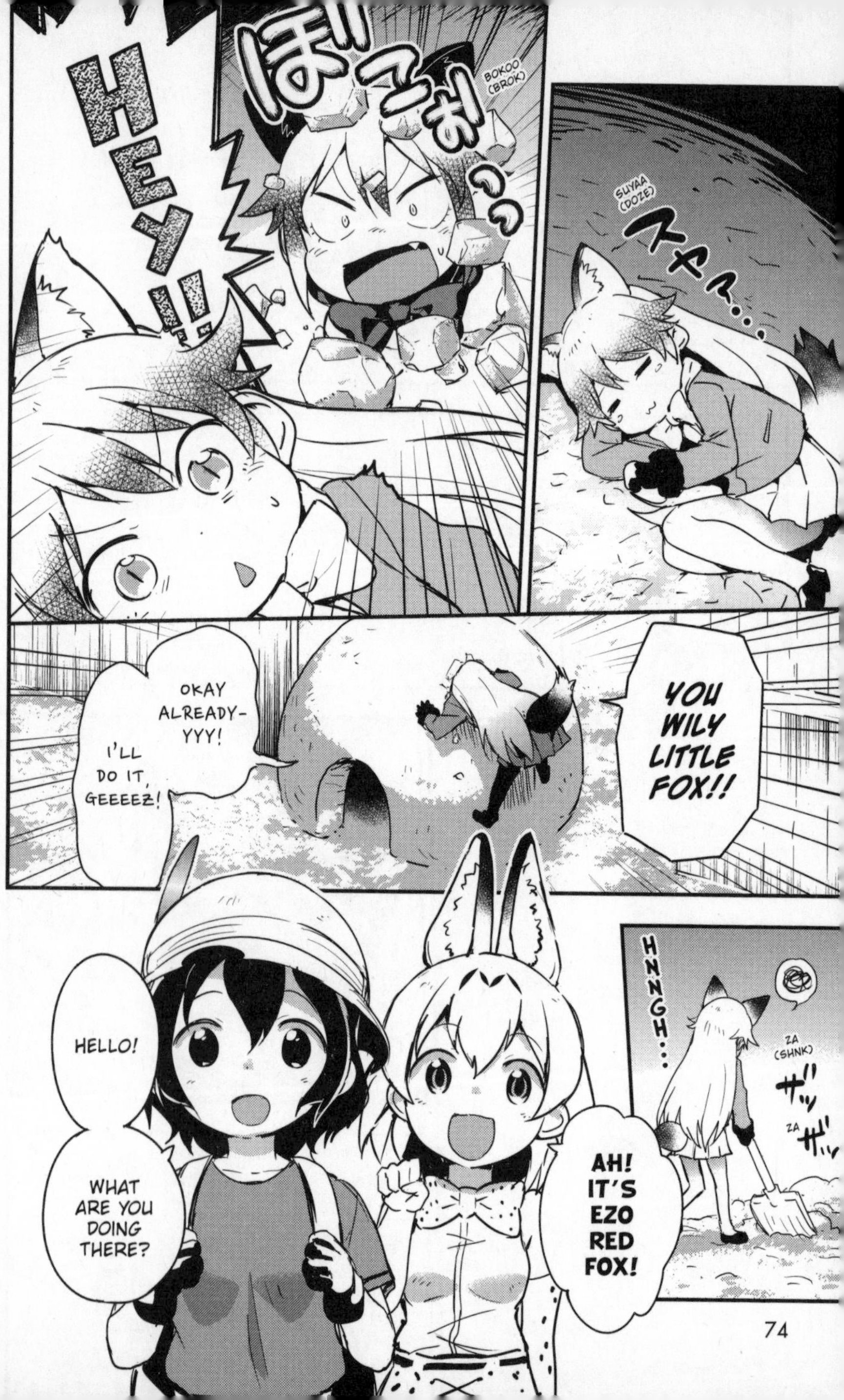
SUYAA (DOZE)
スヤァ…
ぼこぉっ
BOKOO (BROK)
HEY!!
YOU WILY LITTLE FOX!!
OKAY ALREADY-YYY!
I'LL DO IT, GEEEEZ!
HNNGH…
ZA (SHNK)
ザッ
ZA
ザッ
AH! IT'S EZO RED FOX!
HELLO!
WHAT ARE YOU DOING THERE?

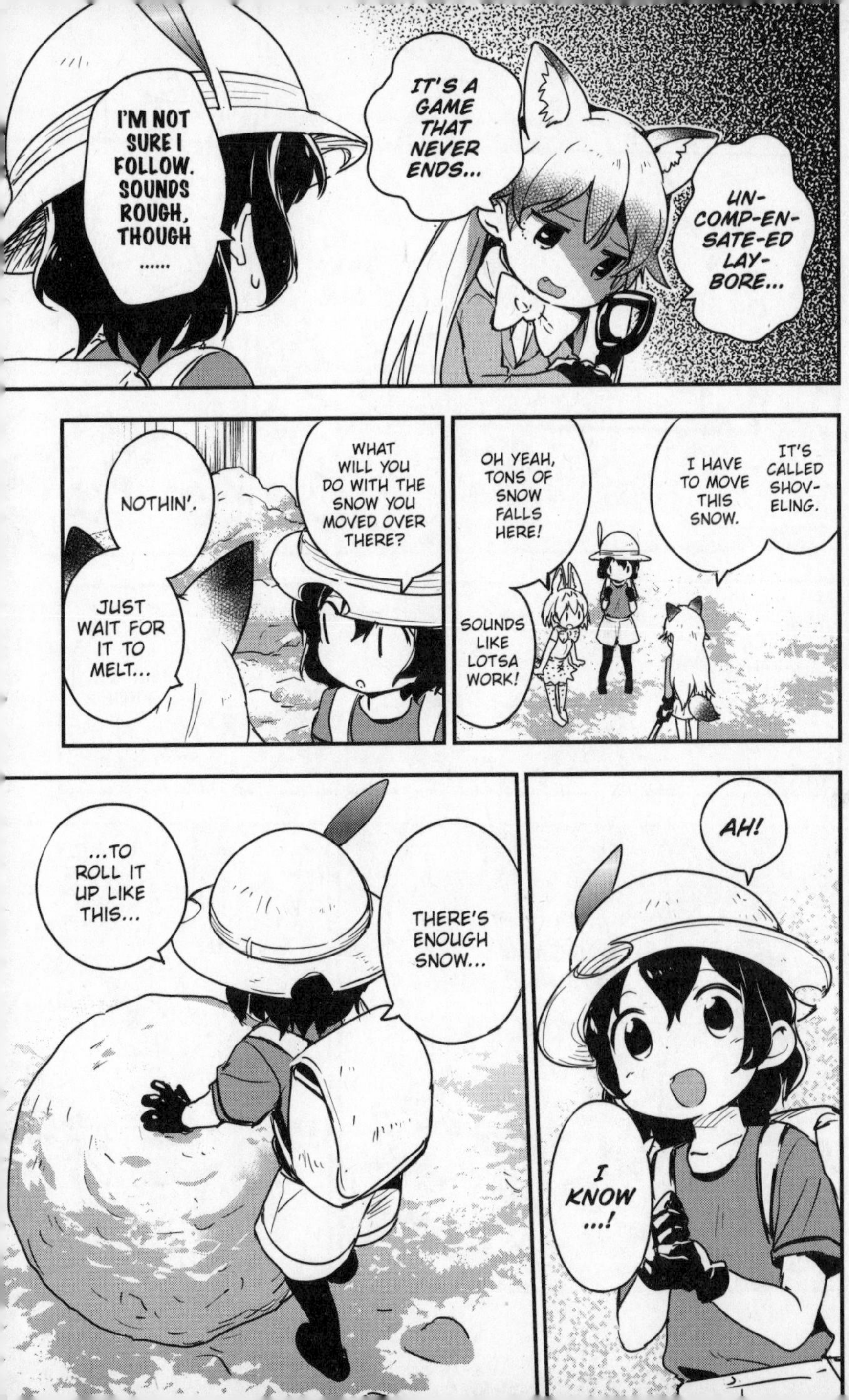
UN-COMP-EN-SATE-ED LAY-BORE...
IT'S A GAME THAT NEVER ENDS...
I'M NOT SURE I FOLLOW. SOUNDS ROUGH, THOUGH ......
IT'S CALLED SHOV-ELING.
I HAVE TO MOVE THIS SNOW.
OH YEAH, TONS OF SNOW FALLS HERE!
SOUNDS LIKE LOTSA WORK!
WHAT WILL YOU DO WITH THE SNOW YOU MOVED OVER THERE?
NOTHIN'.
JUST WAIT FOR IT TO MELT...
AH!
I KNOW ...!
THERE'S ENOUGH SNOW...
...TO ROLL IT UP LIKE THIS...

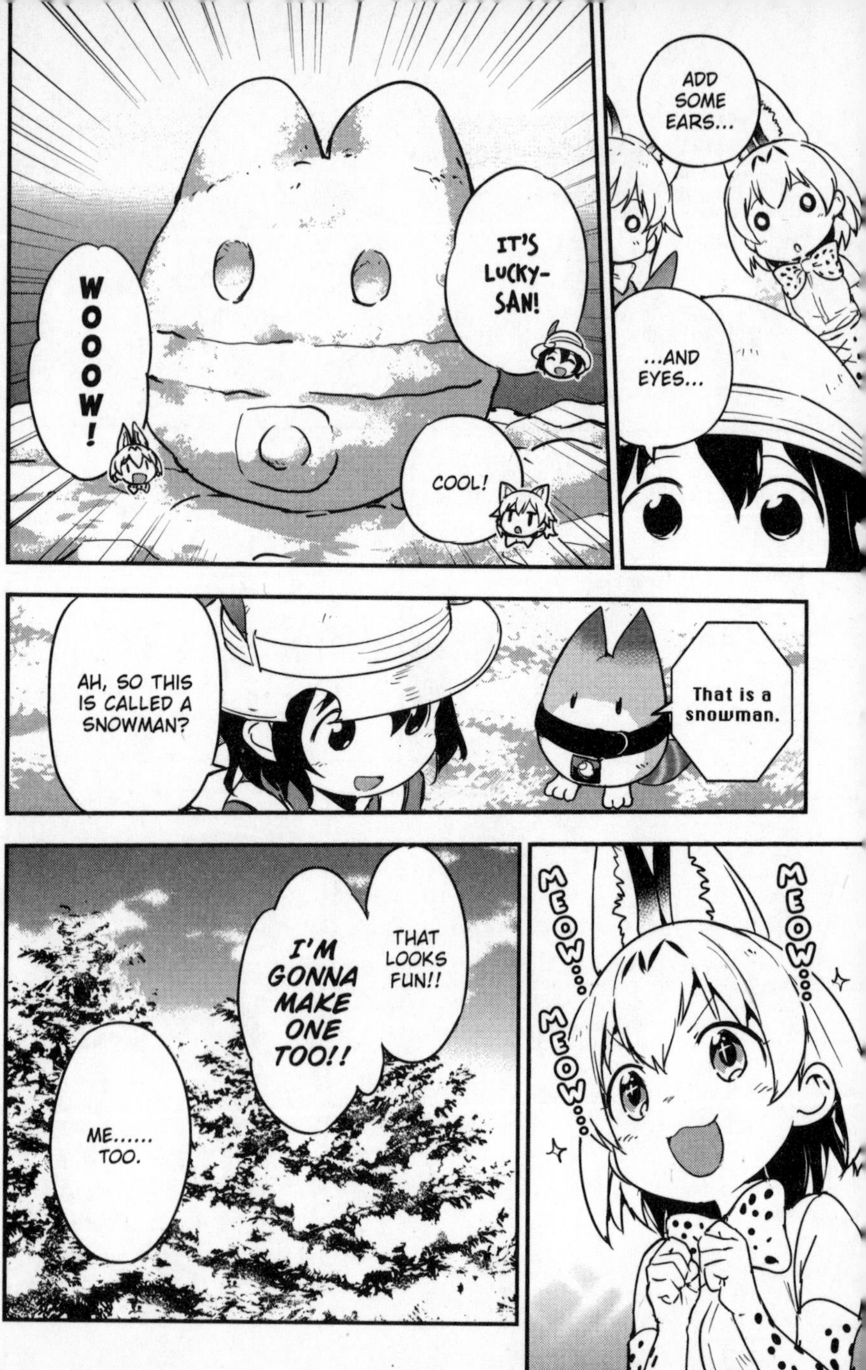
ADD SOME EARS...
...AND EYES...
IT'S LUCKY-SAN!
WOOOW!
COOL!
That is a snowman.
AH, SO THIS IS CALLED A SNOWMAN?
MEOW...
MEOW...
MEOW...
THAT LOOKS FUN!!
I'M GONNA MAKE ONE TOO!!
ME...... TOO.

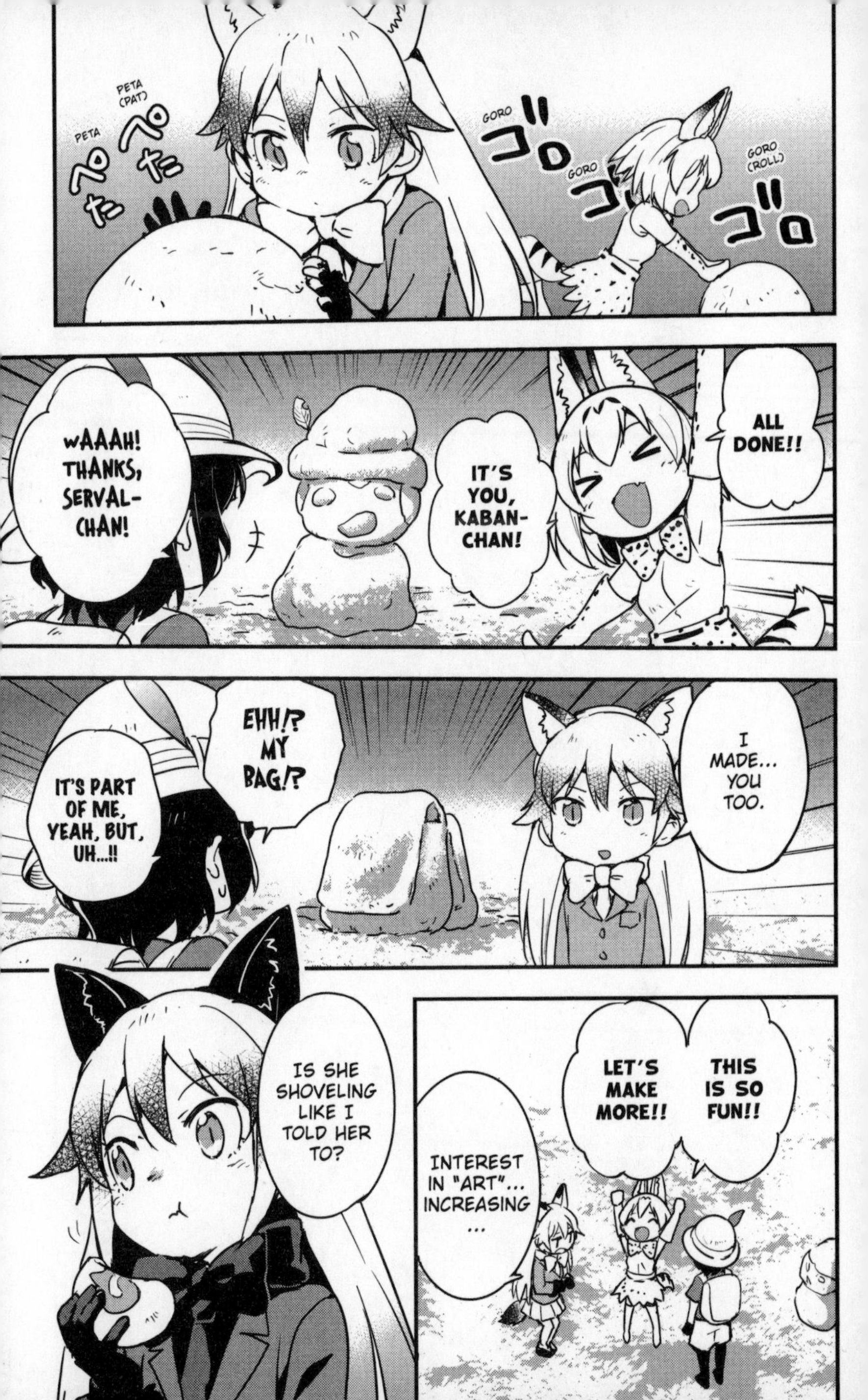
ゴロ GORO (ROLL)
ゴロ GORO
ゴロ GORO
ぺた PETA (PAT)
ぺた PETA
ALL DONE!!
IT'S YOU, KABAN-CHAN!
WAAAH! THANKS, SERVAL-CHAN!
I MADE... YOU TOO.
EHH!? MY BAG!?
IT'S PART OF ME, YEAH, BUT, UH...!!
THIS IS SO FUN!!
LET'S MAKE MORE!!
INTEREST IN "ART"... INCREASING ...
IS SHE SHOVELING LIKE I TOLD HER TO?

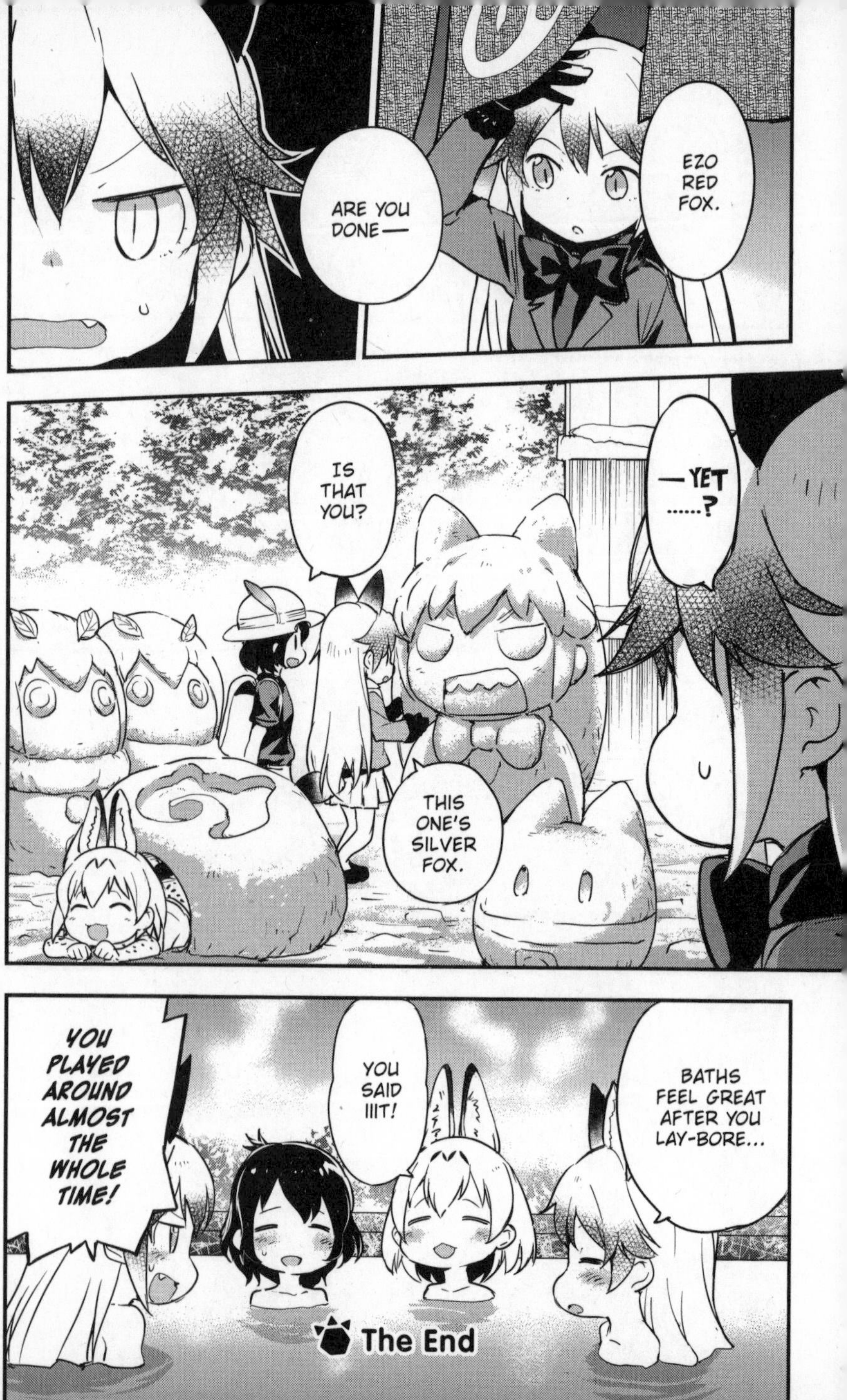
EZO RED FOX.
ARE YOU DONE—
—YET ......?
IS THAT YOU?
THIS ONE'S SILVER FOX.
BATHS FEEL GREAT AFTER YOU LAY-BORE...
YOU SAID IIIT!
YOU PLAYED AROUND ALMOST THE WHOLE TIME!
The End

62 WHAT'S THAT ANIMAL?

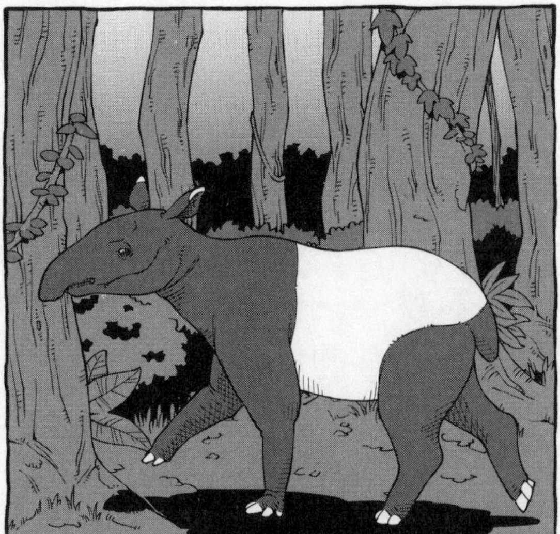

HINT:

Their divided black-and-wh
markings make them easy
identify. However, in the da
of night, only their white pa
is visible, keeping them saf
from their natural predators

Turn the page for the ans

Kemono Friends

Answer

A2
MALAYAN TAPIR

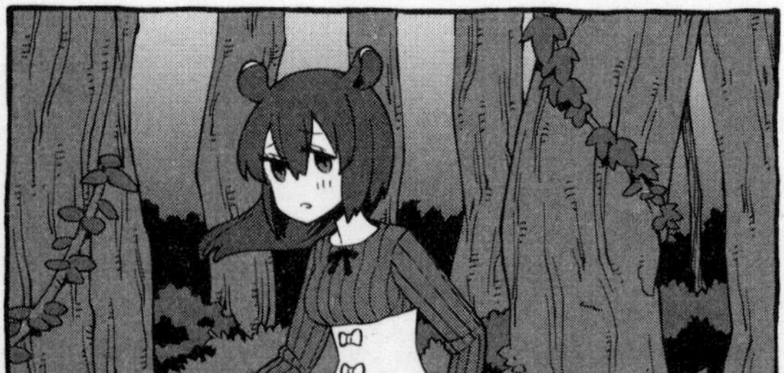

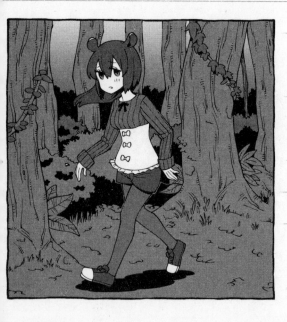

Kanaineko ● I'll Be the Best Ninja I Can Be Today!

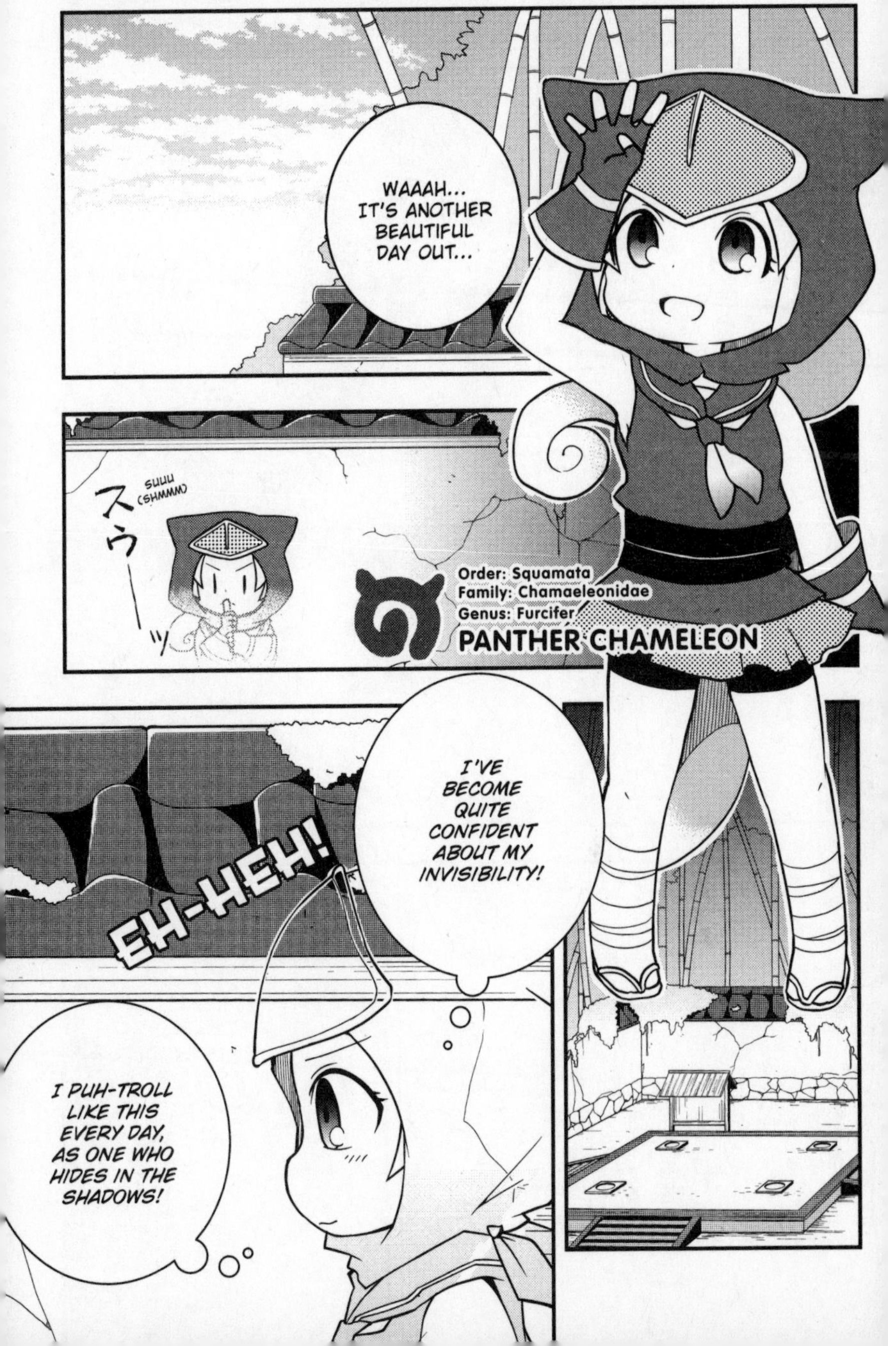
WAAAH... IT'S ANOTHER BEAUTIFUL DAY OUT...
Order: Squamata
Family: Chamaeleonidae
Genus: Furcifer
PANTHER CHAMELEON
スゥーッ
SUUU (SHMMM)
I'VE BECOME QUITE CONFIDENT ABOUT MY INVISIBILITY!
EH-HEH!
I PUH-TROLL LIKE THIS EVERY DAY, AS ONE WHO HIDES IN THE SHADOWS!

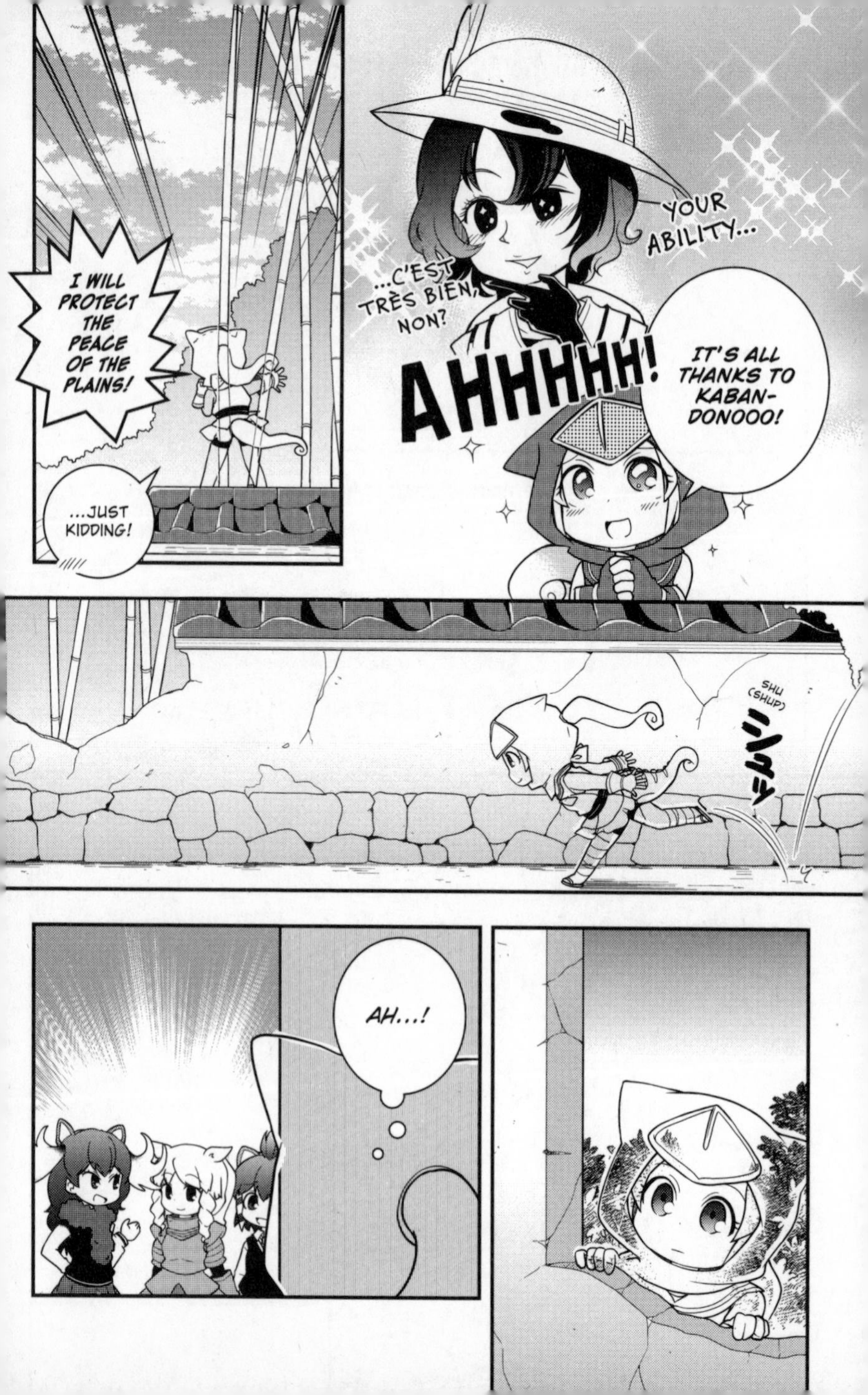
YOUR ABILITY...
...C'EST TRÈS BIEN, NON?
AHHHHH!
IT'S ALL THANKS TO KABAN-DONOOO!
I WILL PROTECT THE PEACE OF THE PLAINS!
...JUST KIDDING!
シュッ
SHU (SHUP)
AH...!

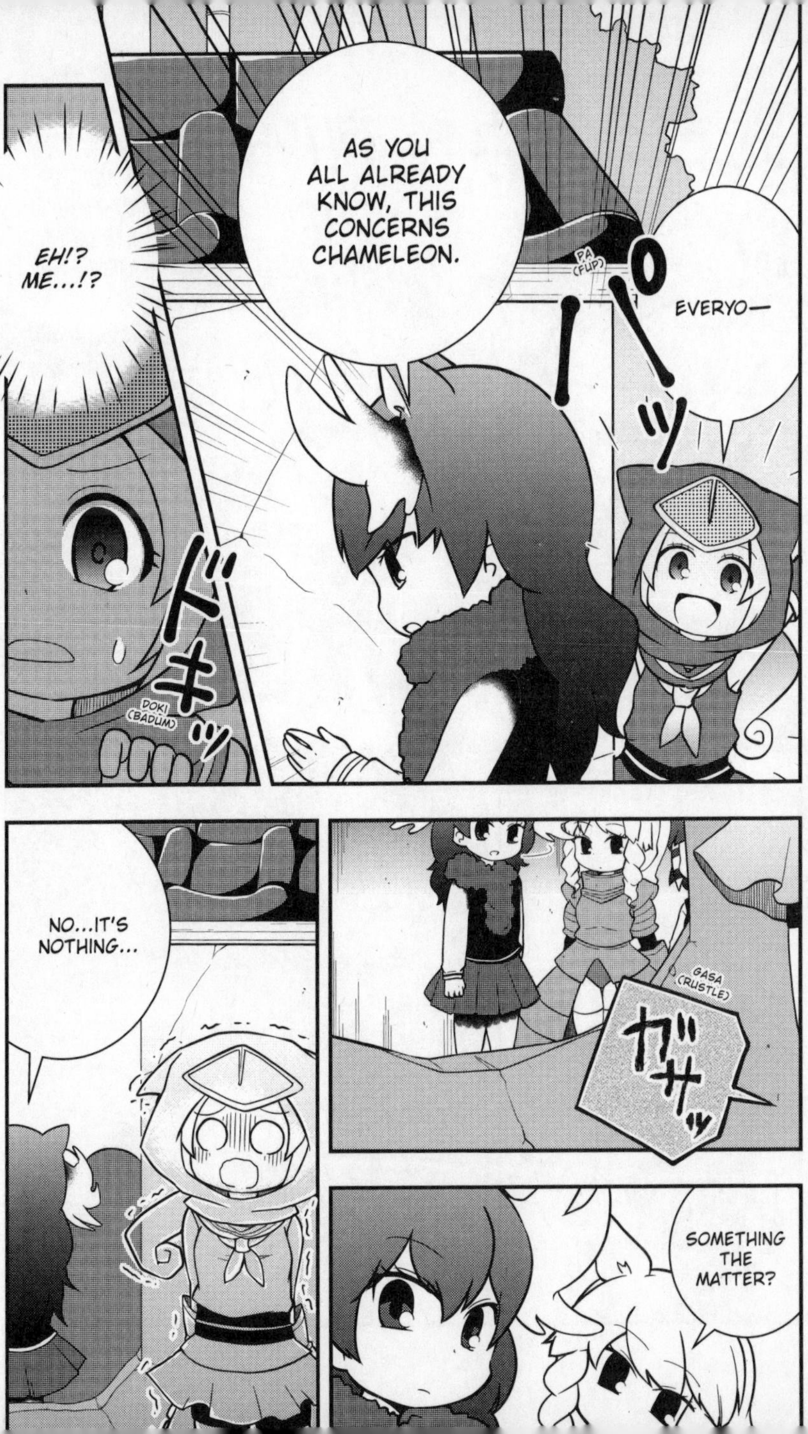
EVERYO—
PA (FUP)
AS YOU ALL ALREADY KNOW, THIS CONCERNS CHAMELEON.
EH!? ME...!?
DOKI (BADUM)
GASA (RUSTLE)
SOMETHING THE MATTER?
NO...IT'S NOTHING...

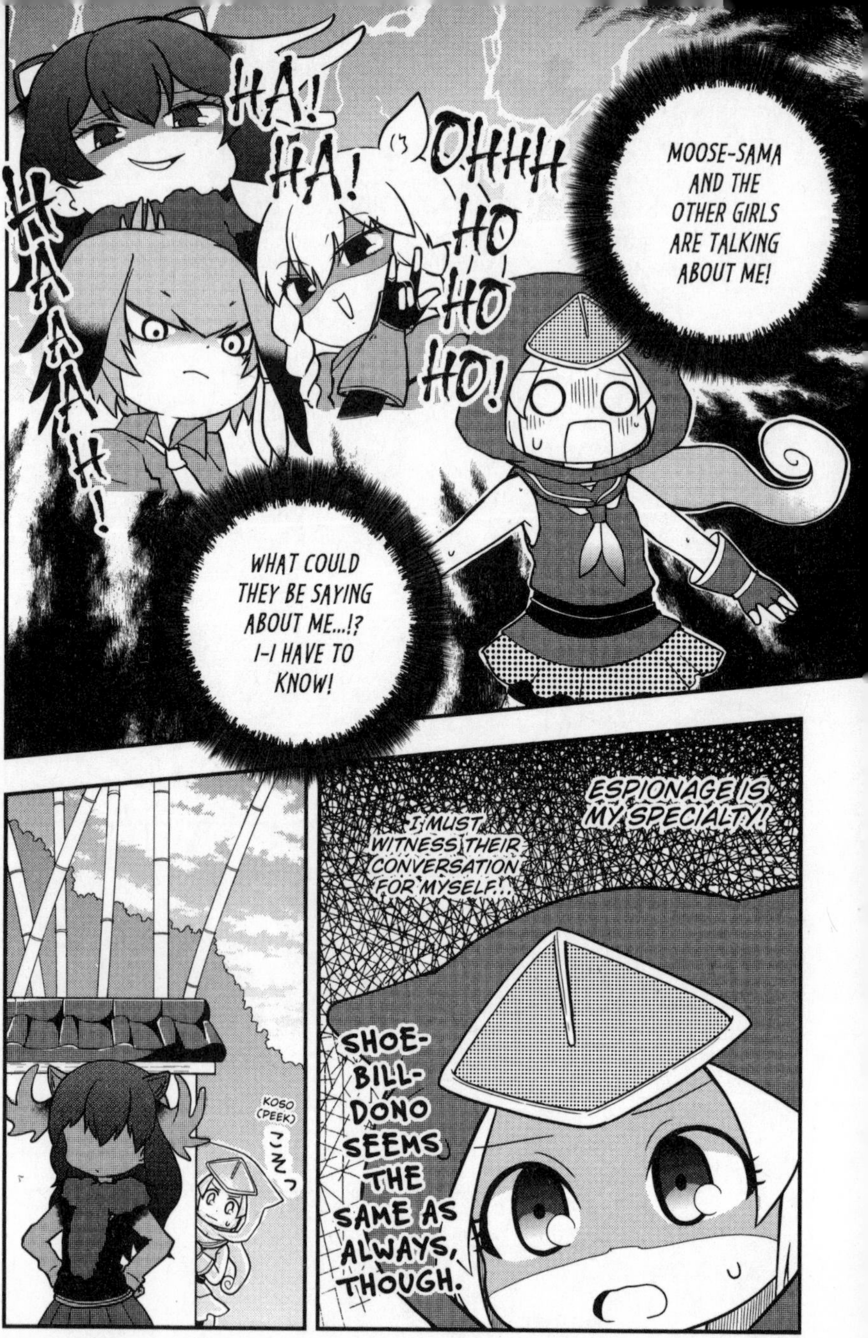
MOOSE-SAMA AND THE OTHER GIRLS ARE TALKING ABOUT ME!
OHHH HO HO HO HO!
HA! HA!
HAAAAH!
WHAT COULD THEY BE SAYING ABOUT ME...!? I-I HAVE TO KNOW!
ESPIONAGE IS MY SPECIALTY!
I MUST WITNESS THEIR CONVERSATION FOR MYSELF...
SHOE-BILL-DONO SEEMS THE SAME AS ALWAYS, THOUGH.
KOSO (PEEK)
こそっ

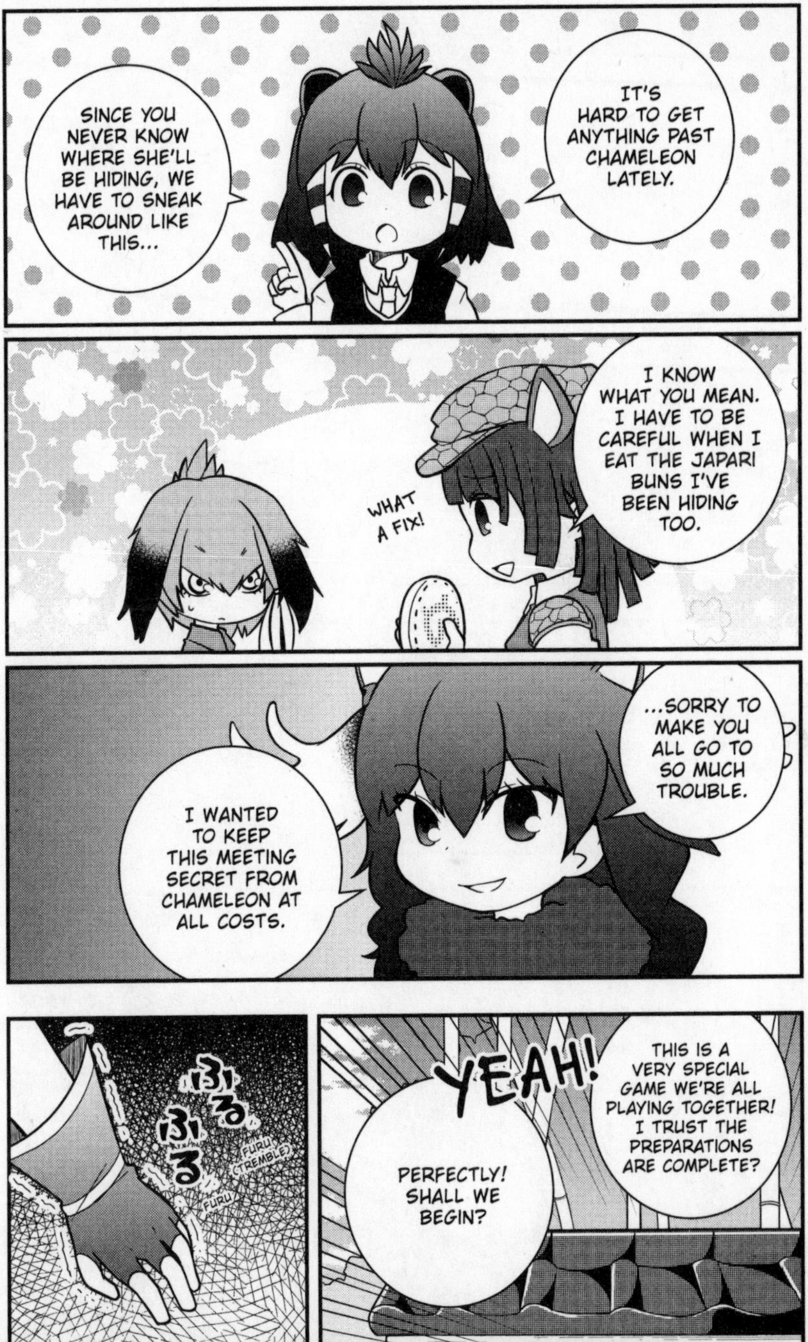
IT'S HARD TO GET ANYTHING PAST CHAMELEON LATELY.
SINCE YOU NEVER KNOW WHERE SHE'LL BE HIDING, WE HAVE TO SNEAK AROUND LIKE THIS...
I KNOW WHAT YOU MEAN. I HAVE TO BE CAREFUL WHEN I EAT THE JAPARI BUNS I'VE BEEN HIDING TOO.
WHAT A FIX!
...SORRY TO MAKE YOU ALL GO TO SO MUCH TROUBLE.
I WANTED TO KEEP THIS MEETING SECRET FROM CHAMELEON AT ALL COSTS.
THIS IS A VERY SPECIAL GAME WE'RE ALL PLAYING TOGETHER! I TRUST THE PREPARATIONS ARE COMPLETE?
YEAH!
PERFECTLY! SHALL WE BEGIN?
ふる
ふる
FURU (TREMBLE)
FURU

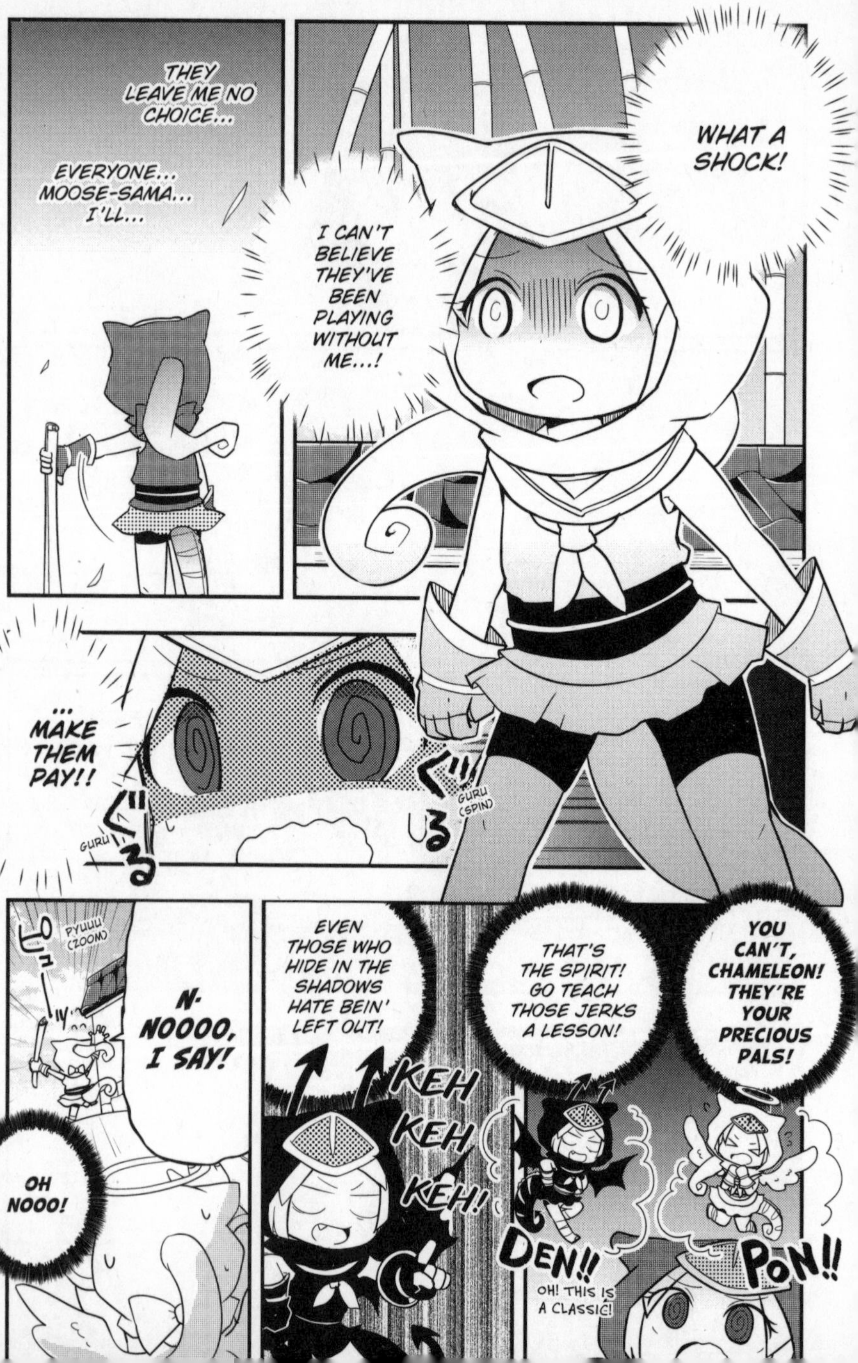
WHAT A SHOCK!
I CAN'T BELIEVE THEY'VE BEEN PLAYING WITHOUT ME...!
THEY LEAVE ME NO CHOICE...
EVERYONE... MOOSE-SAMA... I'LL...
...MAKE THEM PAY!!
GURU (SPIN)
GURU
YOU CAN'T, CHAMELEON! THEY'RE YOUR PRECIOUS PALS!
THAT'S THE SPIRIT! GO TEACH THOSE JERKS A LESSON!
EVEN THOSE WHO HIDE IN THE SHADOWS HATE BEIN' LEFT OUT!
KEH KEH KEH!
DEN!!
PON!!
OH! THIS IS A CLASSIC!
PYUUU (ZOOM)
N-NOOOO, I SAY!
OH NOOO!

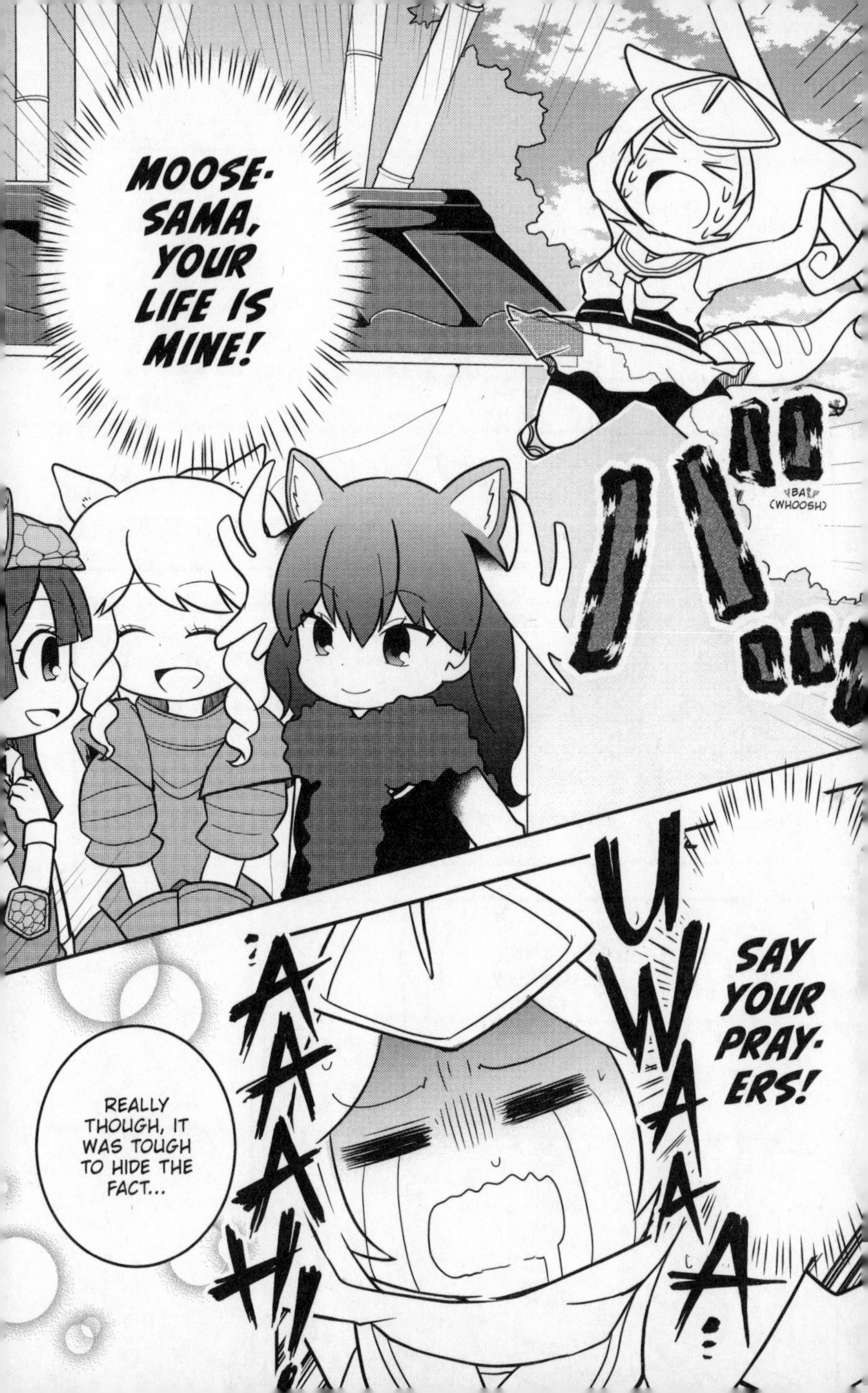
MOOSE-SAMA, YOUR LIFE IS MINE!
BA (WHOOSH)
SAY YOUR PRAYERS!
UWAAA
AAAAH!!
REALLY THOUGH, IT WAS TOUGH TO HIDE THE FACT...

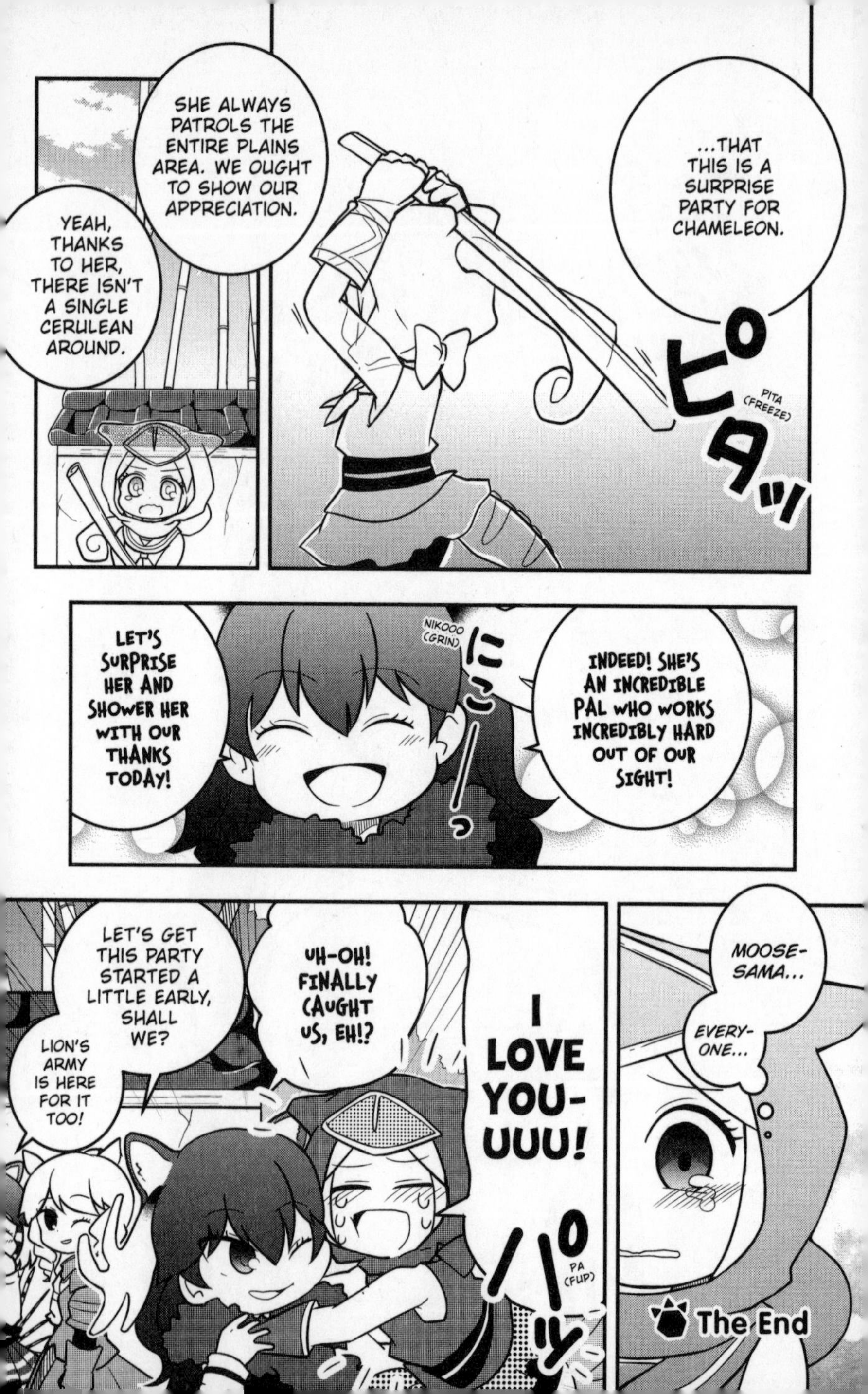
...THAT THIS IS A SURPRISE PARTY FOR CHAMELEON.
ピタッ
PITA (FREEZE)
SHE ALWAYS PATROLS THE ENTIRE PLAINS AREA. WE OUGHT TO SHOW OUR APPRECIATION.
YEAH, THANKS TO HER, THERE ISN'T A SINGLE CERULEAN AROUND.
INDEED! SHE'S AN INCREDIBLE PAL WHO WORKS INCREDIBLY HARD OUT OF OUR SIGHT!
にこーっ
NIKOOO (GRIN)
LET'S SURPRISE HER AND SHOWER HER WITH OUR THANKS TODAY!
MOOSE-SAMA...
EVERY-ONE...
The End
I LOVE YOU-UUU!
パッ
PA (FLIP)
UH-OH! FINALLY CAUGHT US, EH!?
LET'S GET THIS PARTY STARTED A LITTLE EARLY, SHALL WE?
LION'S ARMY IS HERE FOR IT TOO!

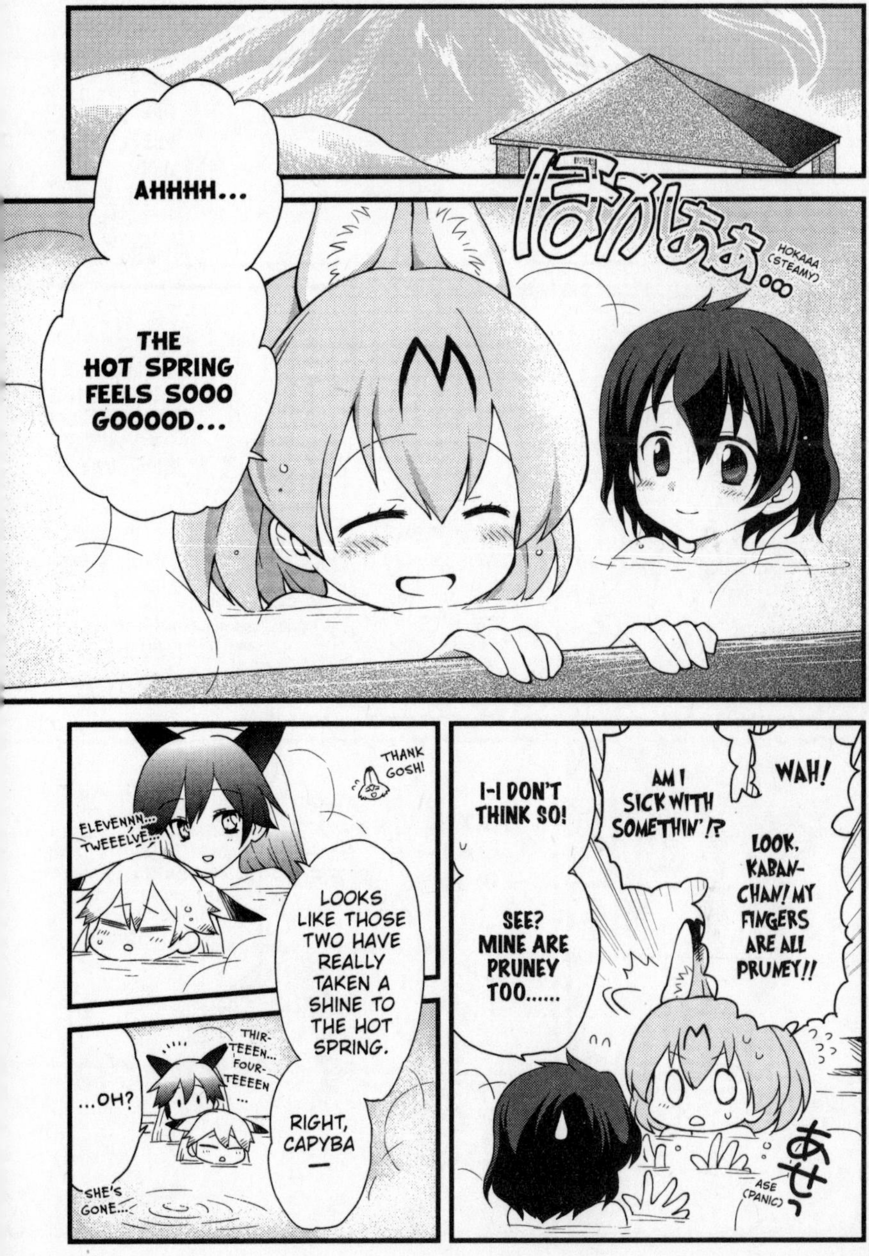
HOKAAA (STEAMY)
AHHHH...
THE HOT SPRING FEELS SOOO GOOOOD...
WAH!
LOOK, KABAN-CHAN! MY FINGERS ARE ALL PRUNEY!!
AM I SICK WITH SOMETHIN'!?
I-I DON'T THINK SO!
SEE? MINE ARE PRUNEY TOO......
ASE (PANIC)
THANK GOSH!
ELEVENNN... TWEEELVE...
LOOKS LIKE THOSE TWO HAVE REALLY TAKEN A SHINE TO THE HOT SPRING.
THIR-TEEEN... FOUR-TEEEEN ...
RIGHT, CAPYBA—
...OH?
SHE'S GONE...

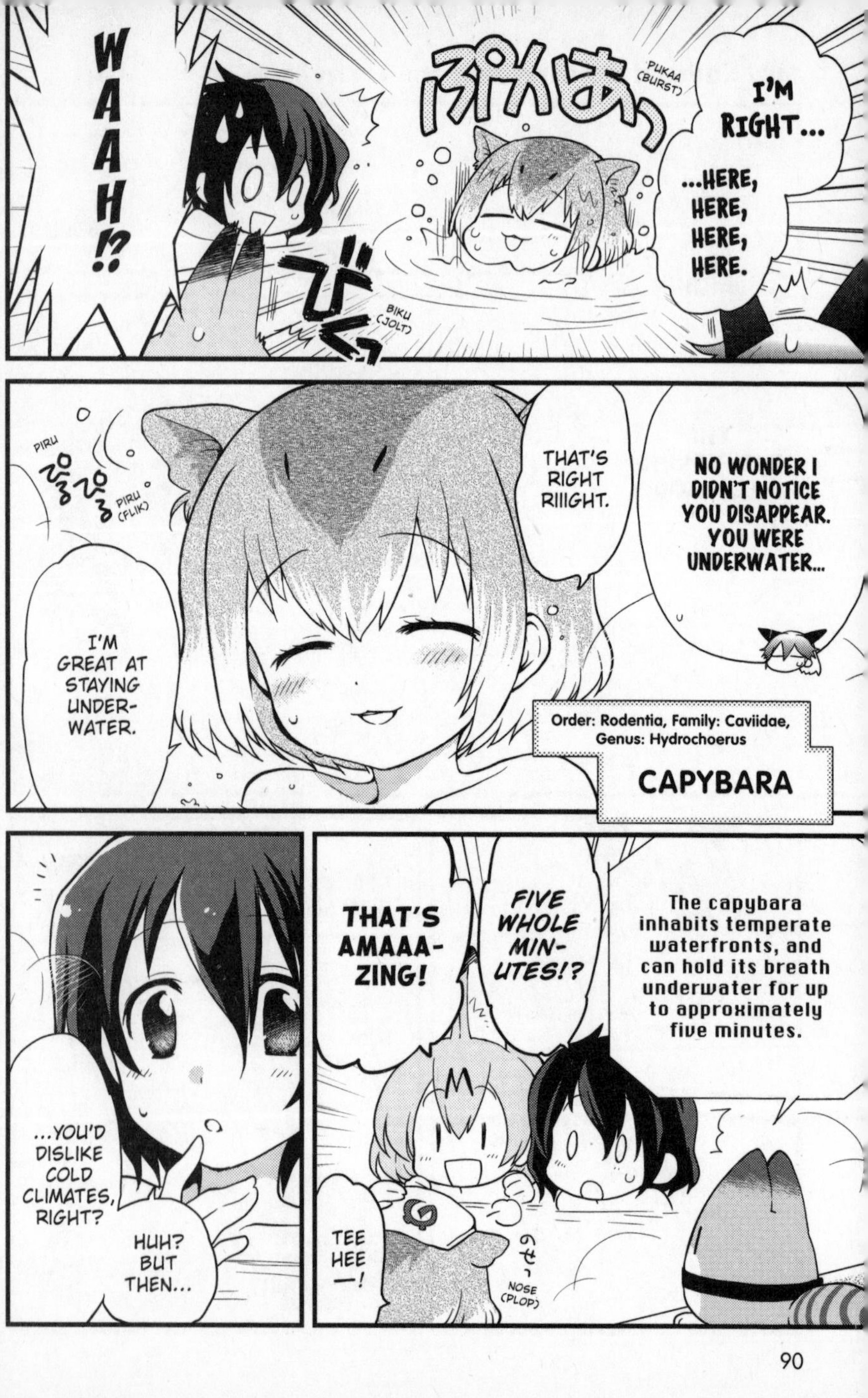
I'M RIGHT...
...HERE, HERE, HERE, HERE.
ぷかあっ
PUKAA (BURST)
びくっ
BIKU (JOLT)
WAAAH!?
NO WONDER I DIDN'T NOTICE YOU DISAPPEAR. YOU WERE UNDERWATER...
THAT'S RIGHT RIIIGHT.
ぴるぴる
PIRU PIRU (FLIK)
I'M GREAT AT STAYING UNDER-WATER.
Order: Rodentia, Family: Caviidae, Genus: Hydrochoerus
CAPYBARA
The capybara inhabits temperate waterfronts, and can hold its breath underwater for up to approximately five minutes.
FIVE WHOLE MIN-UTES!?
THAT'S AMAAA-ZING!
のせっ
NOSE (PLOP)
TEE HEE—!
HUH? BUT THEN...
...YOU'D DISLIKE COLD CLIMATES, RIGHT?

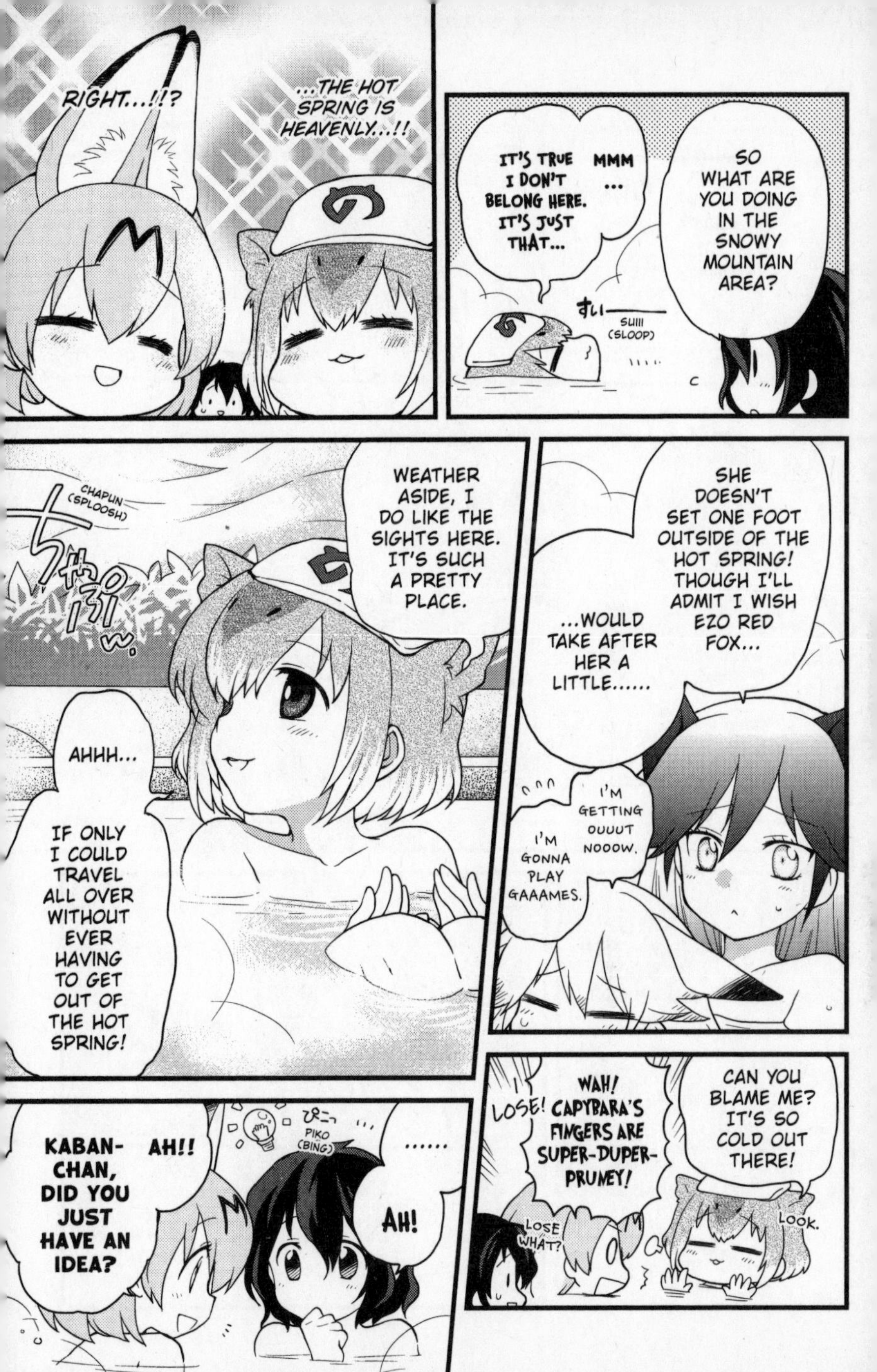
SO WHAT ARE YOU DOING IN THE SNOWY MOUNTAIN AREA?
MMM ...
IT'S TRUE I DON'T BELONG HERE. IT'S JUST THAT...
すぃ——
SUIII (SLOOP)
...THE HOT SPRING IS HEAVENLY...!!
RIGHT...!!?
SHE DOESN'T SET ONE FOOT OUTSIDE OF THE HOT SPRING! THOUGH I'LL ADMIT I WISH EZO RED FOX...
...WOULD TAKE AFTER HER A LITTLE......
I'M GETTING OUUUT NOOOW.
I'M GONNA PLAY GAAAMES.
ちゃぷん
CHAPUN (SPLOOSH)
WEATHER ASIDE, I DO LIKE THE SIGHTS HERE. IT'S SUCH A PRETTY PLACE.
AHHH...
IF ONLY I COULD TRAVEL ALL OVER WITHOUT EVER HAVING TO GET OUT OF THE HOT SPRING!
CAN YOU BLAME ME? IT'S SO COLD OUT THERE!
WAH! CAPYBARA'S FINGERS ARE SUPER-DUPER-PRUNEY!
I LOSE!
LOOK.
LOSE WHAT?
......
ぴこっ
PIKO (BING)
AH!
AH!!
KABAN-CHAN, DID YOU JUST HAVE AN IDEA?

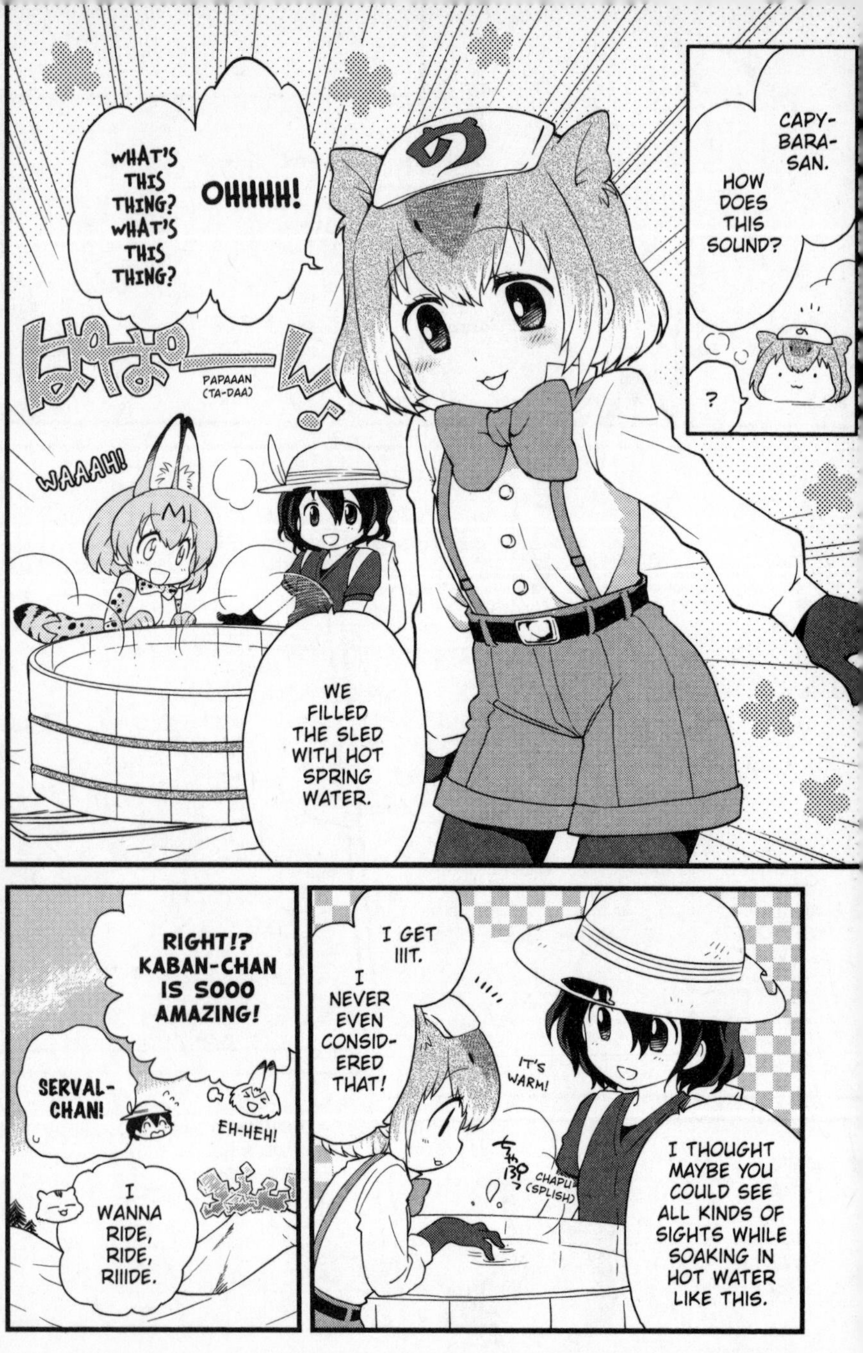
CAPY-BARA-SAN.
HOW DOES THIS SOUND?
?
OHHHH!
WHAT'S THIS THING? WHAT'S THIS THING?
PAPAAAN (TA-DAA)
WAAAH!
WE FILLED THE SLED WITH HOT SPRING WATER.
I GET IIIT.
I NEVER EVEN CONSIDERED THAT!
IT'S WARM!
CHAPU (SPLISH)
I THOUGHT MAYBE YOU COULD SEE ALL KINDS OF SIGHTS WHILE SOAKING IN HOT WATER LIKE THIS.
RIGHT!? KABAN-CHAN IS SOOO AMAZING!
SERVAL-CHAN!
EH-HEH!
I WANNA RIDE, RIDE, RIIIDE.

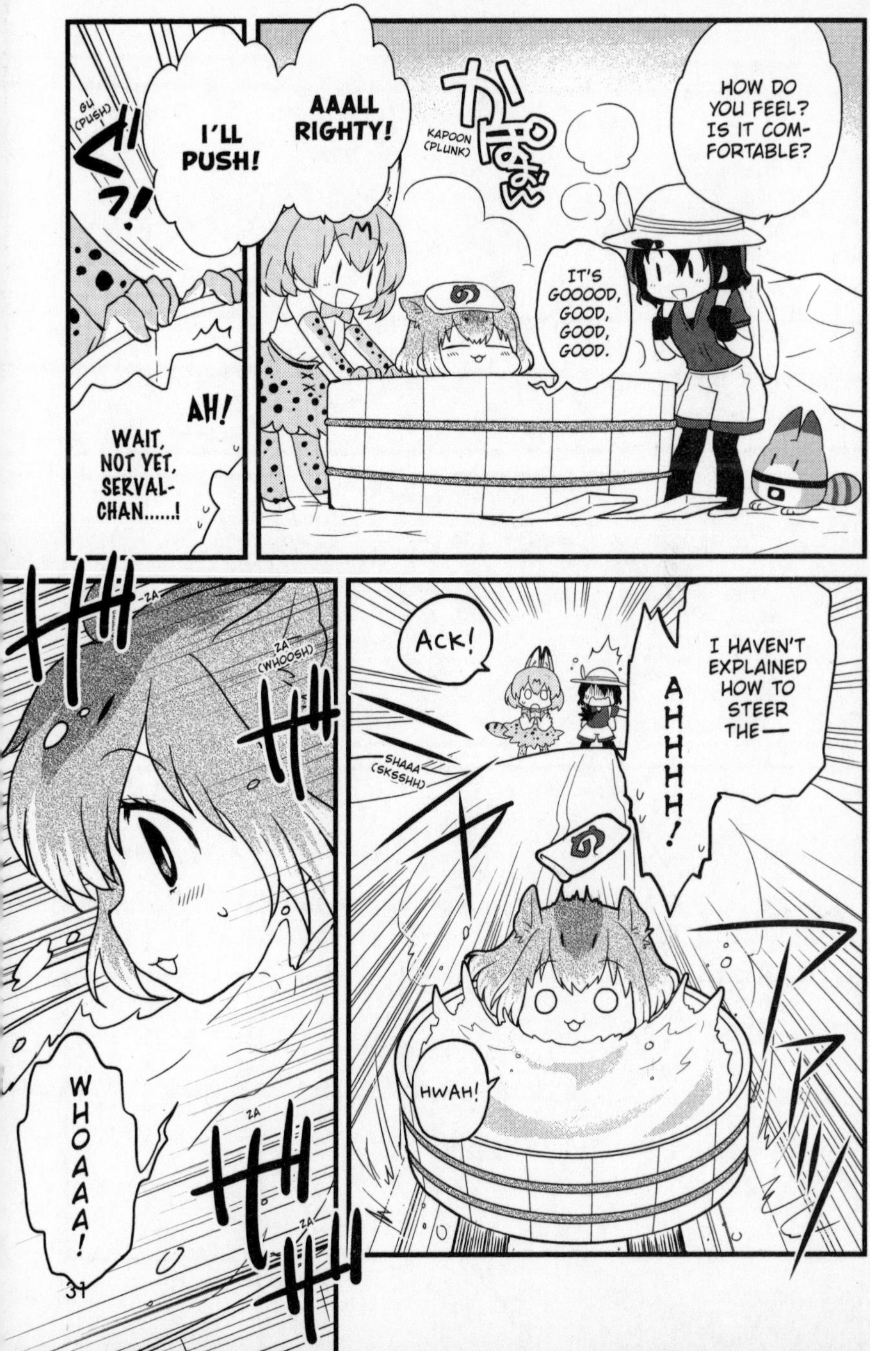
HOW DO YOU FEEL? IS IT COM-FORTABLE?
KAPOON (PLUNK)
IT'S GOOOOD, GOOD, GOOD, GOOD.
AAALL RIGHTY!
I'LL PUSH!
GU (PUSH)
AH!
WAIT, NOT YET, SERVAL-CHAN......!
I HAVEN'T EXPLAINED HOW TO STEER THE—
AHHHHH!
ACK!
SHAAA (SKSSHH)
HWAH!
ZA
ZA (WHOOSH)
WHOAAAA!
ZA
ZA

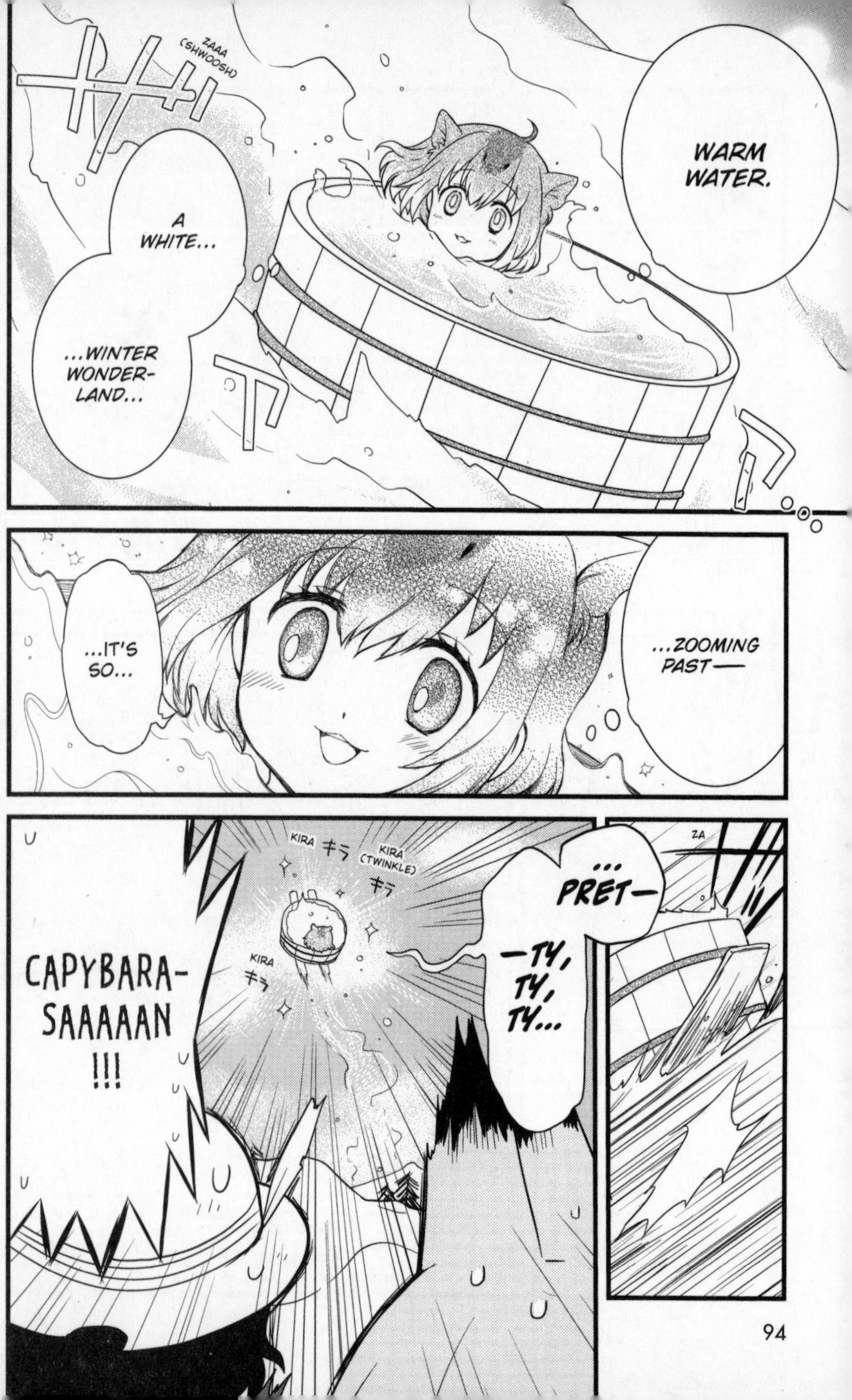
WARM WATER.
ZAAA (SHWOOSH)
A WHITE...
...WINTER WONDER-LAND...
...ZOOMING PAST—
...IT'S SO...
ZA
...PRET—
—TY, TY, TY...
KIRA KIRA (TWINKLE)
KIRA
CAPYBARA-SAAAAAN!!!

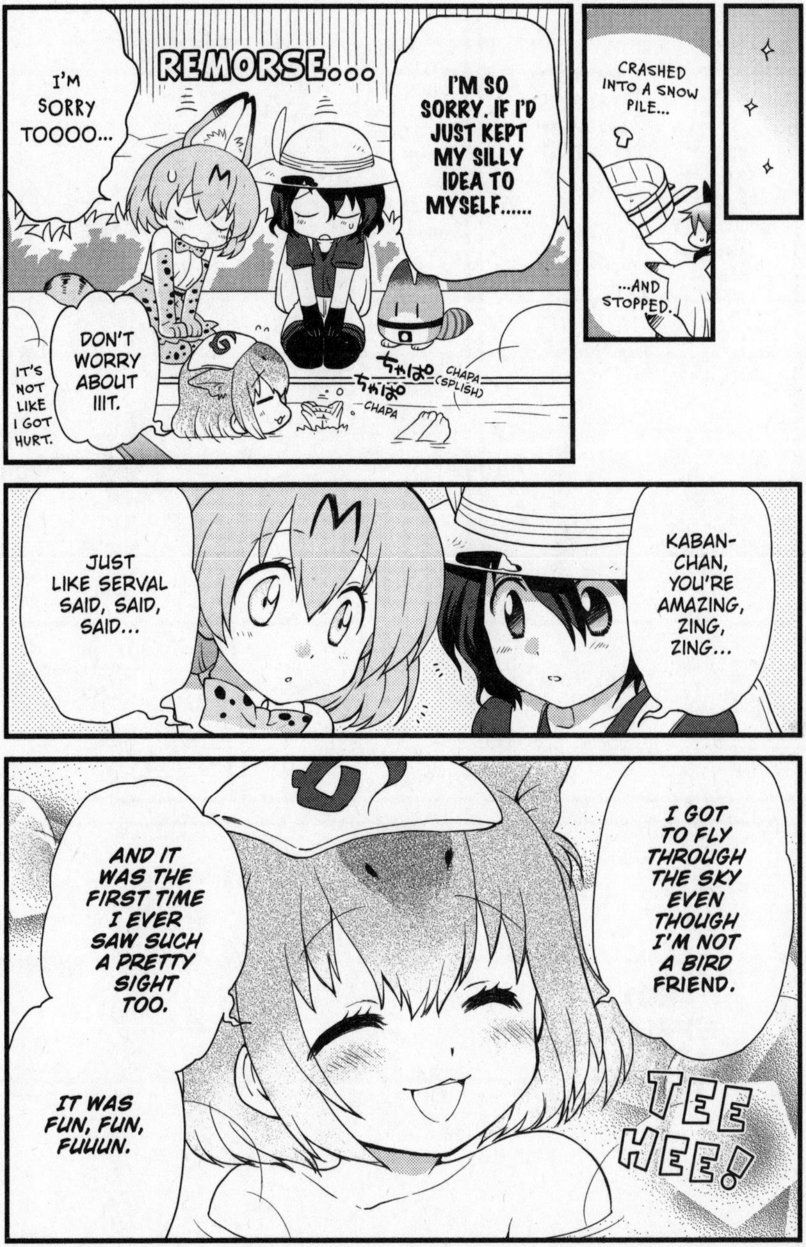
CRASHED INTO A SNOW PILE...
...AND STOPPED.
I'M SO SORRY. IF I'D JUST KEPT MY SILLY IDEA TO MYSELF......
REMORSE...
I'M SORRY TOOOO...
ちゃぽ CHAPA (SPLISH)
ちゃぽ CHAPA
DON'T WORRY ABOUT IIIT.
IT'S NOT LIKE I GOT HURT.
KABAN-CHAN, YOU'RE AMAZING, ZING, ZING...
JUST LIKE SERVAL SAID, SAID, SAID...
I GOT TO FLY THROUGH THE SKY EVEN THOUGH I'M NOT A BIRD FRIEND.
AND IT WAS THE FIRST TIME I EVER SAW SUCH A PRETTY SIGHT TOO.
IT WAS FUN, FUN, FUUUN.
TEE HEE!

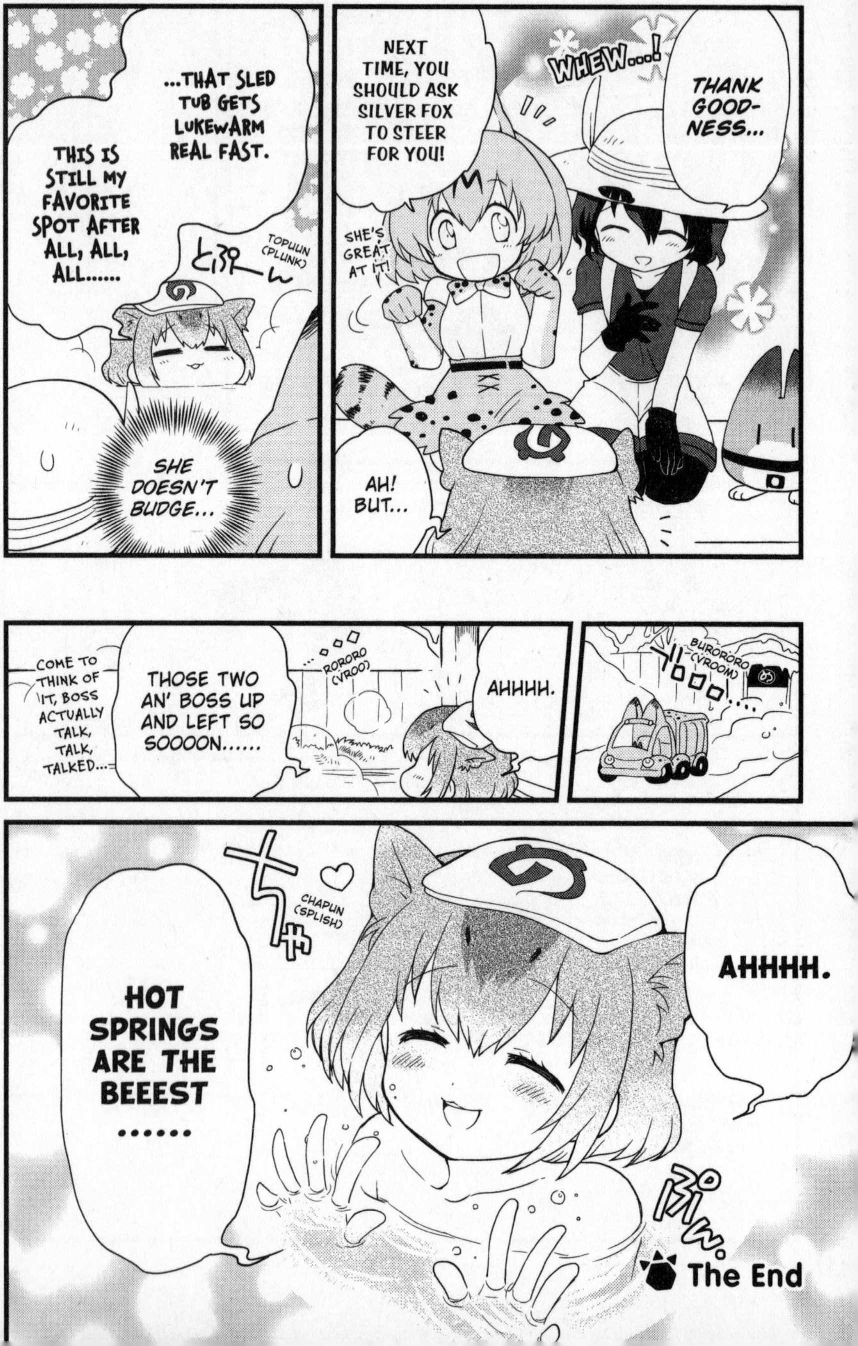

WHEW...!
THANK GOODNESS...
NEXT TIME, YOU SHOULD ASK SILVER FOX TO STEER FOR YOU!
SHE'S GREAT AT IT!
AH! BUT...
...THAT SLED TUB GETS LUKEWARM REAL FAST.
THIS IS STILL MY FAVORITE SPOT AFTER ALL, ALL, ALL......
とぷーん
TOPUUN (PLUNK)
SHE DOESN'T BUDGE...
BUROROROO (VROOM)
AHHHH.
ROROROO (VROO)
THOSE TWO AN' BOSS UP AND LEFT SO SOOOON......
COME TO THINK OF IT, BOSS ACTUALLY TALK, TALK, TALKED...
AHHHH.
CHAPUN (SPLISH)
HOT SPRINGS ARE THE BEEEST ......
The End

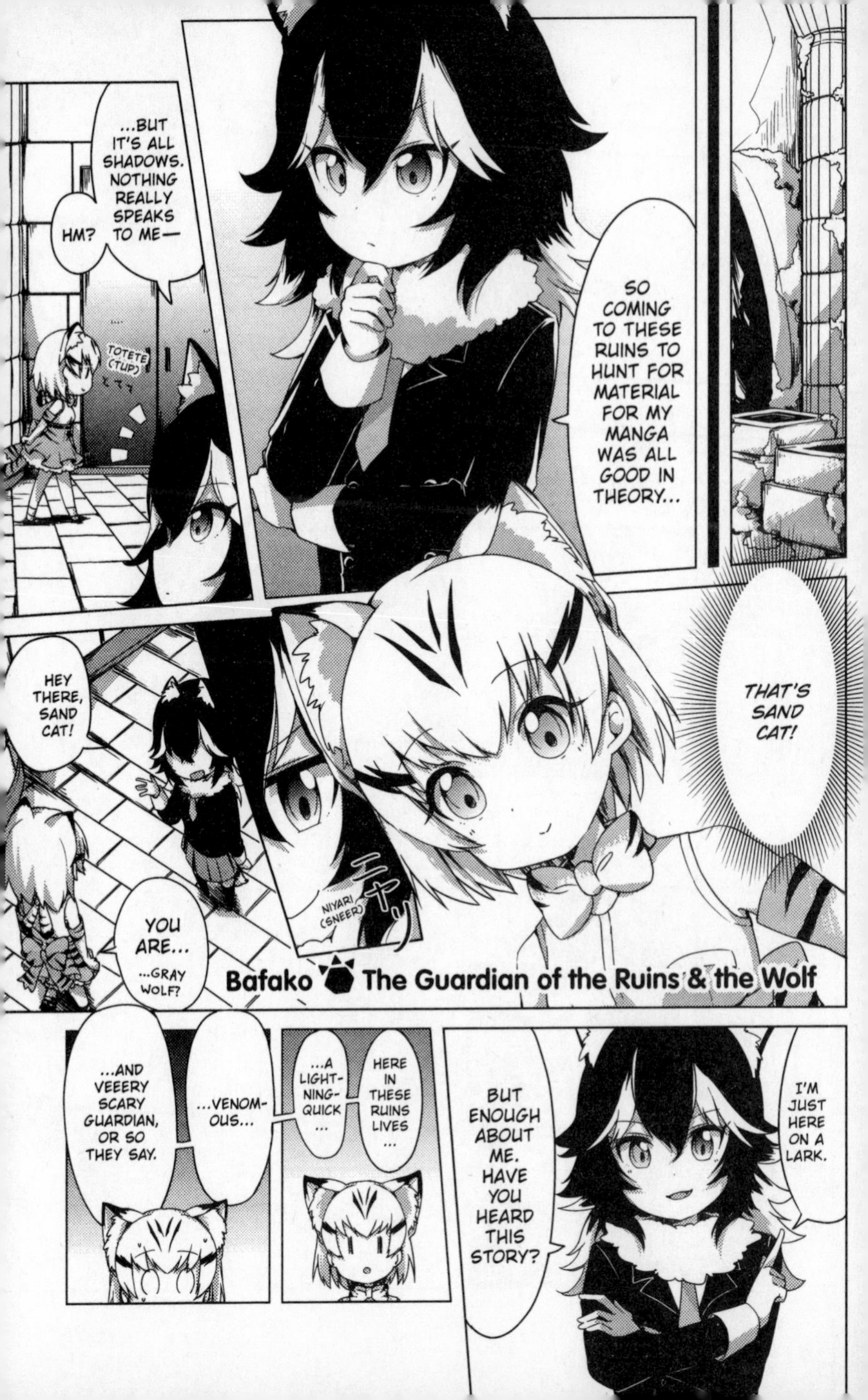
SO COMING TO THESE RUINS TO HUNT FOR MATERIAL FOR MY MANGA WAS ALL GOOD IN THEORY...
...BUT IT'S ALL SHADOWS. NOTHING REALLY SPEAKS TO ME—
HM?
TOTETE (TUP)
THAT'S SAND CAT!
NIYARI (SNEER)
ニヤリ
HEY THERE, SAND CAT!
YOU ARE...
...GRAY WOLF?
Bafako The Guardian of the Ruins & the Wolf
I'M JUST HERE ON A LARK.
BUT ENOUGH ABOUT ME. HAVE YOU HEARD THIS STORY?
HERE IN THESE RUINS LIVES...
...A LIGHTNING-QUICK...
...VENOMOUS...
...AND VEEERY SCARY GUARDIAN, OR SO THEY SAY.

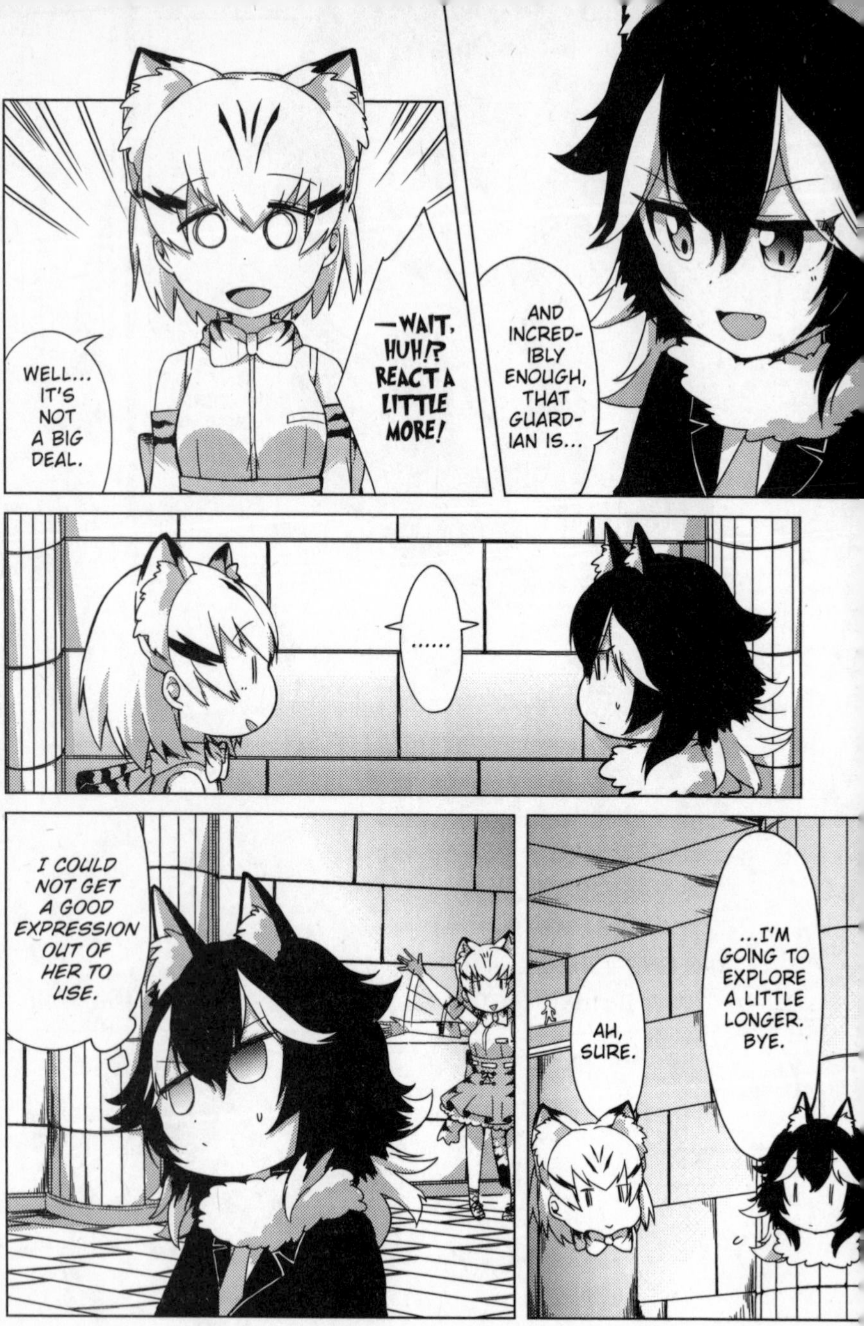
AND INCREDIBLY ENOUGH, THAT GUARDIAN IS...
—WAIT, HUH!? REACT A LITTLE MORE!
WELL... IT'S NOT A BIG DEAL.
......
...I'M GOING TO EXPLORE A LITTLE LONGER. BYE.
AH, SURE.
I COULD NOT GET A GOOD EXPRESSION OUT OF HER TO USE.

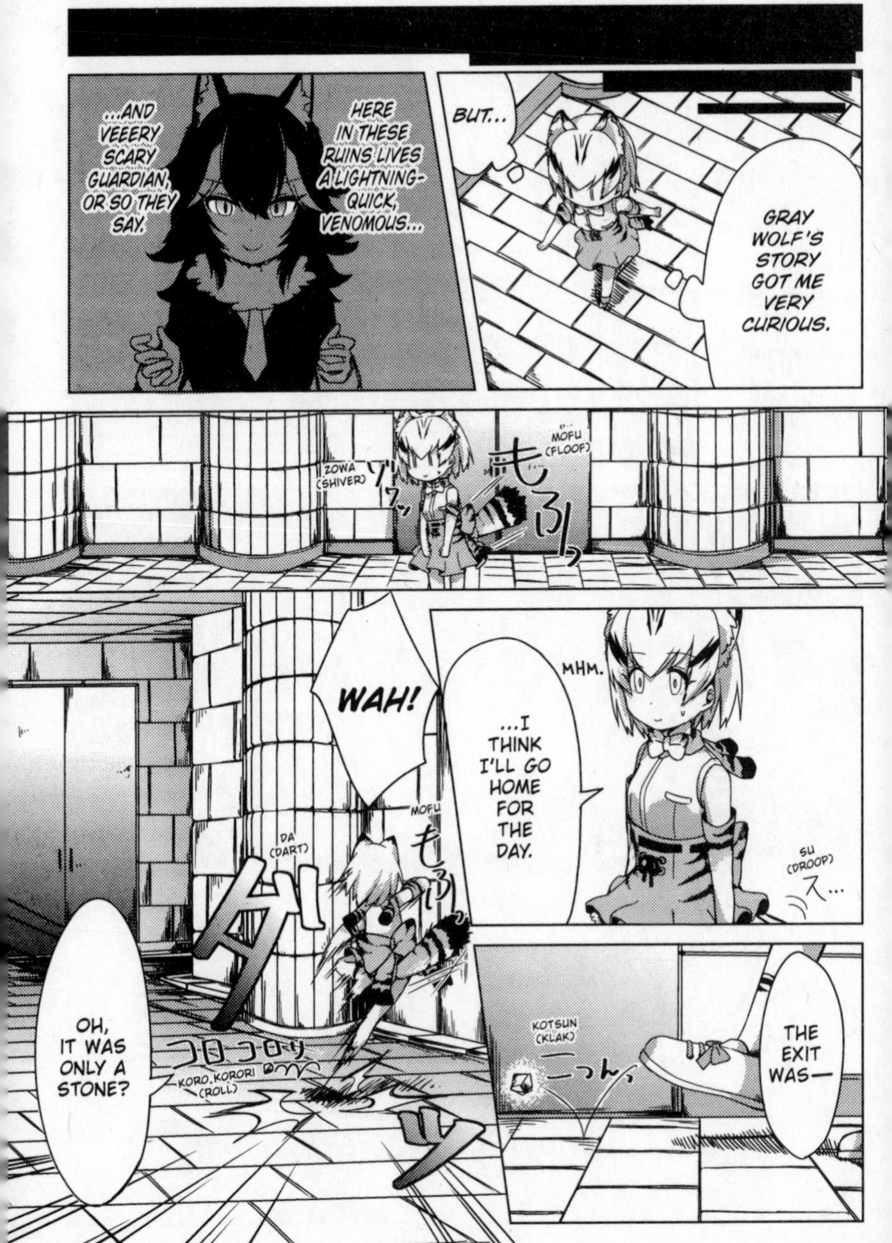
[redacted]
[redacted]
GRAY WOLF'S STORY GOT ME VERY CURIOUS.
BUT...
HERE IN THESE RUINS LIVES A LIGHTNING-QUICK, VENOMOUS...
...AND VEEERY SCARY GUARDIAN, OR SO THEY SAY.
MOFU (FLOOF)
ZOWA (SHIVER)
MHM.
...I THINK I'LL GO HOME FOR THE DAY.
SU (DROOP)
ス…
THE EXIT WAS—
KOTSUN (KLAK)
WAH!
MOFU
DA (DART)
コロコロリ
KORO KORORI (ROLL)
OH, IT WAS ONLY A STONE?

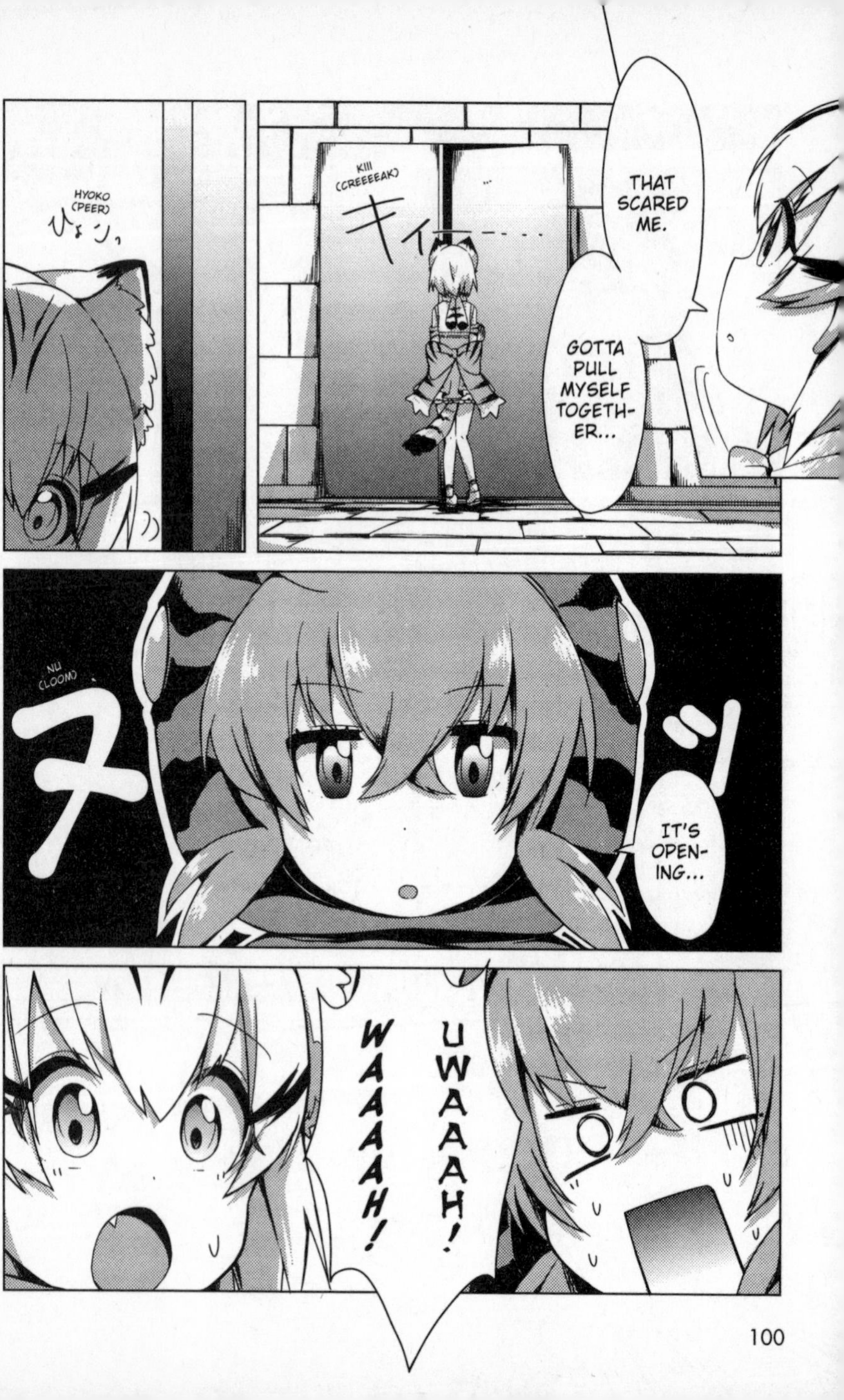
THAT SCARED ME.
GOTTA PULL MYSELF TOGETHER...
KIII (CREEEEAK)
キィ
...
HYOKO (PEER)
ひょこ
NU (LOOM)
ヌッ
IT'S OPENING...
UWAAAAH!
WAAAAAH!

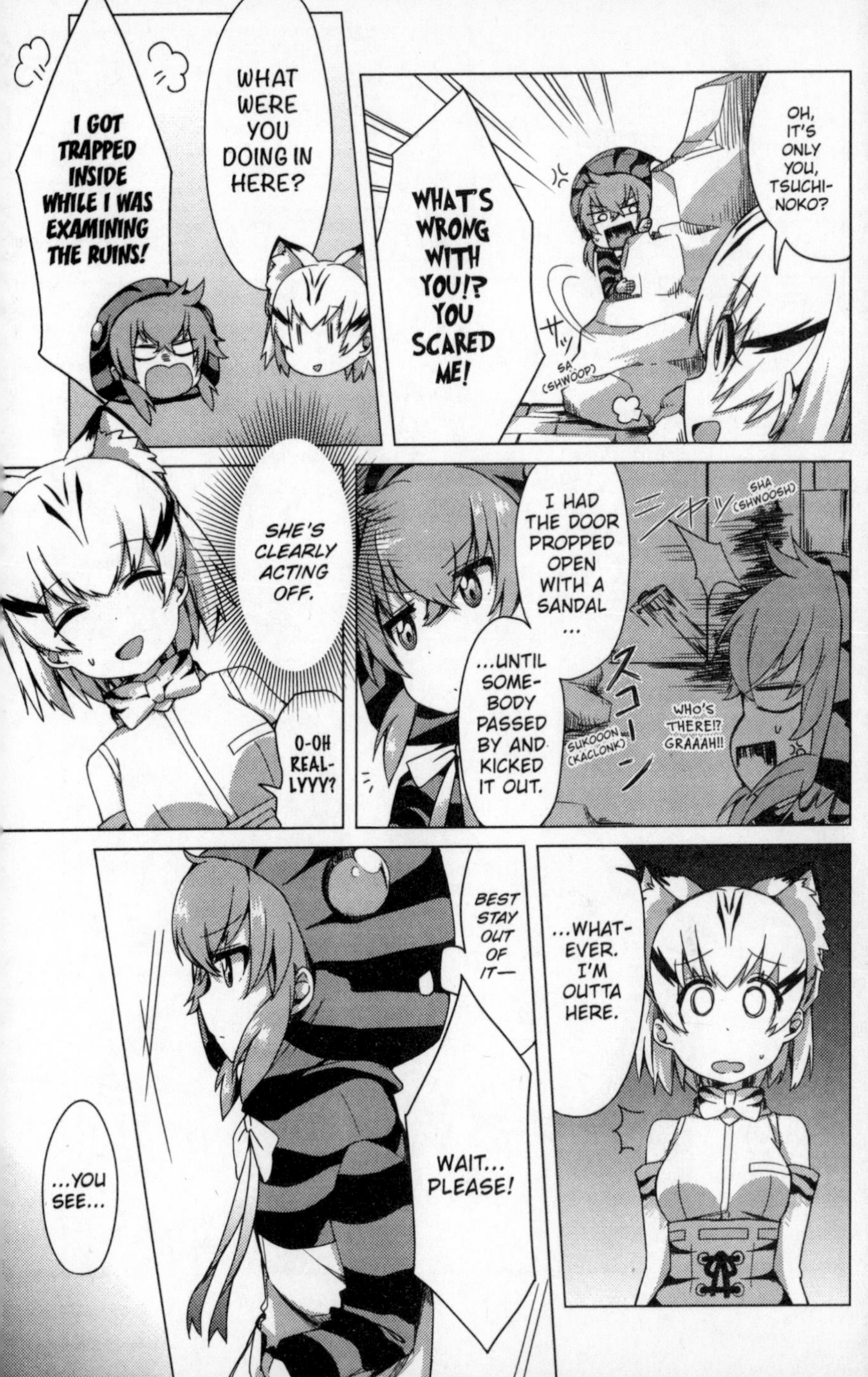
OH, IT'S ONLY YOU, TSUCHINOKO?
WHAT'S WRONG WITH YOU!? YOU SCARED ME!
SA (SHWOOP)
WHAT WERE YOU DOING IN HERE?
I GOT TRAPPED INSIDE WHILE I WAS EXAMINING THE RUINS!
I HAD THE DOOR PROPPED OPEN WITH A SANDAL ...
SHA (SHWOOSH)
...UNTIL SOMEBODY PASSED BY AND KICKED IT OUT.
SUKOOON (KACLONK)
WHO'S THERE!? GRAAAH!!
SHE'S CLEARLY ACTING OFF.
O-OH REAL-LYYY?
...WHAT-EVER. I'M OUTTA HERE.
BEST STAY OUT OF IT—
WAIT... PLEASE!
...YOU SEE...

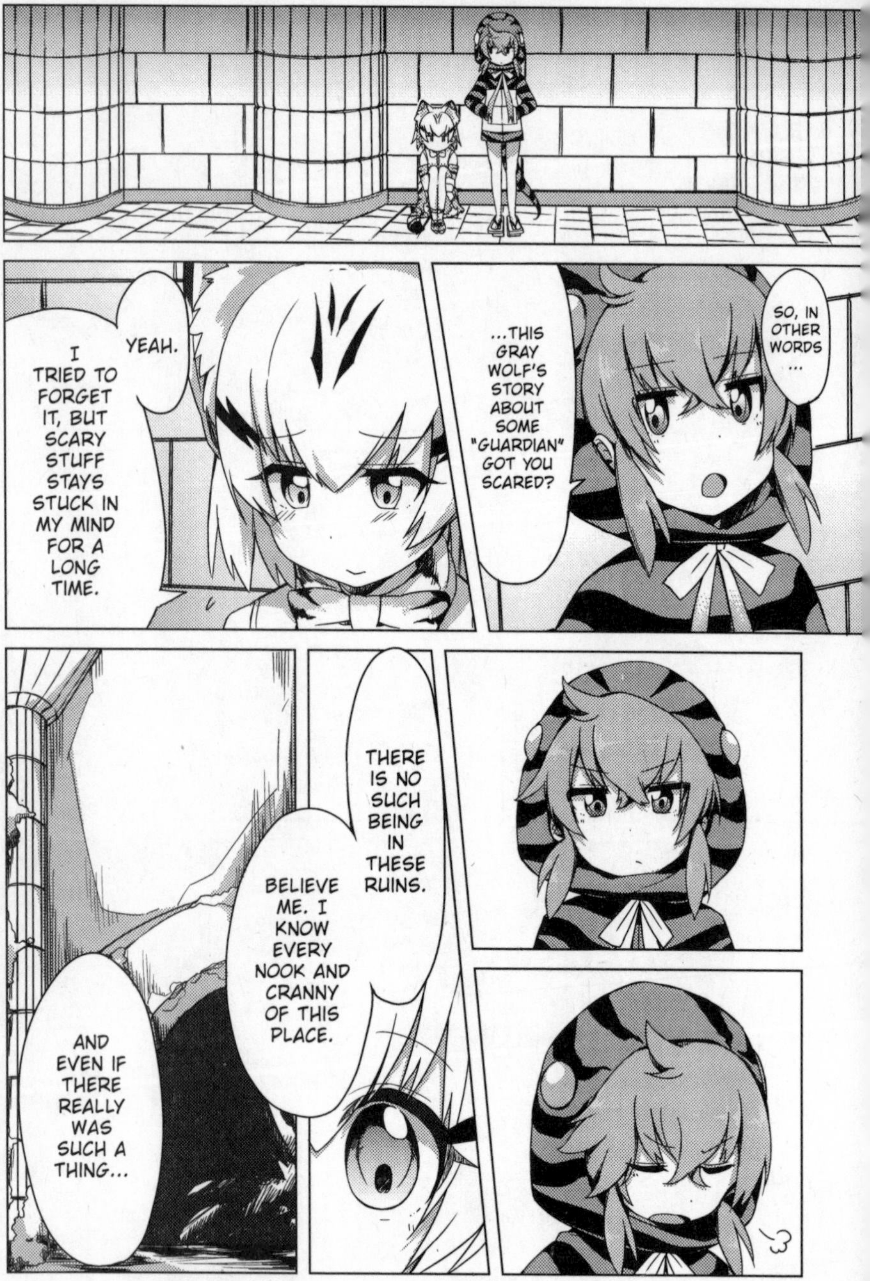
SO, IN OTHER WORDS...
...THIS GRAY WOLF'S STORY ABOUT SOME "GUARDIAN" GOT YOU SCARED?
YEAH.
I TRIED TO FORGET IT, BUT SCARY STUFF STAYS STUCK IN MY MIND FOR A LONG TIME.
THERE IS NO SUCH BEING IN THESE RUINS.
BELIEVE ME. I KNOW EVERY NOOK AND CRANNY OF THIS PLACE.
AND EVEN IF THERE REALLY WAS SUCH A THING...

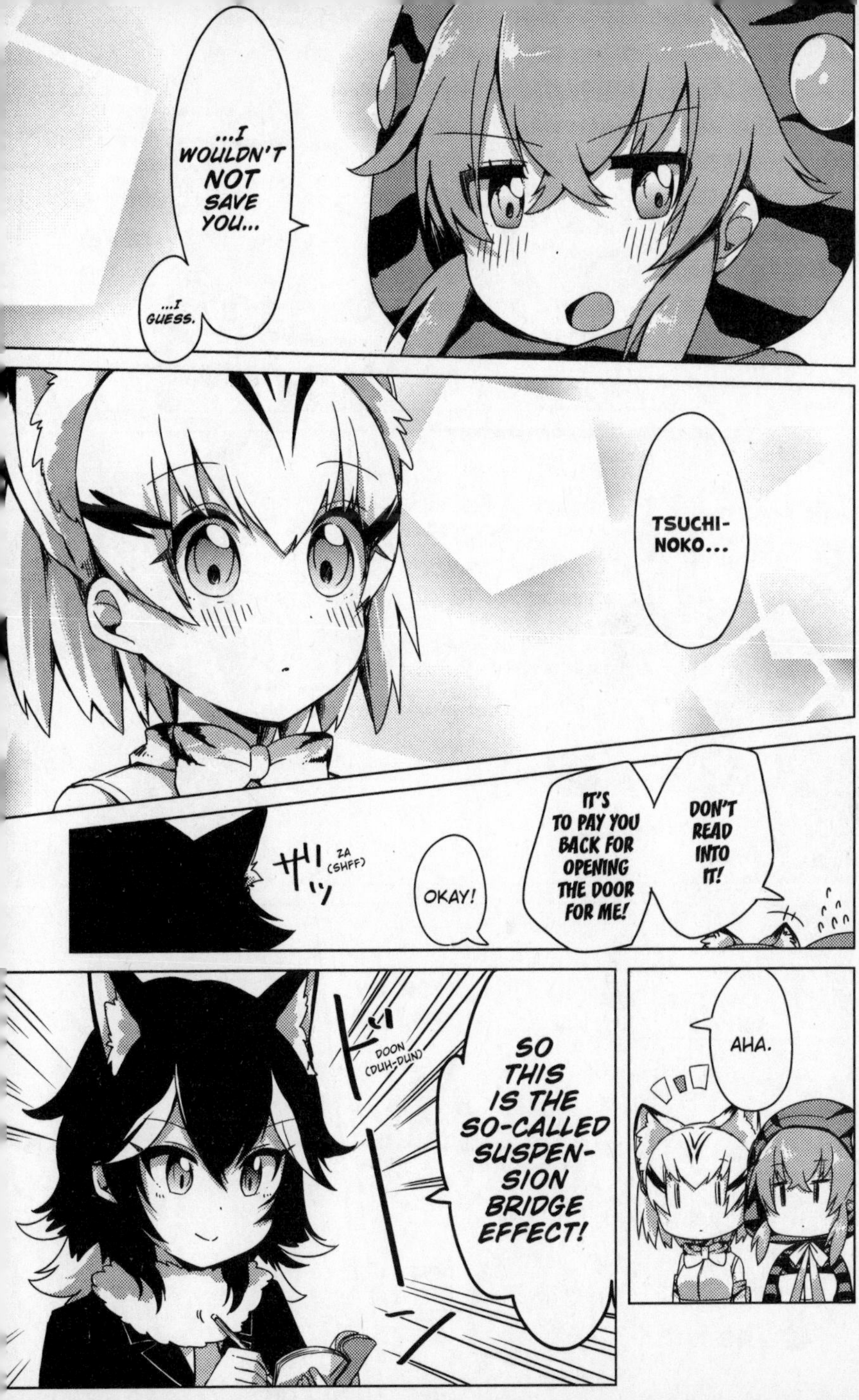
...I WOULDN'T NOT SAVE YOU...
...I GUESS.
TSUCHI-NOKO...
DON'T READ INTO IT!
IT'S TO PAY YOU BACK FOR OPENING THE DOOR FOR ME!
OKAY!
ザッ
ZA (SHFF)
AHA.
ドン
DOON (DUH-DUN)
SO THIS IS THE SO-CALLED SUSPEN-SION BRIDGE EFFECT!

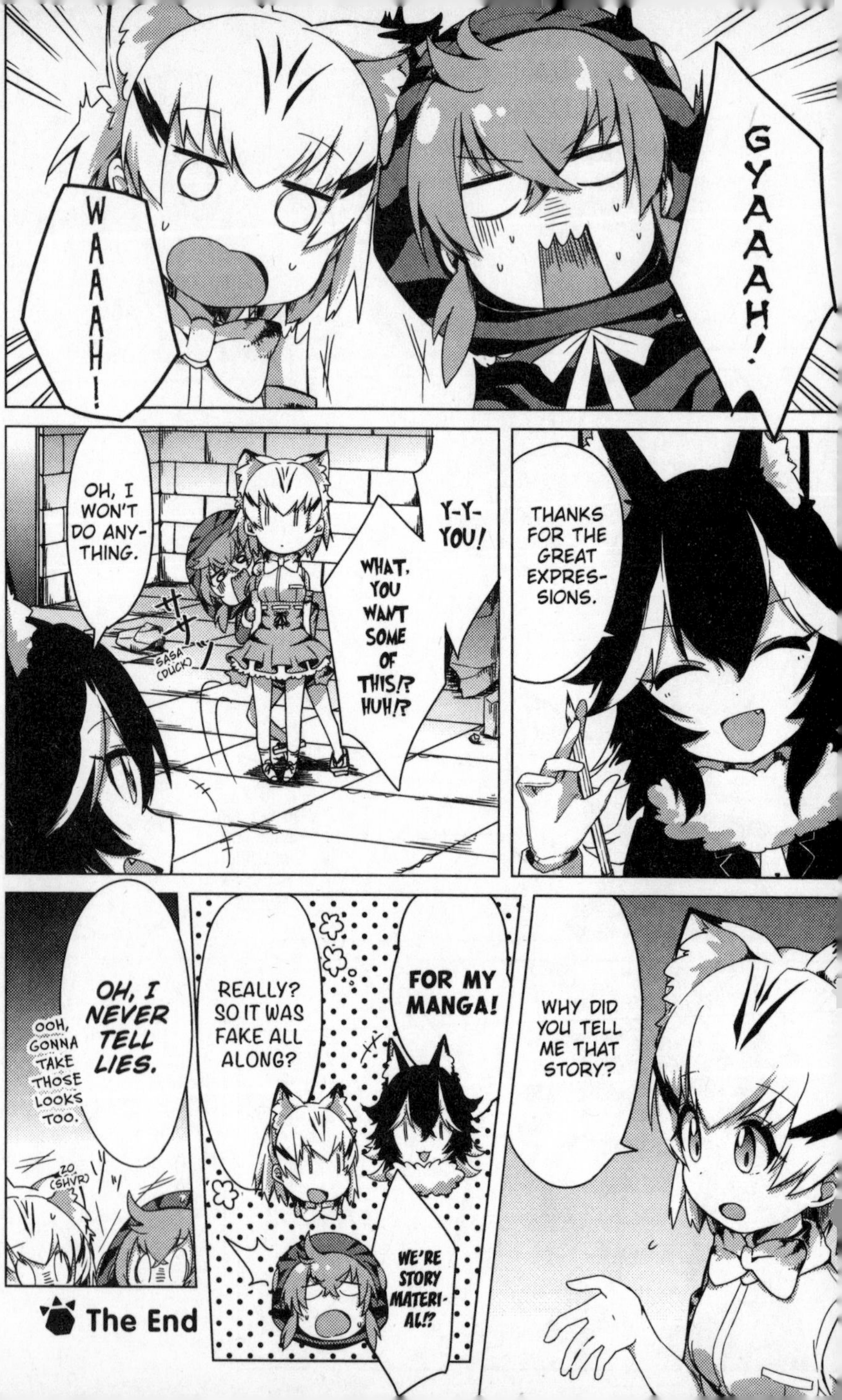
GYAAAH!
WAAAAH!
THANKS FOR THE GREAT EXPRES-SIONS.
Y-Y-YOU!
WHAT, YOU WANT SOME OF THIS!? HUH!?
OH, I WON'T DO ANY-THING.
SASA (DUCK)
WHY DID YOU TELL ME THAT STORY?
FOR MY MANGA!
REALLY? SO IT WAS FAKE ALL ALONG?
WE'RE STORY MATERI-AL!?
OH, I NEVER TELL LIES.
OOH, GONNA TAKE THOSE LOOKS TOO.
ZO (SHVR)

The End

Kiki Special Drinks! All Hands On Deck at Japari Café!!

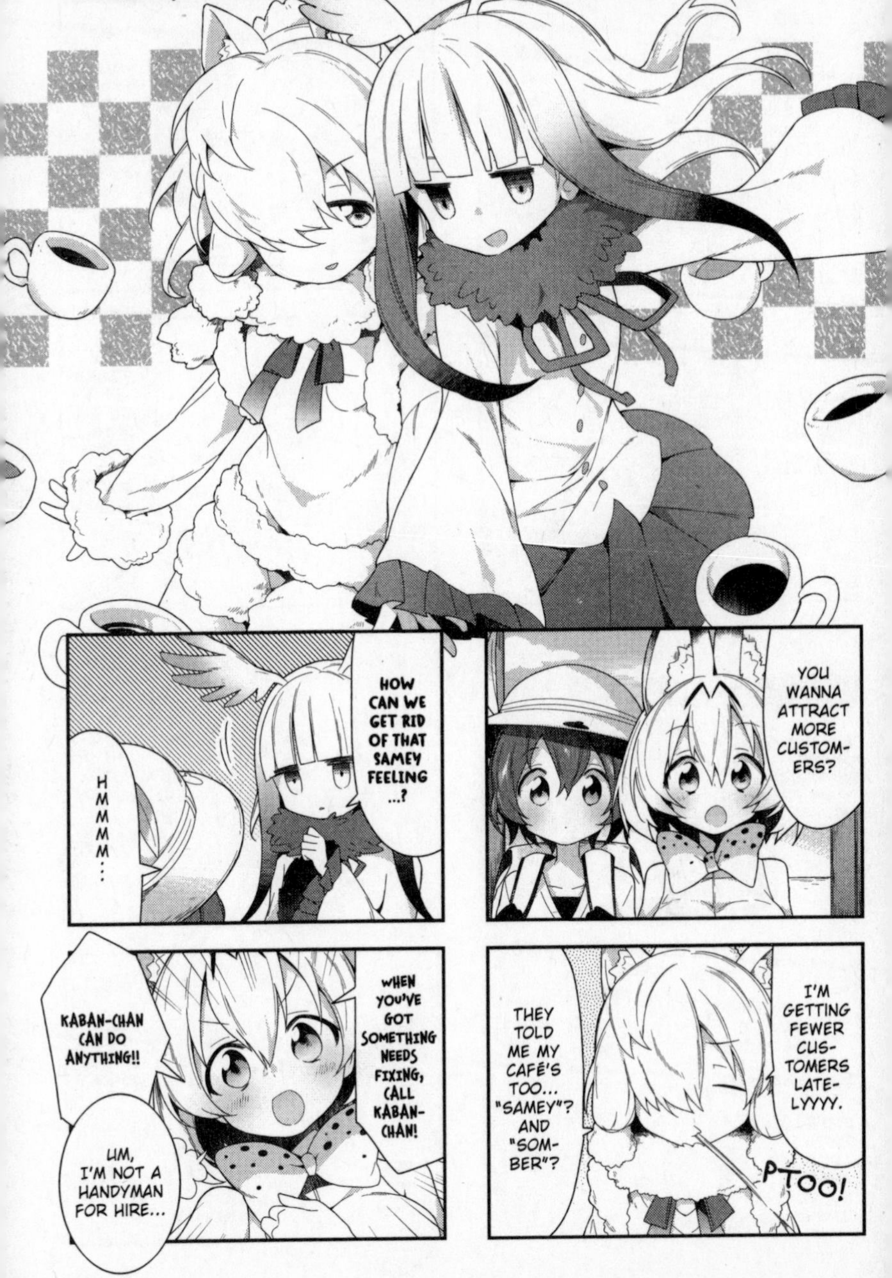
YOU WANNA ATTRACT MORE CUSTOMERS?
HOW CAN WE GET RID OF THAT SAMEY FEELING ...?
HMMMM...
I'M GETTING FEWER CUSTOMERS LATELYYYY.
THEY TOLD ME MY CAFÉ'S TOO... "SAMEY"? AND "SOMBER"?
PTOO!
WHEN YOU'VE GOT SOMETHING NEEDS FIXING, CALL KABAN-CHAN!
KABAN-CHAN CAN DO ANYTHING!!
UM, I'M NOT A HANDYMAN FOR HIRE...

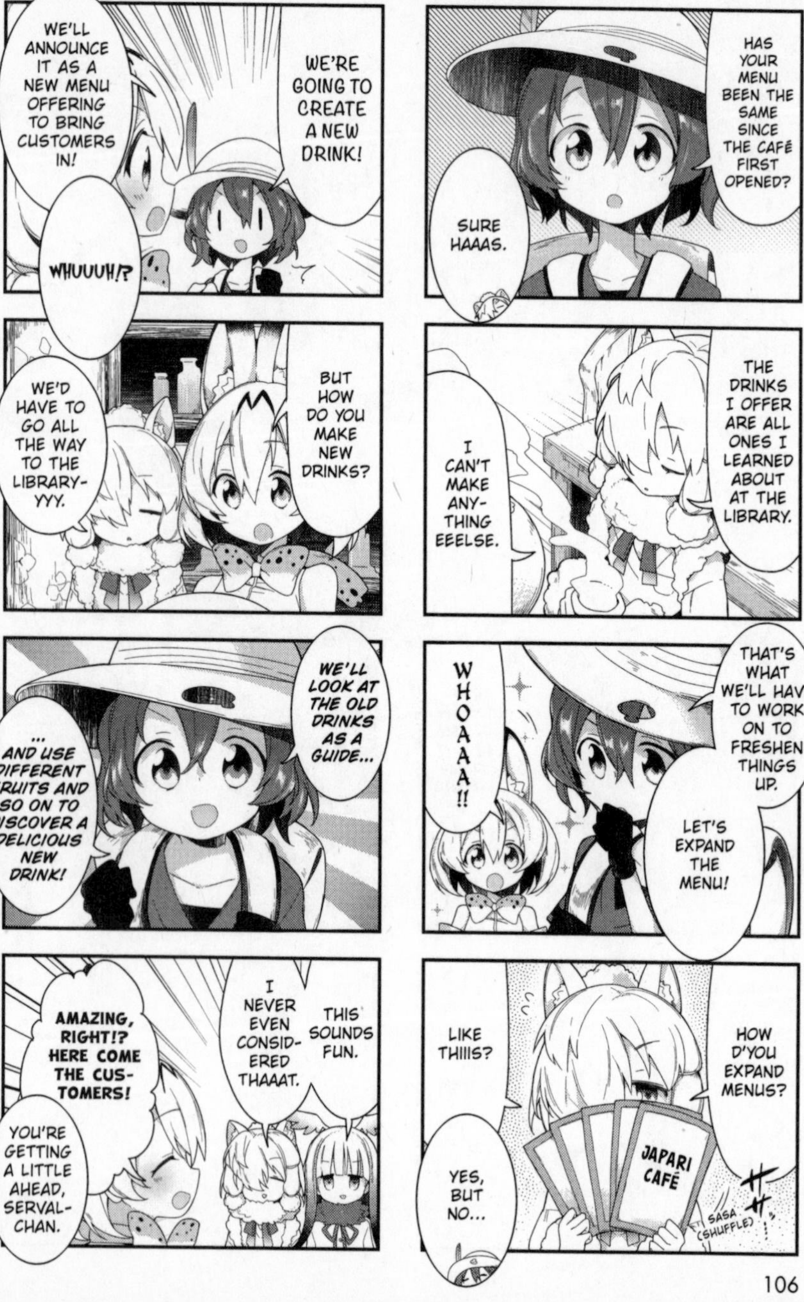
HAS YOUR MENU BEEN THE SAME SINCE THE CAFÉ FIRST OPENED?
SURE HAAAS.
THE DRINKS I OFFER ARE ALL ONES I LEARNED ABOUT AT THE LIBRARY.
I CAN'T MAKE ANY-THING EEELSE.
THAT'S WHAT WE'LL HAVE TO WORK ON TO FRESHEN THINGS UP.
LET'S EXPAND THE MENU!
WHOAAAA!!
HOW D'YOU EXPAND MENUS?
LIKE THIIIS?
JAPARI CAFÉ
SASA (SHUFFLE)
YES, BUT NO...
WE'RE GOING TO CREATE A NEW DRINK!
WE'LL ANNOUNCE IT AS A NEW MENU OFFERING TO BRING CUSTOMERS IN!
WHUUUH!?
BUT HOW DO YOU MAKE NEW DRINKS?
WE'D HAVE TO GO ALL THE WAY TO THE LIBRARY-YYY.
WE'LL LOOK AT THE OLD DRINKS AS A GUIDE...
...AND USE DIFFERENT FRUITS AND SO ON TO DISCOVER A DELICIOUS NEW DRINK!
THIS SOUNDS FUN.
I NEVER EVEN CONSID-ERED THAAAT.
AMAZING, RIGHT!? HERE COME THE CUS-TOMERS!
YOU'RE GETTING A LITTLE AHEAD, SERVAL-CHAN.

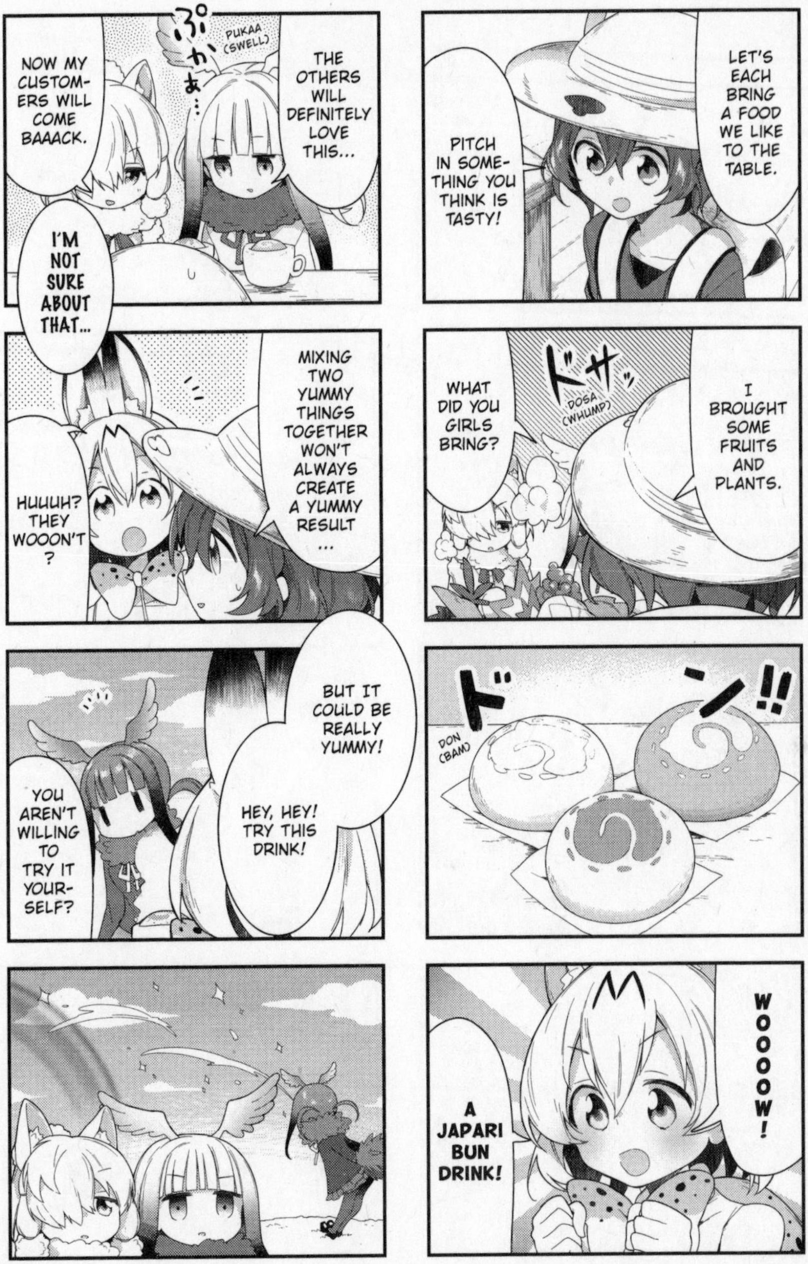
LET'S EACH BRING A FOOD WE LIKE TO THE TABLE.
PITCH IN SOMETHING YOU THINK IS TASTY!
ぷかぁ…
PUKAA (SWELL)
THE OTHERS WILL DEFINITELY LOVE THIS...
NOW MY CUSTOMERS WILL COME BAAACK.
I'M NOT SURE ABOUT THAT...
I BROUGHT SOME FRUITS AND PLANTS.
ドサッ
DOSA (WHUMP)
WHAT DID YOU GIRLS BRING?
MIXING TWO YUMMY THINGS TOGETHER WON'T ALWAYS CREATE A YUMMY RESULT ...
HUUUH? THEY WOOON'T?
ドーン!!
DON (BAM)
BUT IT COULD BE REALLY YUMMY!
HEY, HEY! TRY THIS DRINK!
YOU AREN'T WILLING TO TRY IT YOURSELF?
WOOOOOW!
A JAPARI BUN DRINK!

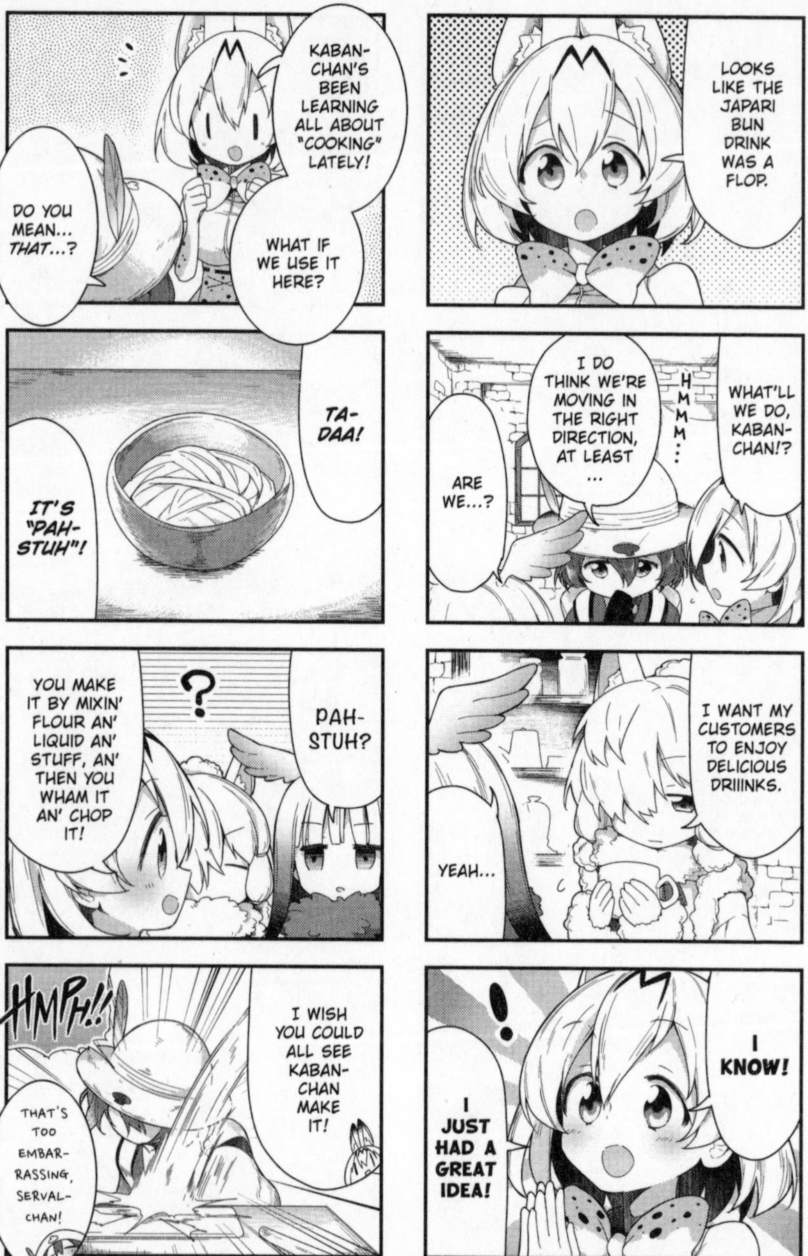
LOOKS LIKE THE JAPARI BUN DRINK WAS A FLOP.
KABAN-CHAN'S BEEN LEARNING ALL ABOUT "COOKING" LATELY!
WHAT IF WE USE IT HERE?
DO YOU MEAN... THAT...?
WHAT'LL WE DO, KABAN-CHAN!?
HMMM...
I DO THINK WE'RE MOVING IN THE RIGHT DIRECTION, AT LEAST...
ARE WE...?
TA-DAA!
IT'S "PAH-STUH"!
I WANT MY CUSTOMERS TO ENJOY DELICIOUS DRIIINKS.
YEAH...
PAH-STUH?
?
YOU MAKE IT BY MIXIN' FLOUR AN' LIQUID AN' STUFF, AN' THEN YOU WHAM IT AN' CHOP IT!
!
I KNOW!
I JUST HAD A GREAT IDEA!
I WISH YOU COULD ALL SEE KABAN-CHAN MAKE IT!
HMPH!!
THAT'S TOO EMBARRASSING, SERVAL-CHAN!

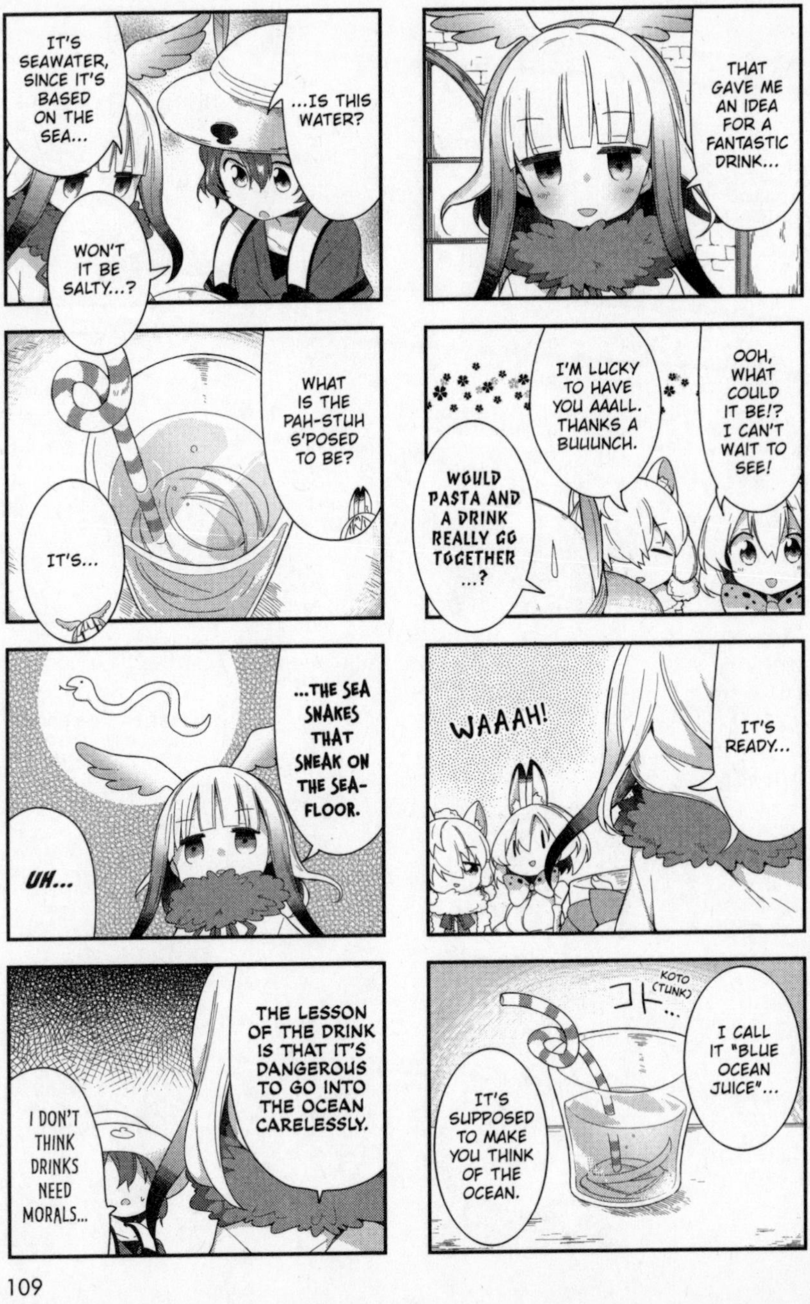
THAT GAVE ME AN IDEA FOR A FANTASTIC DRINK...
OOH, WHAT COULD IT BE!? I CAN'T WAIT TO SEE!
I'M LUCKY TO HAVE YOU AAALL. THANKS A BUUUNCH.
WOULD PASTA AND A DRINK REALLY GO TOGETHER ...?
IT'S READY...
WAAAH!
KOTO (TUNK)
コト...
I CALL IT "BLUE OCEAN JUICE"...
IT'S SUPPOSED TO MAKE YOU THINK OF THE OCEAN.
...IS THIS WATER?
IT'S SEAWATER, SINCE IT'S BASED ON THE SEA...
WON'T IT BE SALTY...?
WHAT IS THE PAH-STUH S'POSED TO BE?
IT'S...
...THE SEA SNAKES THAT SNEAK ON THE SEA-FLOOR.
UH...
THE LESSON OF THE DRINK IS THAT IT'S DANGEROUS TO GO INTO THE OCEAN CARELESSLY.
I DON'T THINK DRINKS NEED MORALS...

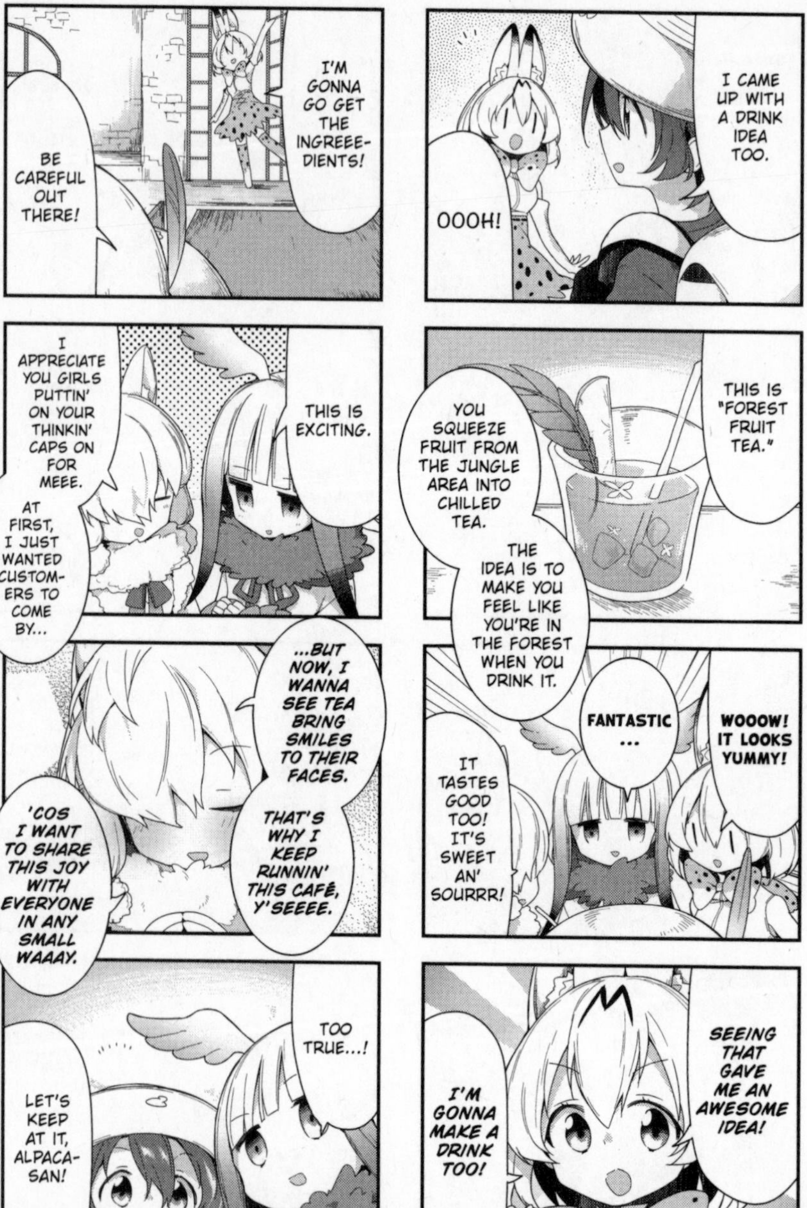
I CAME UP WITH A DRINK IDEA TOO.
OOOH!
THIS IS "FOREST FRUIT TEA."
YOU SQUEEZE FRUIT FROM THE JUNGLE AREA INTO CHILLED TEA.
THE IDEA IS TO MAKE YOU FEEL LIKE YOU'RE IN THE FOREST WHEN YOU DRINK IT.
WOOOW! IT LOOKS YUMMY!
FANTASTIC ...
IT TASTES GOOD TOO! IT'S SWEET AN' SOURRR!
SEEING THAT GAVE ME AN AWESOME IDEA!
I'M GONNA MAKE A DRINK TOO!
I'M GONNA GO GET THE INGREEE-DIENTS!
BE CAREFUL OUT THERE!
THIS IS EXCITING.
I APPRECIATE YOU GIRLS PUTTIN' ON YOUR THINKIN' CAPS ON FOR MEEE.
AT FIRST, I JUST WANTED CUSTOMERS TO COME BY...
...BUT NOW, I WANNA SEE TEA BRING SMILES TO THEIR FACES.
THAT'S WHY I KEEP RUNNIN' THIS CAFÉ, Y'SEEEE.
'COS I WANT TO SHARE THIS JOY WITH EVERYONE IN ANY SMALL WAAAY.
TOO TRUE...!
LET'S KEEP AT IT, ALPACA-SAN!

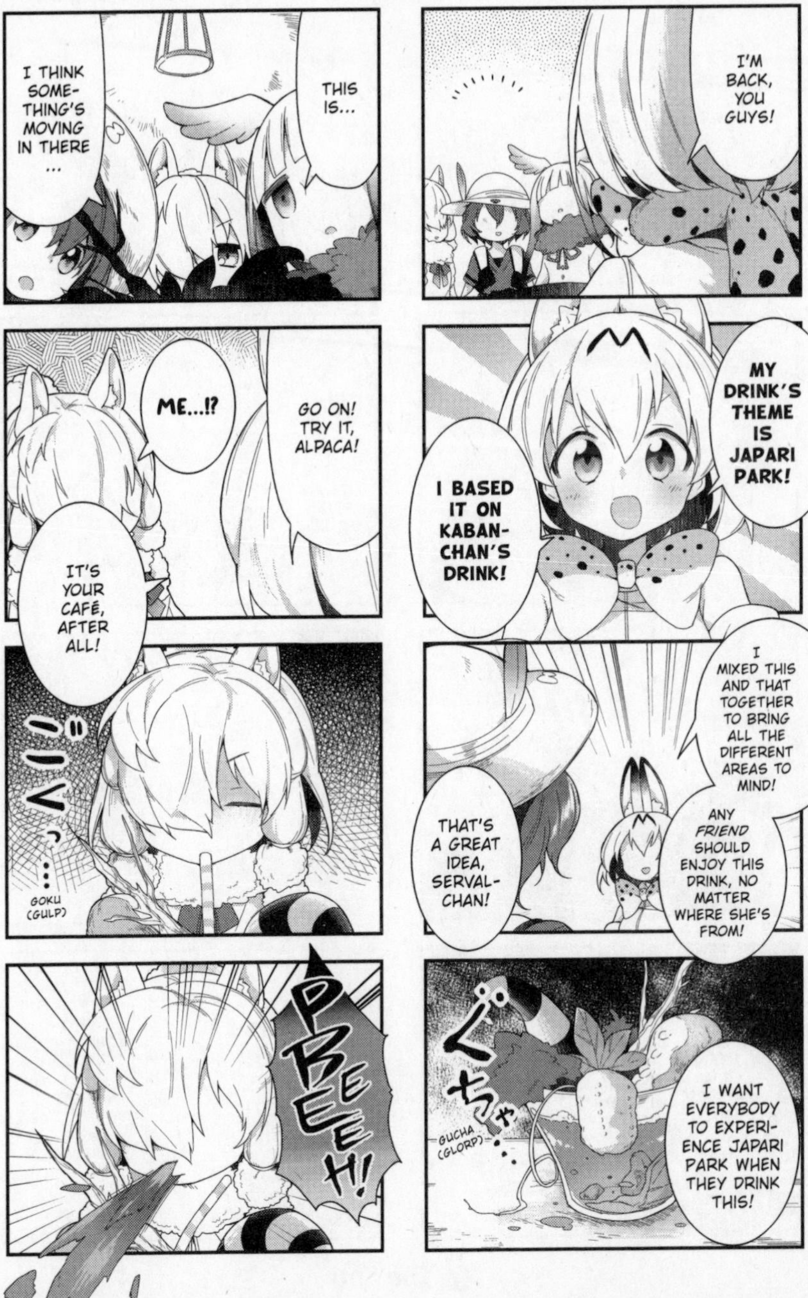
I'M BACK, YOU GUYS!
MY DRINK'S THEME IS JAPARI PARK!
I BASED IT ON KABAN-CHAN'S DRINK!
I MIXED THIS AND THAT TOGETHER TO BRING ALL THE DIFFERENT AREAS TO MIND!
ANY *FRIEND* SHOULD ENJOY THIS DRINK, NO MATTER WHERE SHE'S FROM!
THAT'S A GREAT IDEA, SERVAL-CHAN!
GUCHA (GLORP)
I WANT EVERYBODY TO EXPERIENCE JAPARI PARK WHEN THEY DRINK THIS!
THIS IS...
I THINK SOME-THING'S MOVING IN THERE...
GO ON! TRY IT, ALPACA!
ME...!?
IT'S YOUR CAFÉ, AFTER ALL!
GOKU (GULP)
PBEEEH!

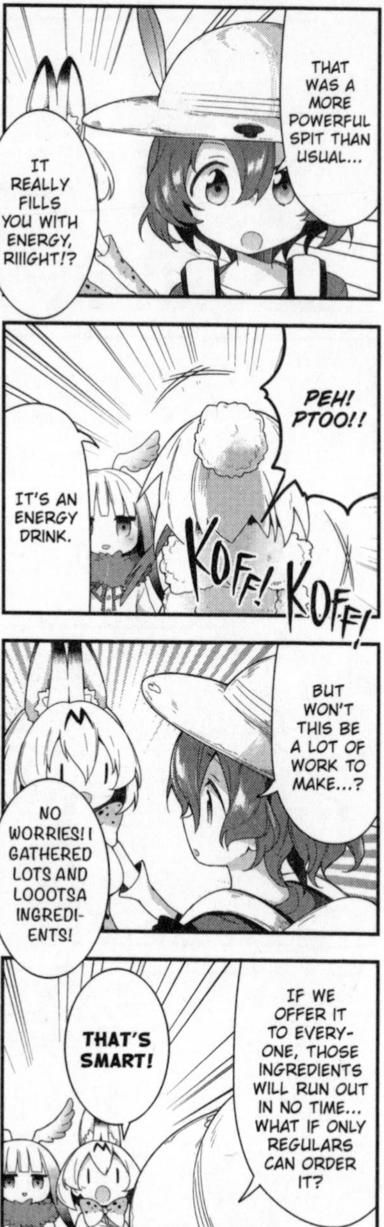
THAT WAS A MORE POWERFUL SPIT THAN USUAL...
IT REALLY FILLS YOU WITH ENERGY, RIIIGHT!?
PEH! PTOO!!
IT'S AN ENERGY DRINK.
KOFF! KOFF!
BUT WON'T THIS BE A LOT OF WORK TO MAKE...?
NO WORRIES! I GATHERED LOTS AND LOOOTSA INGREDIENTS!
IF WE OFFER IT TO EVERY-ONE, THOSE INGREDIENTS WILL RUN OUT IN NO TIME... WHAT IF ONLY REGULARS CAN ORDER IT?
THAT'S SMART!

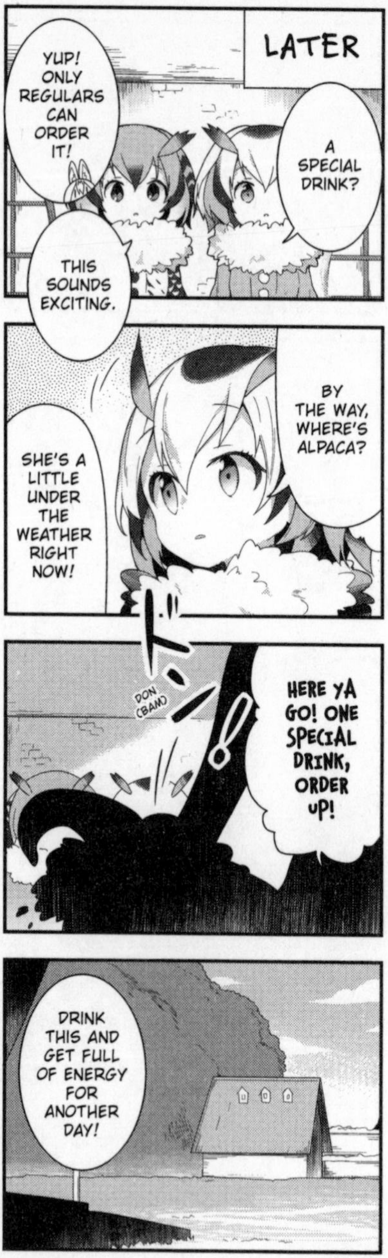
LATER
A SPECIAL DRINK?
YUP! ONLY REGULARS CAN ORDER IT!
THIS SOUNDS EXCITING.
BY THE WAY, WHERE'S ALPACA?
SHE'S A LITTLE UNDER THE WEATHER RIGHT NOW!
HERE YA GO! ONE SPECIAL DRINK, ORDER UP!
DON (BAM)
DRINK THIS AND GET FULL OF ENERGY FOR ANOTHER DAY!

The End

Kemono Friends

Question

63 WHAT'S THAT ANIMAL?

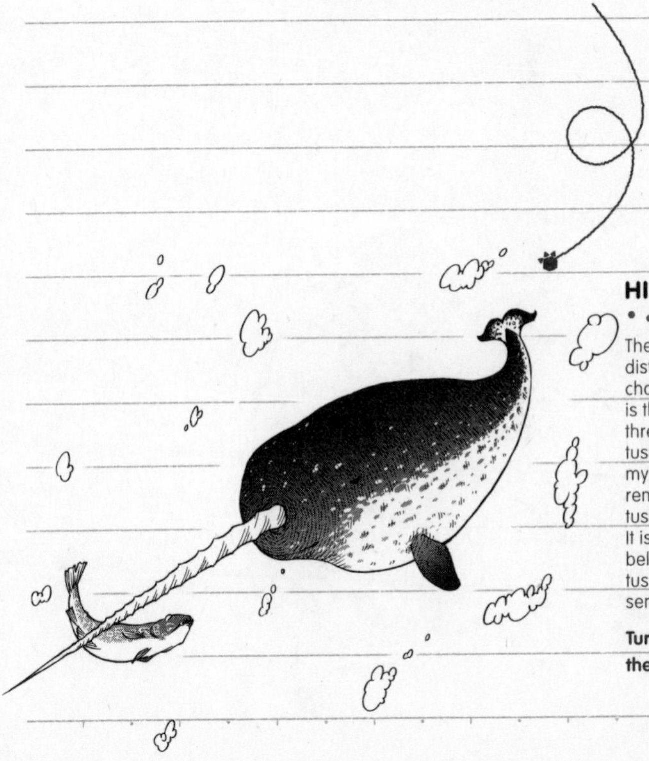

HINT:

Their distinguishing characteristic is their nearly three-meter-long tusk. But many mysteries still remain about the tusk's purpose. It is commonly believed that the tusk is used as a sensory organ.

Turn the page for the answer!

A3
NARWHAL

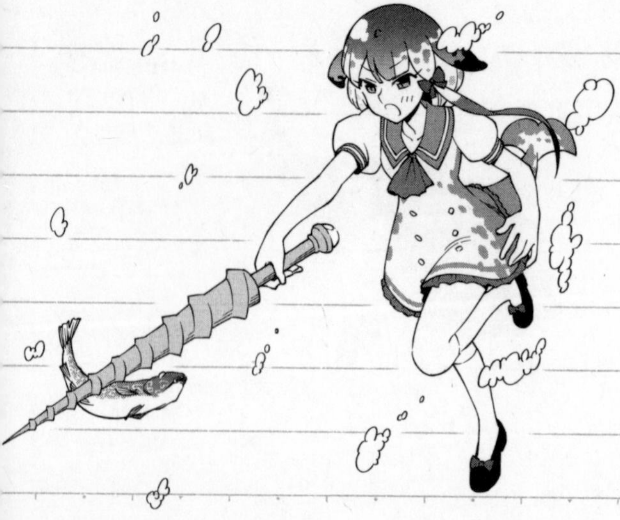

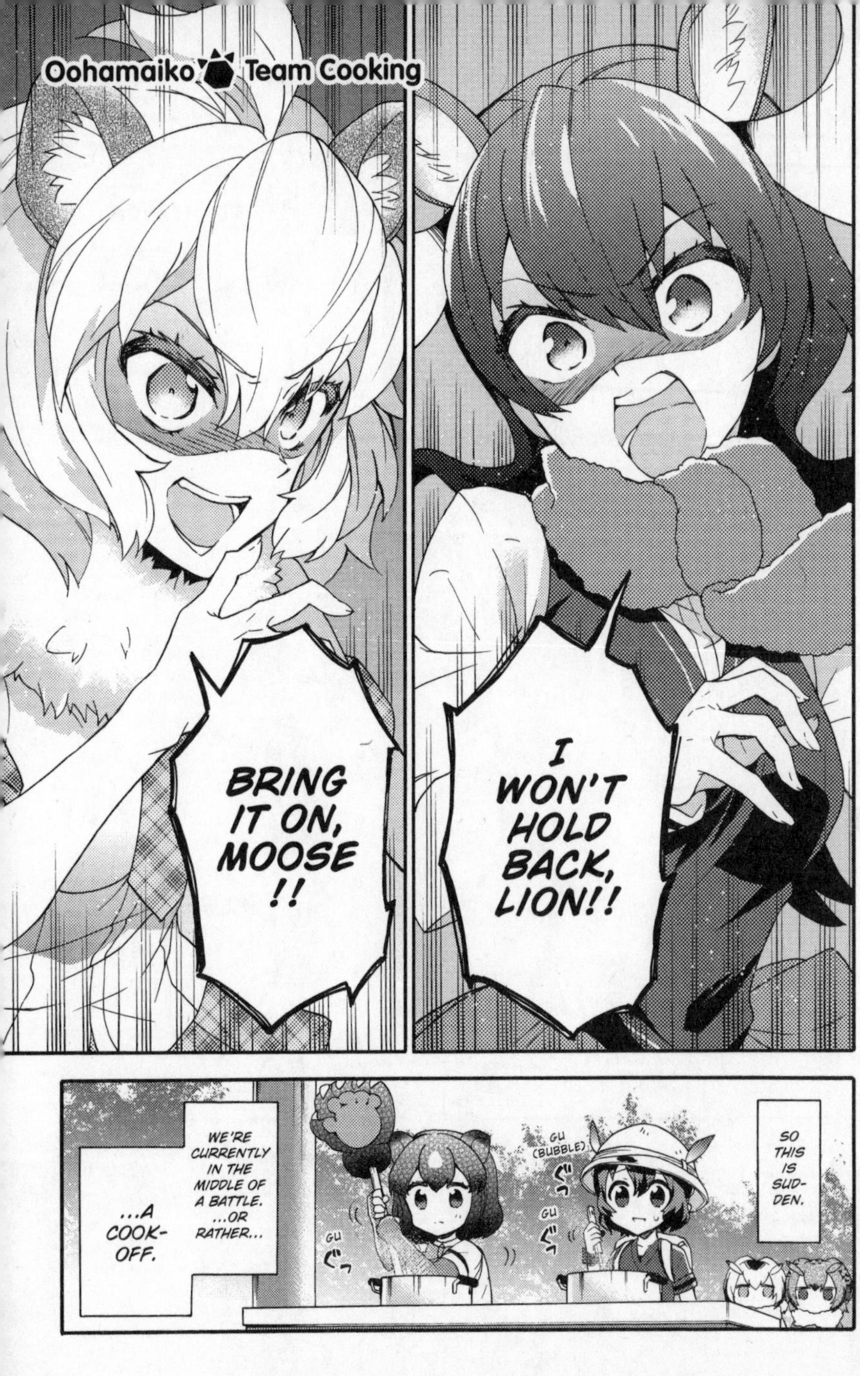
I WON'T HOLD BACK, LION!!
BRING IT ON, MOOSE!!
SO THIS IS SUD-DEN.
GU (BUBBLE)
GU
GU
WE'RE CURRENTLY IN THE MIDDLE OF A BATTLE. ...OR RATHER...
...A COOK-OFF.

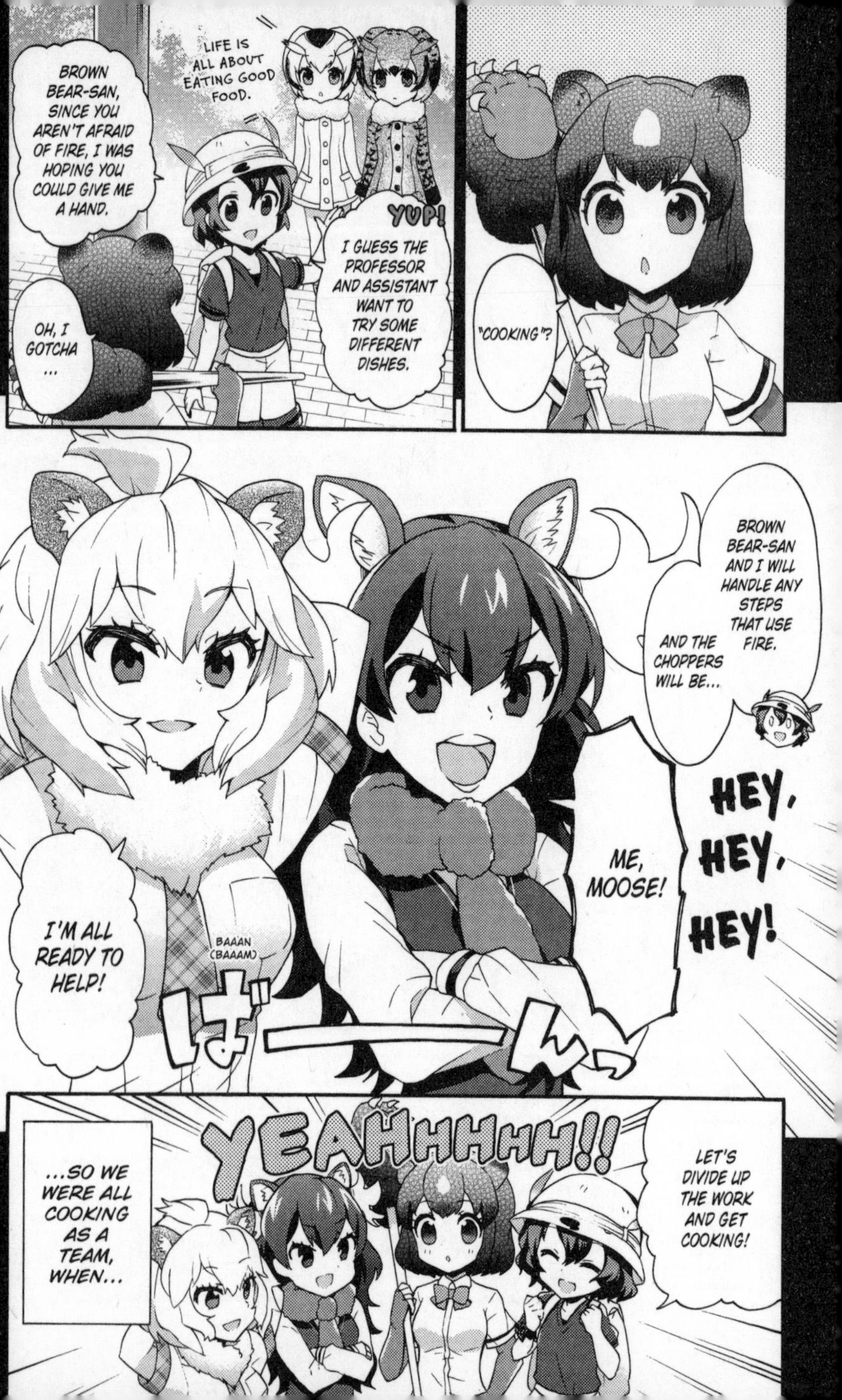
"COOKING"?
LIFE IS ALL ABOUT EATING GOOD FOOD.
BROWN BEAR-SAN, SINCE YOU AREN'T AFRAID OF FIRE, I WAS HOPING YOU COULD GIVE ME A HAND.
YUP!
I GUESS THE PROFESSOR AND ASSISTANT WANT TO TRY SOME DIFFERENT DISHES.
OH, I GOTCHA ...
BROWN BEAR-SAN AND I WILL HANDLE ANY STEPS THAT USE FIRE.
AND THE CHOPPERS WILL BE...
HEY, HEY, HEY!
ME, MOOSE!
I'M ALL READY TO HELP!
BAAAN (BAAAM)
ばーん
LET'S DIVIDE UP THE WORK AND GET COOKING!
YEAHHHHH!!
...SO WE WERE ALL COOKING AS A TEAM, WHEN...

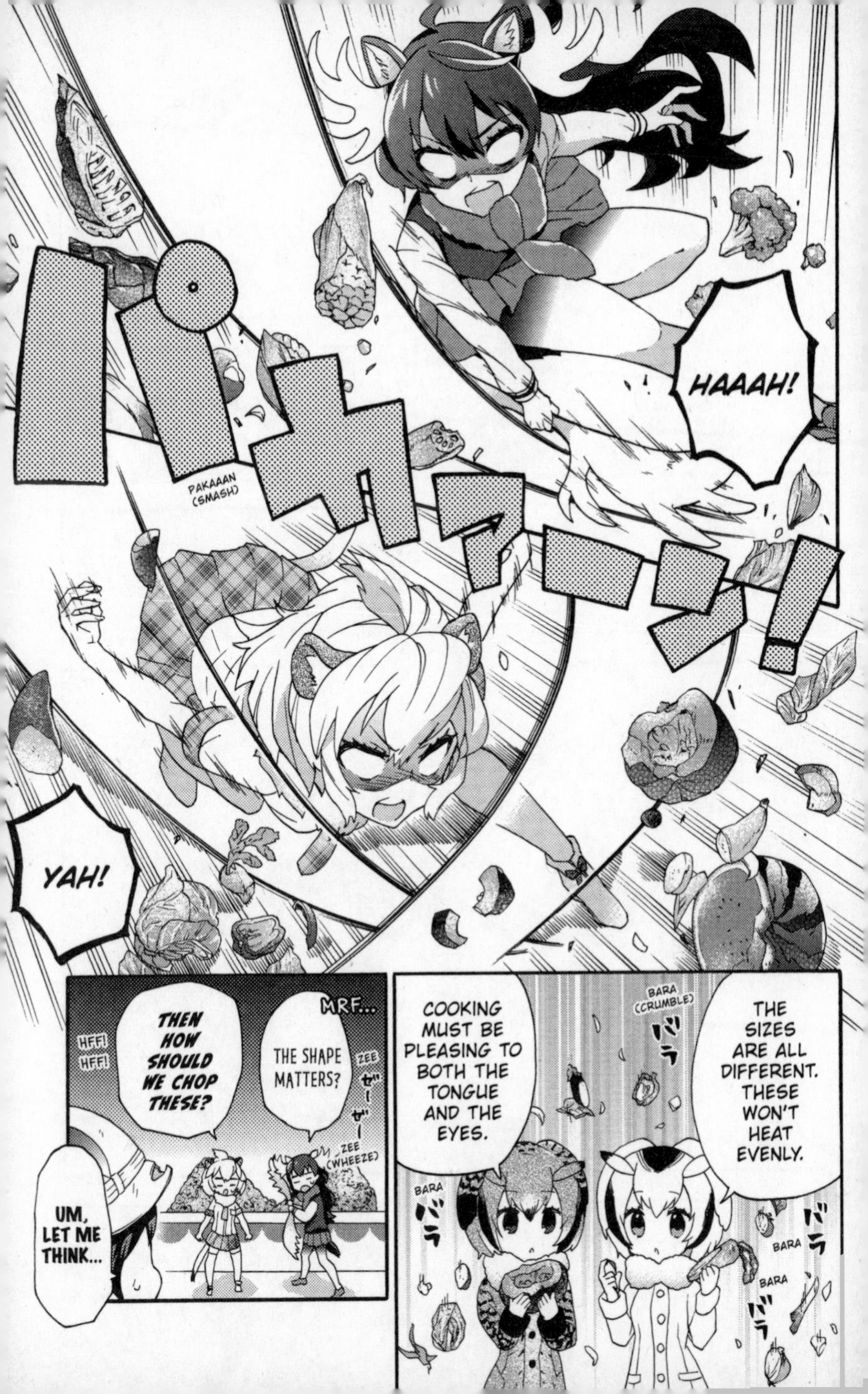
HAAAH!
パカァーンッ!
PAKAAAN (SMASH)
YAH!
THE SIZES ARE ALL DIFFERENT. THESE WON'T HEAT EVENLY.
BARA (CRUMBLE)
バラ
COOKING MUST BE PLEASING TO BOTH THE TONGUE AND THE EYES.
BARA
バラ
BARA
バラ
BARA
バラ
MRF...
THE SHAPE MATTERS?
ZEE
ぜーぜー
ZEE (WHEEZE)
THEN HOW SHOULD WE CHOP THESE?
HFF! HFF!
UM, LET ME THINK...

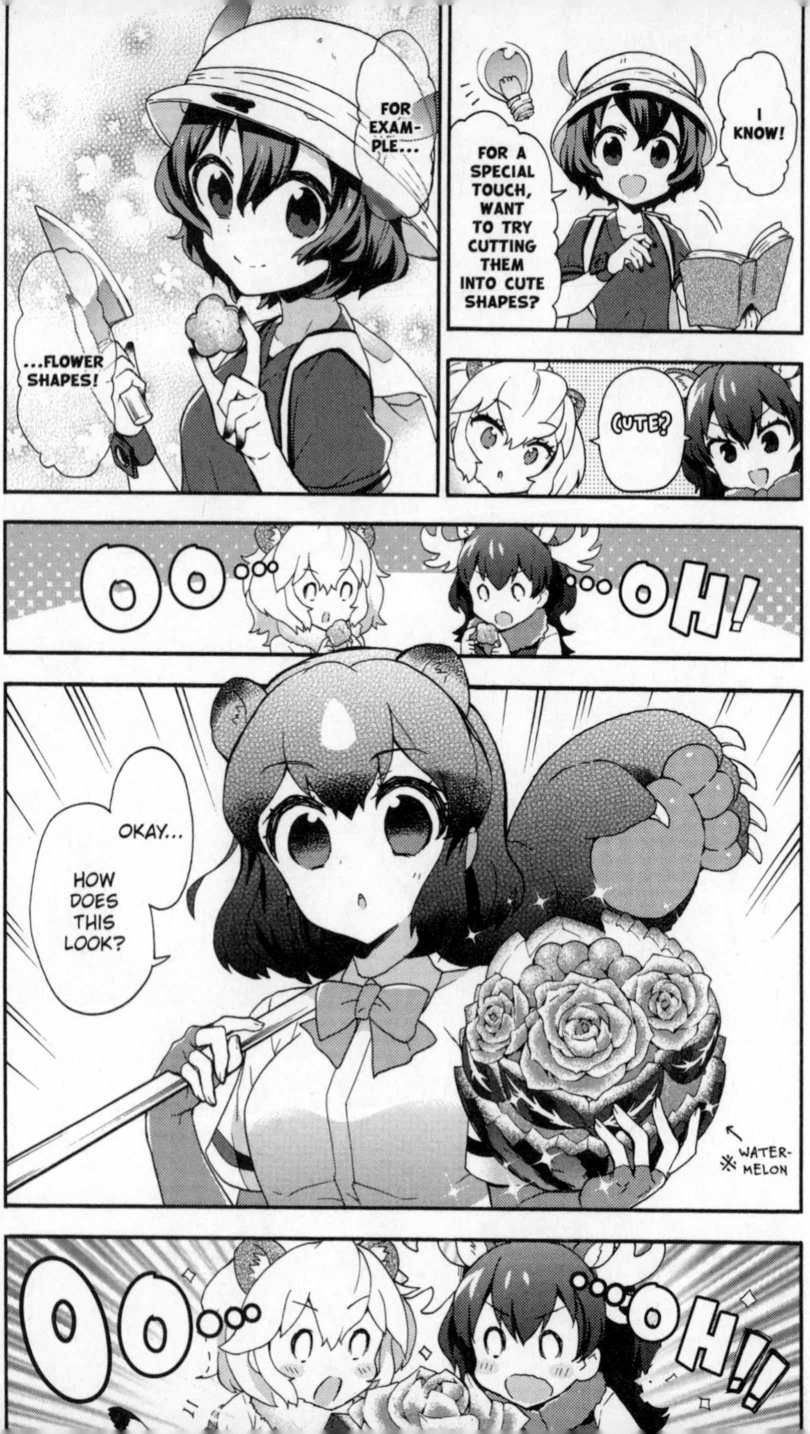
I KNOW!
FOR A SPECIAL TOUCH, WANT TO TRY CUTTING THEM INTO CUTE SHAPES?
CUTE?
FOR EXAM-PLE...
...FLOWER SHAPES!
OO...
...OH!
OKAY...
HOW DOES THIS LOOK?
※WATER-MELON
OO...
...OH!!

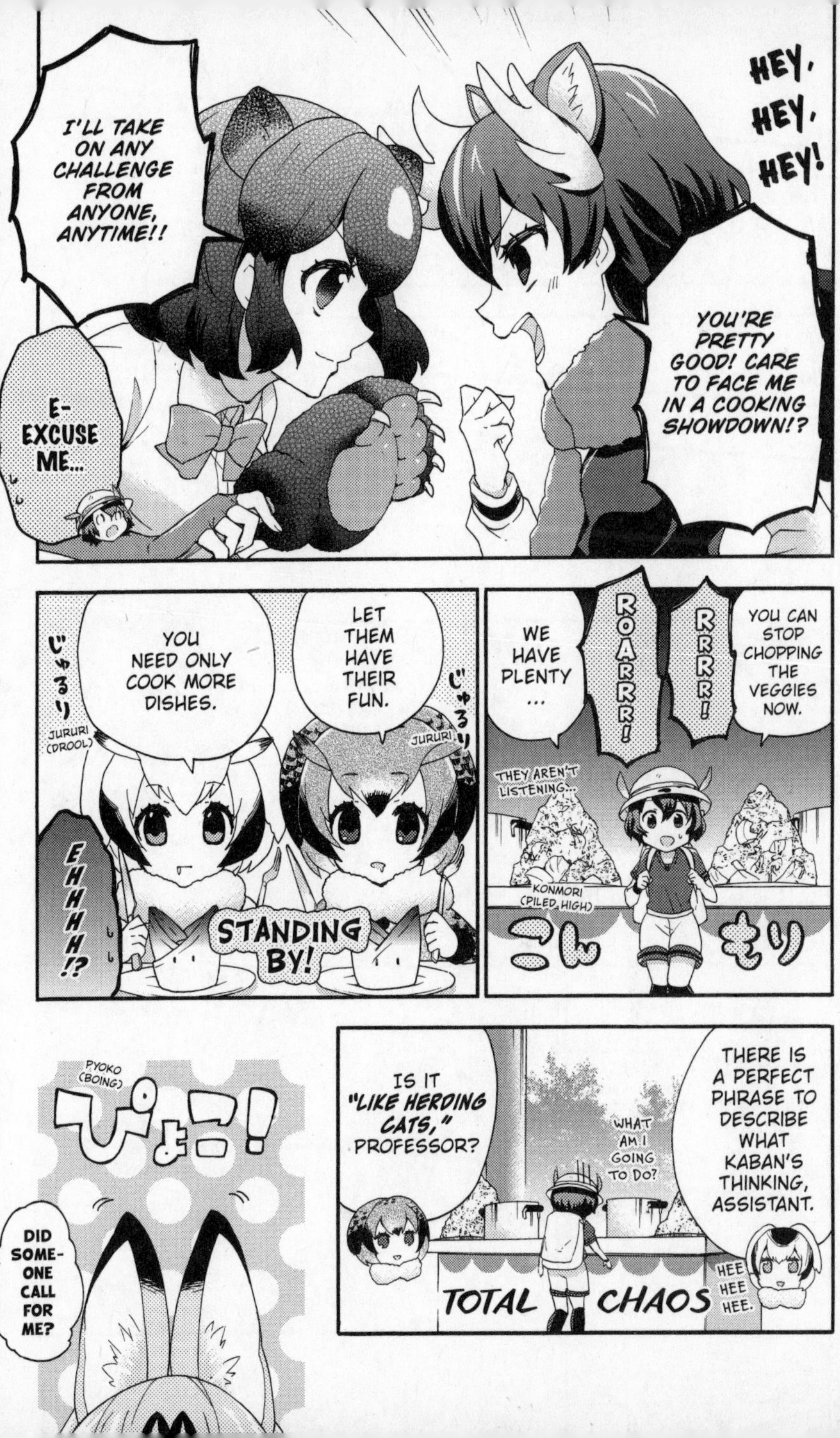
HEY, HEY, HEY!
YOU'RE PRETTY GOOD! CARE TO FACE ME IN A COOKING SHOWDOWN!?
I'LL TAKE ON ANY CHALLENGE FROM ANYONE, ANYTIME!!
E-EXCUSE ME...
YOU CAN STOP CHOPPING THE VEGGIES NOW.
RRRR!
ROARRR!
WE HAVE PLENTY...
THEY AREN'T LISTENING...
KONMORI (PILED HIGH)
こんもり
LET THEM HAVE THEIR FUN.
じゅるり
JURURI
YOU NEED ONLY COOK MORE DISHES.
じゅるり
JURURI (DROOL)
STANDING BY!
EHHHHH!?
THERE IS A PERFECT PHRASE TO DESCRIBE WHAT KABAN'S THINKING, ASSISTANT.
IS IT "LIKE HERDING CATS," PROFESSOR?
WHAT AM I GOING TO DO?
HEE HEE HEE.
TOTAL CHAOS
PYOKO (BOING)
ぴょこ!
DID SOMEONE CALL FOR ME?

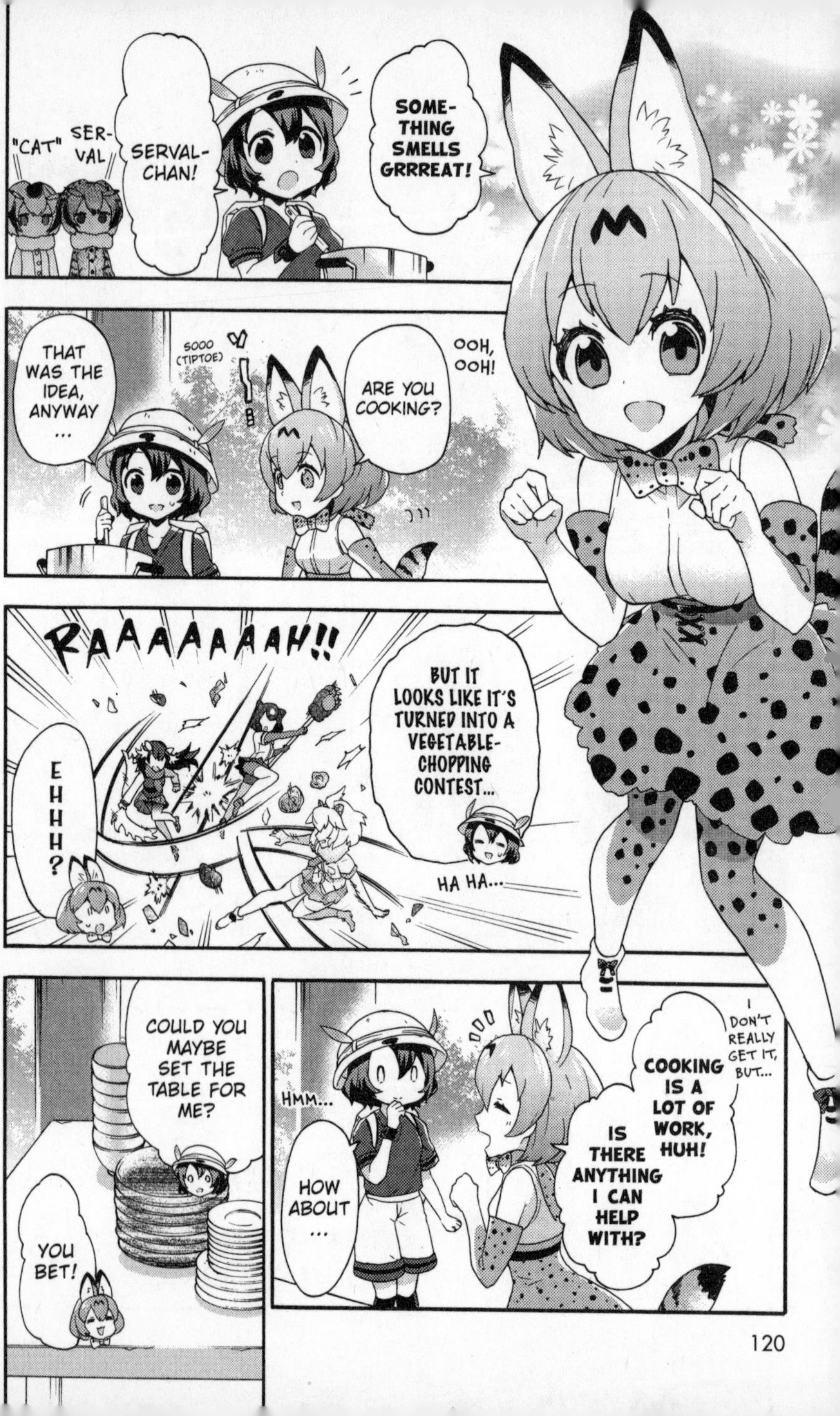
SOMETHING SMELLS GRRREAT!
SERVAL-CHAN!
SERVAL
"CAT"
OOH, OOH!
ARE YOU COOKING?
SOOO (TIPTOE)
THAT WAS THE IDEA, ANYWAY...
RAAAAAAAAH!!
BUT IT LOOKS LIKE IT'S TURNED INTO A VEGETABLE-CHOPPING CONTEST...
HA HA...
EHHHH?
I DON'T REALLY GET IT, BUT...
COOKING IS A LOT OF WORK, HUH!
IS THERE ANYTHING I CAN HELP WITH?
HMM...
HOW ABOUT...
COULD YOU MAYBE SET THE TABLE FOR ME?
YOU BET!

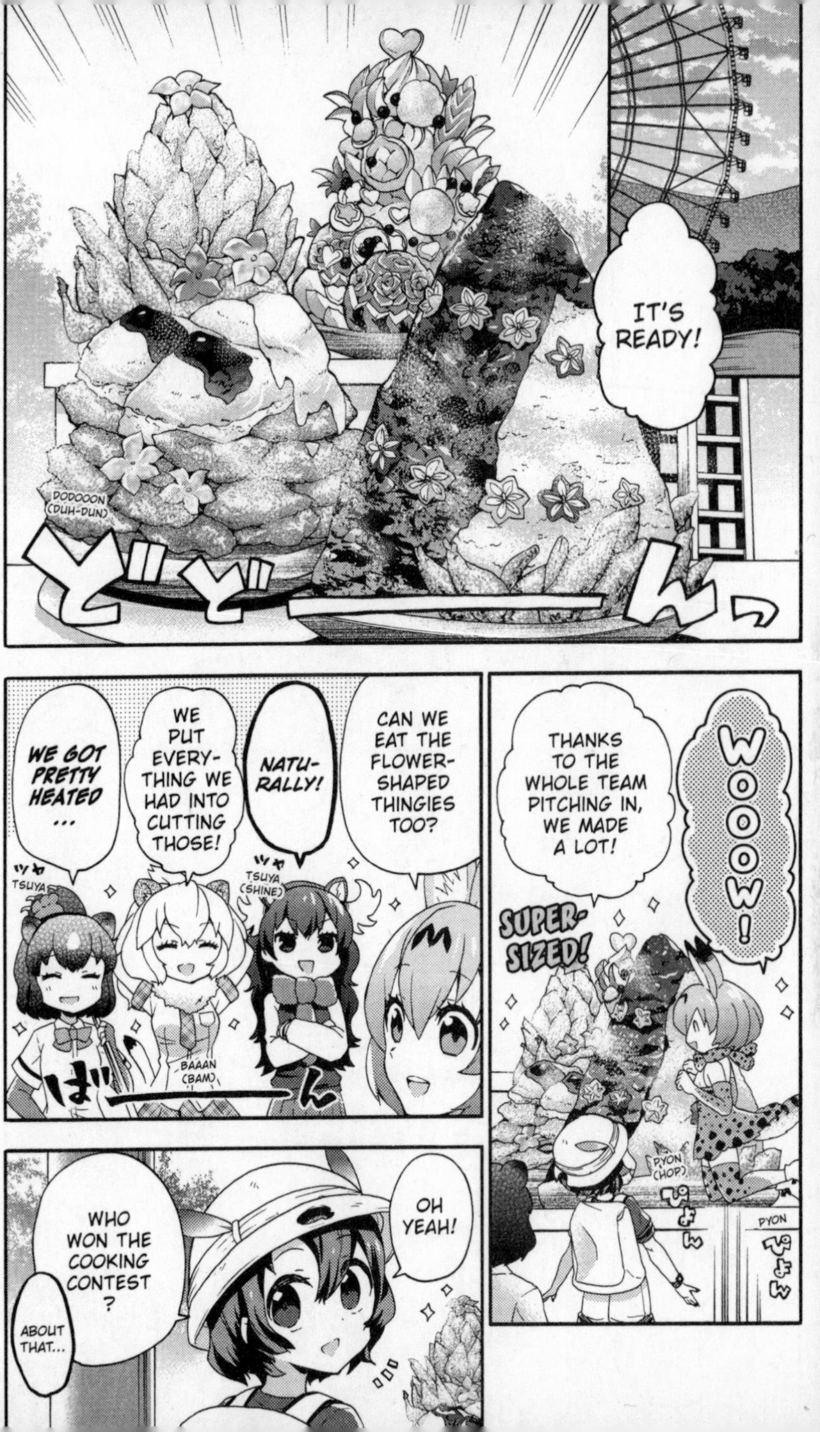
IT'S READY!
DODOOON (DUH-DUN)
どどーーーんっ
WOOOW!
THANKS TO THE WHOLE TEAM PITCHING IN, WE MADE A LOT!
SUPER-SIZED!
PYON (HOP)
ぴょん
PYON
ぴょん
CAN WE EAT THE FLOWER-SHAPED THINGIES TOO?
NATU-RALLY!
ツヤ TSUYA (SHINE)
WE PUT EVERY-THING WE HAD INTO CUTTING THOSE!
WE GOT PRETTY HEATED...
ツヤ TSUYA
BAAAN (BAM)
ばーーーん
OH YEAH!
WHO WON THE COOKING CONTEST?
ABOUT THAT...

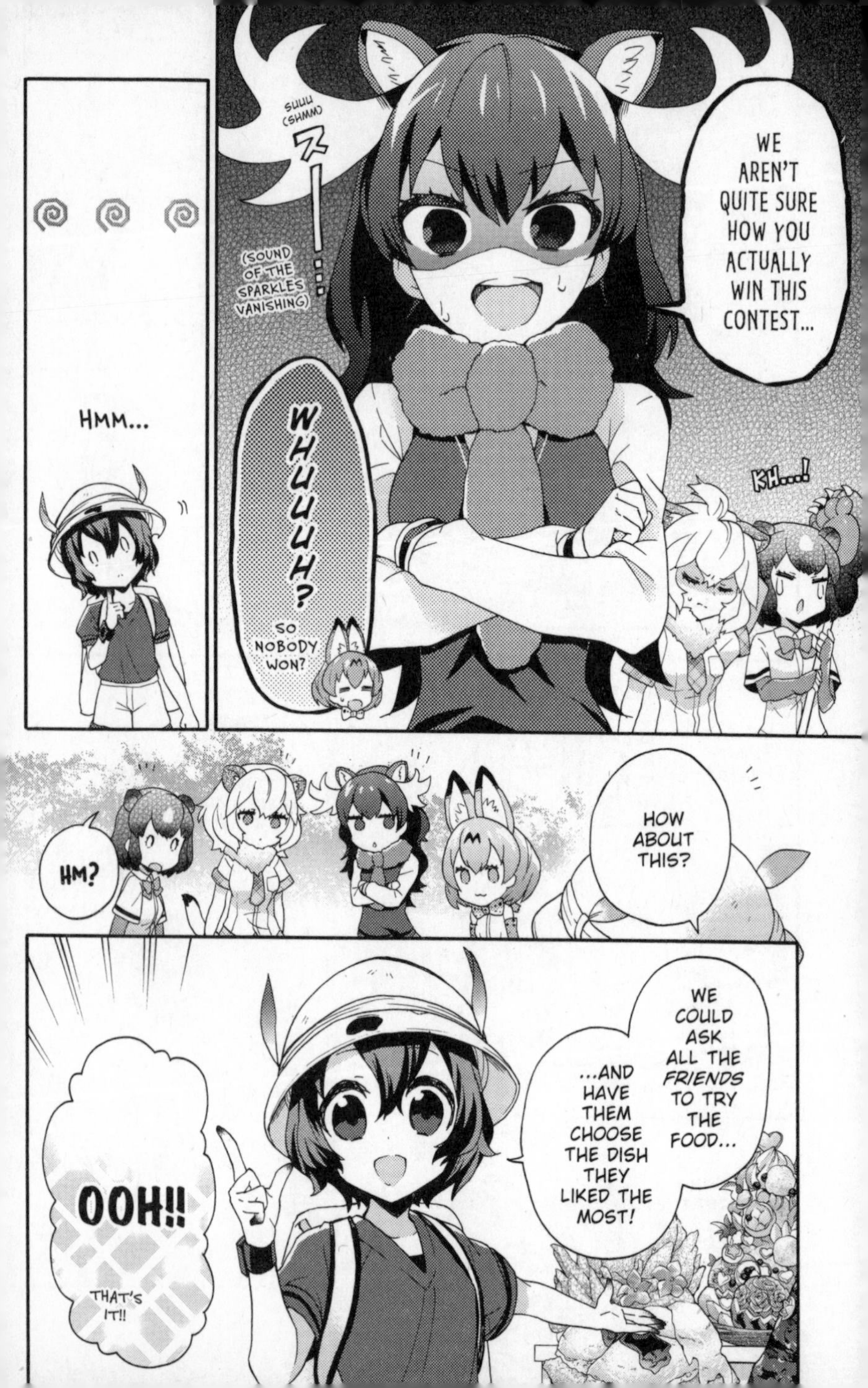
WE AREN'T QUITE SURE HOW YOU ACTUALLY WIN THIS CONTEST...
SUUU (SHMM)
スー
(SOUND OF THE SPARKLES VANISHING)
KH...!
WHUUUUH?
SO NOBODY WON?
HMM...
HOW ABOUT THIS?
HM?
WE COULD ASK ALL THE *FRIENDS* TO TRY THE FOOD...
...AND HAVE THEM CHOOSE THE DISH THEY LIKED THE MOST!
OOH!!
THAT'S IT!!

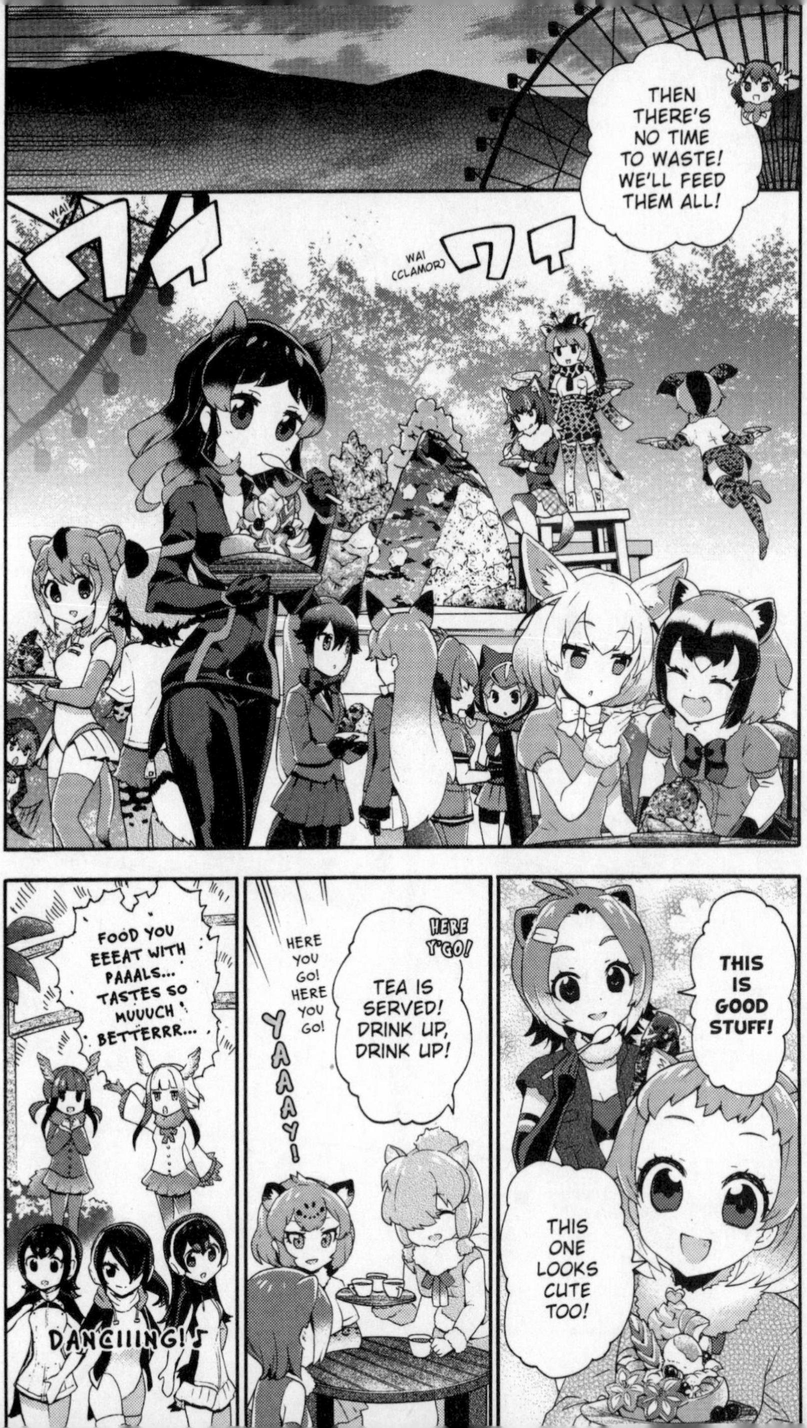
THEN THERE'S NO TIME TO WASTE! WE'LL FEED THEM ALL!
WAI (CLAMOR)
WAI
HERE Y'GO!
TEA IS SERVED! DRINK UP, DRINK UP!
HERE YOU GO! HERE YOU GO!
YAAAAY!
THIS IS GOOD STUFF!
THIS ONE LOOKS CUTE TOO!
FOOD YOU EEEAT WITH PAAALS... TASTES SO MUUUCH BETTERRR...
DANCIIING!

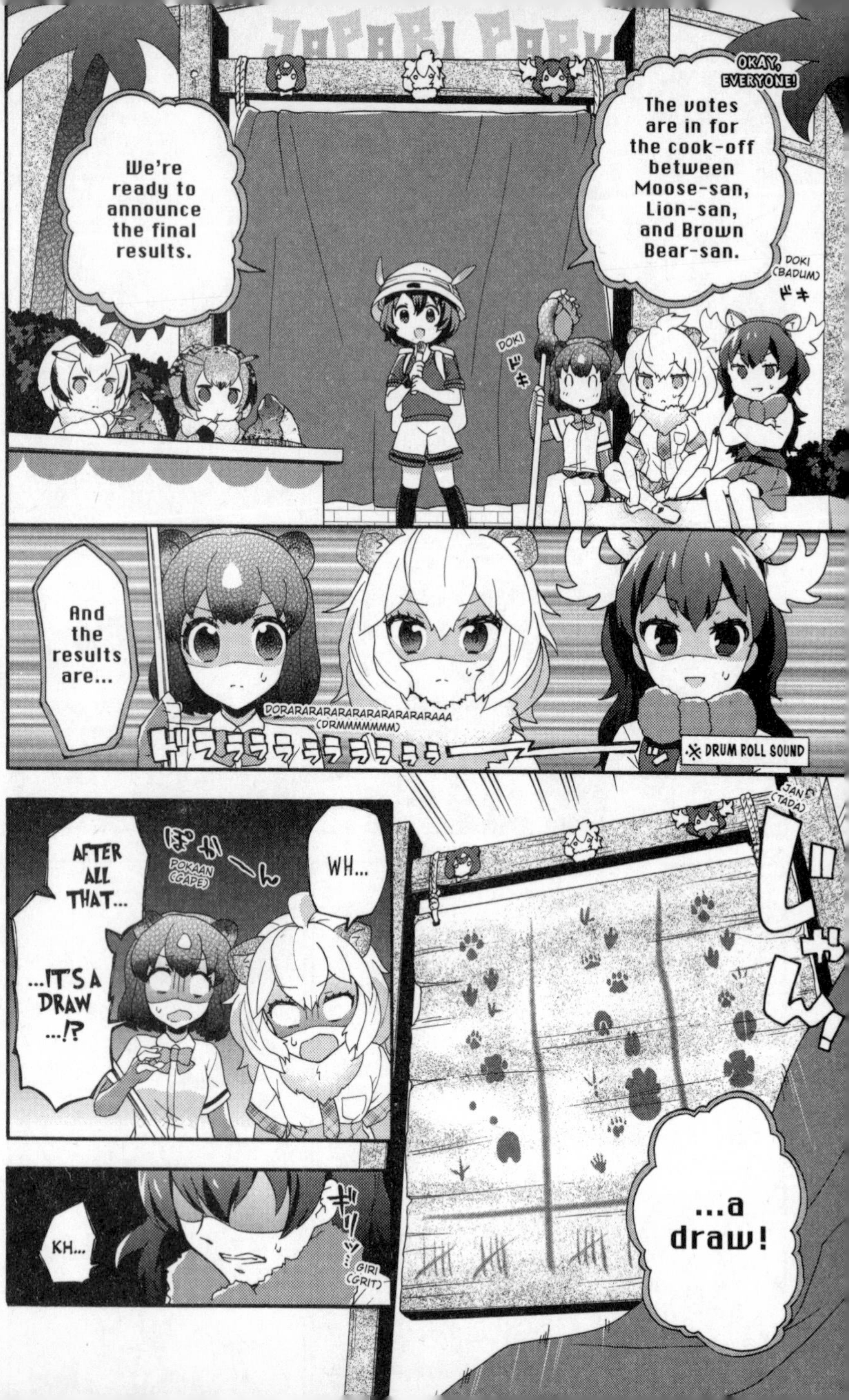
JAPARI PARK
OKAY, EVERYONE!
The votes are in for the cook-off between Moose-san, Lion-san, and Brown Bear-san.
DOKI (BADUM)
ドキ
We're ready to announce the final results.
DOKI
ドキ
And the results are...
DORARARARARARARARARARARAAA (DRMMMMMMM)
※ DRUM ROLL SOUND
JAN (TADA)
じゃーん!
...a draw!
WH...
ぽかーん
POKAAN (GAPE)
AFTER ALL THAT...
...IT'S A DRAW ...!?
ギリッ
GIRI (GRIT)
KH...

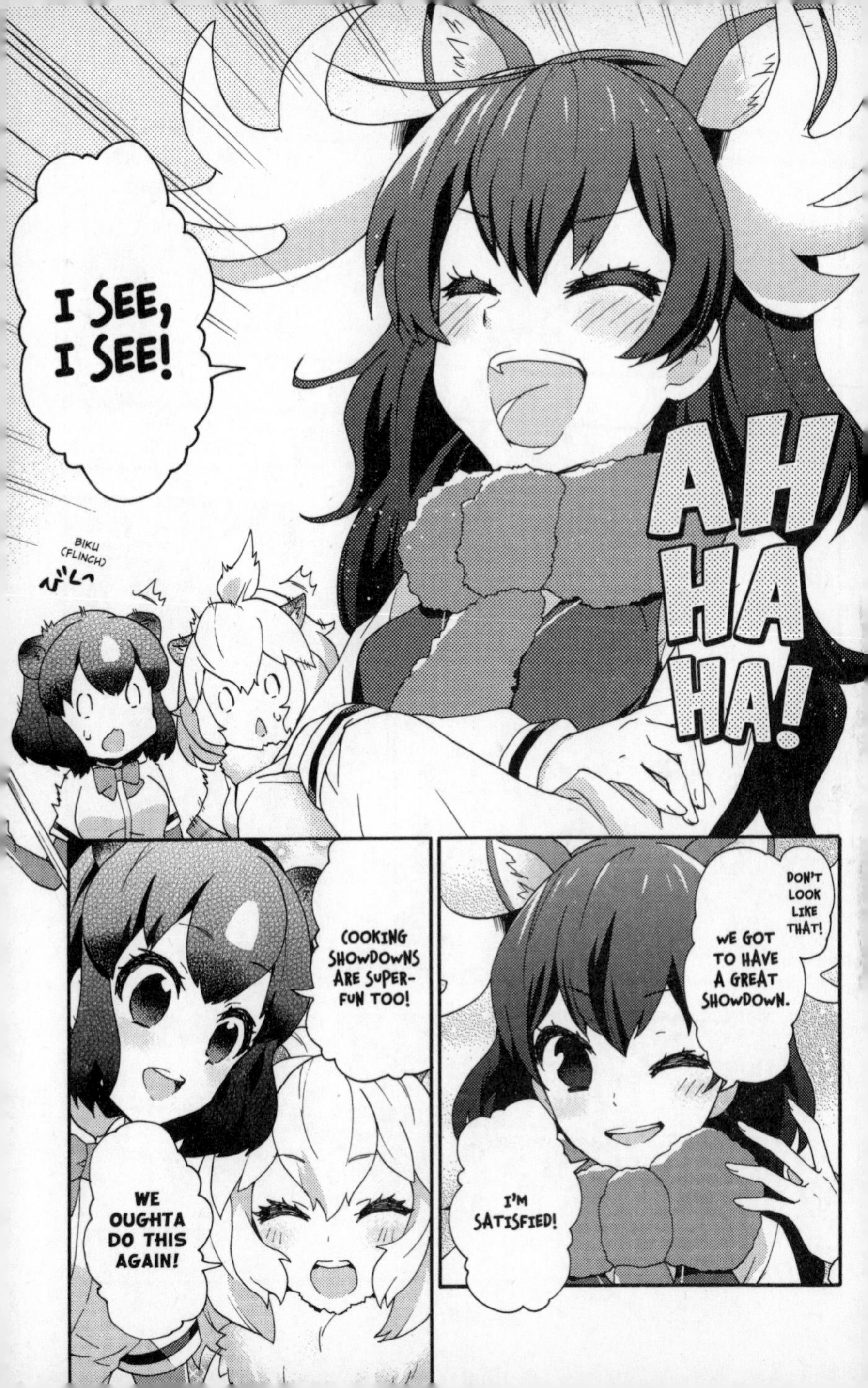
I SEE, I SEE!
AH HA HA HA!
BIKU (FLINCH)
DON'T LOOK LIKE THAT!
WE GOT TO HAVE A GREAT SHOWDOWN.
I'M SATISFIED!
COOKING SHOWDOWNS ARE SUPER-FUN TOO!
WE OUGHTA DO THIS AGAIN!

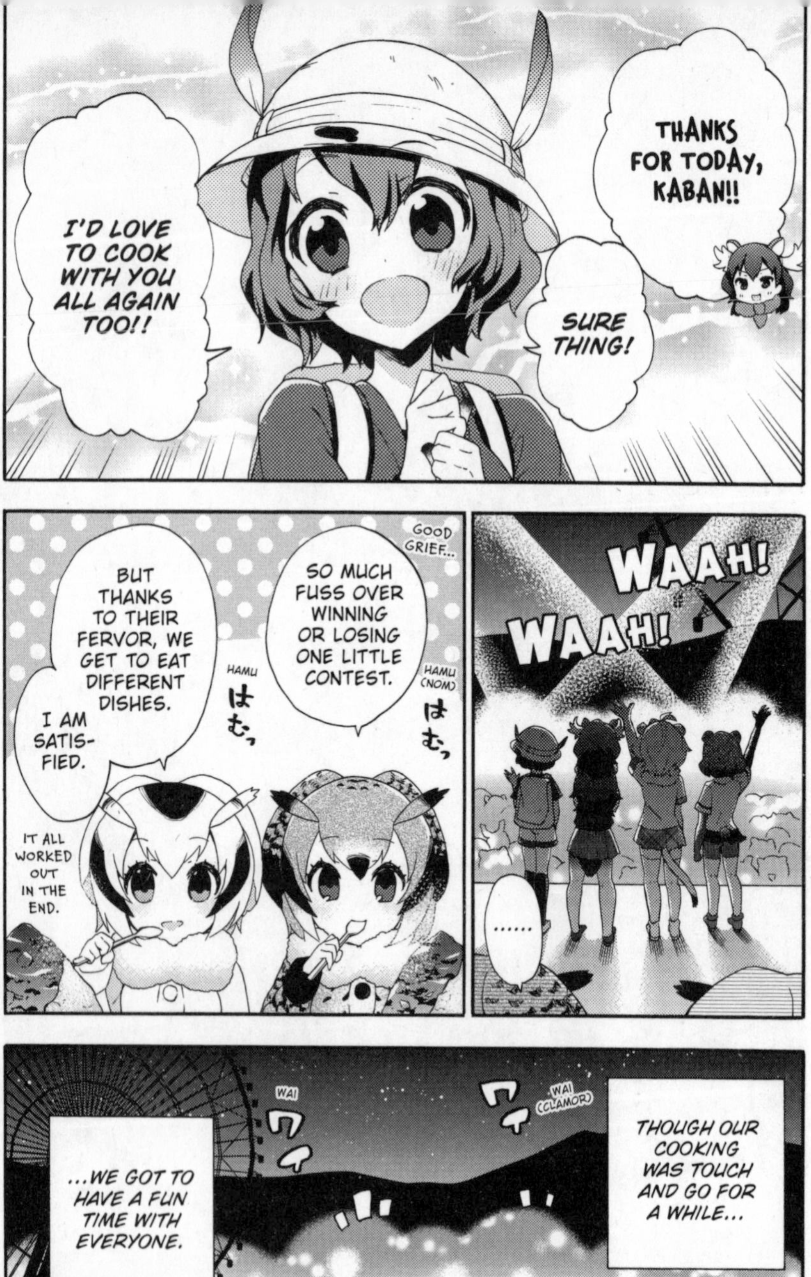
THANKS FOR TODAY, KABAN!!
SURE THING!
I'D LOVE TO COOK WITH YOU ALL AGAIN TOO!!
WAAH!
WAAH!
......
GOOD GRIEF...
SO MUCH FUSS OVER WINNING OR LOSING ONE LITTLE CONTEST.
HAMU (NOM)
はむっ
HAMU
はむっ
BUT THANKS TO THEIR FERVOR, WE GET TO EAT DIFFERENT DISHES.
I AM SATIS-FIED.
IT ALL WORKED OUT IN THE END.
THOUGH OUR COOKING WAS TOUCH AND GO FOR A WHILE...
WAI (CLAMOR)
ワイ
WAI
ワイ
...WE GOT TO HAVE A FUN TIME WITH EVERYONE.

The End

Tsukasa Usui The Melancholy of White Rhino

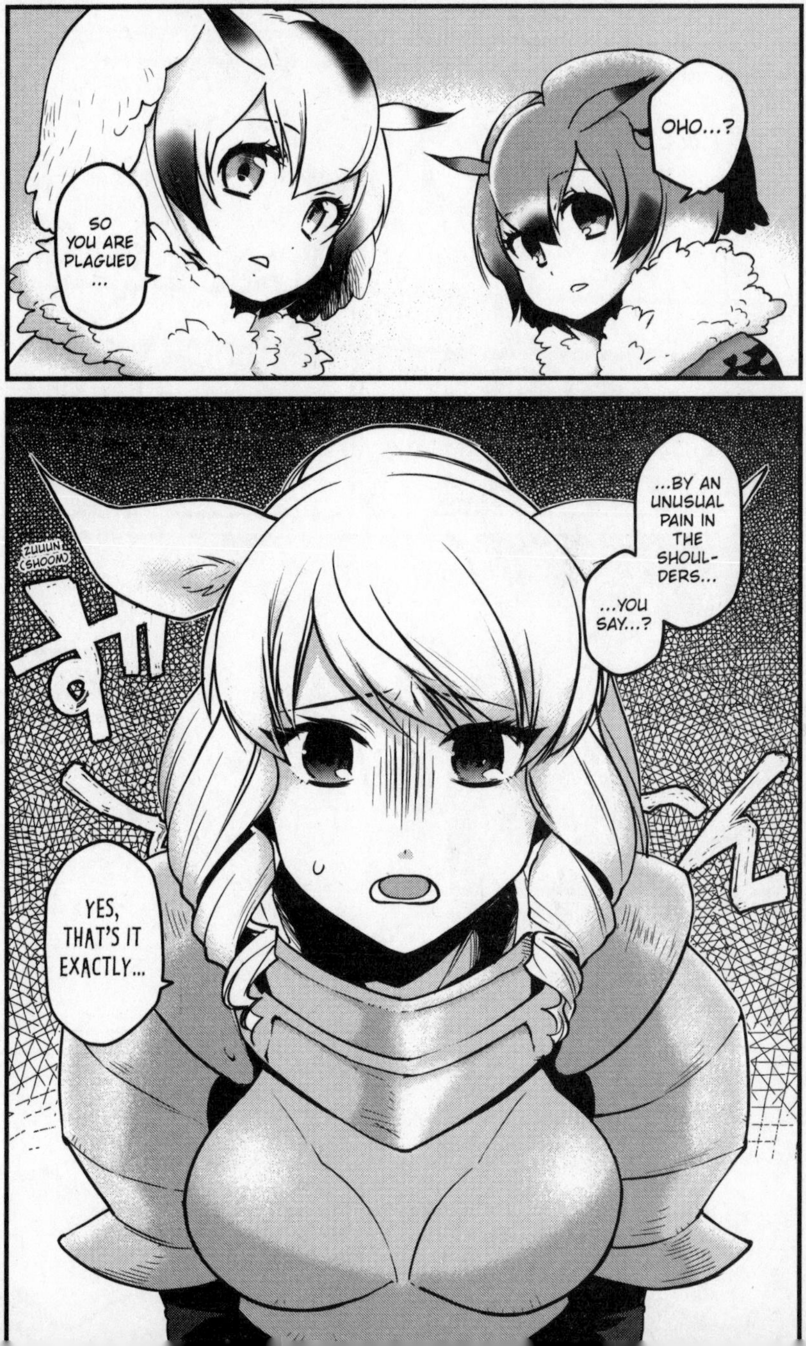
OHO...?
SO YOU ARE PLAGUED ...
...BY AN UNUSUAL PAIN IN THE SHOUL-DERS...
...YOU SAY...?
ZUUUN (SHOOM)
YES, THAT'S IT EXACTLY...

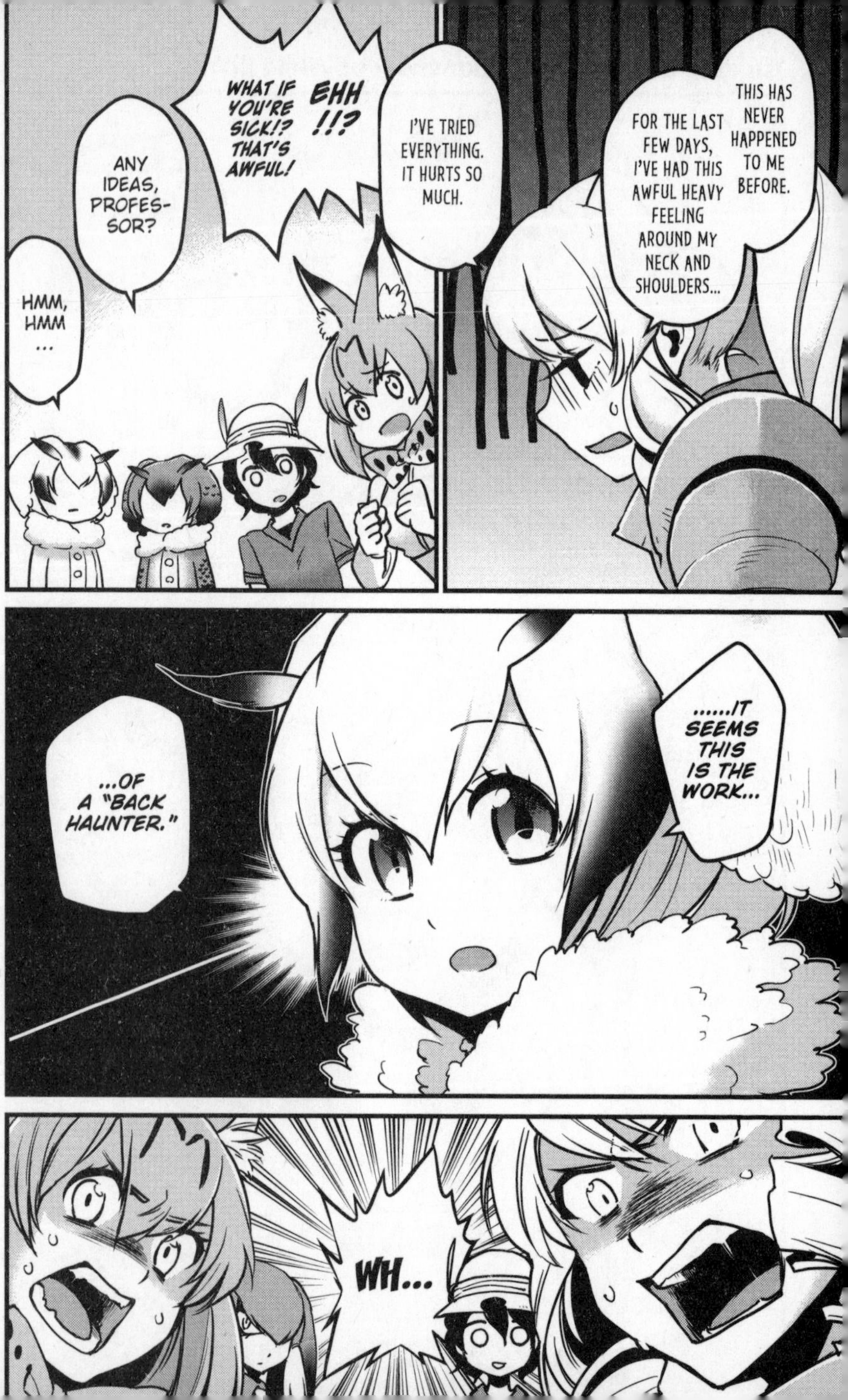
THIS HAS NEVER HAPPENED TO ME BEFORE.
FOR THE LAST FEW DAYS, I'VE HAD THIS AWFUL HEAVY FEELING AROUND MY NECK AND SHOULDERS...
I'VE TRIED EVERYTHING. IT HURTS SO MUCH.
EHH !!?
WHAT IF YOU'RE SICK!? THAT'S AWFUL!
ANY IDEAS, PROFES-SOR?
HMM, HMM ...
......IT SEEMS THIS IS THE WORK...
...OF A "BACK HAUNTER."
WH...

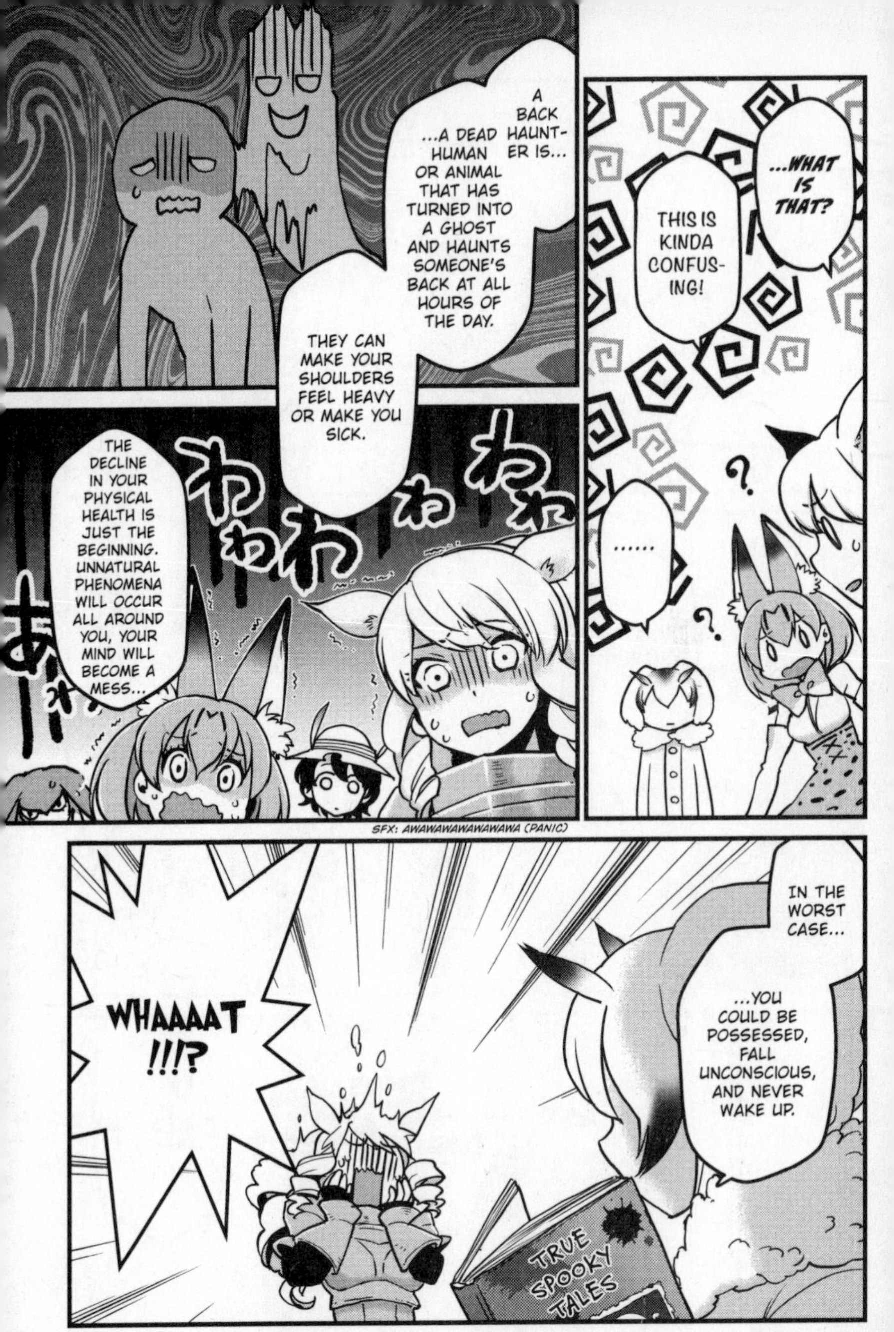
...WHAT IS THAT?
THIS IS KINDA CONFUSING!
......
A BACK HAUNTER IS...
...A DEAD HUMAN OR ANIMAL THAT HAS TURNED INTO A GHOST AND HAUNTS SOMEONE'S BACK AT ALL HOURS OF THE DAY.
THEY CAN MAKE YOUR SHOULDERS FEEL HEAVY OR MAKE YOU SICK.
THE DECLINE IN YOUR PHYSICAL HEALTH IS JUST THE BEGINNING. UNNATURAL PHENOMENA WILL OCCUR ALL AROUND YOU, YOUR MIND WILL BECOME A MESS...
あわわわわわ
SFX: AWAWAWAWAWAWAWA (PANIC)
IN THE WORST CASE...
...YOU COULD BE POSSESSED, FALL UNCONSCIOUS, AND NEVER WAKE UP.
WHAAAAT !!!?
TRUE SPOOKY TALES

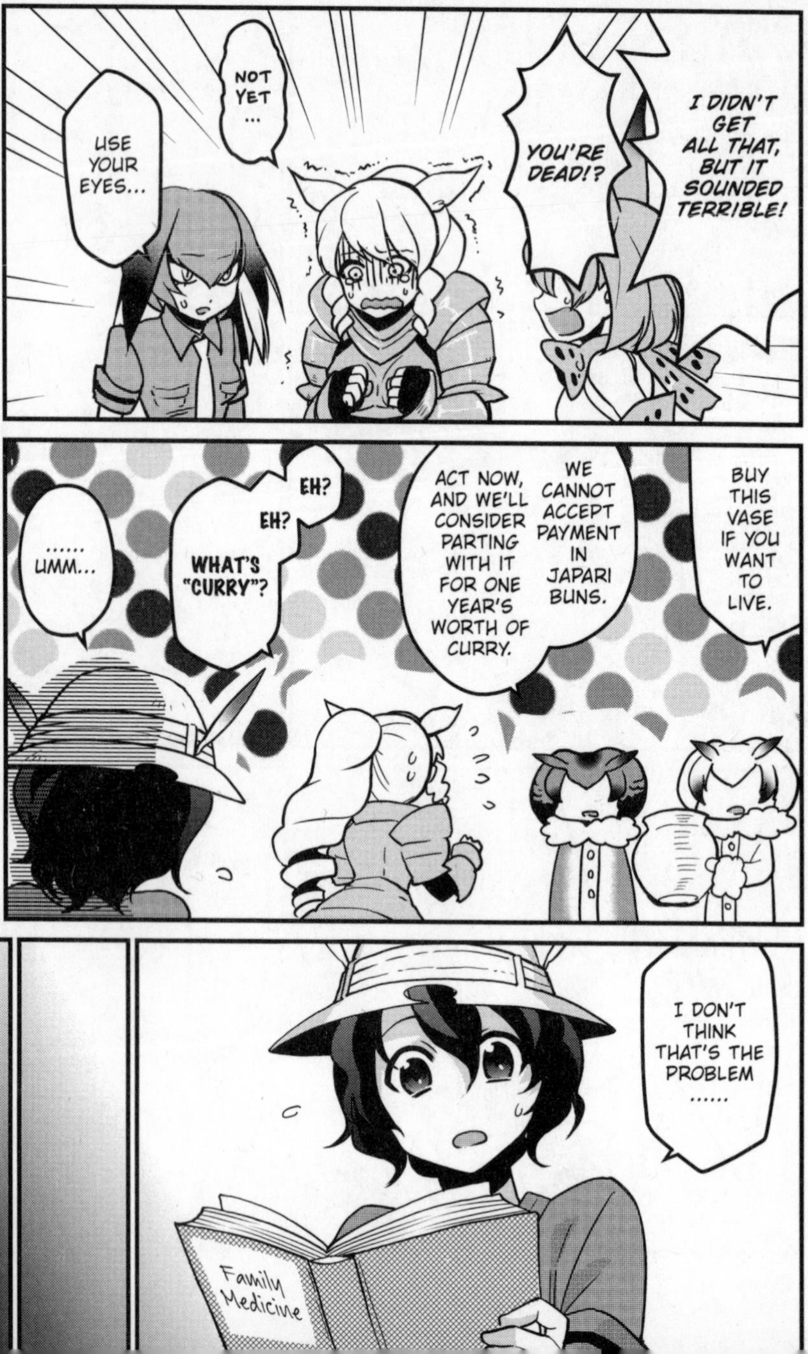
I DIDN'T GET ALL THAT, BUT IT SOUNDED TERRIBLE!
YOU'RE DEAD!?
NOT YET ...
USE YOUR EYES...
BUY THIS VASE IF YOU WANT TO LIVE.
WE CANNOT ACCEPT PAYMENT IN JAPARI BUNS.
ACT NOW, AND WE'LL CONSIDER PARTING WITH IT FOR ONE YEAR'S WORTH OF CURRY.
EH?
EH?
WHAT'S "CURRY"?
...... UMM...
I DON'T THINK THAT'S THE PROBLEM ......
Family Medicine

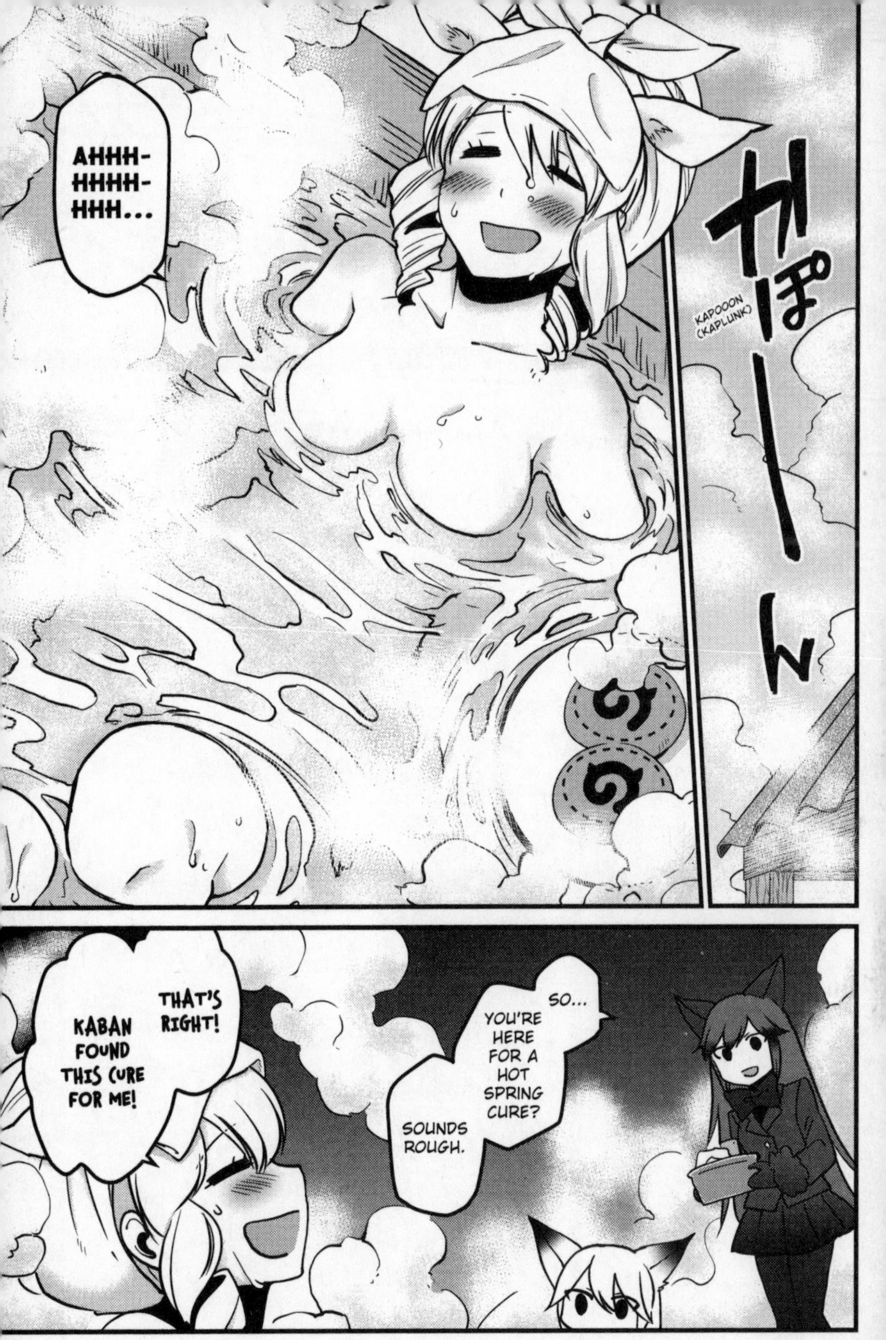
KAPOOON (KAPLUNK)
AHHHHHHHHHHH...
SO... YOU'RE HERE FOR A HOT SPRING CURE?
SOUNDS ROUGH.
THAT'S RIGHT!
KABAN FOUND THIS CURE FOR ME!

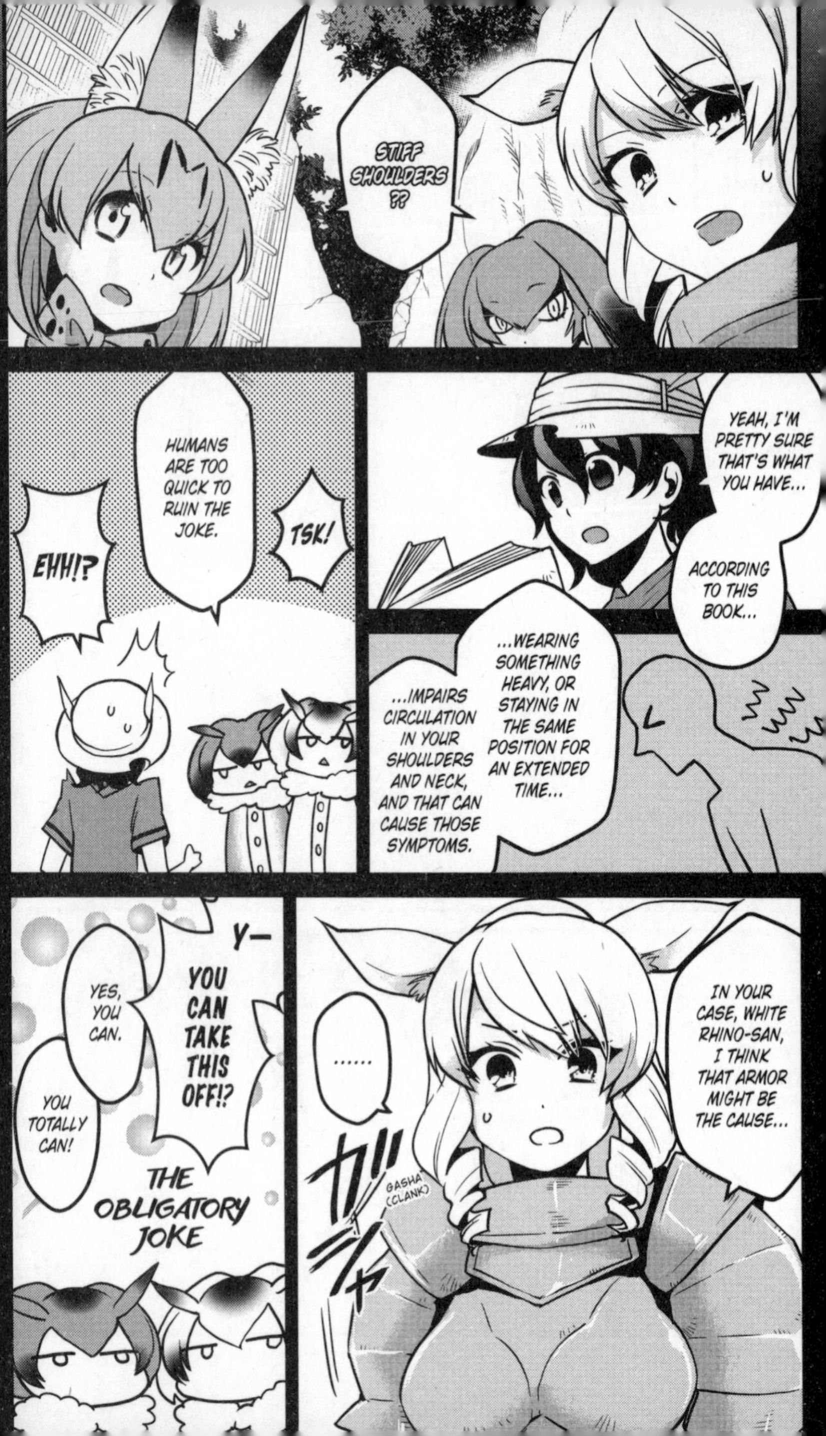
STIFF SHOULDERS ??
YEAH, I'M PRETTY SURE THAT'S WHAT YOU HAVE...
ACCORDING TO THIS BOOK...
...WEARING SOMETHING HEAVY, OR STAYING IN THE SAME POSITION FOR AN EXTENDED TIME...
...IMPAIRS CIRCULATION IN YOUR SHOULDERS AND NECK, AND THAT CAN CAUSE THOSE SYMPTOMS.
TSK!
HUMANS ARE TOO QUICK TO RUIN THE JOKE.
EHH!?
IN YOUR CASE, WHITE RHINO-SAN, I THINK THAT ARMOR MIGHT BE THE CAUSE...
......
GASHA (CLANK)
Y—
YOU CAN TAKE THIS OFF!?
YES, YOU CAN.
YOU TOTALLY CAN!
THE OBLIGATORY JOKE

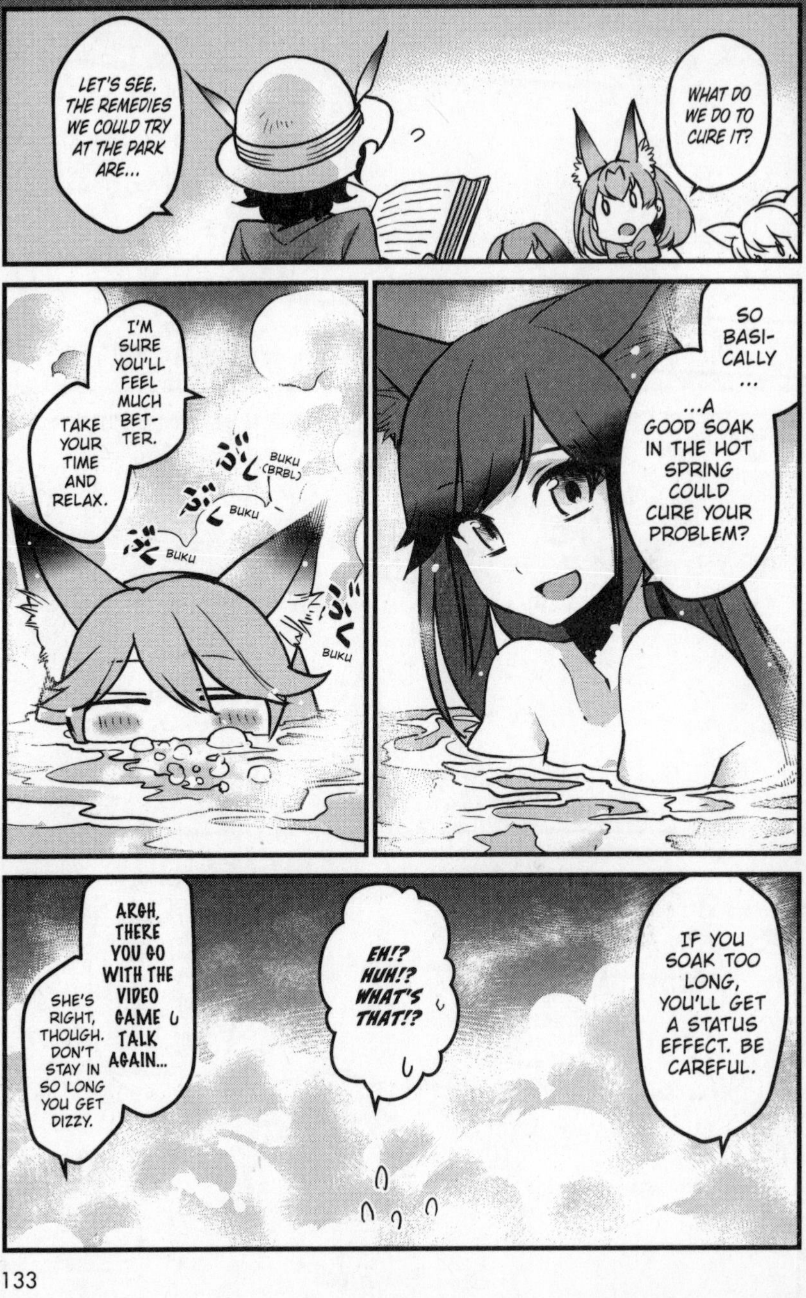
WHAT DO WE DO TO CURE IT?
LET'S SEE. THE REMEDIES WE COULD TRY AT THE PARK ARE...
SO BASICALLY...
...A GOOD SOAK IN THE HOT SPRING COULD CURE YOUR PROBLEM?
I'M SURE YOU'LL FEEL MUCH BETTER.
TAKE YOUR TIME AND RELAX.
BUKU (BRBL)
BUKU
BUKU
BUKU
IF YOU SOAK TOO LONG, YOU'LL GET A STATUS EFFECT. BE CAREFUL.
EH!? HUH!? WHAT'S THAT!?
ARGH, THERE YOU GO WITH THE VIDEO GAME TALK AGAIN...
SHE'S RIGHT, THOUGH. DON'T STAY IN SO LONG YOU GET DIZZY.

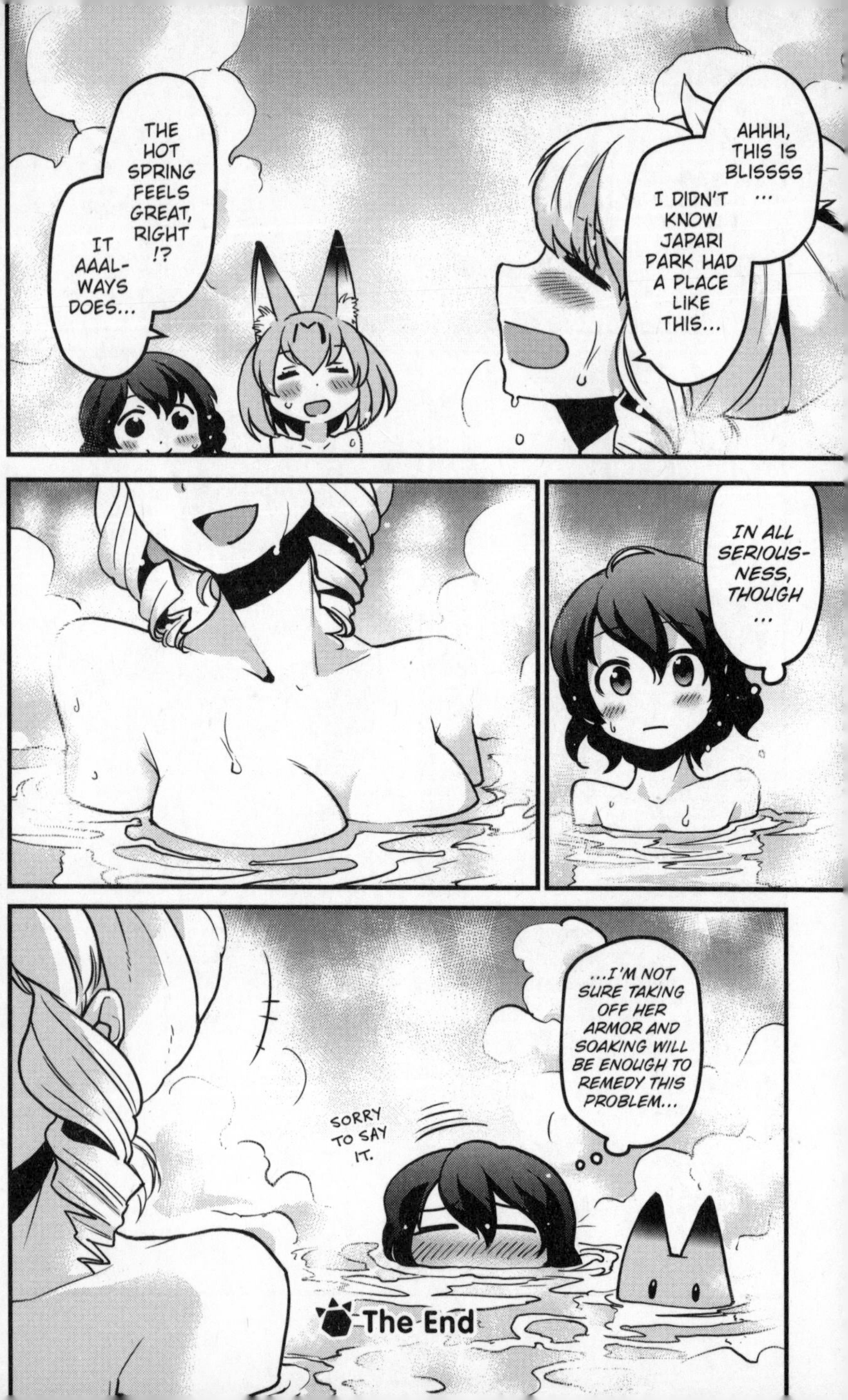
AHHH, THIS IS BLISSSS...
I DIDN'T KNOW JAPARI PARK HAD A PLACE LIKE THIS...
THE HOT SPRING FEELS GREAT, RIGHT!?
IT AAAL-WAYS DOES...
IN ALL SERIOUS-NESS, THOUGH...
...I'M NOT SURE TAKING OFF HER ARMOR AND SOAKING WILL BE ENOUGH TO REMEDY THIS PROBLEM...
SORRY TO SAY IT.
The End

Yajirou Miyaba What Flavor is a Japari Bun?

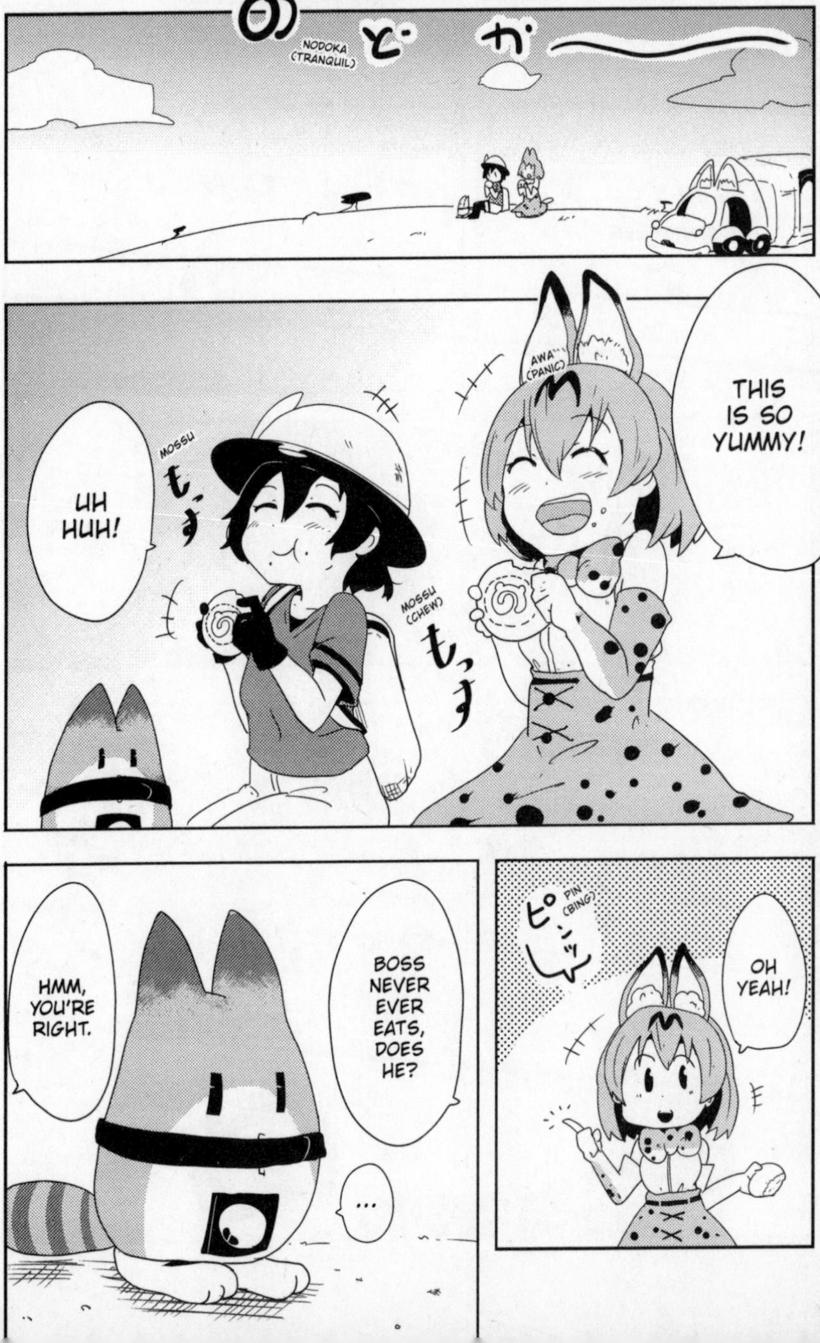
のどか〜〜
NODOKA (TRANQUIL)
THIS IS SO YUMMY!
AWA (PANIC)
MOSSU (CHEW)
もっす
MOSSU
もっす
UH HUH!
PIN (BING)
ピンッ
OH YEAH!
BOSS NEVER EVER EATS, DOES HE?
...
HMM, YOU'RE RIGHT.

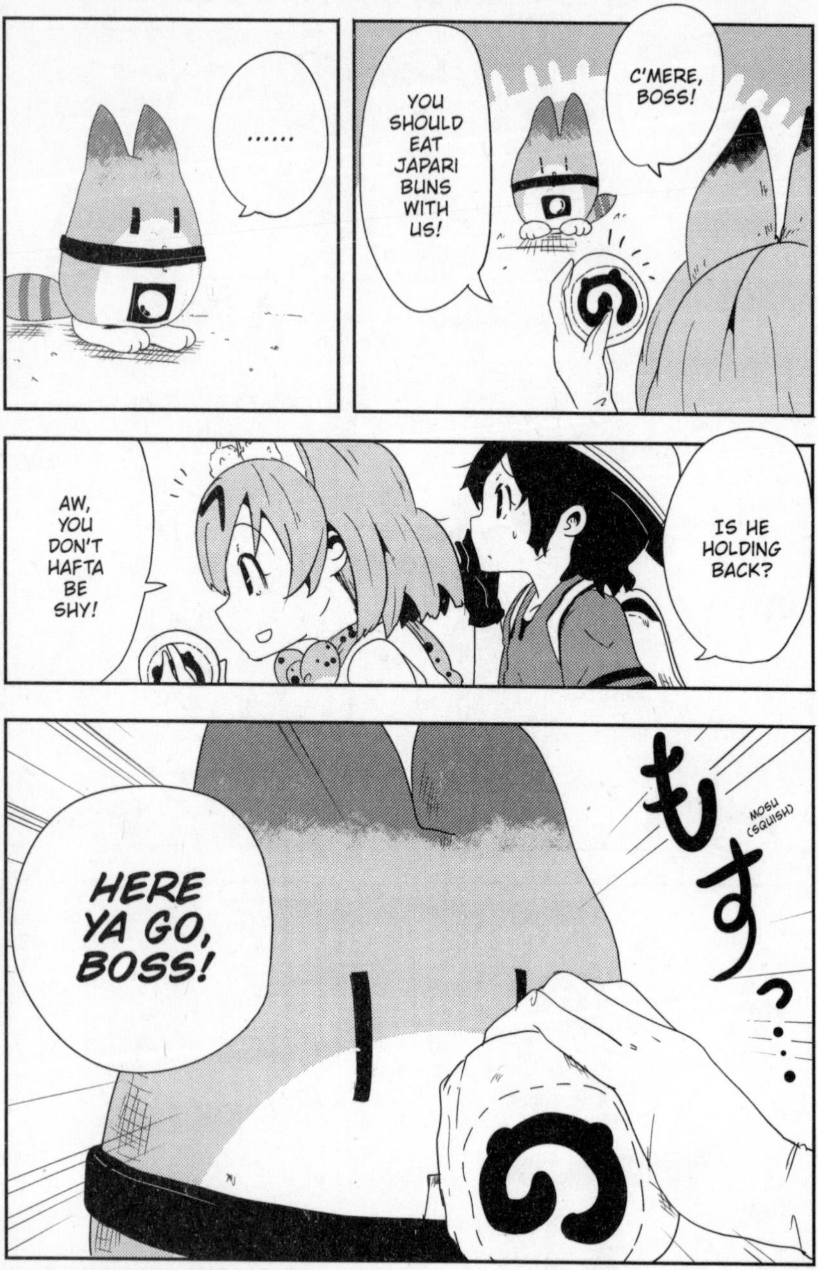
C'MERE, BOSS!
YOU SHOULD EAT JAPARI BUNS WITH US!
......
IS HE HOLDING BACK?
AW, YOU DON'T HAFTA BE SHY!
もすっ...
MOSU (SQUISH)
HERE YA GO, BOSS!

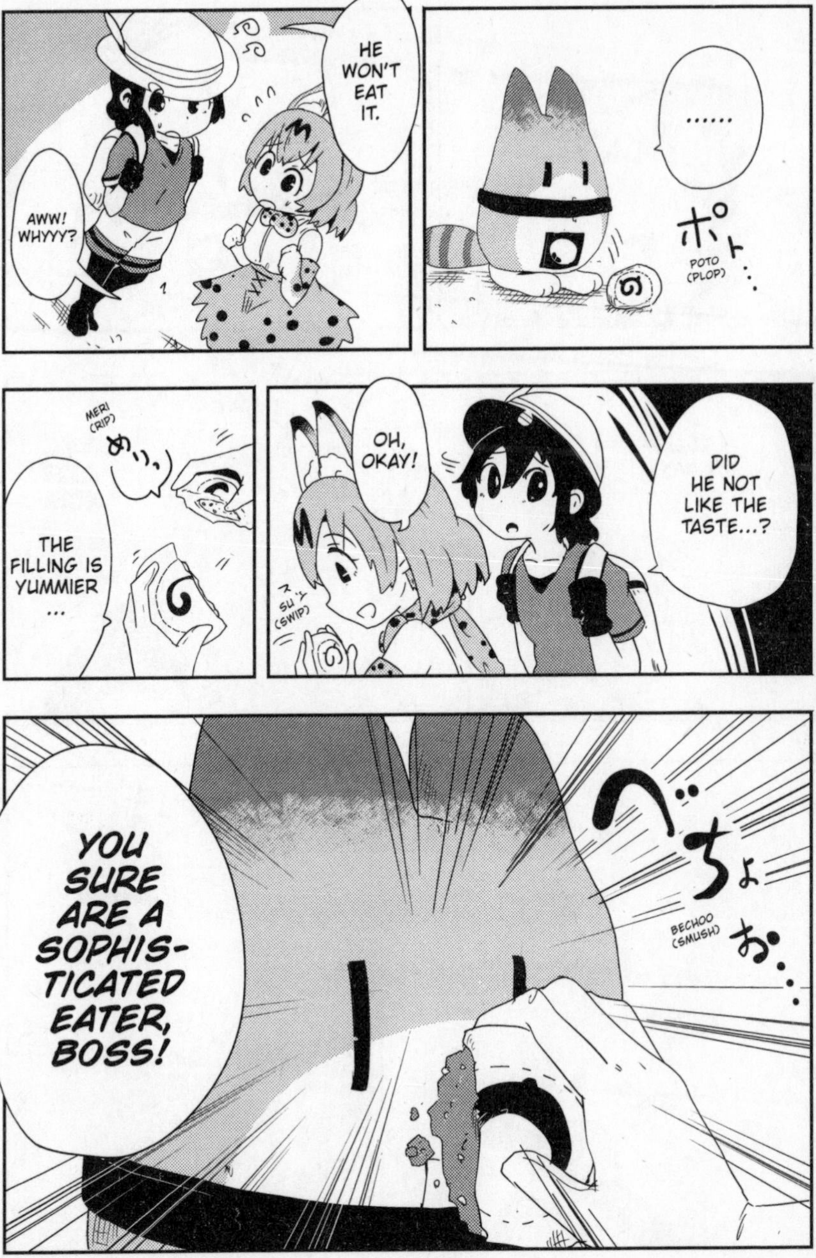

......
ポト…
POTO (PLOP)
HE WON'T EAT IT.
AWW! WHYYY?
DID HE NOT LIKE THE TASTE...?
OH, OKAY!
SU (SWIP)
MERI (RIP)
めりっ
THE FILLING IS YUMMIER ...
べちょぉ…
BECHOO (SMUSH)
YOU SURE ARE A SOPHISTICATED EATER, BOSS!

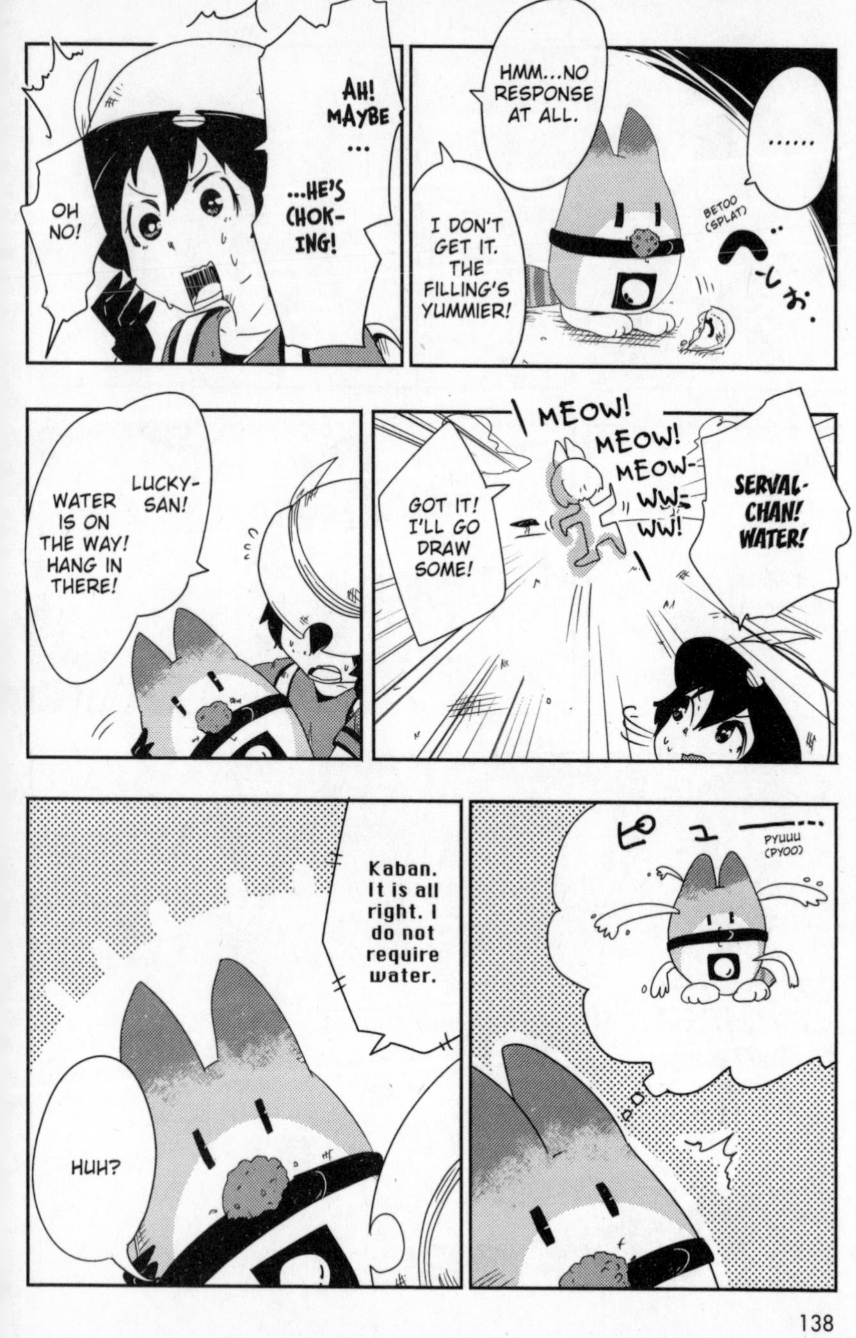
......
HMM...NO RESPONSE AT ALL.
BETOO (SPLAT)
I DON'T GET IT. THE FILLING'S YUMMIER!
AH! MAYBE ...
...HE'S CHOK-ING!
OH NO!
SERVAL-CHAN! WATER!
MEOW! MEOW! MEOW-WWWWW!
GOT IT! I'LL GO DRAW SOME!
LUCKY-SAN!
WATER IS ON THE WAY! HANG IN THERE!
ピュ――…
PYUUU (PYOO)
Kaban. It is all right. I do not require water.
HUH?

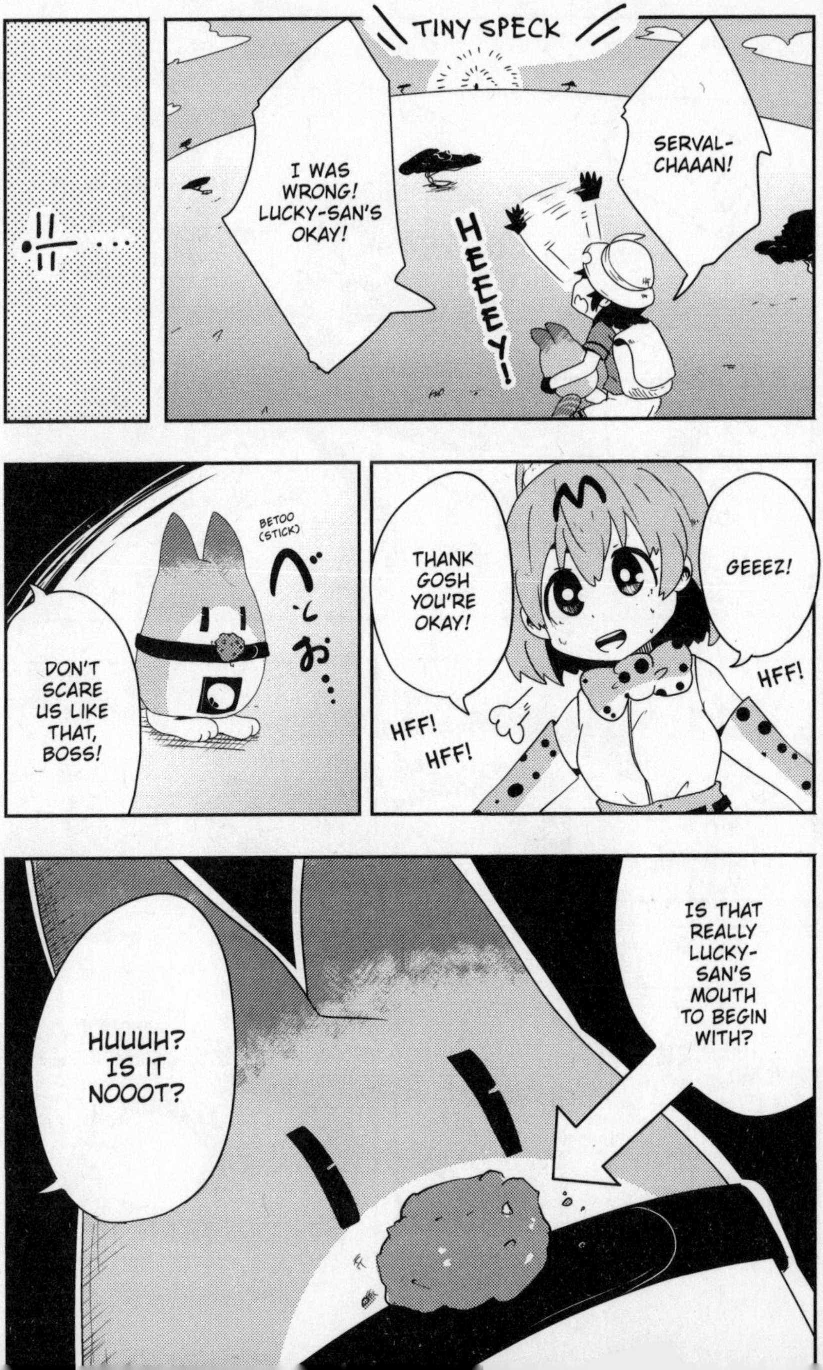
TINY SPECK
SERVAL-CHAAAN!
HEEEEY!
I WAS WRONG! LUCKY-SAN'S OKAY!
!!...
GEEEZ!
HFF!
THANK GOSH YOU'RE OKAY!
HFF! HFF!
べとぉ…
BETOO (STICK)
DON'T SCARE US LIKE THAT, BOSS!
IS THAT REALLY LUCKY-SAN'S MOUTH TO BEGIN WITH?
HUUUH? IS IT NOOOT?

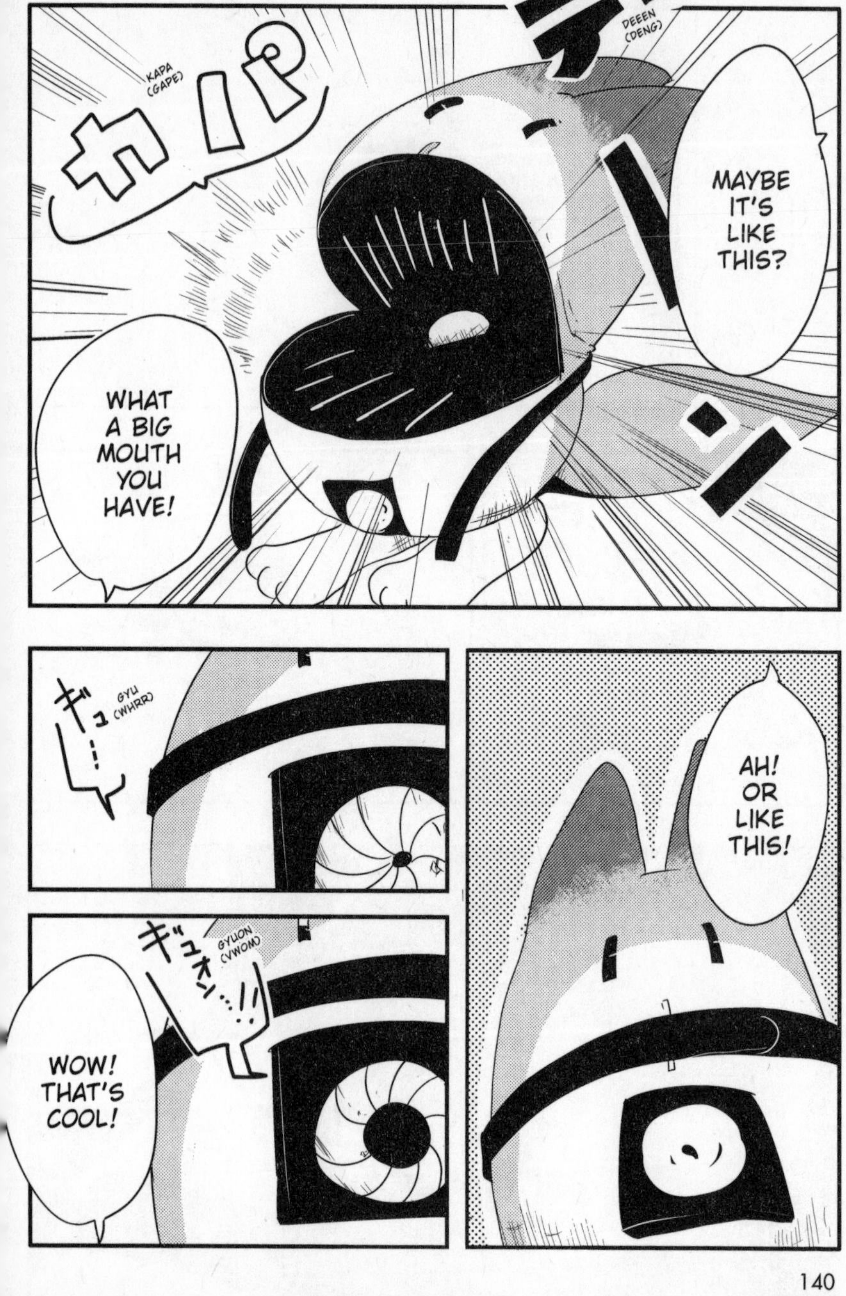
デーン
DEEEN (DENG)
MAYBE IT'S LIKE THIS?
カパ
KAPA (GAPE)
WHAT A BIG MOUTH YOU HAVE!
AH! OR LIKE THIS!
ギュ
GYU (WHRR)
ギュオン
GYUON (VWOM)
WOW! THAT'S COOL!

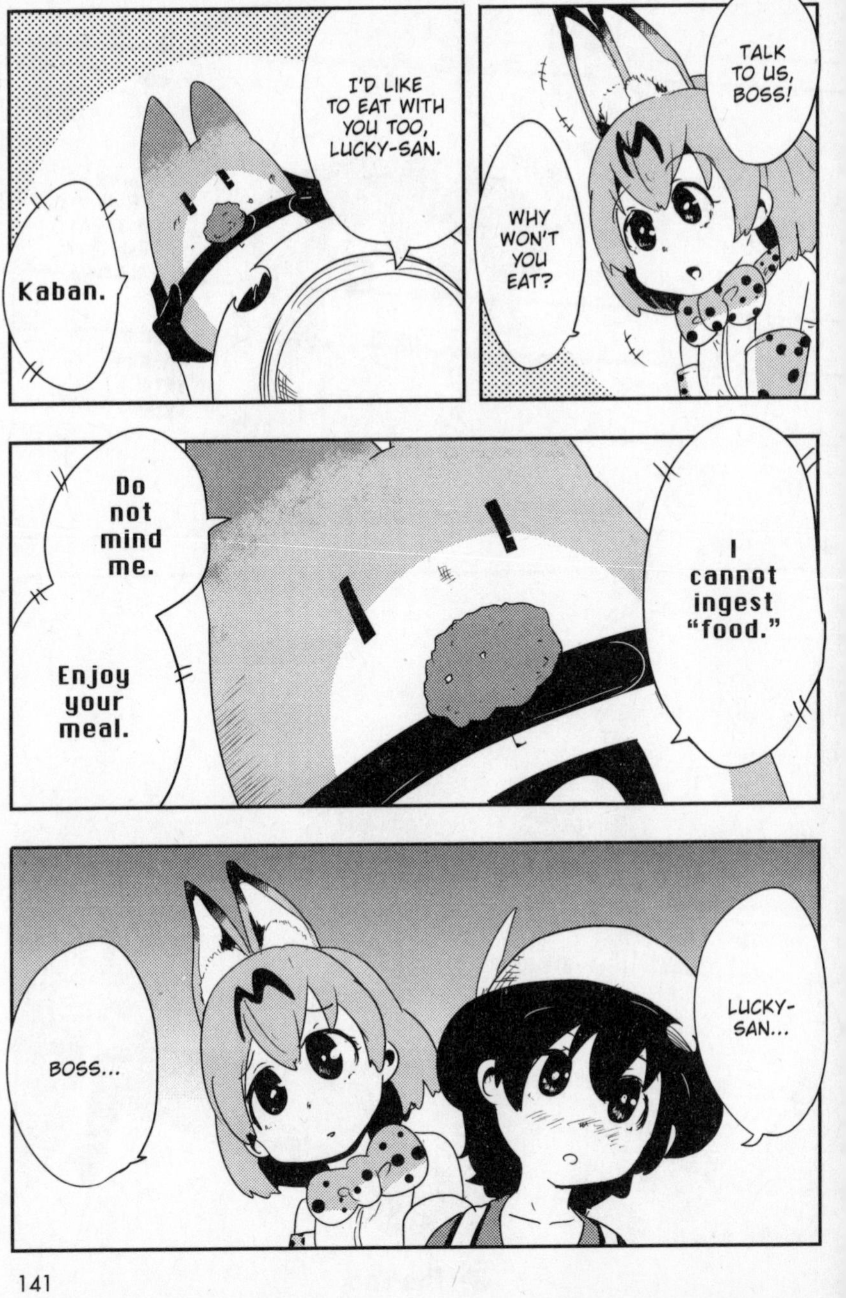
TALK TO US, BOSS!
WHY WON'T YOU EAT?
I'D LIKE TO EAT WITH YOU TOO, LUCKY-SAN.
Kaban.
I cannot ingest "food."
Do not mind me.
Enjoy your meal.
LUCKY-SAN...
BOSS...

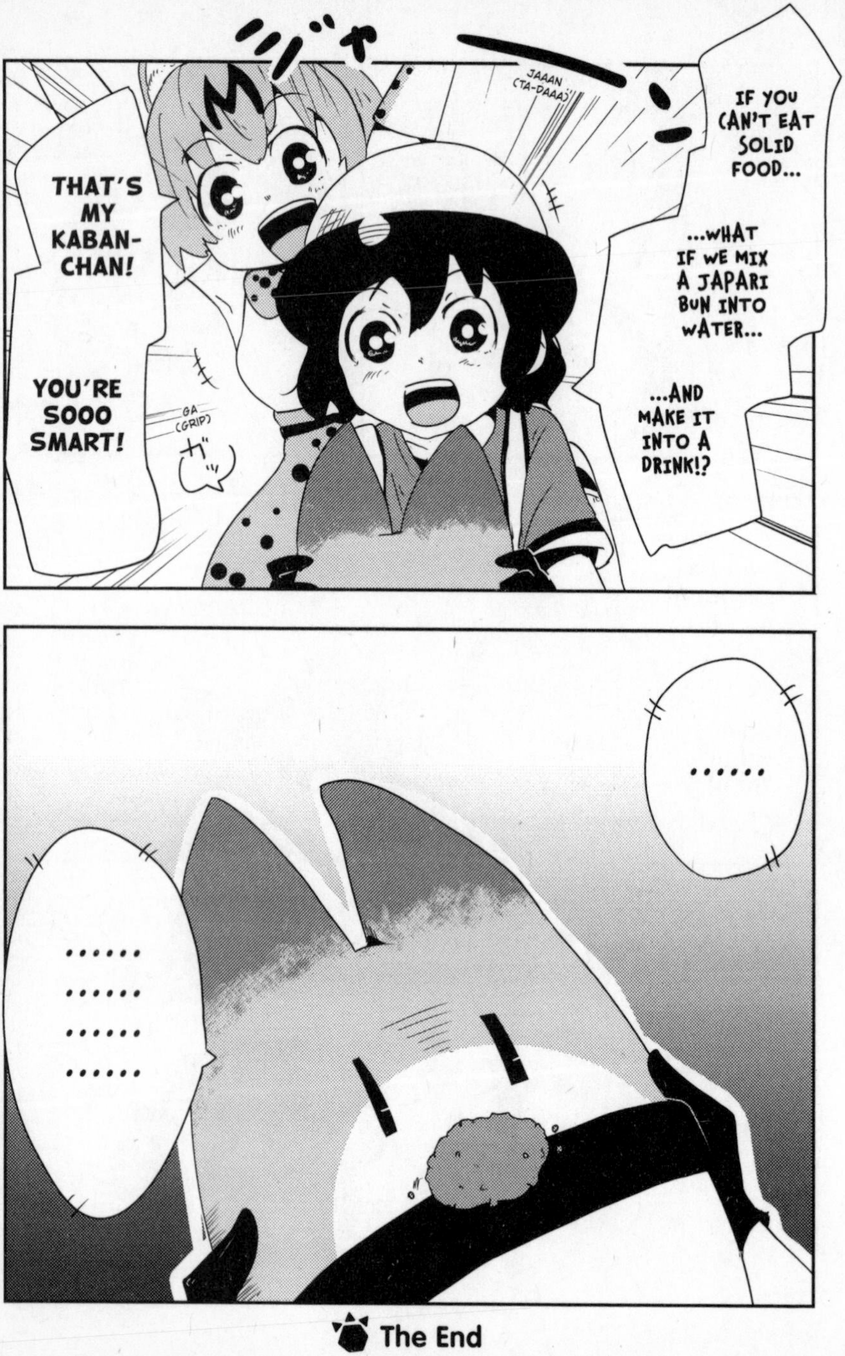
IF YOU CAN'T EAT SOLID FOOD...
...WHAT IF WE MIX A JAPARI BUN INTO WATER...
...AND MAKE IT INTO A DRINK!?
JAAAN (TA-DAAA)
THAT'S MY KABAN-CHAN!
YOU'RE SOOO SMART!
GA (GRIP)
......
......
......
......
......

The End

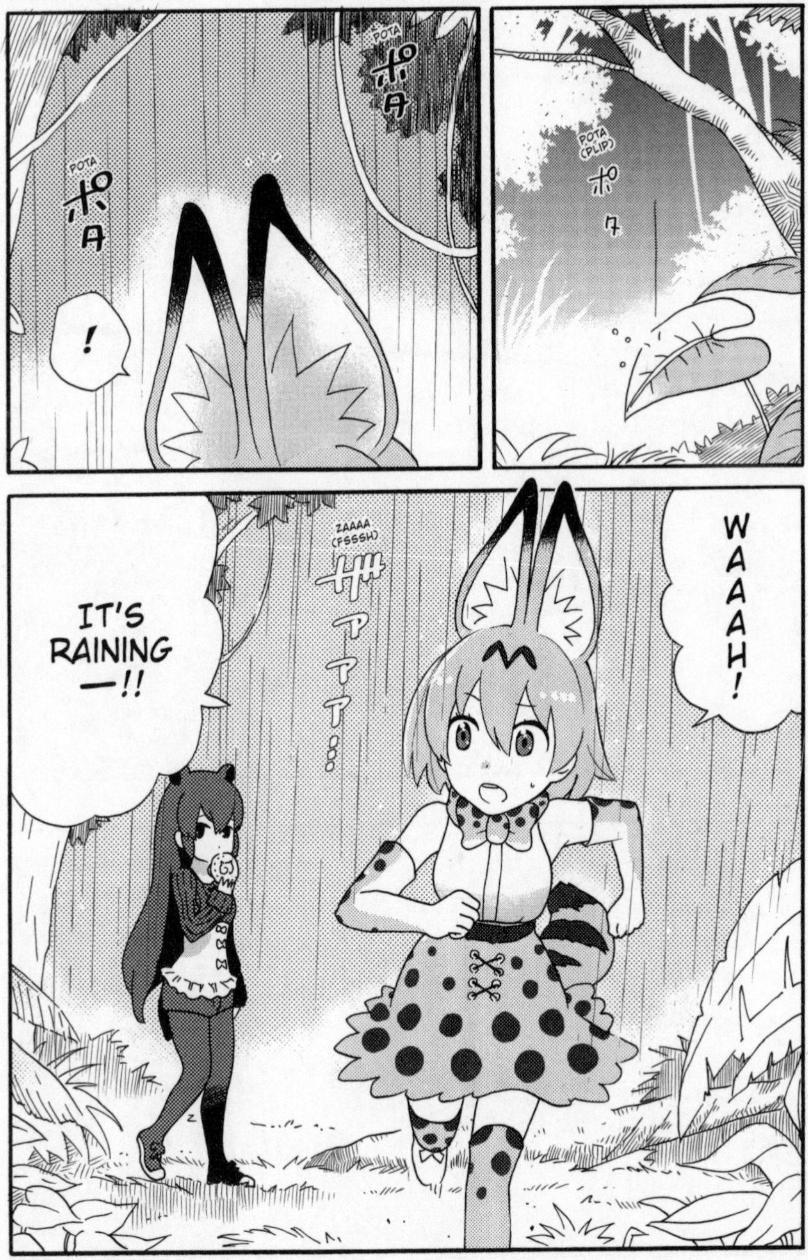
POTA (PLIP)
ポタ
POTA
ポタ
POTA
ポタ
!
WAAAAH!
ZAAAA (FSSSH)
ザァァァ…
IT'S RAINING—!!

Gotsubo x Ryuuji Rain in the Jungle Area

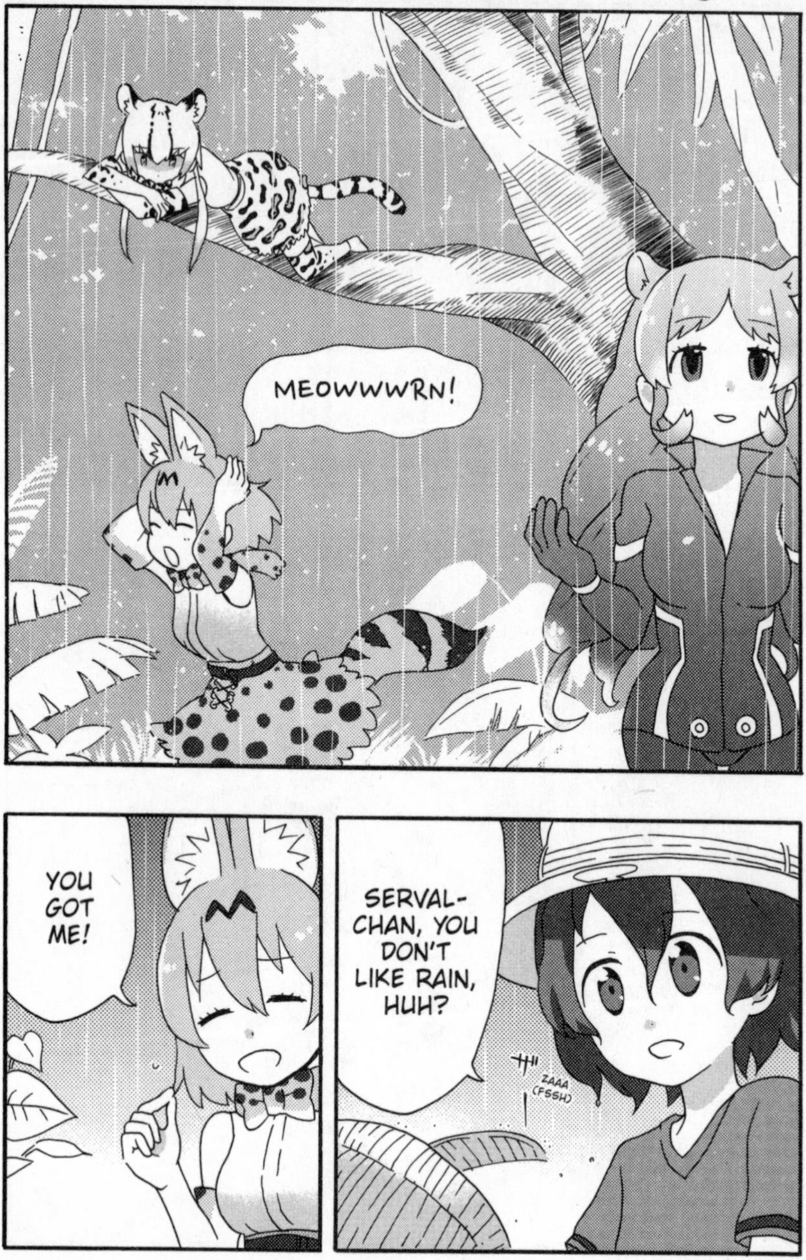
MEOWWWRN!
SERVAL-CHAN, YOU DON'T LIKE RAIN, HUH?
ZAAA (FSSH)
YOU GOT ME!

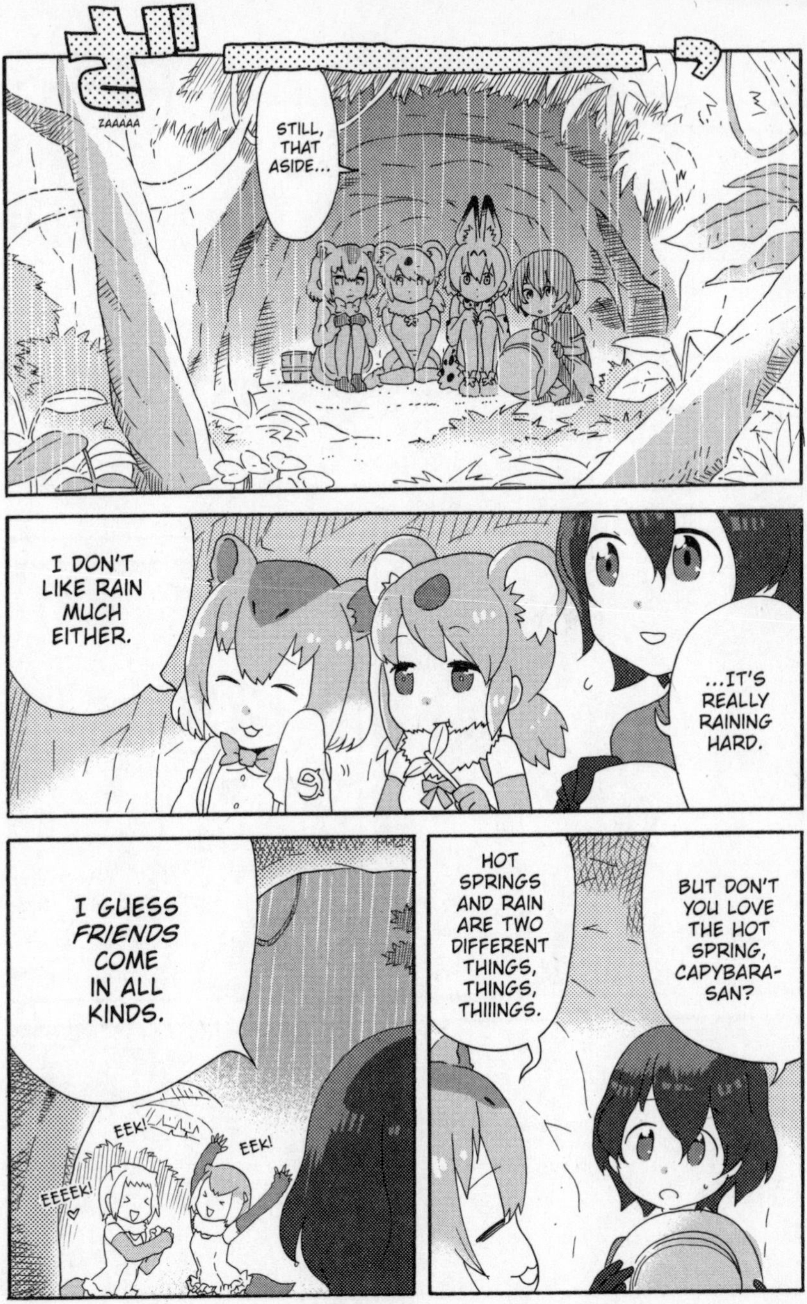
ZAAAAA
STILL, THAT ASIDE...
...IT'S REALLY RAINING HARD.
I DON'T LIKE RAIN MUCH EITHER.
BUT DON'T YOU LOVE THE HOT SPRING, CAPYBARA-SAN?
HOT SPRINGS AND RAIN ARE TWO DIFFERENT THINGS, THINGS, THIIINGS.
I GUESS *FRIENDS* COME IN ALL KINDS.
EEK!
EEK!
EEEEK!

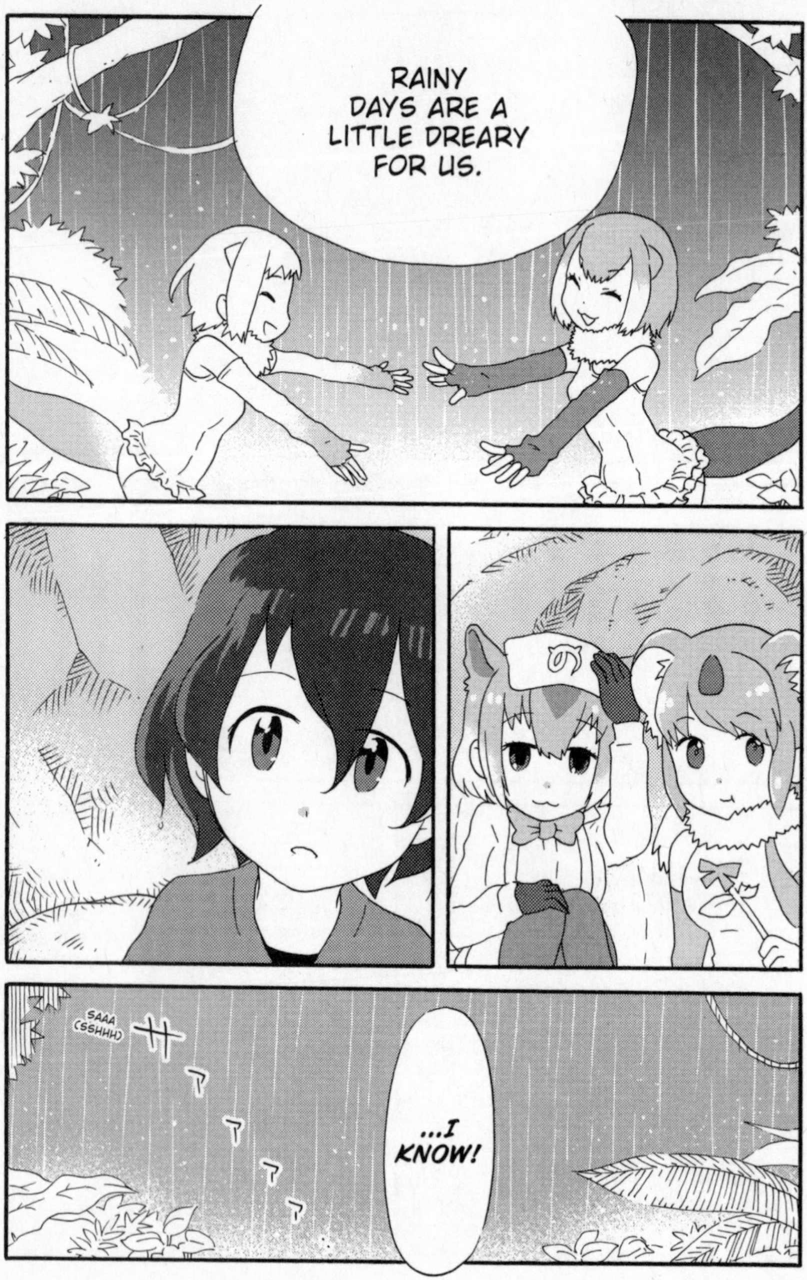
RAINY DAYS ARE A LITTLE DREARY FOR US.
SAAA (SSHHH)
...I KNOW!

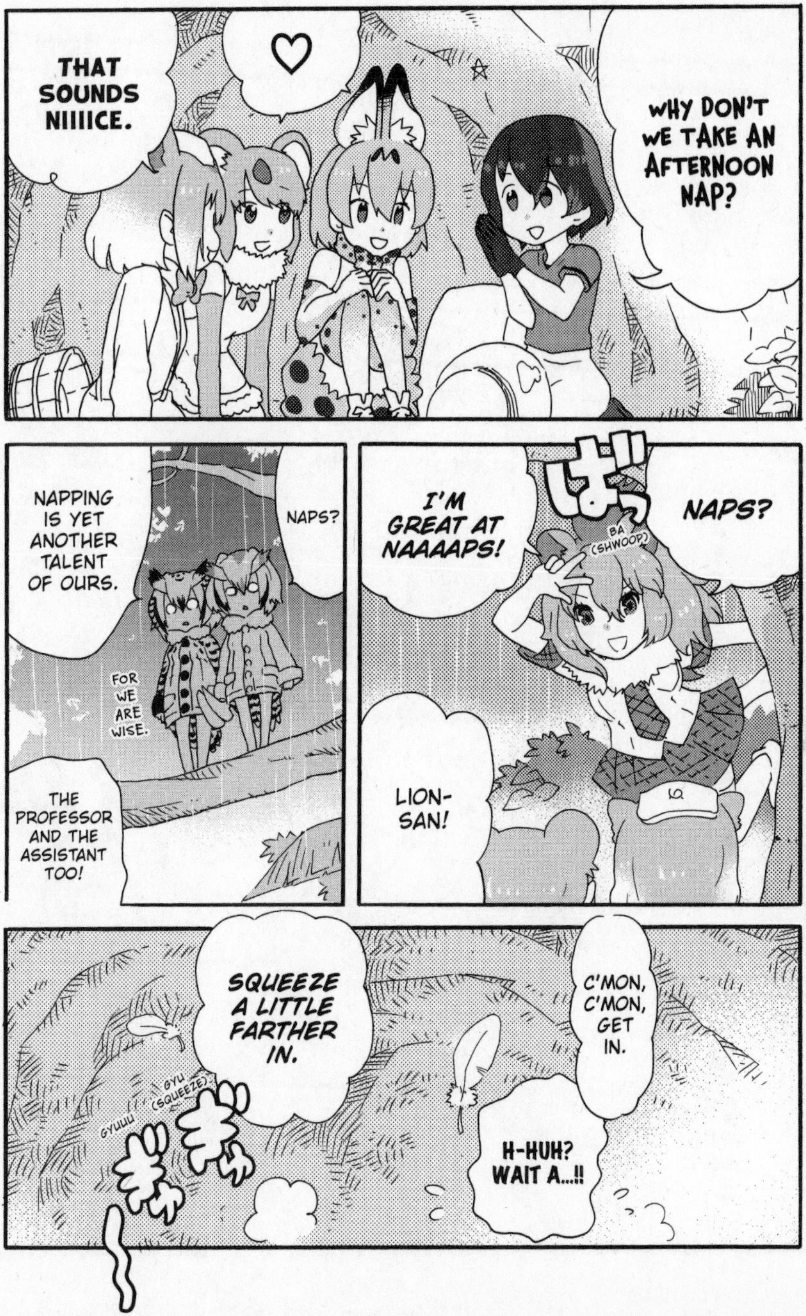
WHY DON'T WE TAKE AN AFTERNOON NAP?
♡
THAT SOUNDS NIIIICE.
NAPS?
ばっ
BA (SHWOOP)
I'M GREAT AT NAAAAPS!
LION-SAN!
NAPS?
NAPPING IS YET ANOTHER TALENT OF OURS.
FOR WE ARE WISE.
THE PROFESSOR AND THE ASSISTANT TOO!
C'MON, C'MON, GET IN.
SQUEEZE A LITTLE FARTHER IN.
H-HUH? WAIT A...!!
GYU (SQUEEZE)
GYUUU

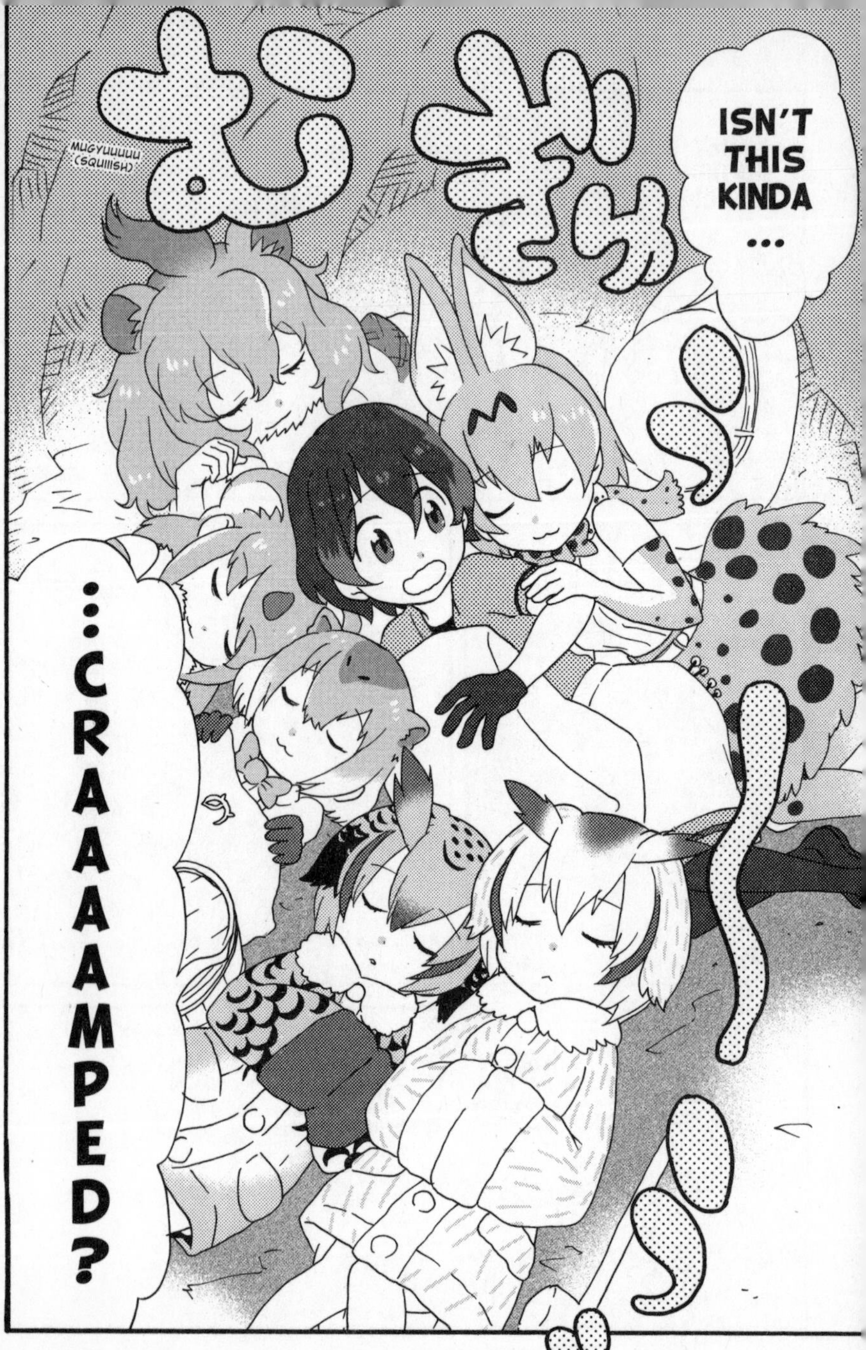
ISN'T THIS KINDA ...
むぎゅ
MUGYUUUUU (SQUIIISH)
...CRAAAAMPED?

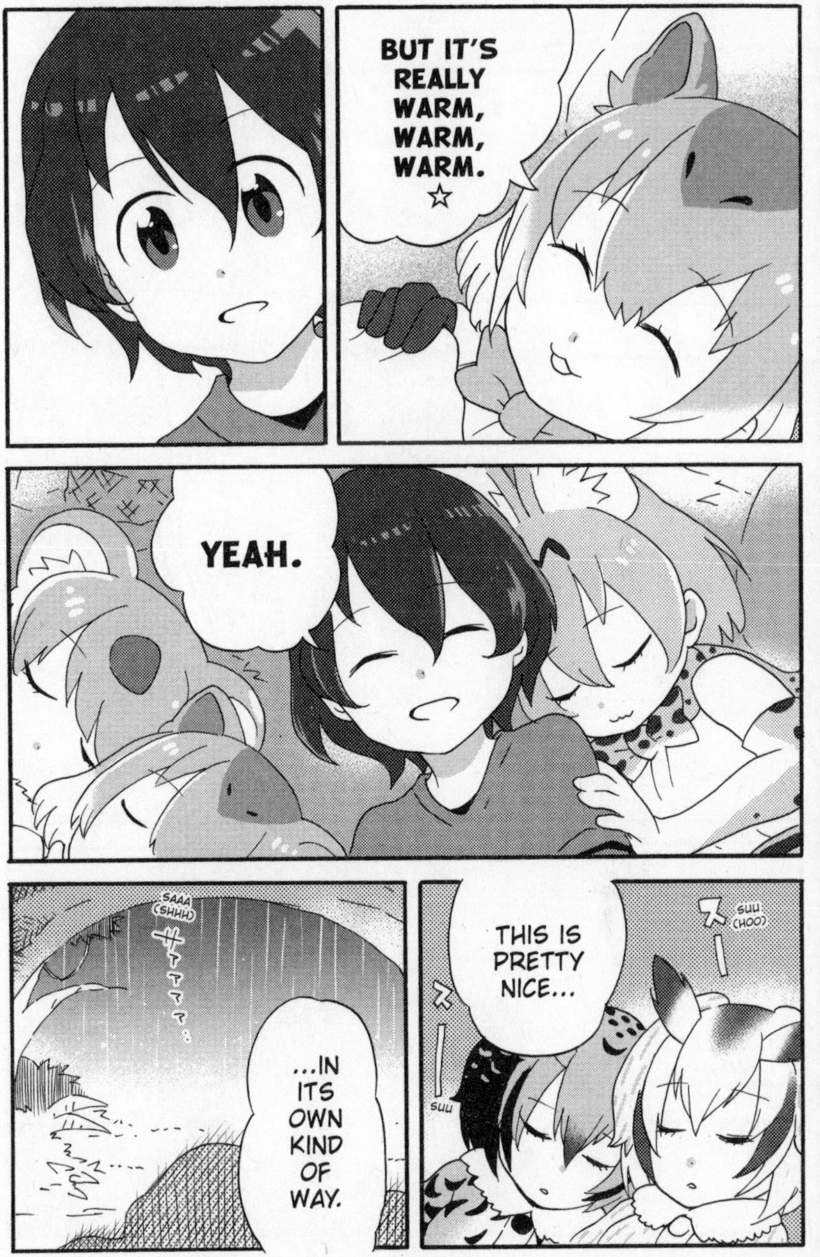
BUT IT'S REALLY WARM, WARM, WARM. ☆
YEAH.
スー
SUU (HOO)
THIS IS PRETTY NICE...
スー
SUU
SAAA (SHHH)
ザァァァ…
...IN ITS OWN KIND OF WAY.

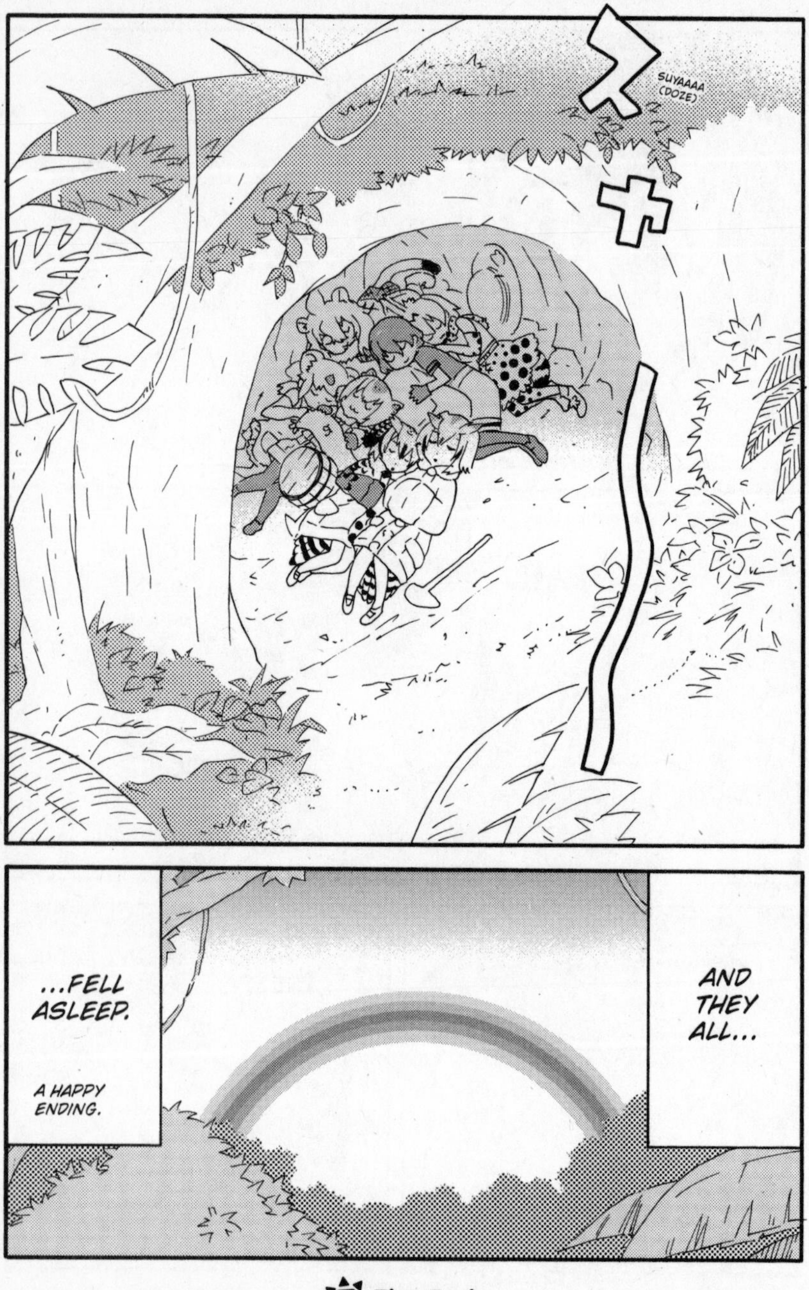

スヤー
SUYAAAA (DOZE)
AND THEY ALL...
...FELL ASLEEP.
A HAPPY ENDING.

The End

Kemono Friends
Question

 WHAT'S THAT
ANIMAL?

HINT

One of the most intelligent birds, with a distinct deep "Caw-caw" cry. Not the same as the bird that cries "Graa-graa."

Turn the page for the answer!

Kemono Friends

Answer

A4

JUNGLE CROW

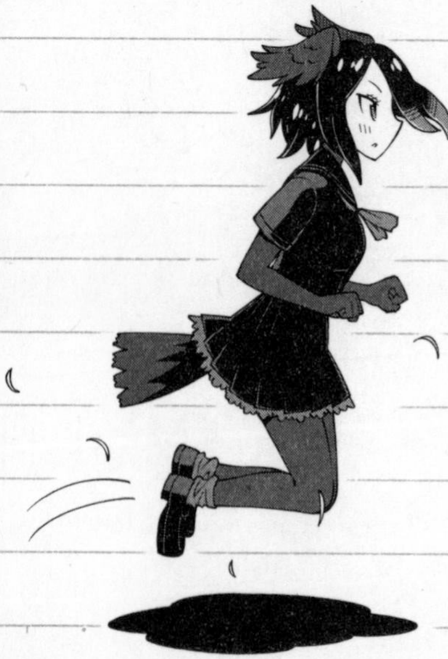

THE PROFESSOR, THE ASSISTANT & FERMENTATION

Gratin Bird

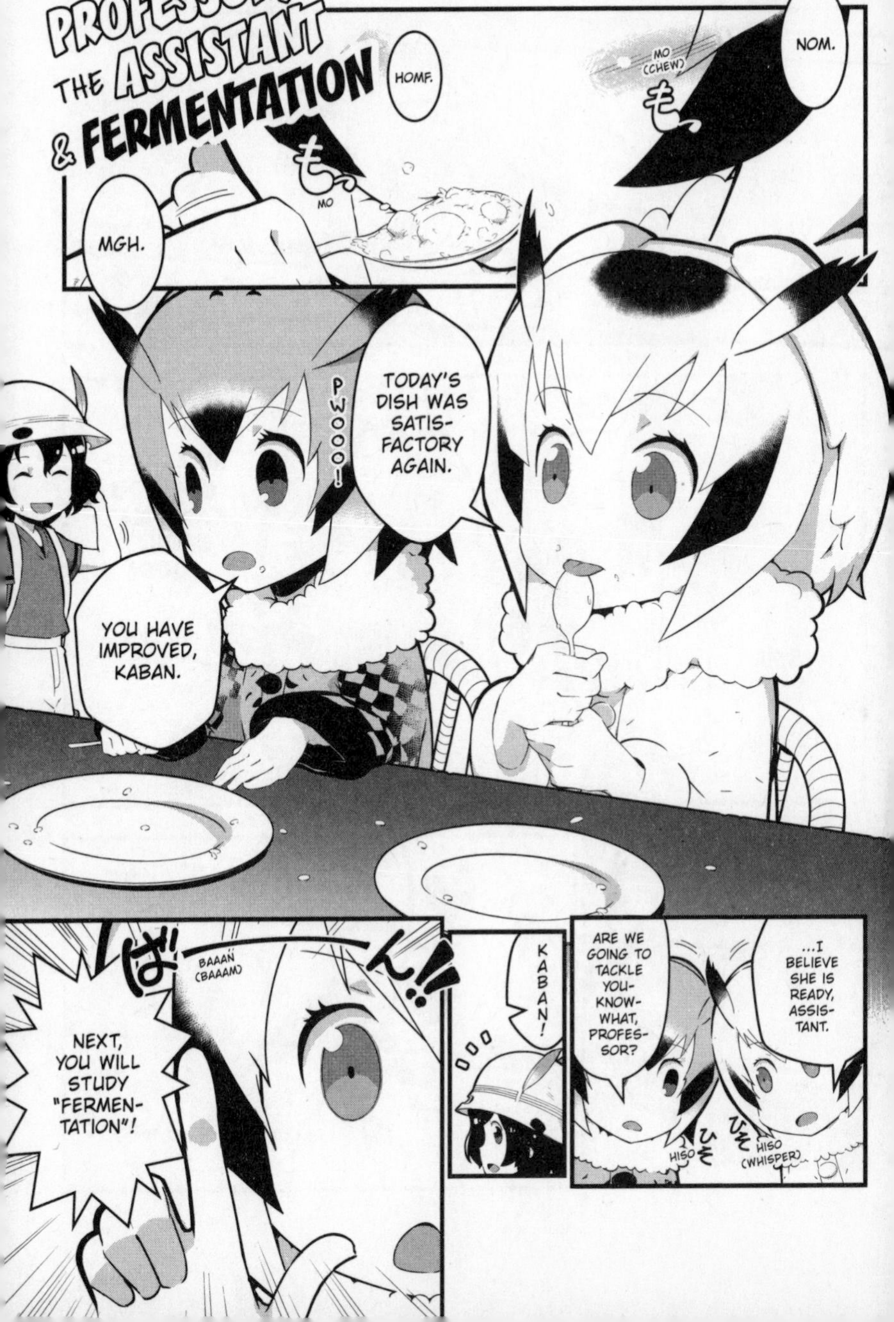
NOM.
MO (CHEW)
もっ
HOMF.
もっ
MO
MGH.
TODAY'S DISH WAS SATIS-FACTORY AGAIN.
PWOOO!
YOU HAVE IMPROVED, KABAN.
...I BELIEVE SHE IS READY, ASSIS-TANT.
ARE WE GOING TO TACKLE YOU-KNOW-WHAT, PROFES-SOR?
ひそ
HISO (WHISPER)
ひそ
HISO
KABAN!
ばーーん!!
BAAAN (BAAAM)
NEXT, YOU WILL STUDY "FERMEN-TATION"!

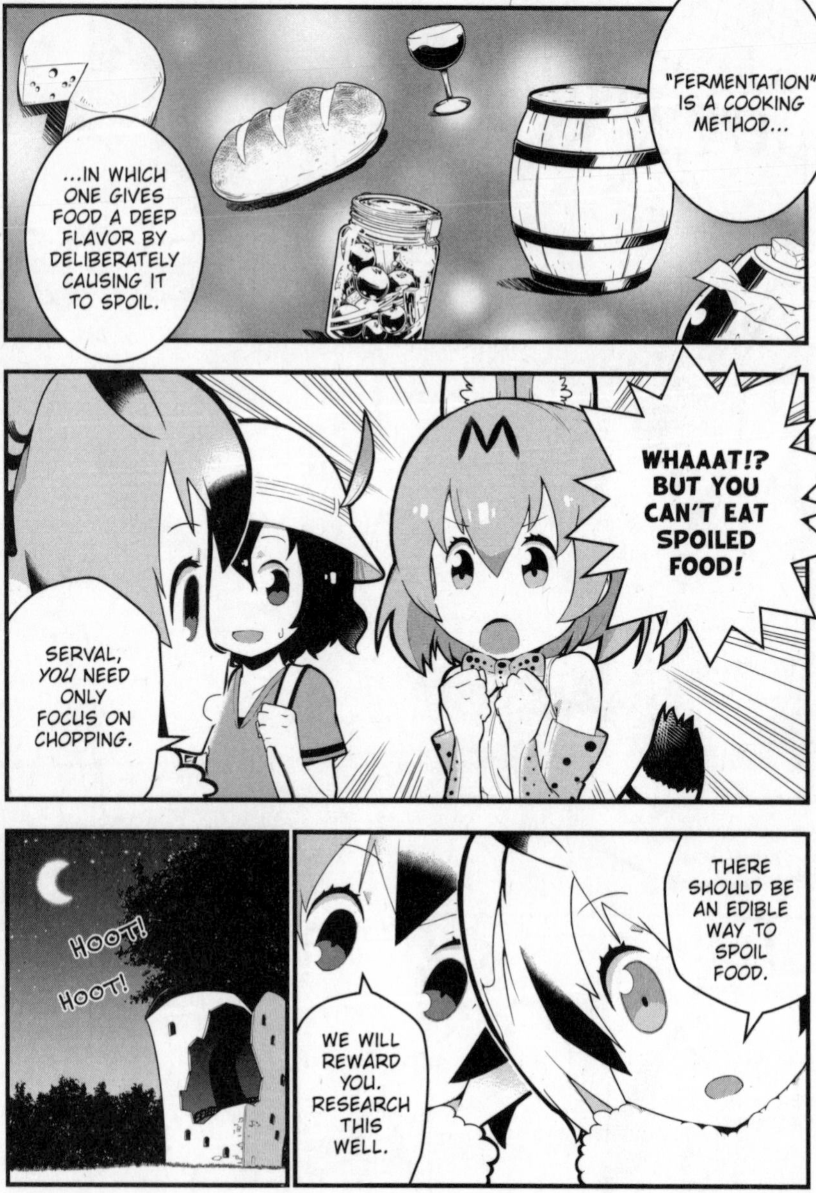
"FERMENTATION" IS A COOKING METHOD...
...IN WHICH ONE GIVES FOOD A DEEP FLAVOR BY DELIBERATELY CAUSING IT TO SPOIL.
WHAAAT!? BUT YOU CAN'T EAT SPOILED FOOD!
SERVAL, *YOU* NEED ONLY FOCUS ON CHOPPING.
THERE SHOULD BE AN EDIBLE WAY TO SPOIL FOOD.
WE WILL REWARD YOU. RESEARCH THIS WELL.
HOOT!
HOOT!

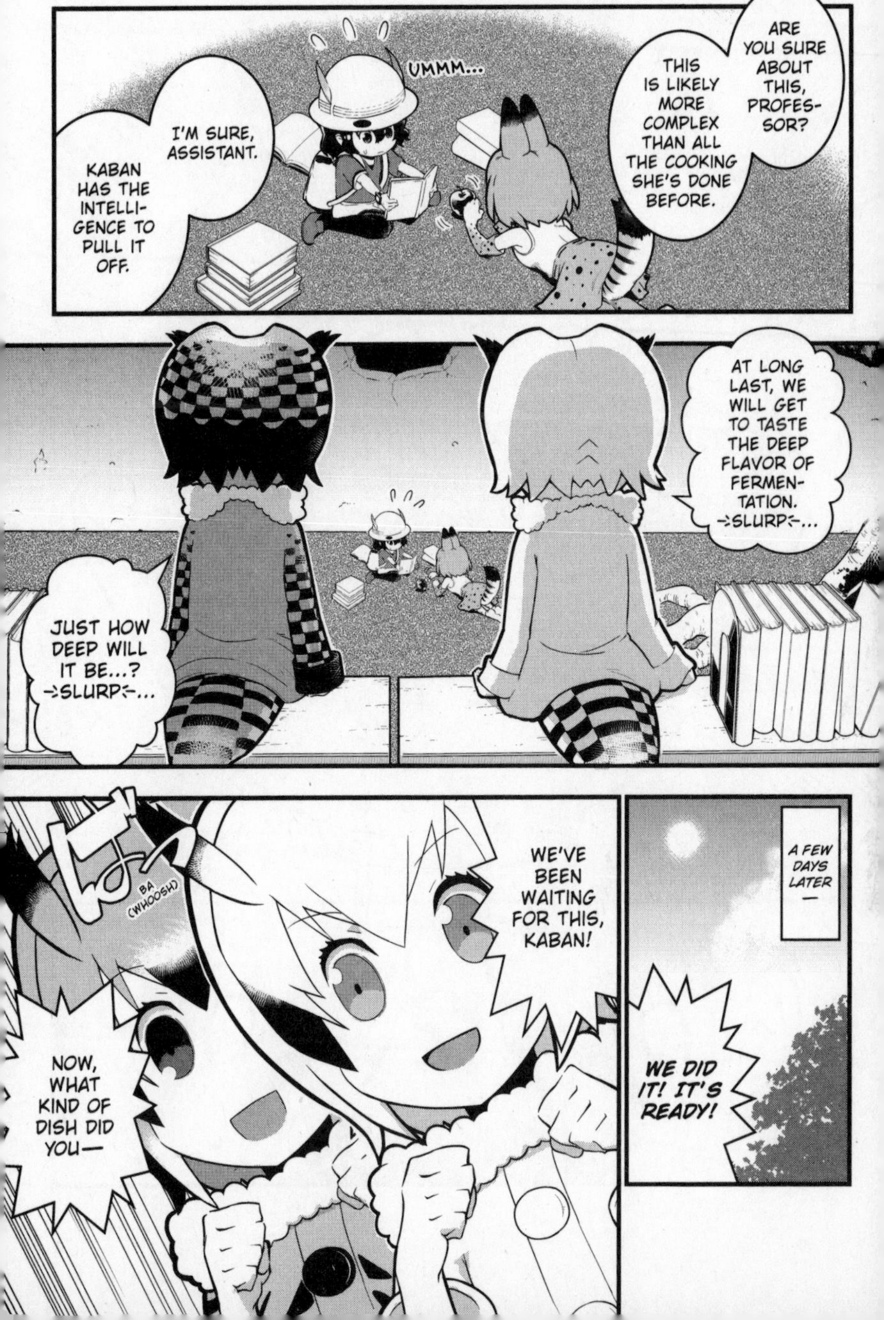
ARE YOU SURE ABOUT THIS, PROFESSOR?
THIS IS LIKELY MORE COMPLEX THAN ALL THE COOKING SHE'S DONE BEFORE.
UMMM...
I'M SURE, ASSISTANT.
KABAN HAS THE INTELLIGENCE TO PULL IT OFF.
AT LONG LAST, WE WILL GET TO TASTE THE DEEP FLAVOR OF FERMENTATION. ~SLURP~...
JUST HOW DEEP WILL IT BE...? ~SLURP~...
A FEW DAYS LATER—
WE DID IT! IT'S READY!
WE'VE BEEN WAITING FOR THIS, KABAN!
BA (WHOOSH)
NOW, WHAT KIND OF DISH DID YOU—

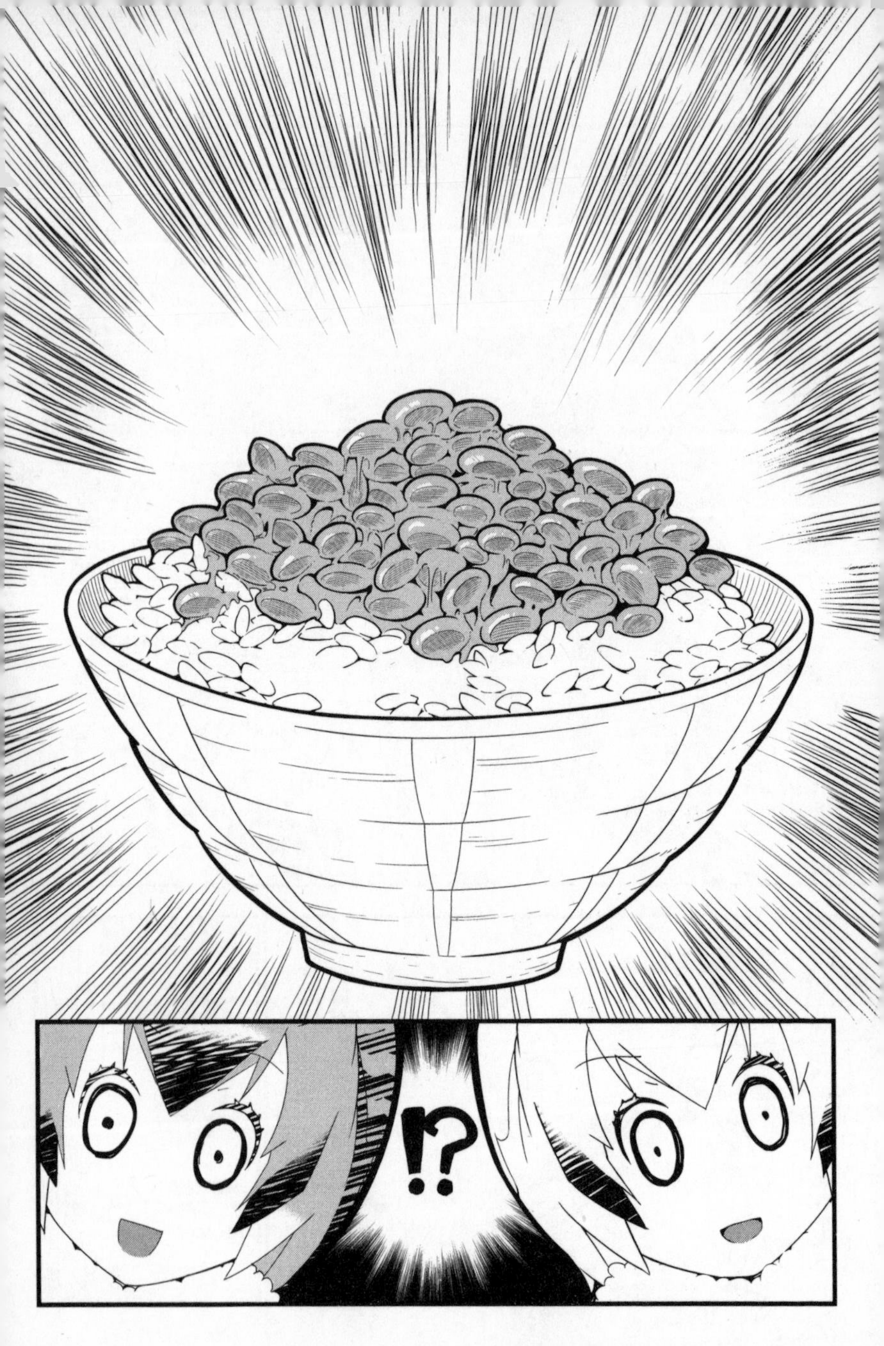
!?

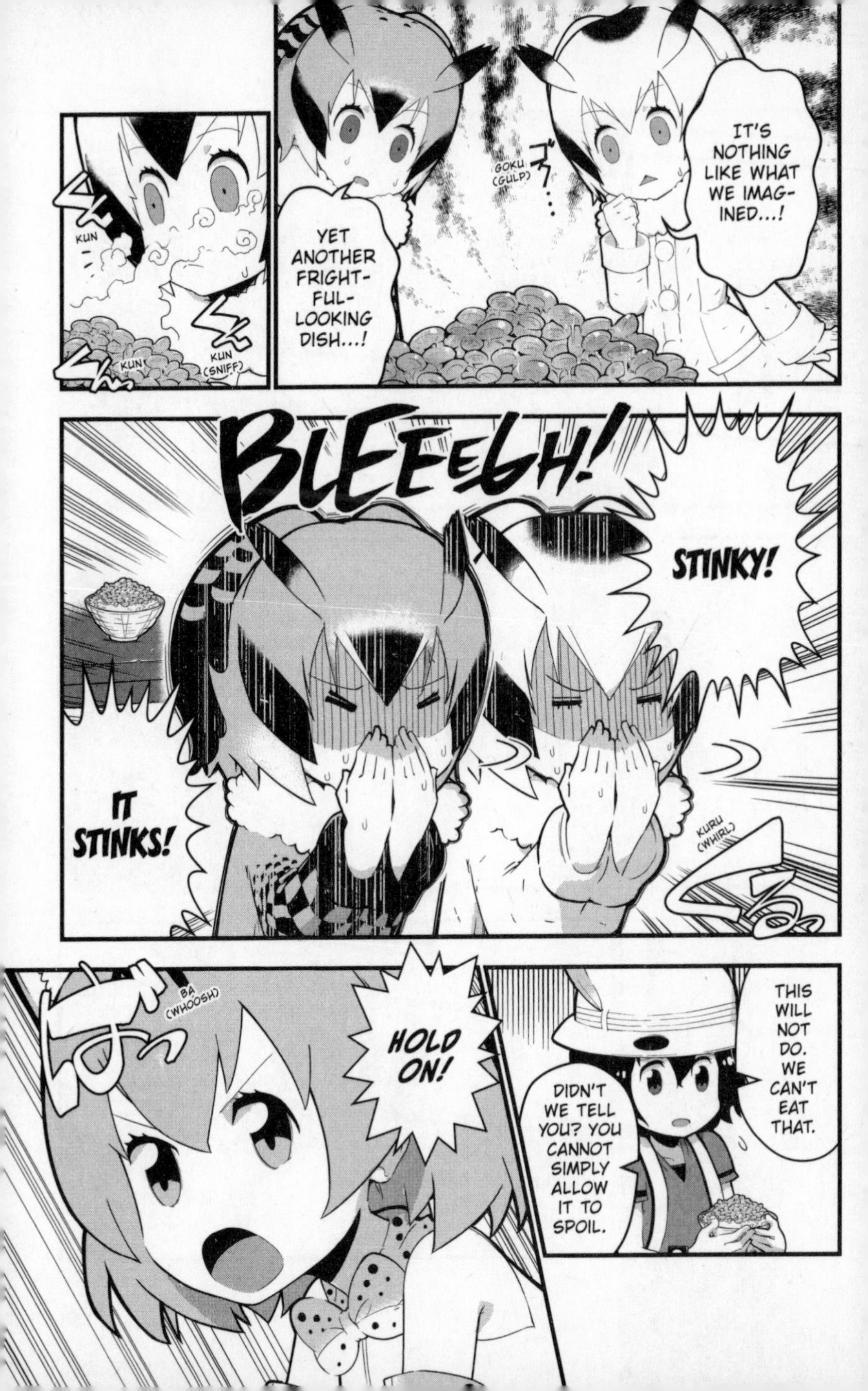
IT'S NOTHING LIKE WHAT WE IMAG-INED...!
GOKU (GULP)
YET ANOTHER FRIGHT-FUL-LOOKING DISH...!
KUN
KUN (SNIFF)
KUN
BLEEEGH!
STINKY!
KURU (WHIRL)
IT STINKS!
THIS WILL NOT DO. WE CAN'T EAT THAT.
DIDN'T WE TELL YOU? YOU CANNOT SIMPLY ALLOW IT TO SPOIL.
HOLD ON!
BA (WHOOSH)

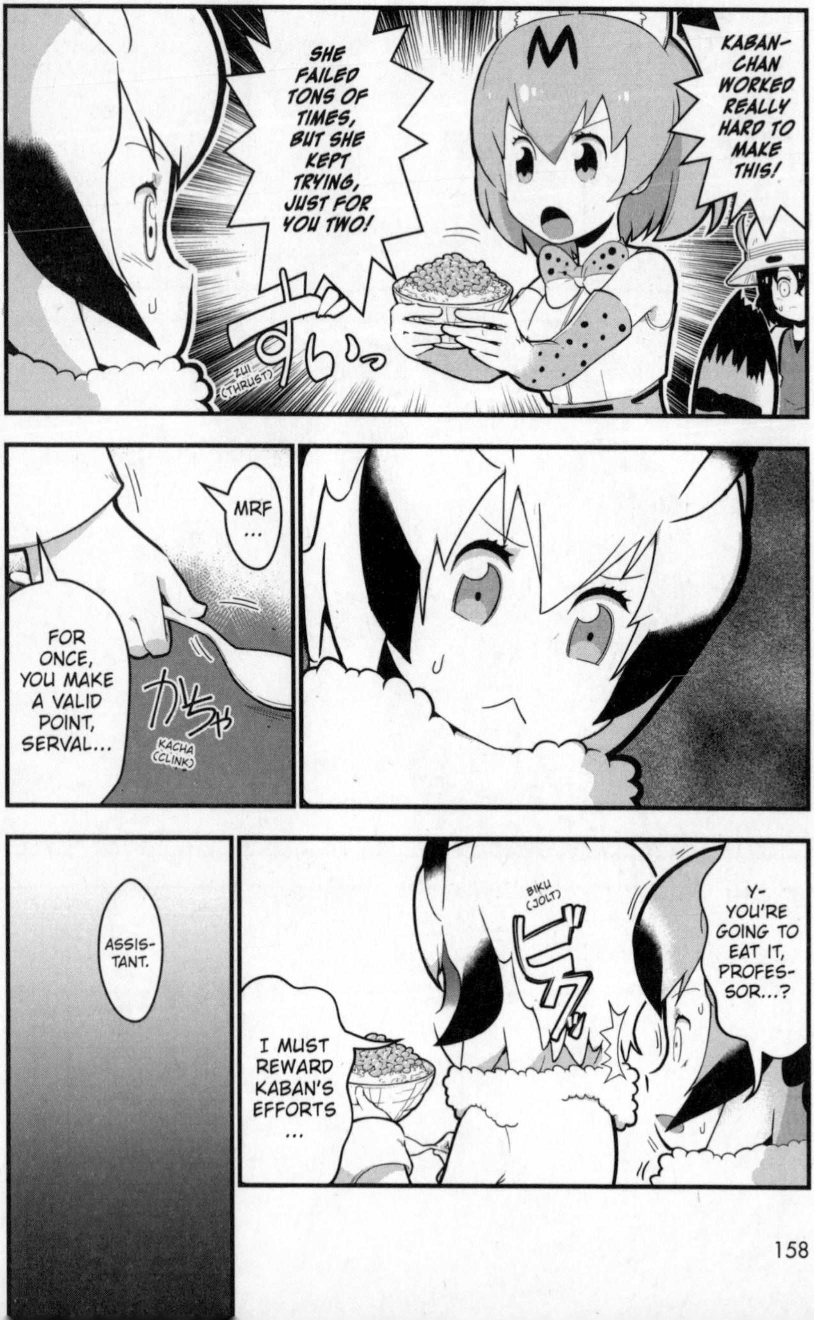
KABAN-CHAN WORKED REALLY HARD TO MAKE THIS!
SHE FAILED TONS OF TIMES, BUT SHE KEPT TRYING, JUST FOR YOU TWO!
ZUI (THRUST)
MRF...
FOR ONCE, YOU MAKE A VALID POINT, SERVAL...
KACHA (CLINK)
Y-YOU'RE GOING TO EAT IT, PROFESSOR...?
BIKU (JOLT)
I MUST REWARD KABAN'S EFFORTS...
ASSISTANT.

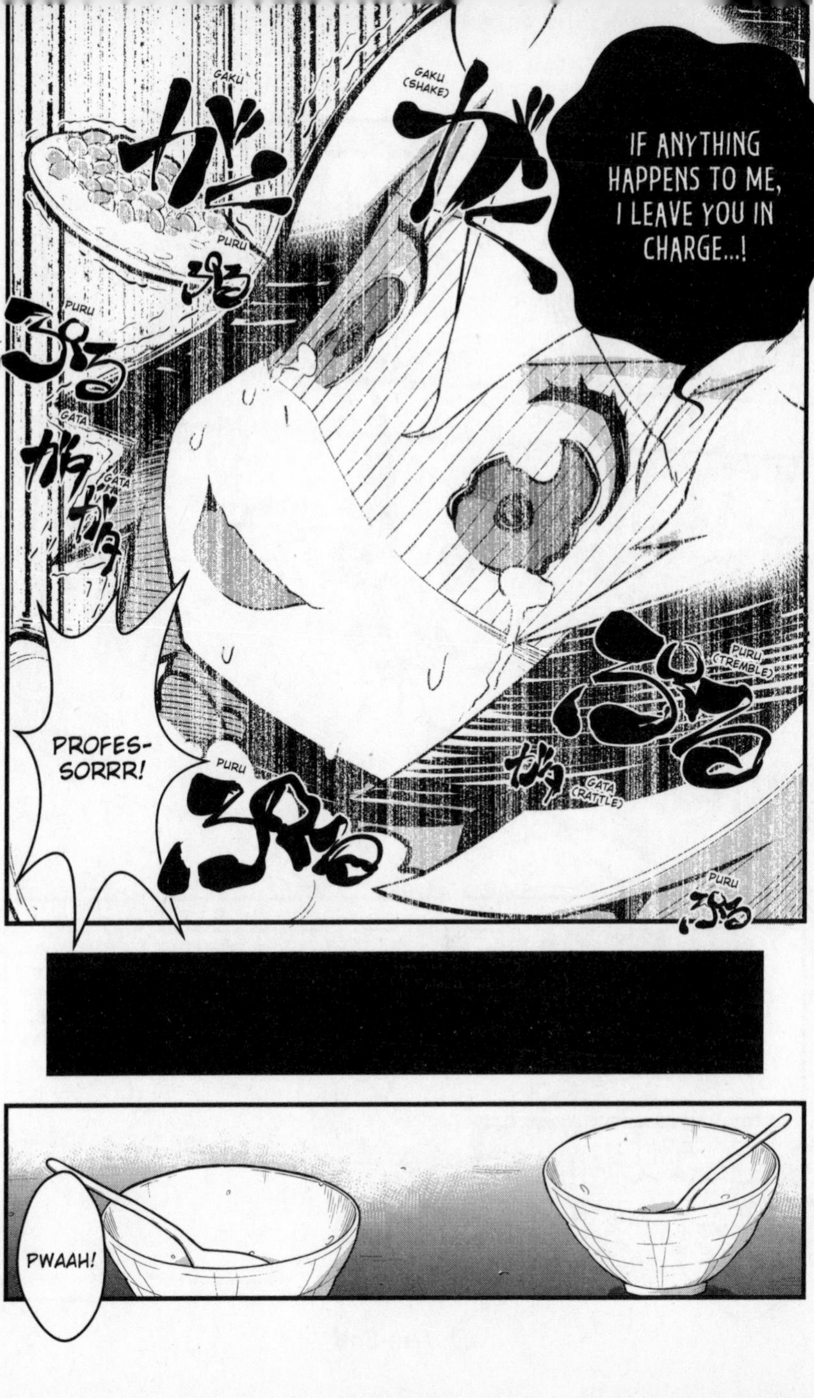
IF ANYTHING HAPPENS TO ME, I LEAVE YOU IN CHARGE...!
GAKU (SHAKE)
GAKU
PURU
PURU
GATA
GATA
PURU (TREMBLE)
GATA (RATTLE)
PURU
PURU
PROFES-SORRR!
PWAAH!

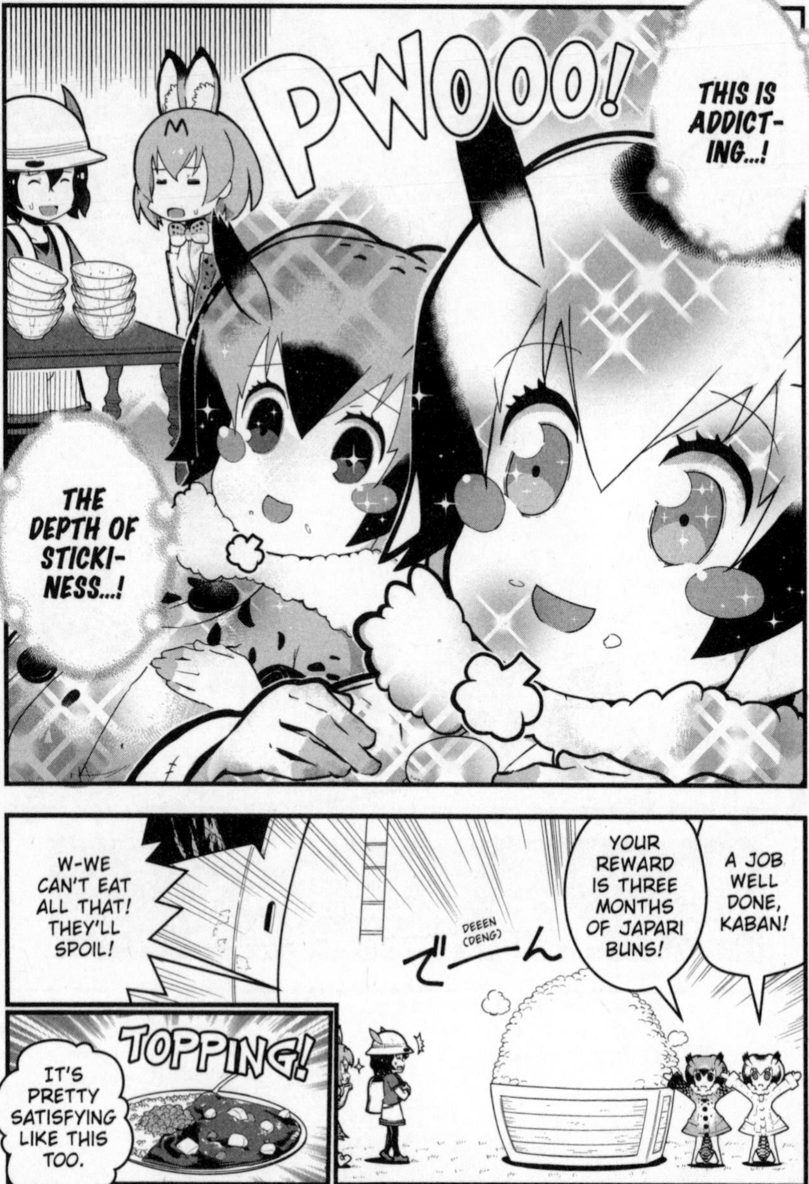
PWOOO!
THIS IS ADDICT-ING...!
THE DEPTH OF STICKI-NESS...!
A JOB WELL DONE, KABAN!
YOUR REWARD IS THREE MONTHS OF JAPARI BUNS!
でーん
DEEEN (DENG)
W-WE CAN'T EAT ALL THAT! THEY'LL SPOIL!
TOPPING!
IT'S PRETTY SATISFYING LIKE THIS TOO.

The End

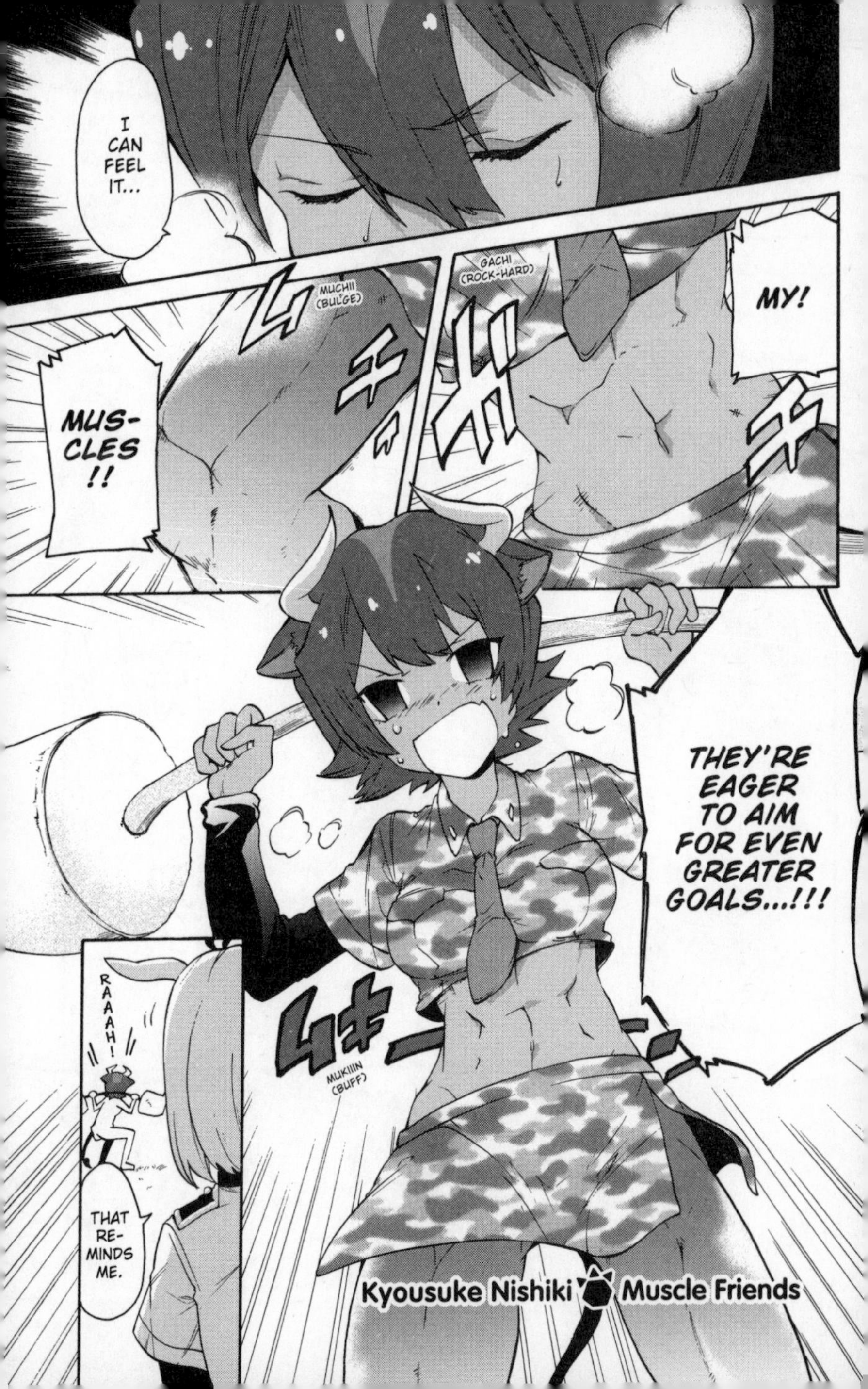
I CAN FEEL IT...
GACHI (ROCK-HARD)
MY!
MUCHII (BULGE)
MUS-CLES!!
THEY'RE EAGER TO AIM FOR EVEN GREATER GOALS...!!!
MUKIIIN (BUFF)
RAAAAH!
THAT RE-MINDS ME.
Kyousuke Nishiki Muscle Friends

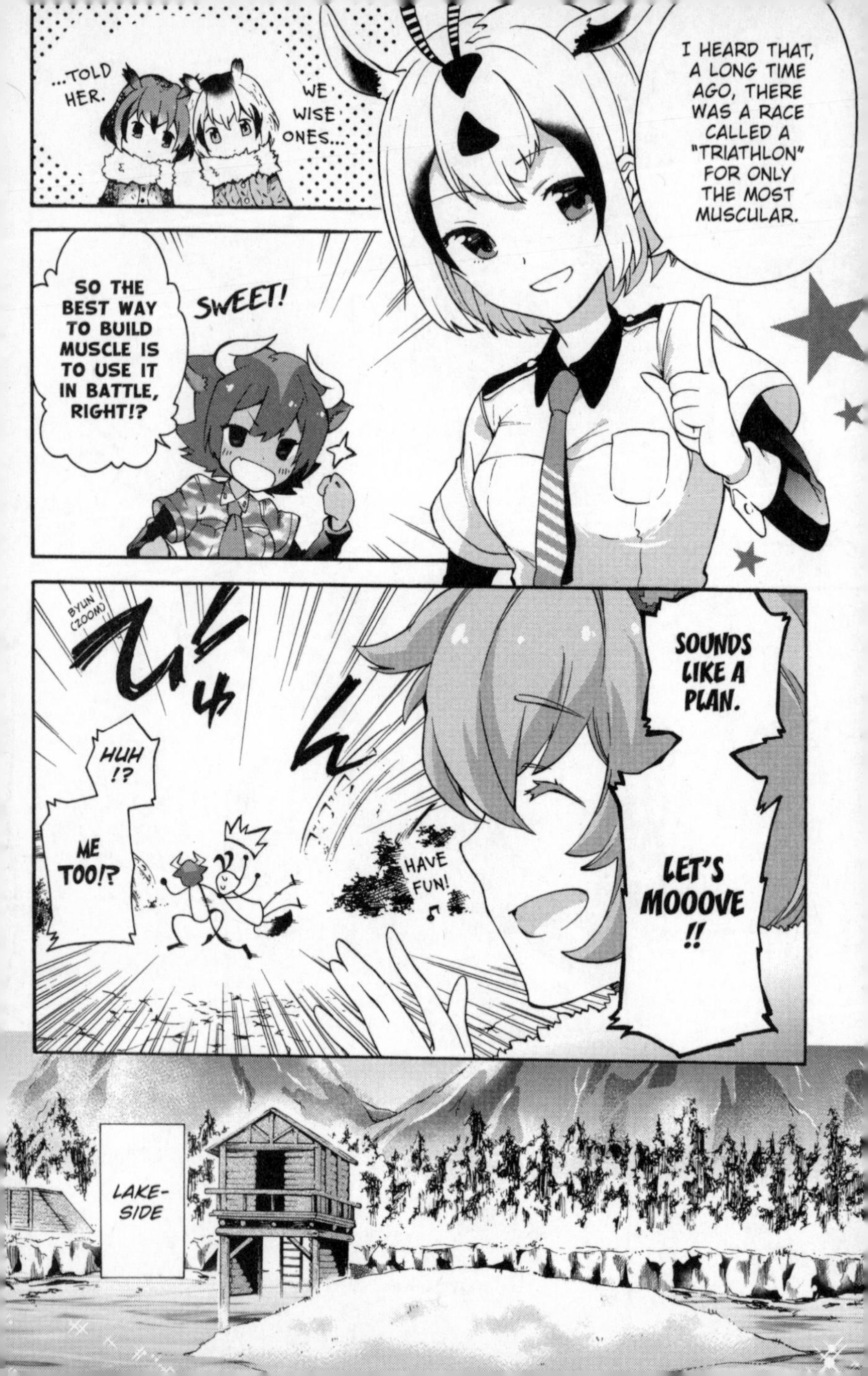

I HEARD THAT, A LONG TIME AGO, THERE WAS A RACE CALLED A "TRIATHLON" FOR ONLY THE MOST MUSCULAR.
WE WISE ONES...
...TOLD HER.
SWEET!
SO THE BEST WAY TO BUILD MUSCLE IS TO USE IT IN BATTLE, RIGHT!?
SOUNDS LIKE A PLAN.
LET'S MOOOVE!!
HAVE FUN!
BYUN (ZOOM)
HUH!?
ME TOO!?
LAKE-SIDE

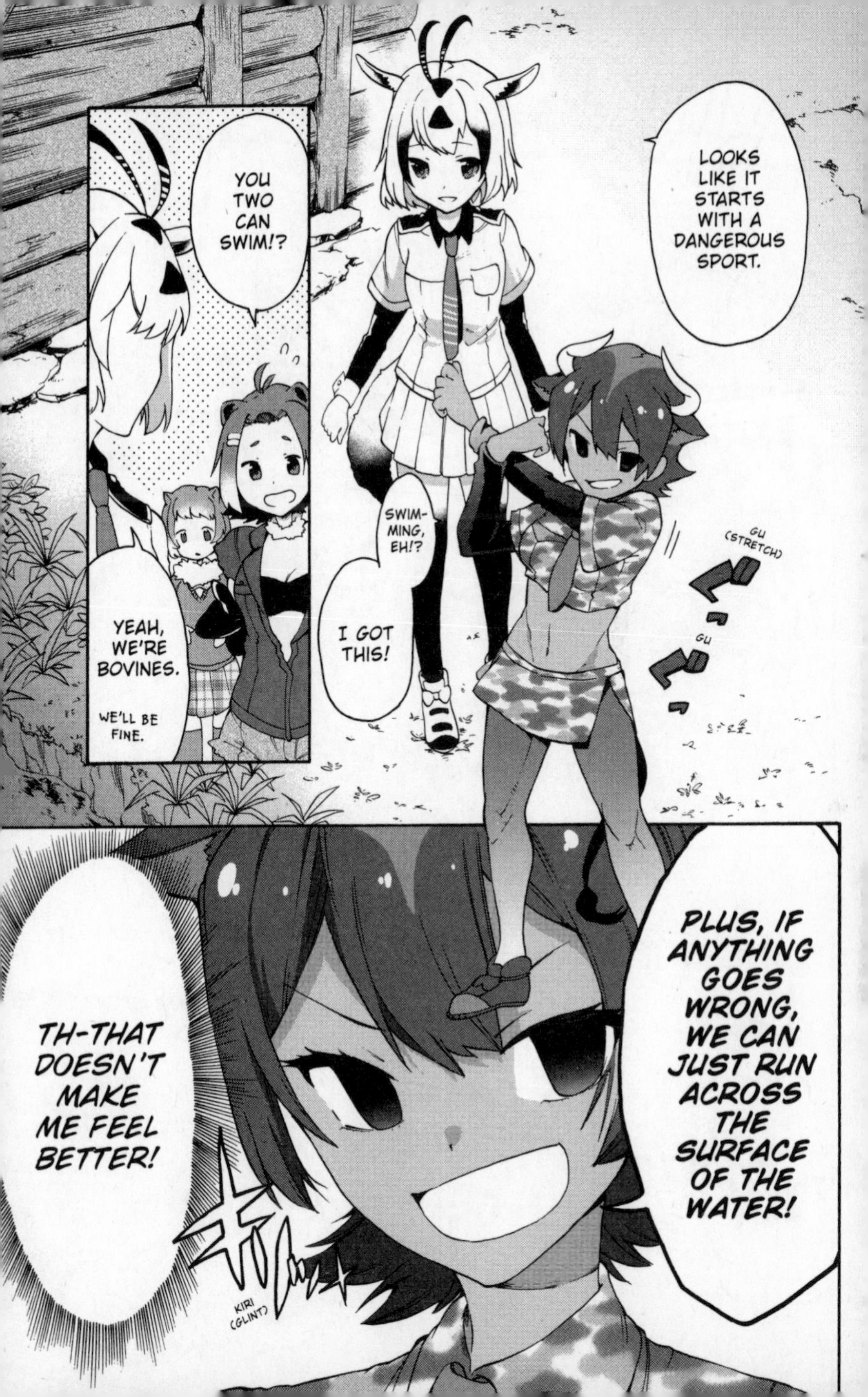
LOOKS LIKE IT STARTS WITH A DANGEROUS SPORT.
SWIMMING, EH!?
I GOT THIS!
GU (STRETCH)
GU
YOU TWO CAN SWIM!?
YEAH, WE'RE BOVINES.
WE'LL BE FINE.
PLUS, IF ANYTHING GOES WRONG, WE CAN JUST RUN ACROSS THE SURFACE OF THE WATER!
KIRI (GLINT)
TH-THAT DOESN'T MAKE ME FEEL BETTER!

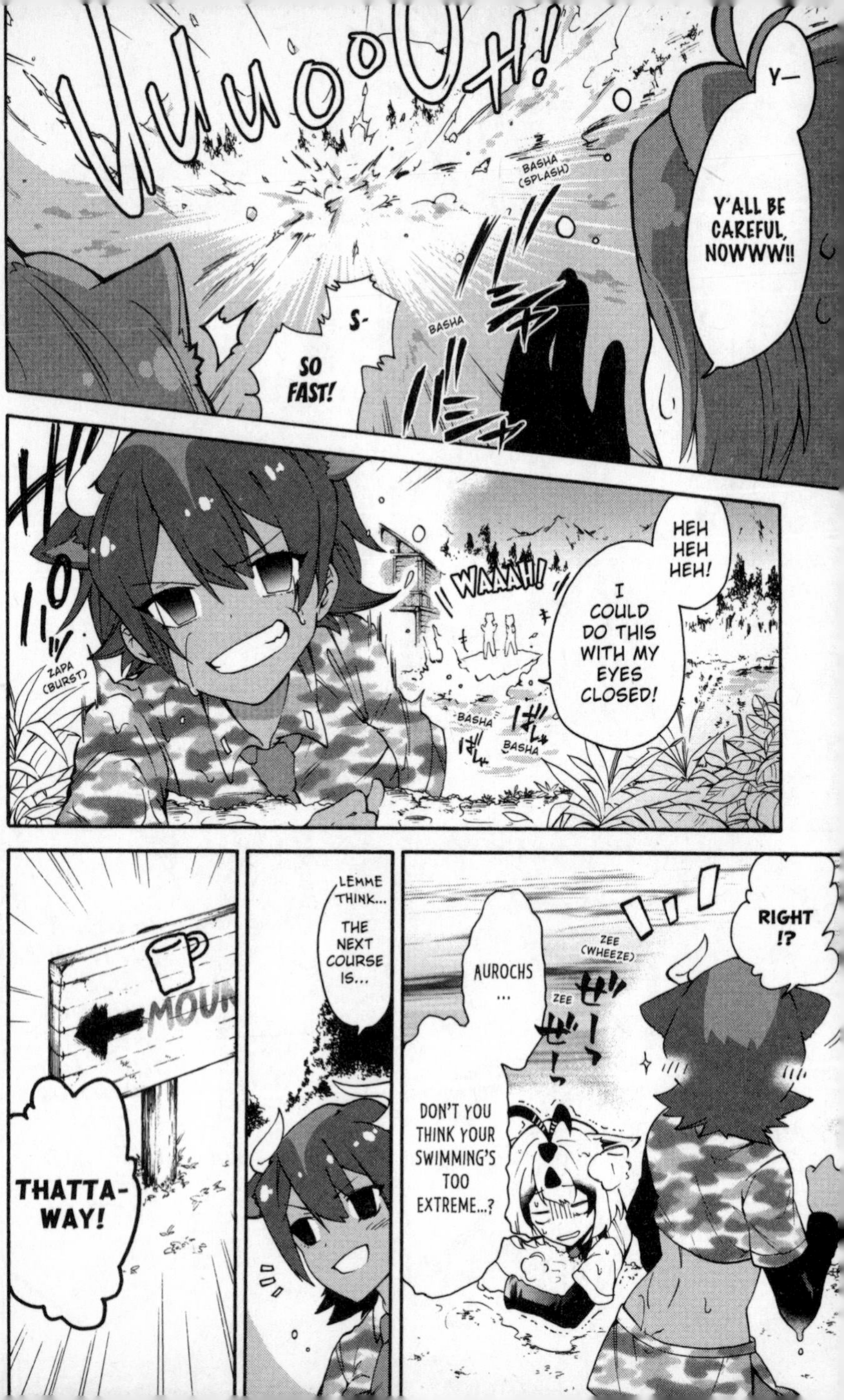
Y—
Y'ALL BE CAREFUL, NOWWW!!
VUUOOUH!
BASHA (SPLASH)
BASHA
S-
SO FAST!
HEH HEH HEH! I COULD DO THIS WITH MY EYES CLOSED!
WAAAH!
BASHA
BASHA
ZAPA (BURST)
RIGHT !?
ZEE (WHEEZE)
ZEE
AUROCHS ...
DON'T YOU THINK YOUR SWIMMING'S TOO EXTREME...?
LEMME THINK... THE NEXT COURSE IS...
MOUN
THATTA-WAY!

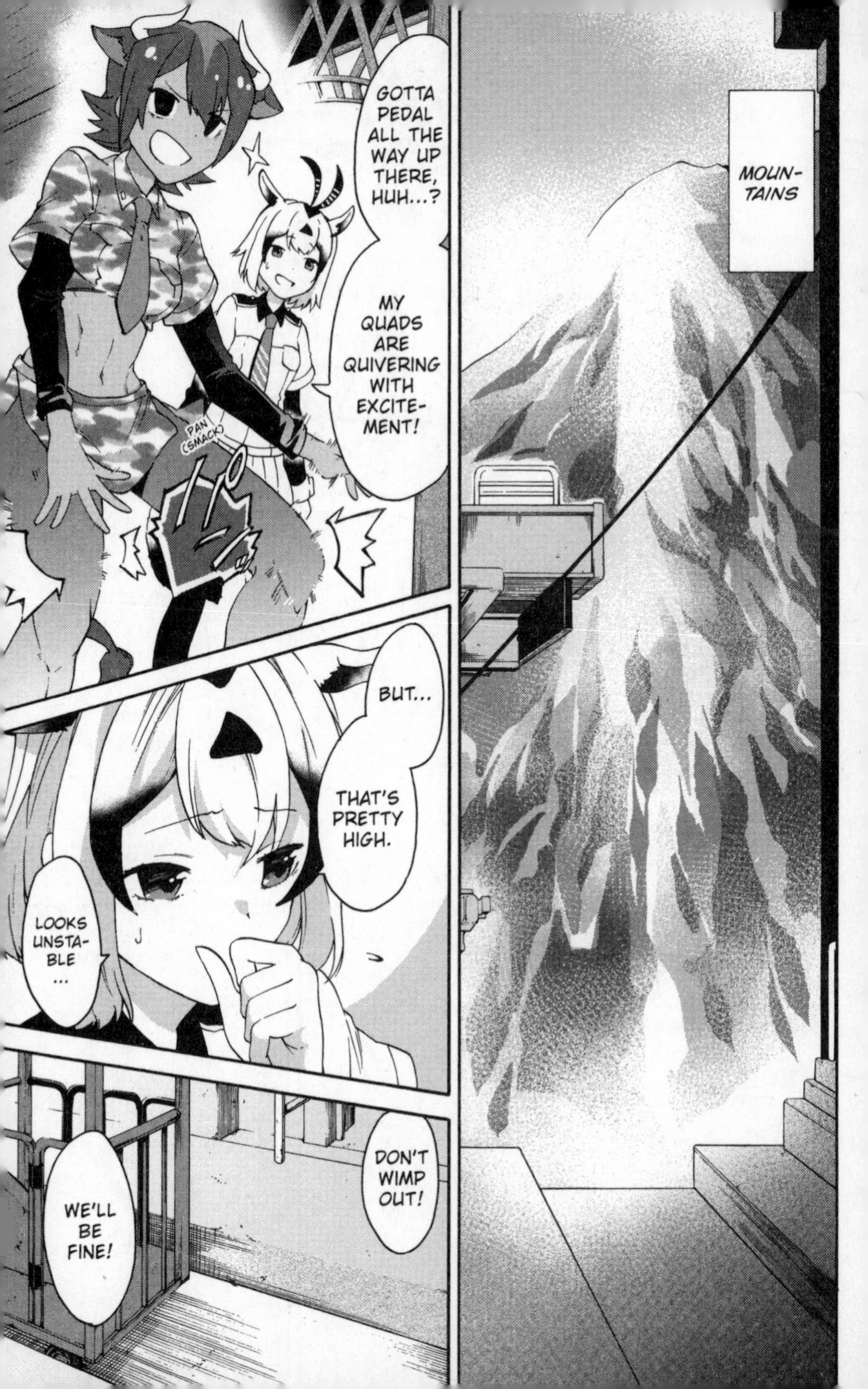
MOUNTAINS
GOTTA PEDAL ALL THE WAY UP THERE, HUH...?
MY QUADS ARE QUIVERING WITH EXCITEMENT!
PAN (SMACK)
BUT...
THAT'S PRETTY HIGH.
LOOKS UNSTABLE...
DON'T WIMP OUT!
WE'LL BE FINE!

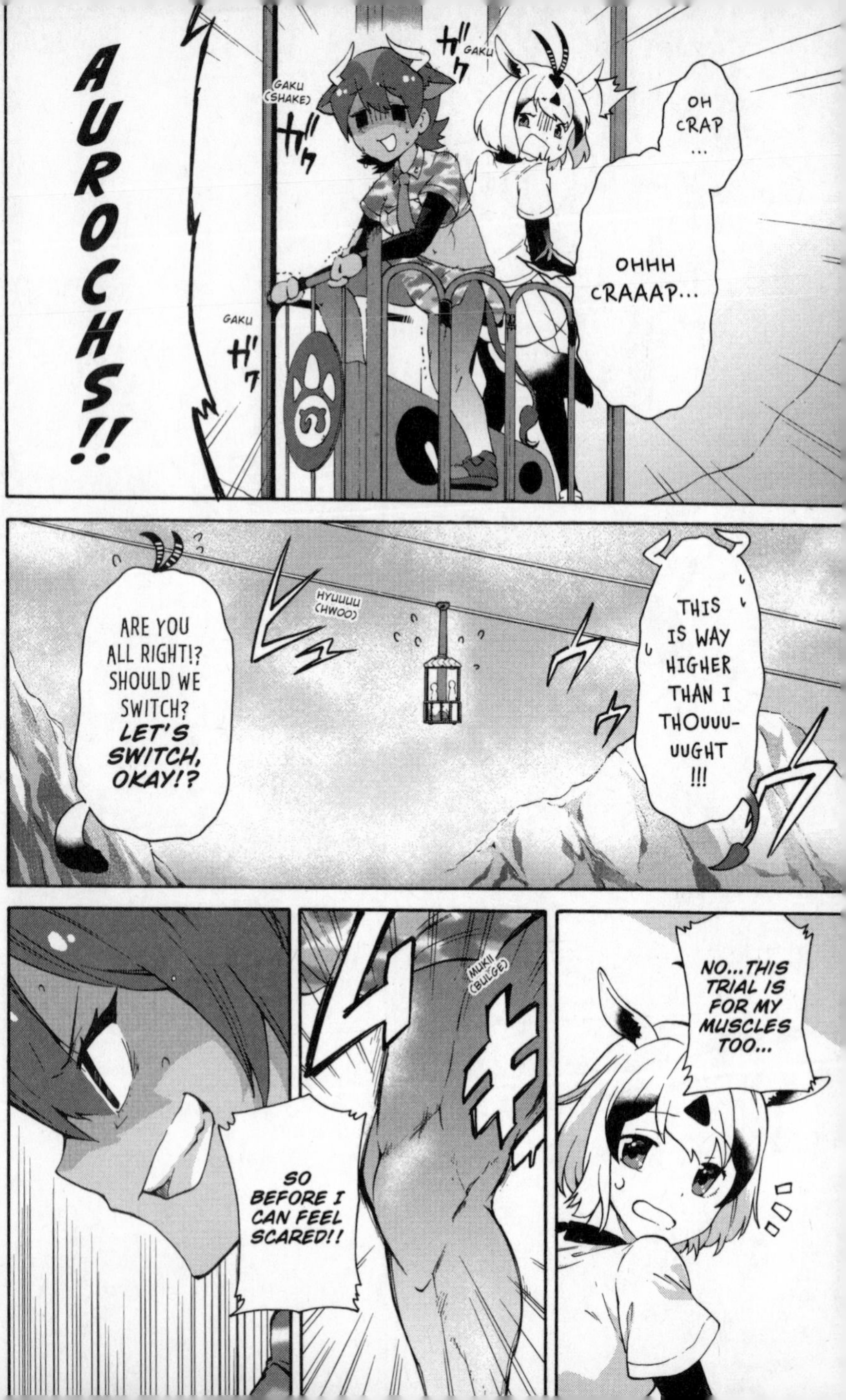
OH CRAP...
GAKU
GAKU (SHAKE)
OHHH CRAAAP...
AUROCHS!!
GAKU
THIS IS WAY HIGHER THAN I THOUUU-UUGHT!!!
HYUUUU (HWOO)
ARE YOU ALL RIGHT!? SHOULD WE SWITCH? LET'S SWITCH, OKAY!?
NO...THIS TRIAL IS FOR MY MUSCLES TOO...
MUKII (BULGE)
SO BEFORE I CAN FEEL SCARED!!

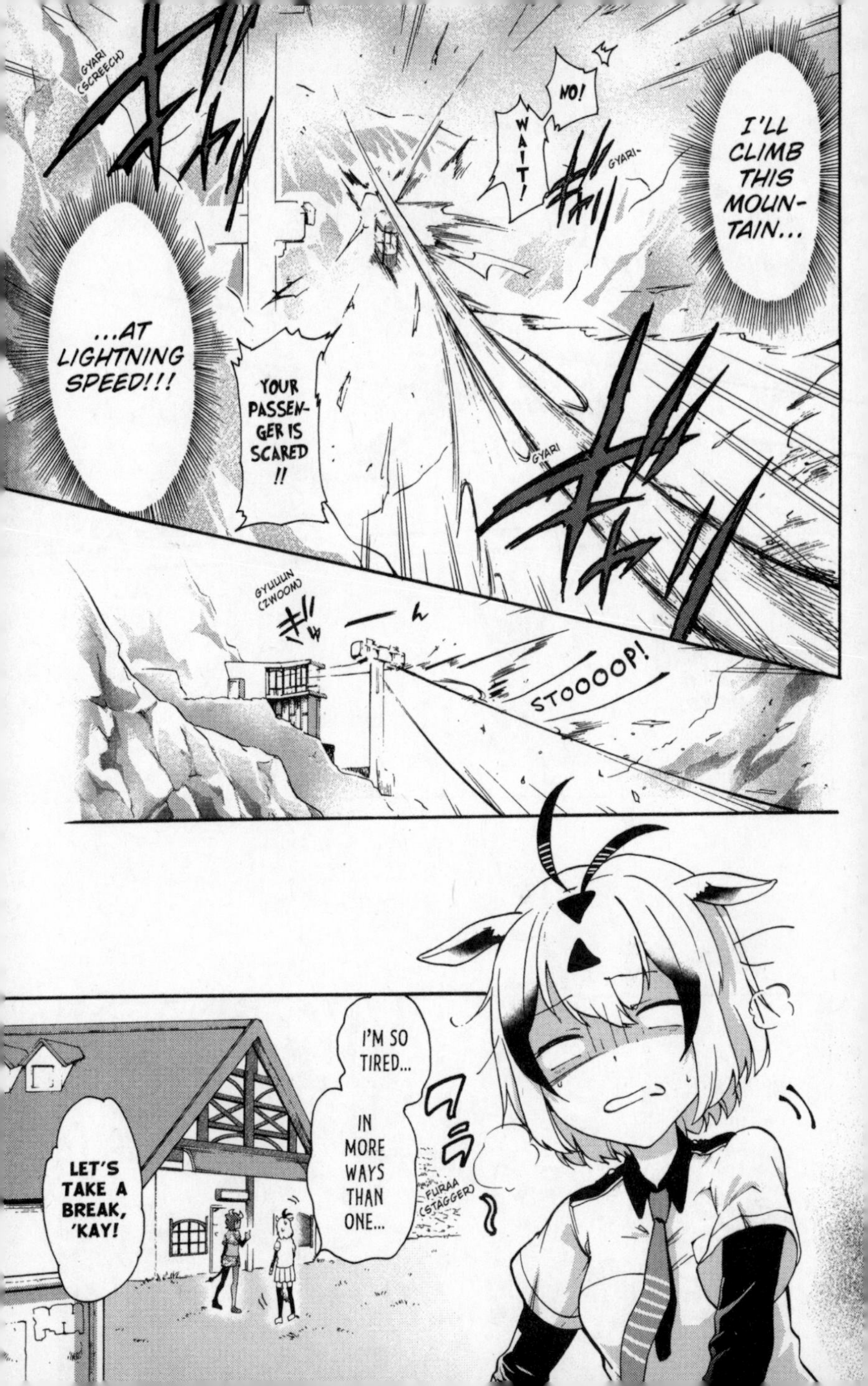
I'LL CLIMB THIS MOUNTAIN...
NO!
WAIT!
GYARI-
GYARI (SCREECH)
...AT LIGHTNING SPEED!!!
YOUR PASSENGER IS SCARED!!
GYARI
STOOOOP!
GYUUUN (ZWOOM)
FURAA (STAGGER)
I'M SO TIRED...
IN MORE WAYS THAN ONE...
LET'S TAKE A BREAK, 'KAY!

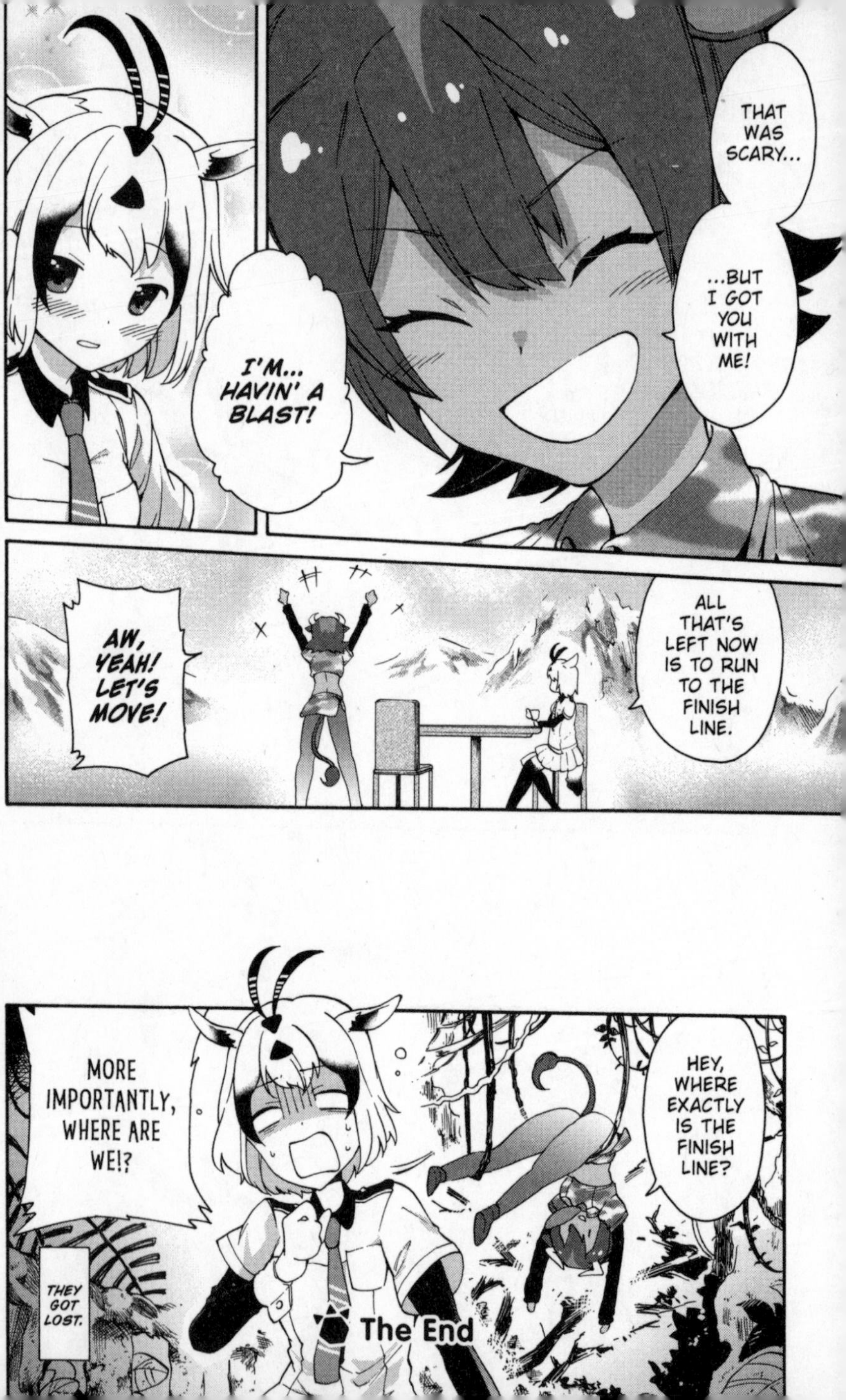
THAT WAS SCARY...
...BUT I GOT YOU WITH ME!
I'M... HAVIN' A BLAST!
ALL THAT'S LEFT NOW IS TO RUN TO THE FINISH LINE.
AW, YEAH! LET'S MOVE!
HEY, WHERE EXACTLY IS THE FINISH LINE?
MORE IMPORTANTLY, WHERE ARE WE!?
THEY GOT LOST.
The End

Kemono Friends

Question

65 WHAT'S THAT ANIMAL?

HINT

Often mistaken for the tanuki (the Japanese raccoon dog) because of their similar appearance. Like the tanuki, they play dead (also known as "thanatosis") when they feel surprised or threatened.

Turn the page for the answer!

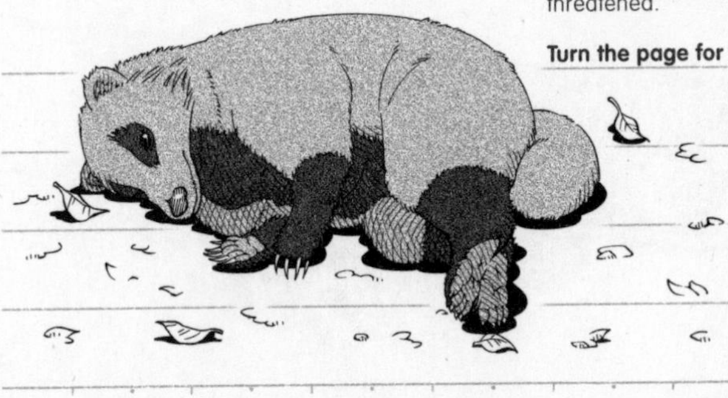

Kemono Friends

Answer

A5 JAPANESE BADGER

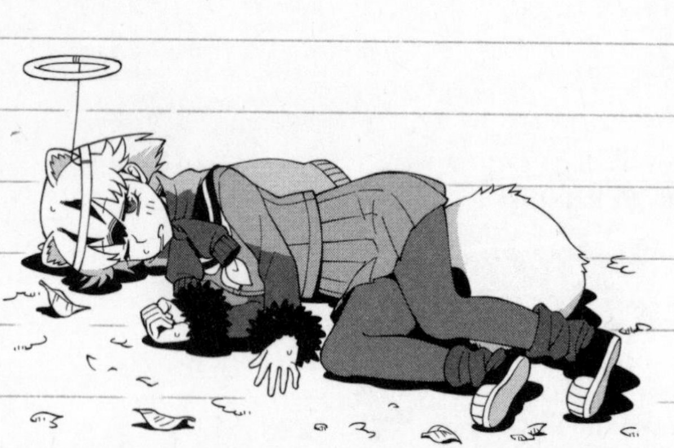

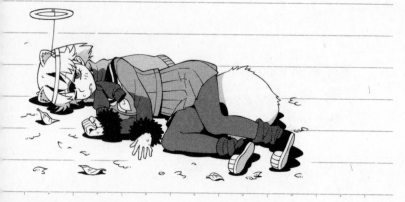

COMMENTS

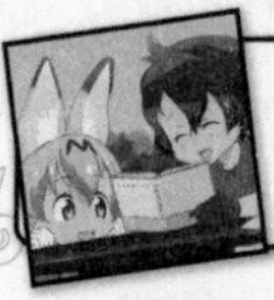

irodori

When I heard that a lot of manga artists would be participating in this book, I decided to feature the library. I'd love to relax and read manga somewhere like that.

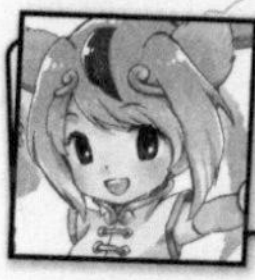

Rin Asano

I especially love the mid-episode zookeeper segments. I want to watch animated descriptions of all the Friends.

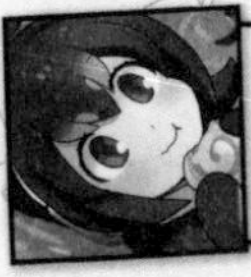

mato

The Friends' designs are all so unbelieeevably fuuun to draw! Thank you!

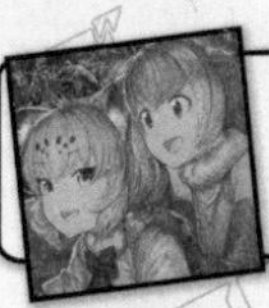

Koruse

I'm honored to participate in an anthology for a property I love and cherish so much! I adore the *Kemono Friends* world and characters!

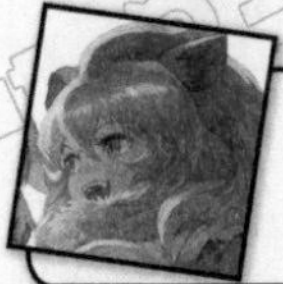

lack

The frenemy relationship between Moose and Lion is ridiculously cute. I adore it.

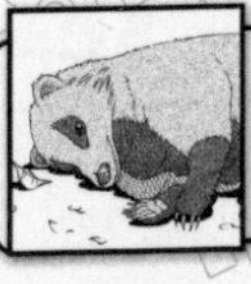

Nijio Rokuno

I actually love drawing animals, so getting to do animal pages this time was fun for me! Thank you very much!

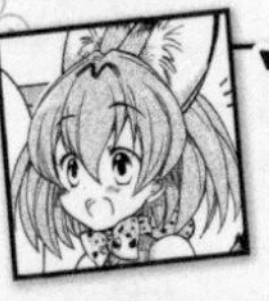

Rei Idumi

Hello! I had so much fun drawing for this. Thank you! Out of the PPP members, I'm a Princess fan all the way. All the characters are so cute that I end up just staring at them with a smile on my face before I know it...! I can't wait to see where it goes in the future!

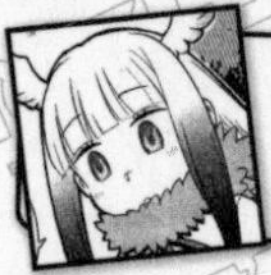

Yasuyuki·Kosaka

This manga was inspired by Alpaca's "[climbing the mountain] is a piece of cake, even if you're carrying things" line in the anime. I hope you enjoy it.

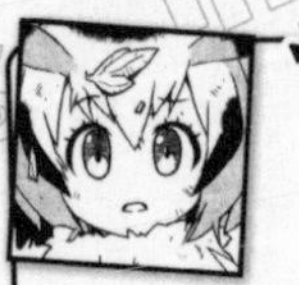

Tomohiro Marukawa

Roar! So with that out of the way, I had the privilege of drawing a Professor Scops and Assistant Eagle-chan manga. The Mojimoji-kun music was stuck in my head while I drew it. 'Cos I'm an old Friend.

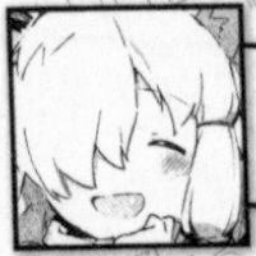

rin

I love Episode 3! Alpaca-chan and Boss are just too cute.

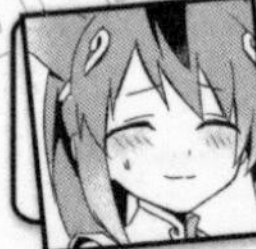

Ikumi·Hino

The Friends are so endearing.
I hope I managed to draw them looking cute and cool.
Thank you so much for inviting me to participate in this fantastic project!

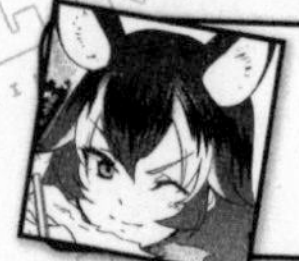

Kabocha

It's been a really long time since I last drew manga. I thought Shoebill-san was a silent character, and then she spoke in this freaking adorable voice, and the contrast of it got me good. I got to draw my favorite three—Shoebill, Wolf, and Moose—so I'm highly satisfied.

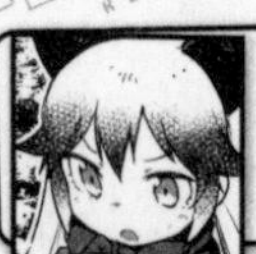

Keiji Watarai

I drew the fox duo. One's responsible, the other's lazy...It's fun to imagine what life at the hot spring inn is normally like for this pair.

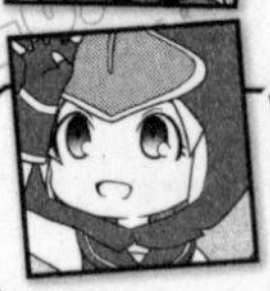

Kanaineko

I've enjoyed *KF* since the mobile game—suffice it to say I was very happy for the chance to participate in a *KF* anthology!

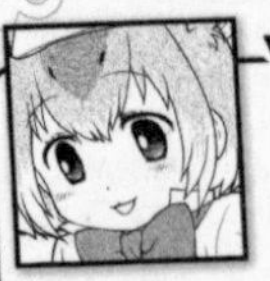

Miki·Kodama

I was so happy for the chance to participate in this anthology!
Capybaras are cute! I tried to show my passion for them in my story.
Of course the Friend Capybara-san is adorable, but the original animal Capybara-sans are totally adorable too.

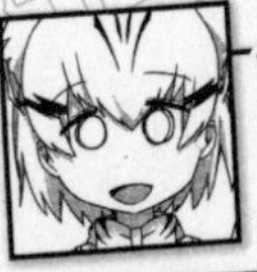

Bafako

It was so very fun to get to participate in this anthology book!!!
By the way, my favorite part is...well, I guess it's not a big deal...

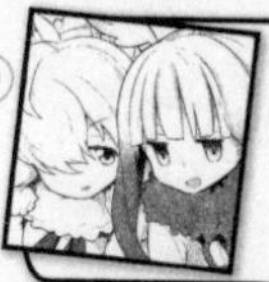

Kiki

I'm so glad I got to be in the *KF* anthology!
I want to become a Friend like Serval-chan who can see others' good qualities and live a fuuun life. Wooow!

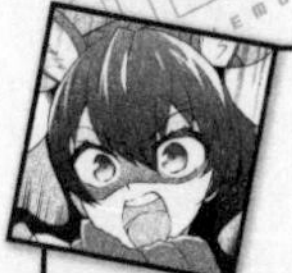

Oohamaiko

The Friends all have different placements of the highlights in their eyes, their eyelashes, etc., and they're all so cute in their own ways! I wanted to draw as many Friends as possible and had tons of fun doing it!

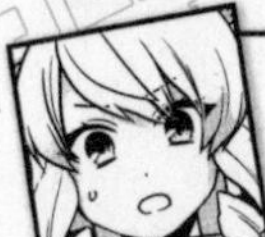

Tsukasa Usui

I recently became a Friend who can wake up early in the morning.
I'd like to keep this up and stay diurnal somehow.

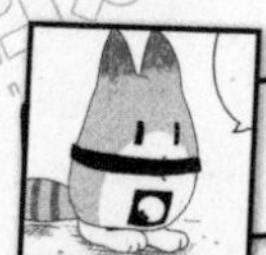

Yajirou Miyaba

Both carnivores and herbivores can eat Japari buns, so seriously, what flavor are they?

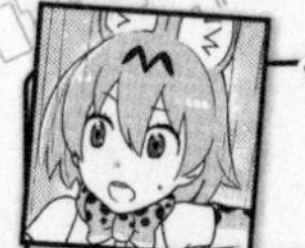

Gotsubo x Ryuuji

Yoshizaki-sensei's character designs are so truly great. We can't help but admire them. We had fun drawing so many cute girls.

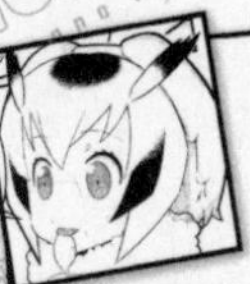

Gratin Bird

Hello, I'm Gratin Bird. I love the Professor and Assistant! They're so cute! For this story, I hesitated over whether to top the natto with spring onions. Apparently, onions are toxic to a lot of animals. So could the Friends eat them?

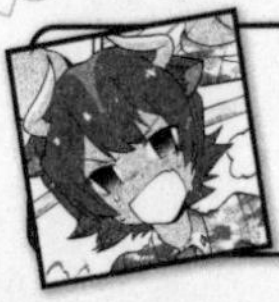

Kyousuke Nishiki

I never dreamed I'd get to be a part of this...
Thank you so much! I love Aurochs-chan's muscles.

Translation Notes

TITLE

Kemono means "beast," and it is also used to refer to anthropomorphic animal characters in the anime community.

PAGE 3

Rock-paper-scissors has its own regional conventions in Japan, where it is known as *janken*. When two players use the same shape, they say, "*Aiko deshou.*" ("Looks like there's a tie.") and throw again. Since Americans just start over when that happens, this line was changed to "Rock, paper, scissors, shoot."

PAGE 20

Kirin is the Japanese word for "giraffe"—the detective Friend— while also working as a "glint" onomatopoeia.

PAGE 21

Sandstar is the mysterious substance that created Friends and Ceruleans, occasionally erupting from the volcano on Japari Island. Friends revert back to normal animals if all their sandstar is absorbed by a Cerulean, and they can apparently use up much of their reserves and become woozy through overexertion as Crested Ibis does here.

PAGE 35

The Japanese word for a body pillow is **dakimakura**. *Daki* means "hug," as the Assistant soon explains, but the Professor confuses it for a homonym meaning "despicable."

PAGE 52

Saiyuki is the Japanese name for the classic sixteenth-century Chinese novel *Journey to the West*.

PAGE 67

Gray Wolf's original joke is more of a pun than the wordplay in the translation. She asks for her food fried fresh *(agetate)*, but the other person in the story thinks she wants raised hands *(agetate)*, at which point Wolf gives up *(oteage*, which figuratively means throwing in the towel, but literally means throwing up your hands).

PAGE 77
Since the Friends don't know what kind of animal she is, **Kaban-chan's** name comes from her "distinguishing characteristic," her bag *(kaban* in Japanese)...which is why Ezo Red Fox made a bag out of the snow.

PAGE 103
The **suspension bridge effect,** also known as "misattribution of arousal," is a psychological phenomenon where people mislabel their physical responses to a scary situation as the (similar) symptoms of romantic attraction. The name comes from a study which found that men who were asked to participate in a quick psychological experiment immediately after crossing an unsteady suspension bridge were much more likely to call the young female experimenter later for "questions about the study" than men who used a sturdier bridge.

PAGE 117
The **"pakaan!"** sound effect is a reference to the sound effect that would appear in the original *Kemono Friends* mobile game when an enemy is defeated.

PAGE 119
The **cat idiom** in the original Japanese was *neko no te mo karitai* ("I'd even take help from a cat.")—and Serval shows up in the next panel to lend a hand.

PAGE 130
In Japan, lucky **vases** that can supposedly make you win the lottery, drive away evil spirits, get you a promotion at work, etc., are the go-to example of spiritual-pressure scams to sell products at ridiculously high prices.

PAGE 156
Kaban has cooked up the traditional Japanese dish **natto**—sticky fermented soybeans with a powerful smell and flavor. It's considered a love-it-or-hate-it food and is often eaten on rice.

Translated as **Professor Scops**, the Professor is sometimes called "Professor Konoha" in Japanese. This originates from the name of her animal type, the African northern white-faced **scops**-owl *(afurika ookonohazuku)*, probably because Konoha can be a given name in Japanese. Similarly, the Eurasian **eagle**-owl Assistant is sometimes called "Assistant Mimi-chan" because the animal's name in Japanese is *washimimizuku*. These nicknames originated in the first *Kemono Friends* mobile game.

Mojimoji-kun was a segment on comedy duo Tunnels' long-running comedic variety show/game show *Tunnels no Minasan no Okage Deshita* ("Brought to You by the Members of Tunnels") in which the characters Mojio and Mojimi would spell out a word *(moji)* with their bodies, then play various games. The segment first aired back in 1989.

PAGE 173
Yoshizaki-sensei refers to Mine Yoshizaki, the concept designer for *Kemono Friends*.

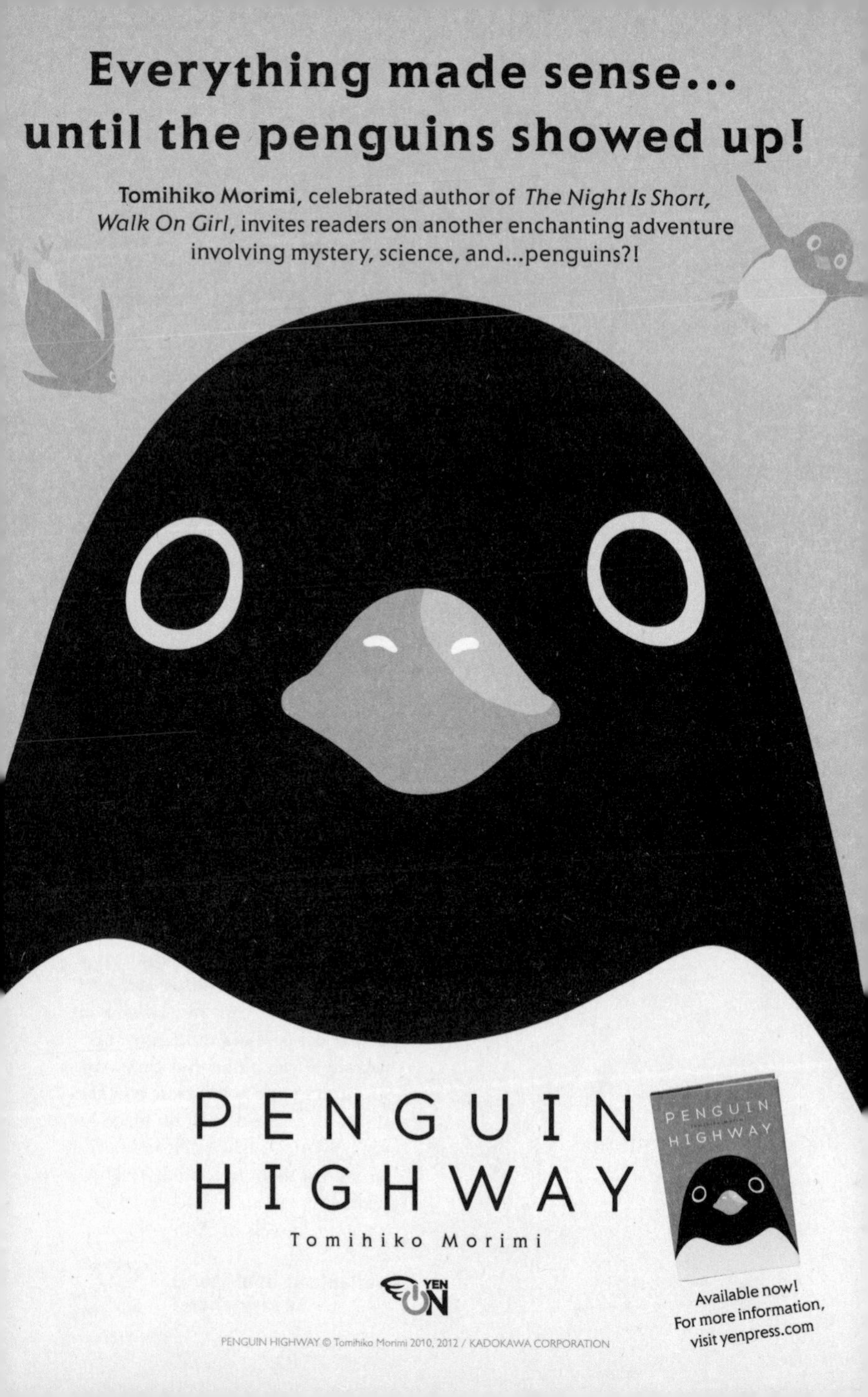
Everything made sense... until the penguins showed up!
Tomihiko Morimi, celebrated author of The Night Is Short, Walk On Girl, invites readers on another enchanting adventure involving mystery, science, and...penguins?!
PENGUIN HIGHWAY
Tomihiko Morimi
YEN ON
PENGUIN HIGHWAY
Available now!
For more information, visit yenpress.com
PENGUIN HIGHWAY © Tomihiko Morimi 2010, 2012 / KADOKAWA CORPORATION

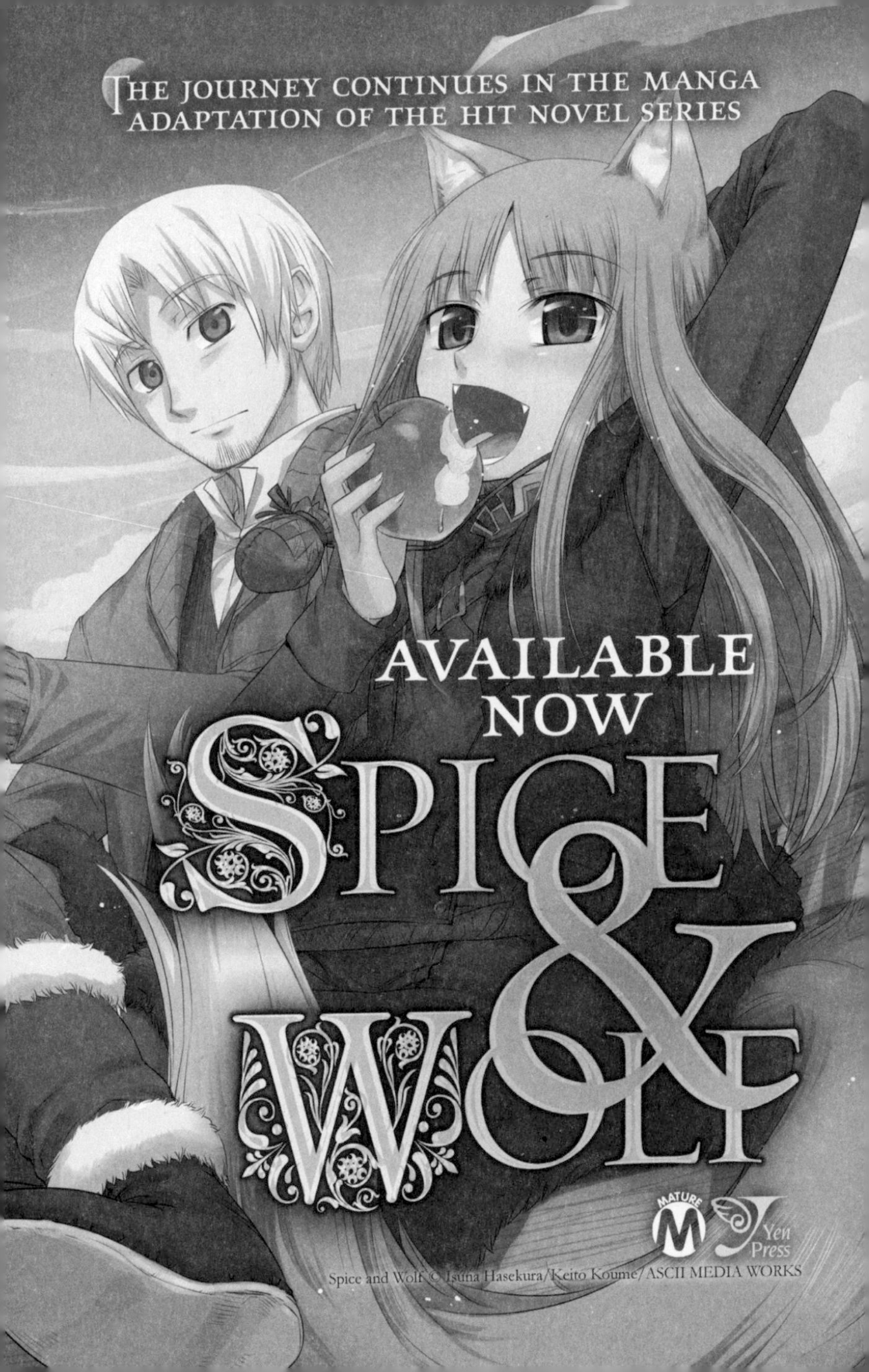
THE JOURNEY CONTINUES IN THE MANGA
ADAPTATION OF THE HIT NOVEL SERIES
AVAILABLE
NOW
SPICE & WOLF
MATURE
M
Yen Press
Spice and Wolf © Isuna Hasekura/Keito Koume/ASCII MEDIA WORKS

Hello! This is YOTSUBA!

Guess what? Guess what? Yotsuba and Daddy just moved here from waaaay over there!

And Yotsuba met these nice people next door and made new friends to play with!

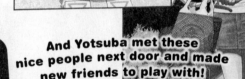

The pretty one took Yotsuba on a bike ride!
(Whoooa! There was a big hill!)

And Ena's a good drawer!
(Almost as good as Yotsuba!)

And their mom always gives Yotsuba ice cream!
(Yummy!)

**And...
        And...   OHHHH!**

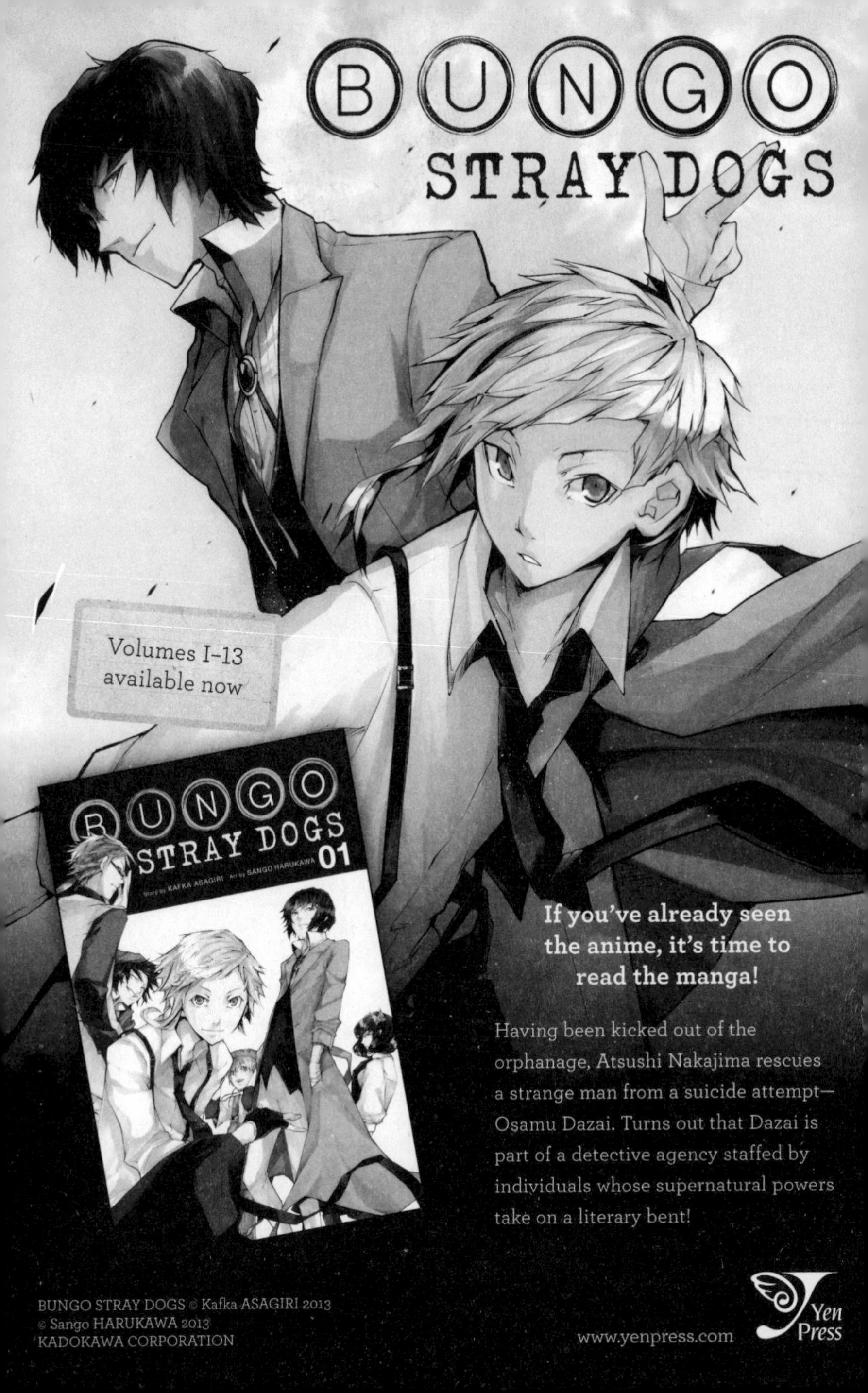
BUNGO STRAY DOGS
Volumes 1–13 available now
BUNGO STRAY DOGS 01
Story by KAFKA ASAGIRI Art by SANGO HARUKAWA
If you've already seen the anime, it's time to read the manga!
Having been kicked out of the orphanage, Atsushi Nakajima rescues a strange man from a suicide attempt—Osamu Dazai. Turns out that Dazai is part of a detective agency staffed by individuals whose supernatural powers take on a literary bent!
BUNGO STRAY DOGS © Kafka ASAGIRI 2013
© Sango HARUKAWA 2013
KADOKAWA CORPORATION
www.yenpress.com
Yen Press

KEMONO FRIENDS À LA CARTE

Japari Park Edition 2

CREATED BY: KEMONO FRIENDS PROJECT
EDITED BY: SHOUNEN ACE EDITORIAL DEPT.

Translation: Amanda Haley • Lettering: Rochelle Gancio

KEMONO FRIENDS COMIC A la Carte -JAPARIPARK HEN- Vol. II
©Kemono Friends Project
First published in Japan in 2017 by KADOKAWA CORPORATION, Tokyo.
English translation rights arranged with KADOKAWA CORPORATION, Tokyo through TUTTLE-MORI AGENCY, INC.

English translation © 2020 by Yen Press, LLC

Yen Press
150 West 30th Street, 19th Floor
New York, NY 10001

Visit us at yenpress.com
facebook.com/yenpress
yenpress.tumblr.com
twitter.com/yenpress
instagram.com/yenpress

First Yen Press Edition: January 2020

Yen Press is an imprint of Yen Press, LLC.
The Yen Press name and logo are trademarks of Yen Press, LLC.

The publisher is not responsible for websites (or their content) that are not owned by the publisher.

Library of Congress Control Number: 2019947804

ISBNs: 978-1-9753-8684-9 (paperback)
        978-1-9753-8685-6 (ebook)

10 9 8 7 6 5 4 3 2 1

WOR

Printed in the United States of America